MALTA
The Order of St John

Thomas Freller

PHOTOGRAPHY
Daniel Cilia

MIDSEA BOOKS

4 CONTENTS

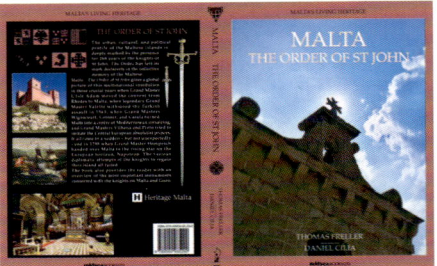

Front Cover:
The façade of the chapel of St Anne on Fort St Angelo.

Back Cover:
Top: The coat of arms of the eight langues of the Order of St John.
Top centre: St Agatha's Tower, Mellieha.
Bottom centre: Painting of a *corso* battle.
Bottom: The main altar of the conventual church of St John.
Right: The sword and dagger of the Religion.

Images on previous pages:
Page 1: The eight-pointed cross of the knights sculpted under the apse of the passage to the chapel of the langue of Castille, Leon, and Portugal in St John's Co-Cathedral.

Pages 2-3:
A contemporary etching recording the capture of four Turkish galleons by the Order's fleet.

Images on the Time Chart on pages 10–11 (from left to right):
Top: The siege of Nicaea, 1097; Frederick II, 1194–1250; Grand Master d'Aubusson supervises the repairs of the fortifications; Grand Master l'Isle Adam in Malta, 1530; last grand master in Malta, Hompesch, 1797; present Grand Master Festing in audience with Pope Benedict XVI.

Bottom: The walls of Jerusalem; the Crac des Chevaliers in Syria; Hagia Sophia interior, Turkey; Magisterial Palace, Fort St Angelo, Malta; aerial photo of Valletta; the knights' symbol projected on Fort St Angelo during the celebrations of Malta's entry in the EU in 2004.

CONTENTS 4
Prologue 6
TIME CHART 10
CHAPTER 1 12
THE OCCIDENT, THE CHIVALRIC ORDERS, AND THEIR SPIRITUAL ROOTS
    The Hospitallers – from a brotherhood to an Order 17
    The Hospitallers become a Chivalric Order 24
    Internal changes and the international background 28
    The 'aristocratization' of an institution 31

CHAPTER 2 34
THE HOSPITALLERS IN RHODES
    Hospitallers, Templars, and the rulers of the occident – an uneasy partnership 35
    Rhodes – the new headquarters . 41
    New orientations 43
    Under Ottoman pressure 51

CHAPTER 3 56
ON THE ROAD TO MALTA
    The Order and its rule – Power, statutes, and organization 57
    From Rhodes to Malta – Aspects of a continuation 67
    The decision for Malta and its global implications 79

CHAPTER 4 84
THE HOSPITALLERS IN MALTA –
A DIFFICULT BEGINNING
 Malta and Sicily – The legal
 and social background 85
 Sieges and heroes 88
 The *corso* – Backbone of
 a society and state 103
 Upheavals and changes 121

CHAPTER 5 128
THE GLOBAL PICTURE AND THE
MEDITERRANEAN ENVIRONMENT

CHAPTER 6 150
MALTA AND THE IMPACT OF THE
RULE OF THE HOSPITALLERS
 Social and demographic
 changes 151
 New economic perspectives 164
 Behind the scene 175
 New cultural horizons 181
 Creating identities – Religion
 and politics 189

CHAPTER 7 192
THE EIGHTEENTH CENTURY – LAST
SPLENDOUR AND DARK CLOUDS
 New horizons and a dangerous
 road 193
 End of an epoch 209
 New arrangements and a
 complicated resurrection 212

CHAPTER 8 232
GRAND MASTERS OF THE ORDER
OF ST JOHN RULING OVER THE
MALTESE ISLANDS
 The Order's structure 242

SITES
 Location Map 246
VALLETTA
 Valletta General 248
 St John's Co-Cathedral 258
 The Magisterial Palace 282
THE GRAND HARBOUR CONURBATION
 Fort St Elmo 296
 Fort St Angelo 298
 Fort St Michael 304
 Floriana 306
 The Cottonera Lines 308
 Fort Ricasoli 312
THE MINOR PALACES AND FORTIFICATIONS
 Mdina 314
 Verdala Palace 318
 The Palace and Gardens of
 San Anton 324
 Fort Manoel 326
 Fort Tigné 328
 The Gozo *castello* 330
 Fort Chambray 334
 The Wignacourt Aqueduct 336
 The Coastal Fortifications 338

APPENDICES
 Sources and recommended
 reading 350
 Photo Credits 355
 Index 356

A bas-relief sculpture representing the Order as Minerva, the goddess of war and wisdom, crushing Moorish slaves beneath her feet. Chapel of the langue of Provence, St John's Co-Cathedral, Valletta.

Malta – The Order of St John does not – and cannot – focus only on the achievements of the Hospitallers in Malta and Gozo. It also aims to give a more global picture of this multinational institution in those crucial years when Grand Master L'Isle Adam moved the convent from Rhodes to Malta, when legendary Grand Master Valette withstood the Turkish assault in 1565, when Grand Masters Wignacourt, Cotoner, and Carafa turned Malta into a centre of Mediterranean corsairs, and Grand Masters Vilhena and Pinto tried to imitate the Central European absolutist princes. It all came to a sad end in 1798 when Grand Master Hompesch handed over Malta to the rising star on the European horizon Napoleon and, in 1800, it became a British colony.

By then the Hospitallers could look back to a centuries-old and chequered history. Originally a charitable, monastic institution devoted to the care of Christian pilgrims in the Holy Land, by the middle of the twelfth century there was a gradual transformation of the Hospitallers into a military Order. With the fall of Acre to the Mamelukes in 1291, the Order moved to Cyprus and then, in 1306, to Rhodes. On 1 January 1523 – after a six-month siege – the Order was evicted from that island by the superior forces of Sultan Suleiman the Magnificent. After seven years of protracted negotiations the Order was invested with the islands of Malta and Gozo and the North African fortress of Tripoli 'in perpetual, noble, full, and free enfeoffment'.

The genesis and development of a cosmopolitan institution like the Order of St John cannot be understood without looking back at its Palestinian roots and its international role. It was not only Malta which they transformed into the 'Epitome of Europe', as an eighteenth-century English visitor put it. Through its history, the Order was an important factor of European and Latin-Christian culture, whether it was in Palestine, in Rhodes, or in Malta. Although for 700 years the Order's headquarters were – purposely – placed on the borders of the occidental world and Latin Christendom with the 'infidel world', the institution never existed in a sort of vacuum or independence. On the contrary, the Sovereign Military

Order of St John of Jerusalem, commonly known as the Order of Malta was deeply rooted in western thinking and the knights were closely connected with the political and cultural situation and climate with the more important political units of the west: France, the German empire, England, the Italian States, Castille, and Aragon.

Between the twelfth and the eighteenth century, the Order went through many changes, re-structurings, inner tensions, and political and economic ups-and-downs. However, until the Order was forced to leave Malta, it never lost the extraordinary esteem of the western world. Among the European Catholic aristocracy, this esteem rose even more when, in the sixteenth and seventeenth centuries, the new concepts of Lutheranism, humanism, mercantilism, and absolutism threatened their old prerogatives and identity. The Order and its noble knights appeared as an echo of the golden times of chivalry and a *locus amoenus* of Christian values. The Order itself very cleverly instrumentalized these visions, as will be seen later.

It was no coincidence that the days of the Order's military power and sovereignty state ended when a new epoch in history started with the French Revolution, the beginning of European nationalism, and industrialization. The old aristocratic chivalric Order became an anachronism as the commercial power of the bourgeoisie and the concept of national states developed. The Order's very structure and ideology since its transition from a brotherhood of Hospitallers into a chivalric institution had been clearly anti-bourgeois. In spite of some oblique moves and exceptions, its exclusive structure composed of members of the old European aristocracy lingered on until the Order's last days in Malta. Until that fateful 12 June 1798 when Napoleon Bonaparte swept the Order out of Malta – besides its charitable aims and tasks – the identity of its members was based on two main columns: (1) a stylization of the knights as military defenders of Latin Christendom in a perpetual war against the infidels, and (2) the knights as guarantors of the traditional religious, ideological, and feudal structure of Catholic Europe. This must have led to clashes with the new forces of bourgeois enterprise and liberalism and with the new intellectuals and statesmen of the enlightenment who favoured the prerogatives of the state over those of any religious institution. Most of the European nobility then still found their ideological and political home – when they were already threatened by the new developments – as well as their social home and legitimization in these old anachronistic concepts.

And still – that the Order in its form and structure basically established in the twelfth and thirteenth centuries kept on existing as a state and a military power more or less without deeper interior changes five more centuries simultaneously documents an astonishing continuity of political and spiritual culture in

Christian Europe. The survival of the chivalric Order seems to testify to the spiritual and cultural continuity of the Crusades up to the Counter Reformation. Despite the uncertainty of a period of upheaval, the Order attracted Protestants as well as Catholics. This interest by Prussians, Scandinavians, and Protestants from central and south Germany to become members document that, in early modern times, both Catholics and Protestants were interested to join mainly for reasons of fame and career and to acquire military and naval experience. From a more global point of view the end of the Order's rule over Malta in 1798 and the taking over of the island by a 'pre-imperialistic' state – Napoleon's France – can be interpreted as a symbol of the end of an epoch.

This book also tries to show how deeply Malta was transformed and shaped through the presence of the Order. In fact Malta's cultural identity cannot be understood without understanding the effects of the knights' rule. The beginning was not easy. The Maltese islands are located in the narrowest part of the Mediterranean Sea, between North Africa and Sicily, on the border between the European and the Semitic areas of culture. Even more than that of Sicily, the history of Malta has been characterized by periods of cultural changes, providing ethnographical and ethnological breaks. After the high middle ages, Malta had more or less become an integral part of European Mediterranean culture, although linguistically it remained in the Arab world. The frontier position of Malta has resulted in a blend of cultural and political manifestations. A southern European Roman Catholic culture dominated the islands from late medieval times onwards. This culture was implemented by the Aragonese (1283–1530) and strengthened by influences from Sicily and by the knights of St John (1530–1798).

The granting of the Maltese archipelago by Emperor Charles V in March 1530 to the Order as a free and noble fief violated the agreements of the fourteenth and fifteenth centuries between the crown of Aragon and the Maltese Universitas, the body which managed domestic affairs. The Universitas was the guardian of the ancient rights, freedoms, and privileges of the Maltese. There was one Universitas in Malta and one in Gozo. In 1397 the Universitas of Malta had won a charter that testified that the islands were to be definitely incorporated in the royal *demanium* and were not to be ceded any more to foreign lords. This was confirmed in 1428. Despite this political violation, the knights' rule contributed to the distinction and uniqueness of this typical 'blend of *Malteseness*', not the least the survival of the language which, contrary to, for example, the neighbouring island of Pantelleria, was not absorbed into the Italian hemisphere.

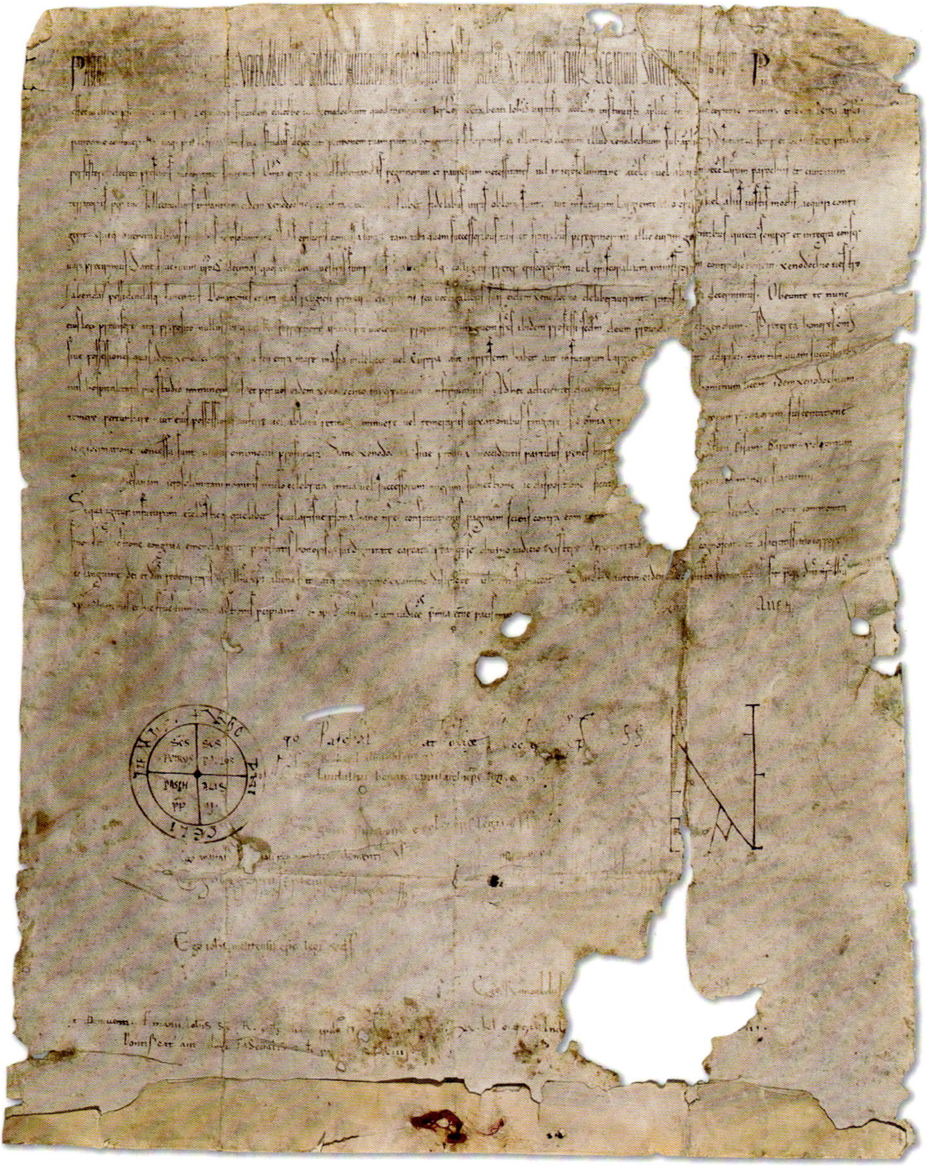

PROLOGUE 9

The papal bull Pie postulatio voluntatis *of Pope Paschal II. Dated 15 February 1113, it approved the foundation of the hospital and placed the institution under the protection of the Holy See.*
Now at the National Library of Malta.

10 Timechart

Our dateline shows the amazing continuity of the history of the knights of St John through various periods and upheavals of Occidental and Oriental history. The institution's beginning dates back to the time of the First Crusade and the deep Christian-Muslim antagonism of the time. The Order survived the loss of Jerusalem and the Holy Land, the expulsion from Rhodes and from Malta, and several wanderings through Europe which shows that its spiritual kernel must have been inseparably linked with Occidental Christian culture. This survival was only possible through political, economic, and

| 1000 AD | 1100 | 1200 | 1300 | 1400 | 1 |

JERUSALEM

CYPRUS

RHODES

| 1000 AD | 1100 | 1200 | 1300 | 1400 | 1 |

THE FIRST CRUSADE

THE BLACK DEATH

END OF G

SALADIN CONQUERS JERUSALEM

COSTANTINOPLE FALLS

DEATH OF FREDERICK II

DISCOVE AMERI

TIMECHART 11

intellectual adaptations. That the institution has survived to this day as a world-wide active charitable Order is thanks to a drastic changes in its profile and to its intellectual strength to adapt to a changing environment of the national states. One of the columns of the Order's old *raison d`être*, the war against the infidels, has been abandoned. Other columns, such as the taking care of the sick and the needy, are very much alive. The time of the Order's rule over Malta – as described in this book – was perhaps the most prestigious and glorious period of the honorable institution's millennial history.

|1600|1700|1800|1900|2000|

ILE   MALTA   EXILE   ROME

|1600|1700|1800|1900|2000|

GDOM OF   WAR OF THE SPANISH   FIRST WORLD
ADA   SUCCESSION   WAR

OTESTANTISM   INDEPENDENCE OF   SECOND WORLD
IN EUROPE   THE UNITED STATES   WAR

    THIRTY YEARS   FRENCH   EUROPEAN
       WAR   REVOLUTION   UNION

The eleventh and twelfth centuries were a period of clashes between the emperor and the popes and of considerable political and economical dynamization. The Occidental expansion into the south and east of the Mediterranean was an aspect of this.

Chapter 1

The Occident, the Chivalric Orders, and their Spiritual Roots

To understand Hospitaller Malta, one has to look back to the second half of the eleventh and the early twelfth century which saw a new orientation and spiritual interpretation of poverty and the concept of serving of the *pauperes commilitones Christi*. This is documented by the formation of several new Orders, congregations, and institutions like the Premonstratensians, Cistercians, Cartusians, Gilbertines, Lords of the Cross, Humilates, Antonites, and Trinitarians which generally took over the rules of St Benedict or St Augustine. To a certain extent this background and development also can be applied on the emerging of the chivalric Orders. However, other events contributed to the foundation of the Templars, the Teutonic knights, and the knights of St John.

The eight-pointed cross of the knights sculpted under the apse of the passage to the chapel of the langue of Castille, Leon, and Portugal in St John's Co-Cathedral.

14   THE CHIVALRIC ORDERS, AND THEIR SPIRITUAL ROOTS

Sketch of the Templar symbol and piebald pennant by Benedictine monk illustrator Matthew Paris (c.1200–59).

The term 'order' comes from the Latin *Ordo* meaning 'order', 'rule', and 'institution' and is used for groups of people who have chosen to live according to an obligatory 'order'. In the medieval Latin-Christian world, these Orders developed highly refined and strict ethical rules as well as ambitious tasks and aims to reach. Quite early in their history the idea was established that a man could only be member of one Order, to which he had to remain faithful all his life. Therefore every new member of an Order had to do a vow to obey its rules and to promise to fulfil its tasks and goals. This procedure also comprises the acceptance of punishment in case the vows, statutes, and rules of the Order and institution were not respected or obeyed.

One important reason for the genesis and establishment of the monastic chivalric Orders was the crusades. The formation of these Orders was a deeply international affair. From their beginning their members came from several Latin-Christian countries, and they cherished a certain amount of independence – also from the power of the king of Jerusalem. An exception was the Teutonic Order whose members were mainly recruited from German lands and had strong ties with the Hohenstaufen dynasty. The spiritual climate and *Zeitgeist* of the eleventh and twelfth centuries, with their movement of ecclesiastical reforms, the questioning of the ecclesiastic policy of the emperor, and the European expansionist tendencies caused by a significant demographic increase were important aspects which favoured the birth and growth of the chivalric Orders. That their foundation in the twelfth century was not limited to the Holy Land is documented by the subsequent foundation of the three important Spanish chivalric Orders: the Orders of Alcantara, Calatrava, and Santiago. There were, however, important differences. Although it was significant that they were formed in a country whose destiny and development in high medieval times was determined by a 'Holy War' between Christians and Muslims, the Spanish Orders from the beginning had strong ties with the kingdom. This feature distinguished them from the Hospitallers or the Templars.

Although originally intended for the Templars, Bernard of Clairvaux's treatise *Liber ad Milites Templi, de laude novae militiae*, written between 1130 and 1136, can be considered as the spiritual, ethical, and ideological basis for 'monks of war'

in general. As in St Bernard's propagandistic clerical treatises, the idea of a knight as a martyr killed in the fight with the infidels is interpreted as a sort of fulfilment of earthly life, a death which is the best way to have one's sins forgiven and to gain heaven. St Bernard had created possibly the most convincing justification for the symbiosis of *Militia Dei* and *Militia Saeculari* and therefore the coalition of chivalric life and life in an Order. Several later clerics and medieval intellectuals followed and built upon these thoughts and theories. However, the emphasis of this new model of an institution – despite of all military tasks by the *Militia Saeculari* – is laid on the spiritual aspect of the *Militia Dei*.

Some historians have pointed out the correlation between the new concept of the fighting knights of

A medieval manuscript portraying St Bernard of Clairvaux who wrote the treatise Liber ad Milites Templi, de laude novae militiae *(In Praise of the New Knighthood) between 1130 and 1136.*

The Chivalric Orders, and their Spiritual Roots

Christ and the contemporary internal reform of the Church. In fact in several important aspects, these models of knightly and ecclesiastical virtues and functions appear more and more identical. Significantly this close relation is reflected in the belief that the Templars and the knights of St John originally took their rules from the Augustinians and the Benedictines respectively, reforming them according to their own needs. This opinion that the Hospitallers took over the Augustinian rule – although shared by the majority of the older and modern historians – is, however, to be dealt with care. The term 'a rule of St Augustine' first appeared in 1067 and it is still not clear if it defines a proper text or refers to a general form of living.

Moreover, since St Augustine appears as the author of several texts which refer to certain rules, until further research is carried out, it is hardly possible to define what was understood as a rule of St Augustine in the early twelfth century. The *consuetudines* of the different institutions have still to be clarified. With regard to the close relationship of the new chivalric Orders to canons and monks – besides the most likely use of the same rules – the term *Militia Dei* was used for all these institutions. The protection and the care of pilgrims were not only taken over by the new chivalric Orders but also by brotherhoods and communities of canons and other clerics.

St Augustine, *fresco by Sandro Botticelli, 1480; in the church of Ognissanti, Florence.*

SHAPING OF AN INSTITUTION   17

The Amalfi Cross, which eventually became the Maltese cross, is found all over Amalfi. The eight-pointed cross is allegedly a symbol used by the knights to denote the eight obligations or aspirations of the knights: have faith; repent of sins; give proof of humility; love justice; be merciful; be sincere and whole-hearted; and endure persecution.

The historical flag of Amalfi.

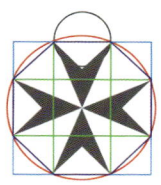

The geometric construction of the Order's cross.

The Hospitallers – from a Brotherhood to an Order

In this theoretical concept, the *Militia Saecularis* appears clearly subordinated as an instrument to the proper aim of the *Militia Dei*: the fight for God and the Latin Christian religion.

Theories which try to find direct connections between the hospital for pilgrims founded in Jerusalem in 603 by Abbot Probus by order of Pope Gregory the Great or that founded by order of Charlemagne and described by the Franconian monk Bernard in 870 with the later foundation of the merchants of Amalfi and the institution of the brotherhood of the Hospitallers are not based on solid archival ground. The works of medieval and early modern historians of the Order which trace back the roots of the Order to biblical or at least early medieval times have to be considered as significant manifestations of the strong will of legitimization and a growing confidence in a glorious past. From the scientific point of view, they are just fantasies. More solid evidence is an anonymous Amalfitanian chronicle of the late eleventh century about the pilgrimage of Archbishop John of Amalfi (*c*.1070–81) to Palestine and the report of William of Tyre written around 1180. Both sources mention two Amalfitan hospitals with personnel in existence in Jerusalem before 1080 and which catered for pilgrims. The controversially interpreted history of the Amalfitan foundations of monasteries, convents, and hospitals in Jerusalem in the eleventh century cannot be discussed here in detail. What is surely is that the Amalfitans built a monastery (S. Maria Latina) for male pilgrims and a convent (S. Maria Magdalena) for female ones in the second half of the eleventh century.

Most likely S. Maria Latina and S. Maria Magdalena were dedicated to the care of the pilgrims from the very beginning. That explains why William of Tyre and the anonymous chronicler of Archbishop John of Amalfi's pilgrimage describe them as hospitals. Still no documents have been found to support William's claim of a direct continuity between the Amalfitan institutions and the famous hospital of the brotherhood of St John. This would mean that the Amalfitanian hospitals would have survived the conquest of Jerusalem by the Seljuks between 1070 and 1078. There are, however, some not unimportant reasons to believe that there was a Christian hospital in permanent use since the mid-eleventh century and throughout the period of Muslim rule over the city.

The Crusaders' conquest of Jerusalem in 1099 led to the decisive step of separating the hospitals from the convents and monasteries of S. Maria de Latina and S. Maria Magdalena, as documented in Frutolf and Ekkehard's *Chronica necnon anonymi Chronica imperatorum* and Albert of Aachen's *Historia Hierosolymitana*. Both sources clearly separate the terms of *monasteria* and *hospitalia* and refer to taxes and donations exclusively made to the hospitals. From then on the hospitals became independent

Blessed Gerard, feeding the sick from Giacomo Bosio, Histoire des Chevaliers de l'Ordre de S. Iean de Hierusalem, edited by J. Baudoin (Paris, 1643).

jurisdictional bodies. This innovative step of separation can only be fully understood in the context with the softening of the frontiers between the spheres of laymen and clerics.

The two papal bulls of July 1112 and February 1113 by Paschal II confirmed the property of the convent of S. Maria de Latina in Jerusalem and the property of the hospital and herewith documented their separation. Thanks to this separation, a steadily growing amount of donations went exclusively to the benefit of the hospital. Still there is no reference or indication of a rule of the brethren of the hospital and it can be assumed that, in the beginning of the twelfth century, this institution

Shaping of an Institution

Portrait (detail) of Blessed Gerard in the first entry of the Cronologia dei Grandi Maestri del Sovrano Militare Ordine di Malta dal Beato Frà Gerardo Sasso ad oggi.

was a community of laymen. In the papal bull of February 1113, a certain brother 'Gerard' is mentioned as *institutor* of the hospital. Later in the historical works on the Order, this Gerard is wrongly styled as founder of the Order and its first grand master. The terms 'founder' and 'grand master' of the Order are certainly false as there was then no fixed rule for the brethren of the hospital. But, in consideration of his importance and his alleged role as the founder of the institution, it is understandable that in early modern times the langues of Provence and of Italy respectively claimed that he came from their lands. Concrete details about the life of Blessed Gerard are enshrouded in the mists of history.

Further confusion abounds because, in the first decades of the

THE BLESSED GERARD

For the members of the Order of St John the figure of the Blessed Gerard or 'Gerard' as he appears in the archival documents, is of special importance. In the history books and chronologies of the Order, he is often listed as 'Grand Master' and 'founder' of the institution. This, however, is false as in the early 12th century the brethren of the hospital had no fixed rule yet. Although the langues of Provence and of Italy claim that he came from their lands concrete details about his life are lacking.

twelfth century, not only the hospital but also the Holy Sepulchre and the monastery at Mount Tabor had chiefs called Gerard. It is most likely that Gerard, the *institutor* of the hospital, came from central or southern Italy, maybe even from Amalfi itself. The genesis of this false interpretation and stylization of Gerard as the founder of the Order of St John – which was current until very recently – seems to have been Jacob of Vitry's *Historia orientalis*, a work composed in the early thirteenth century. By then the Order had been established and, adopting the new spiritual and ideological climate, Gerard is styled as 'a man who dedicated his life entirely to God and the Christian religion; and who established the saintly rules of the new institution. He also took care that these rule were strictly observed by every member.'

Moreover, the bull issued by Pope Paschal II in February 1113 cannot be considered as the 'foundation charter for the new Order' as is maintained so often in older literature. This bull just contains a general papal declaration of protection, an exemption from tithes, and the permission to elect the head of the institution in a free manner. The papal privileges only confirm the previous documents issued by the patriarch of Jerusalem and the archbishop of Caesarea. In fact those rights were guaranteed to many clerical institutions in the twelfth century. The hospital remained subordinated to the patriarch of Jerusalem. There was still no exemption from the hierarchy of the diocese when, following the death of Gerard in September 1120, 'Raimundus de Podio' appeared as new head of the brotherhood. In the documents he also appears as 'Raymond de Podio' or 'Raymond de Puy' which suggests a French origin.

In the following decades the importance of the institution grew further: numerous early-twelfth-century records of donations and privileges guaranteed the hospital a solid material and jurisdictional basis and positions. Amongst the most important of these documents are two diplomas issued by King Baldouin of Jerusalem in 1100 and 1112 which acknowledge that the hospital had possessions and houses in Jerusalem, Acre, Nablus, and Jaffa. The deeds of the patriarch of Jerusalem and the archbishop of Caesarea exempted the brotherhood of St John from paying tithes to the bishops in Palestine. To Pope Paschal II's exemption from the paying of tithes in 1113, in 1135 Pope Innocent II added the jurisdictional exemption of the hospital and the brotherhood of St John from the hierarchy of the diocese. In medieval eyes, this was a most important step and contributed considerably to the popularity of the Hospitallers.

Godfrey de Bouillon meeting the Blessed Gerard at his hospital in Jerusalem. Antoine Favray, Museum of Fine Arts, Valletta.

22 THE CHIVALRIC ORDERS, AND THEIR SPIRITUAL ROOTS

In the mid-twelfth century, the brotherhood already had rich possessions in Palestine and Syria as well as in Sicily, South and North Italy, and France. During Raymond de Puy's forty years of activity as head of the institution, the road towards an independence as an Order was undertaken. This meant a largely universal exemption from the ecclesiastical hierarchy, the establishment of its own fixed rules, and the taking up of military 'chivalric' tasks. These were the decisive steps towards a sovereign chivalric Order. The exact date when priests and clerics started to take up service in the hospital and the resultant adoption of the rule of St Augustine – with the inclusion of some elements of the rule of the Benedictines – has not yet been determined.

The Order's growing importance and popularity is echoed by more and more comments and authentic sources. In 1102 the English pilgrim Saewulf reports about an *ecclesia sancti Joannis* in Jerusalem connected with the hospital. After 1139 Pope Innocent II officially allowed the hospital to take priests in its service for one or two years. These priests were, so to say, 'guest priests'. The acquisition and new foundation of more hospitals and the privilege of 1137 to build own churches and churchyards made it obvious that the brotherhood could not do without clerics. In October 1154 Pope Anastasius IV permitted the hospital to have its own right for clerics.

Raymond de Puy called the First Capitolo Generale *after he took over the role of Master of the Hospital in 1120.*
Lionello Spada (1576–1622) fresco, Summer Room, Grand Master's Palace, Valletta.

Raymond de Puy offers the help of the Hospitallers to Baldouin II of Jerusalem in 1120.
Lionello Spada (1576–1622) fresco, Summer Room, Grand Master's Palace, Valletta.

In medieval eyes, an exempt institution implied a decisive attraction: liberation from being subject to the threat of excommunication and interdiction by the diocese and local clergy. With donations and gifts to the hospital, one could gain pastoral support and – even more importantly – a regular and official ecclesiastic blessing and burial. Maybe the most spectacular document of this mentality of religious donations for personal spiritual salvation is the testament by Alfonso I of Aragon of 1131 in which he bequeathed huge tracts of his lands to the Hospitallers, the Templars, and the Holy Sepulchre.

These growing tasks and responsibilities required the Hospitallers to employ more laymen and clerics.

The privilege *Christianae fidei religio* issued by Pope Anastasius IV in October 1154 documented the ecclesiastical confirmation of the hospitaller brotherhood of St John as an Order, laying the basis for a deep transformation of the internal structure and ideology of the institution. Although now almost in all jurisdictional aspects equal to the Templars in terms of function and structure, the Order of St John and the mainly military oriented Order of the Templars were perceived as clearly different.

The Hospitallers become a Chivalric Order

In 1136 King Fulques of Jerusalem transferred to the Hospitallers possessions in the south of Palestine, including the strategic castle of Beit-Jibrin, near Ascalon. The Hospitallers therefore became directly concerned with duties to colonize this border region of the Christian kingdom of Palestine, resulting in a move towards militarization. In subsequent years more castles and other possessions in Palestine and Antioch were transferred in the hands of the Hospitallers. More important was the fact that these possessions were often transferred with their feudal rights which meant that the new lords were also expected to take their military protection which, however, then were not yet taken over by the Hospitallers but by recruited servants and subsequently by mercenaries and knights from Italy, France, and Spain.

This military role soon became the Hospitallers' primary obligation. In the 1140s and 1150s there occur more and more references to the participation of military contingents in the service of the Hospitallers fighting against the increasing pressure of the Muslims. But it was not before 1182 that, in the statutes of Roger de Moulins, there appeared a definite reference to *fratres armorum*. When Raymond de Puy died in 1160 there

King Fulques, third king of Jerusalem hands over the castle of Beit-Jibrin, near Ascalon in c.1136 to Raymond de Puy. Lionello Spada (1576–1622) fresco, Summer Room, Grand Master's Palace, Valletta.

In 1142 the Hospitallers were handed over a stronghold in the county of Tripoli (now central Syria). The castle became to be known as Le Crac des Chevaliers. The appearance of the fort as seen today is mostly from the reconstructions done on the structure by the Order after the great earthquakes of 1170 and 1202.

were three different groups – not classes – unified under the term of the hospital: (1) the brethren who traditionally concentrated on the aspect of *caritas* (2) the clerics responsible for the pastoral work, and (3) the recently established section of the mercenaries and knights taking care of the military defence of the possessions and protecting the pilgrims. Historians like Berthold von Waldstein-Wartenberg are certainly mistaken when they claim that the Hospitallers had a special 'class' of 'servants' in the middle of the twelfth century. There is no archival evidence that there were criteria of social rank or status in the institution at the time.

It is yet unclear if military duty was then only carried out by paid troops or if some Hospitaller brethren also took part. It was evident, however, for the people of the late twelfth century – with their pragmatic-religious *Weltanschauung* – that membership in the Order of St John offered the double privileges of a charitable as well as a military Order. For centuries it was the charitable aspect which was pointed out. In fact the term *'miles et frater Hospitalis'* appears relatively rarely in early documents which might indicate that the unification of monastic and military duties in one Order then still appeared strange, if not outrageous. From 1148 onwards there are mainly references to *fratres Hospitalis*, a term commonly used in numerous medieval reports and pilgrim accounts with reference to members of the Order. This was still the case when the Order moved to Rhodes.

The complex and difficult transformation of the Hospitallers into a military Order is documented by various sources. Still in the 1170s Pope Alexander III and several chroniclers condemned the militarization of the Order. There must

A satellite photo of Jerusalem showing the large area which belonged to the Order of St John of Jerusalem in the 12th century. This area has ever since been called 'Muristan' which is Kurdish for hospital (cf. Arab [انات‌سرامیب] bīmārestān and Persian himeristan).

have been a lively discussion also between the members about the future course of the institution. Certainly there was also pressure from outside, namely the diocese of Palestine and the *Curia* in Rome. A papal mandate of 1170 directed the Hospitallers to concentrate again on charitable duties. Despite the increasing *de facto* militarization of the Order, the statutes fixed under the new head of the institution Roger de Moulins in 1181 still stress the task to take care of the *domini infermi* – 'our lords, the sick'.

With the Holy Land in the limelight of occidental and oriental interest, the situation became more and more dynamic. The growing Mameluke and Saracen threat to Christian Palestine and Syria made the militaristic orientation of the Order appear quite useful and therefore acceptable. There are more and more indications of the unification of the Order's charitable and military duties after 1160. Around 1165 the priest and pilgrim Johannes of Würzburg travelled to Jerusalem and reported about the military defensive duties of the Hospitallers: his account provides an important insight into the scope of the medical service and administration of the Order's hospital in Jerusalem which then extended to several buildings. Johannes saw no fewer than 2,000 patients in them. Still his report does not make clear if the Hospitallers' military forces

MILITARY DUTIES 27

consisted of paid mercenaries or included fighting brethren. A contemporary letter by the head of the Order Gilbert d'Assailly (1163–69) is clearer: it includes a reference to *fratres nostri religioni milicium commiscentes* which may indicate that there were already members who were active in the military.

The medieval monastic chivalric Orders had had their roots in the movement of the crusades in the late eleventh and early twelfth century; they all started as communities of people who freely joined to carry out duties, acts, and deeds. In the case of the Templars and the Hospitallers, joining was connected with fulfilling strictly stipulated criteria. New members had to prove an impeccable way of life; when at the turn of the twelfth and thirteenth centuries the Hospitallers established the class of knights, the professed knights had to be of free and noble birth. In late medieval times membership in the Order was seen as a distinction of character and class but never as an acknowledgment of proven deeds or honours. Another universally characteristic of the monastic chivalric order was their hierarchical structure.

According to Brancadoro Perini, Master Gilbert d'Assailly was of outstanding temperament. However, he exhausted the Order's budget on military campaigns and he had to borrow money. The huge debt filled him with remorse and, grief-stricken, he abdicated from the office of master in 1169.
Portrait from Histoire des chevaliers hospitaliers de S. Jean de Jérusalem *by Abbé Vertot (1655–1735) and engraved by Laurent Cars (1699–1771).*

From early on these Orders wished to document their exclusiveness and singularity and to give an outward sign of their inner unity. Every member was expected to carry visible signs or marks of his respective Order. The universally accepted and renowned sign of the brotherhood of the hospital of St John of Jerusalem and later the Order of St John was the eight-pointed cross. The eight points of the cross are supposed to be connected with the eight beatitudes of the sermon of the mount. Besides the eight-pointed cross, the bar cross was also used. Since their time in Rhodes, the knights have worn a red cloak on their armour, the so-called *sopraveste* or surcoat with a white bar cross. This form of the cross was also used on the official flag of the Order and the coat of arms of the grand masters.

Internal changes and the international background

The internal changes of the Hospitallers into a chivalric Order are reflected in the question of the identity of their original patron saint which also documents to which extent the institution was a part of the balance of power and interests in the Holy Land. Like the question of the continuity of the Amalfitan foundations of the convents and hospitals in the eleventh century and the hospital of the brotherhood in Jerusalem, the question of the patron is also not completely solved. It is not clear whether the St John who was the patron saint of the hospital was originally St John the Almoner (*beati Joannis Elegmon Alexandrini patriarchas*), as maintained by William of Tyre in his *Historia* written between 1165 and 1180, or whether it was St John the Baptist (*sancti Joannis Baptistae*) from the very beginning. We get some important information from the writings of contemporaries. The English pilgrim Saewulf, when visiting Jerusalem in 1102, mentions a *'hospitale, ubi monasterium habetur praeclarum in honore sancti Joannis Baptistae dedicatum'*. This reference to the Baptist is confirmed eleven years later in Paschal II's papal bull. The historians Jonathan Riley Smith and Berthold Waldstein-Wartenberg believe that there was a change of the patron saints from the Alexandrian Patriarch St John the Almoner to St John the Baptist who was better known in the Western Latin Church immediately after the Crusaders conquered Jerusalem in 1099.

However, if one keeps in mind the massive opposition in the twelfth century against the unification of monastic-clerical principles with the military-chivalric concept and against the softening of the traditional class system, a new explanation crops up. As bishop of Tyre and therefore as a member of the episcopacy of the Holy Land, William of Tyre was one of the many strong pleaders for the traditional *ordo* and against the establishment of the new Orders of 'monks of war'. In this connection it would appear logical to point to St John the Almoner as the patron of the hospital and of the brotherhood as an unmistaken indication for the new institution to concentrate only on the tasks of charity.

In fact it was William of Tyre who, around 1170, had strongly recommended the newly founded Order of St John to abandon its military activities and to turn back exclusively to the care of the sick and pilgrims. This was also repeated by Pope Alexander III after 1178 when the seemingly unstoppable development of the Hospitallers into a military chivalric Order was becoming more and more obvious. We only have to remember how many medieval texts and 'traditions' were later the object of ideologically and politically motivated revisions. Especially in

The Hospitallers' hospitals and castles in the Crusader States from 1135 to 1285.

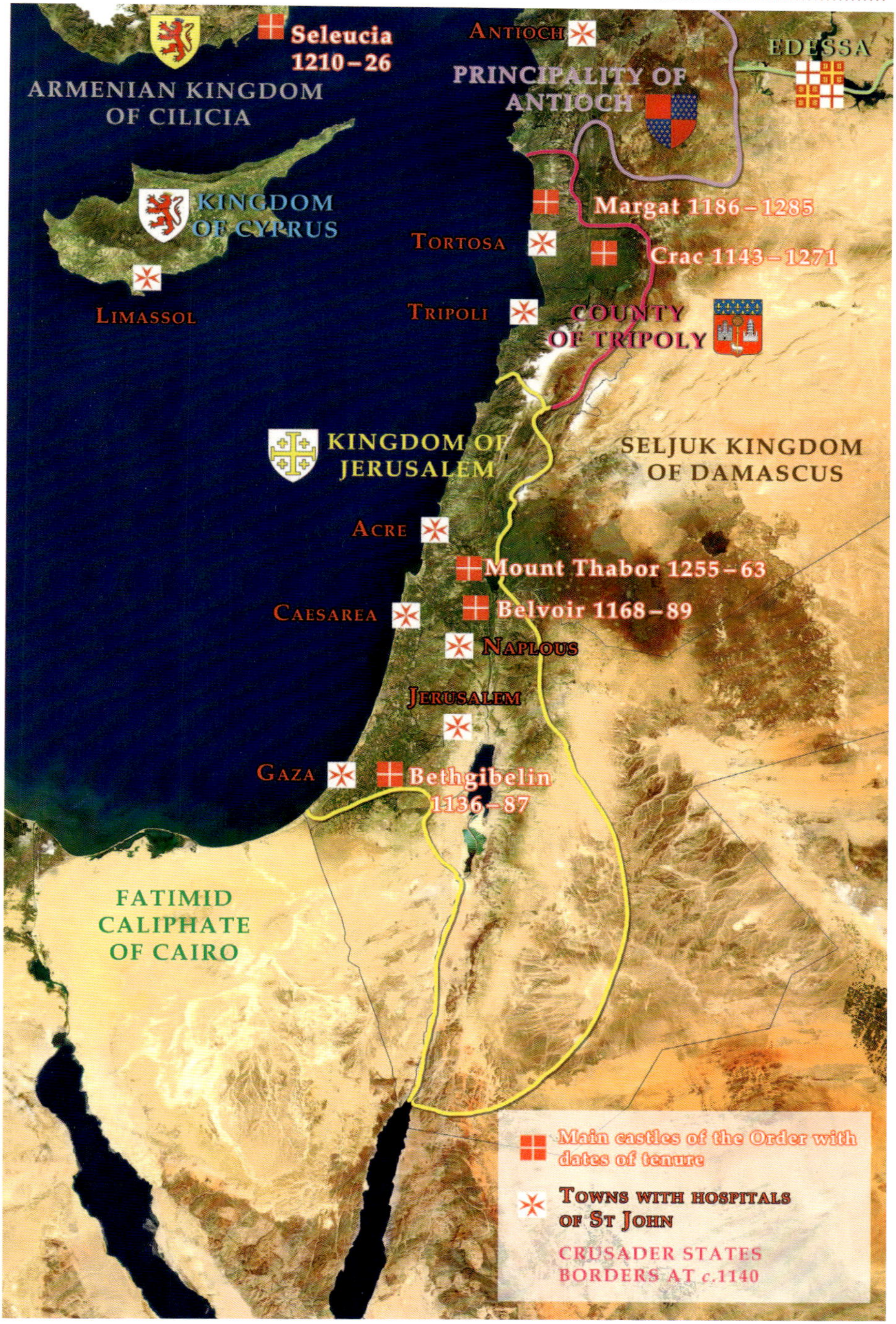

Seleucia 1210–26
ANTIOCH
EDESSA
ARMENIAN KINGDOM OF CILICIA
PRINCIPALITY OF ANTIOCH
KINGDOM OF CYPRUS
Margat 1186–1285
TORTOSA
Crac 1143–1271
LIMASSOL
TRIPOLI
COUNTY OF TRIPOLY
KINGDOM OF JERUSALEM
SELJUK KINGDOM OF DAMASCUS
ACRE
Mount Thabor 1255–63
CAESAREA
Belvoir 1168–89
NAPLOUS
JERUSALEM
GAZA
Bethgibelin 1136–87
FATIMID CALIPHATE OF CAIRO
Main castles of the Order with dates of tenure
TOWNS WITH HOSPITALS OF ST JOHN
CRUSADER STATES BORDERS AT c.1140

the case of such important questions for medieval men, like the patron of an institution or the spiritual and theological legitimization of an institution, one has to read contemporary bulls, annals, chronicles, and historical treatises with great care.

The 1154 exemption from the hierarchy of the diocese and the increasing militarization of the Order must have had some influence on the position of the head of the Order in international politics, as well as the hierarchy of the Order itself. In the first decades of the twelfth century the head of the hospital was often called *provisor*. Some decades later, when describing the siege of Ascalon, William of Tyre – not without some personal political reason – listed the institution's head Raymond de Puy [above] as the lowest in the rank of the ecclesiastical dignitaries in the Holy Land, behind the abbots and the head of the Templars. This is, however, misleading and underestimates the real importance of the Hospitallers' head. When, after 1154, with the papal exemptions and established statutes, the Order became increasingly sovereign, the title *venerabilis magister hospitalis* appeared, a title surely meant to demonstrate the Order's new largely independent and sovereign position. The high-reaching ambitions of the head of the Hospitallers became especially obvious when, in 1157, Raymond de Puy added *Dei gratia* to *venerabilis magister hospitalis*.

The 'aristocratization' of an institution

In late medieval and early modern times – especially in the period when the Hospitallers ruled over Malta – 'aristocratization' became such an important aspect in the profile of the Order. In fact in early modern times the Order's aristocratic aspect was the distinctive feature of the identity of the knights of St John. This was not so in high medieval times. The foundation of a hospital in Jerusalem by the merchants of Amalfi has to be seen in the context of the establishment of contemporary

One of the earliest printed woodcuts of Jerusalem based on contemporary eyewitness sources. It appeared in the first illustrated travel guide to the Holy Land, written by Bernhard von Breydenbach who was accompanied by Dutch artist Erhard Reuwich in 1483.
The hospital is marked in the centre (highlighted in red here).

urban hospitals by communities or town councils. The foundation was a special 'civic' affair and the milieu of the early members of the brotherhood must have been a civic one. Significantly the early sources say nothing about the social background of the *'vir vitae venerabilis et fide insignis'* and the first head of the hospital Gerard, while, in the case of Agnes, the head of the convent S. Maria Magdalena in Jerusalem – also founded by the citizens of Amalfi – they speak of a 'holy and noble-born woman'.

Despite of this original bourgeois character, the unique situation of the Holy Land, the permanent flow of pilgrims, and the special crusading spirit, the Hospitallers must have seemed attractive for nobles. Presumably even in the Order's early phase, some Italian or French nobles must have longed to join the brotherhood of St John. The increasing possession of fiefs and donations

32 THE CHIVALRIC ORDERS, AND THEIR SPIRITUAL ROOTS

of land and the integration in the defence of the country changed the profile of the Hospitallers considerably in the later part of the twelfth century. According to the high medieval class concept, the active and leading role in fighting was reserved for nobles. The mercenaries (*servientes*) or 'guest knights' assumed to cope with the new military duties were surely mostly of noble origin.

The privilege *Christianae fidei religio* issued by Anastasius IV in October 1154 was not only a milestone in establishing the Hospitallers as an Order but was also a decisive step in its 'aristocratization' which made the Hospitallers even more attractive for nobles. To the knight and the nobleman membership now offered the double privilege of a military as well as a charitable Order. On the other hand, when the Hospitallers had to face military duties, they must have been interested to persuade the hired – and surely well-paid – warriors to join the institution, thus guaranteeing a permanent military power as well as a reduction of the military expenses.

Giacomo Bosio's Storia dell'Ordine... *(1589), records that in 1130 Pope Innocent II had decreed that '...the Religion in war should bear a standard with a white cross on a red field'. Pope Alexander IV's Bull of 1259 permitted the knights in war to wear a red mantle bearing a white cross, and the Order began to make systematic use of the bar cross as its emblem. Detail from* Il Miracolo d'Ismeria *(1131) fresco, Lionello Spada (1576–1622), Summer Room, Grand Master's Palace, Valletta.*

These developments certainly required an internal pragmatic restructuring of the Order. Statutes and structures were created to guarantee the soldiers acceptance as full members. In a 'competition' with the Templars, in the following decades more and more nobles were attracted to the Order of St John and the original civic institution became dominated by the nobility. This development did not go unnoticed in Christian Europe. In acknowledgment of their successful activities in the Holy Land, the Hospitallers were showered with donations and property by donors who expected both military protection and spiritual support. Moreover, these donations have to be seen also in the context of the increasing Mameluke and Saracens pressure on Christian Syria and the kingdom of Jerusalem in the late twelfth century. The changing situation also meant that the original rules established under Raymond de Puy were changed and augmented. A new picture emerges in the statutes passed in the chapter-general held under the Order's head Alfonso of Portugal in 1205 in the fortress of Margat. The definite reference to the 'chivalric Order of St John' means that its militarization was officially confirmed.

But by then, in the early thirteenth century, the whole situation in Christian Syria and Palestine had become most fragile and explosive. Soon, in 1291, the Order and all remaining Christians were swept out of their last stronghold, St Jean d'Acre.

The Hospitallers, decision, after the loss of the Holy Land and Syria, not to retreat to Europe's mainland but to establish their convent at the island of Rhodes was a decisive step to guarantee its survival as a sovereign power.

Chapter 2

The Hospitallers in Rhodes

Hospitallers, Templars, and the rulers of the occident – an uneasy partnership

One specific event serves to explain how much the situation of the chivalric Orders in Palestine had changed in the focus of thirteenth-century European politics and therefore in the context of its conflicts and tensions. When, in 1228, Emperor Frederick II – freshly excommunicated by Pope Gregory IX – arrived at the Holy Land and started negotiations with Sultan el-Kamil to achieve a ten years' peace and the handing over of Jerusalem to the Christians, the Hospitallers, besides the patriarch of Jerusalem and the Templars, refused to participate in the ceremonies and to pay homage to the emperor.

These internal Christian antipathies and conflicts were different in nature. The patriarch of Jerusalem considered the ceding of the two

The 1480 Siege of Rhodes. *Unknown French painter c.1485. Oil on wood, transported to canvas. Now at the Epernay Town Hall, France.*
The painting illustrates the moment when 2,500 Turks managed to climb the bastions on 28 July 1480, after 89 days of war. When all seemed lost to Grand Master d'Aubusson and his men, a miraculous apparition in the sky made the Turks turn back.

mosques at Jerusalem to the Muslims and to allow them their own jurisdiction in the city as blasphemous. The Templars and Hospitallers complained that they were not allowed to participate in the negotiations dealing with the restoration of their many castles and fortresses which Sal-ad-Din (*Saladin*) and his successors had conquered. The excommunication of Frederick II gave the Hospitallers and the Templars the pretext to resist the emperor.

The special legal system of the kingdom of Jerusalem and the intentions of its kings to put pressure and dominate over the chivalric Orders contributed considerably to their efforts to achieve ecclesiastic and secular sovereignty and independence. Outside Jerusalem, no feudal lord could be forced to perform military service for its kings who had no power over the military forces of the chivalric Orders – the only institutions who kept their troops permanently under arms. In the twelfth and thirteenth centuries, it became all too clear that the power and sovereignty of the kingdom of Jerusalem – always challenged by the powerful feudal lords, the growing power of the chivalric Orders, and the branches of the Italian maritime metropolises – was very limited. How much the ideological basis of the crusades had already been undermined and corroded in the

The Hospitallers restore a part of the walls of Jerusalem in 1228. Lionello Spada (1576–1622) fresco, Pages' Room, Grand Master's Palace, Valletta.

*Emperor Frederick II, suspicious of his own troops, takes residence in the tents of the Hospitallers and of the Templars. Lionello Spada (1576–1622) fresco, Pages Room, Grand Master's Palace, Valletta.
This is a later unlikely historical interpretation. In general the Hospitallers and Templars had very tense relations with Frederick II.*

middle of the thirteenth century is shown by the activities of the omnipresent agents and trading colonies of Genoa and Venice who did not hesitate to establish close contacts with the Muslim world.

There was anything but Christian unity. To stop Venetian mercantile expansion and to sweep them out of Acre, Genoa allied itself with the Arab rulers in Syria. From 1222 until the end of the Christian presence in Syria and Palestine in 1291, there was constant fighting between Genoa and Venice which had a polarizing effect on the Christian rulers and landlords of Palestine and Syria. Soon the Order of St John – in a paradox opposition to its rules and ideology – sided with the Genoese who were in alliance with the Muslims. The Templars, on the other hand, moved towards Venice. It was only too visible that – contrary to the propaganda of Rome – in the thirteenth century the ideological programme and spiritual foundation of the crusades had given way to a pure policy of power, greed, and personal interests. It would be too simple to explain this development by pointing out the effects of the struggle of the *Curia* against the 'heresy' of Emperor Frederick II and the Hohenstaufen family, the effects of the ambitions and aggressive policy of Charles of Anjou, and the permanent tensions between the Hospitallers and the Templars. The main reasons lay in the new concepts of society and trade as established by the new successful and expanding trading metropolises in Italy, Southern France, and Catalonia, where there was hardly any space for the old concepts of feudalism and religion to tackle politics and questions of power. The economic interchanges between Venice, Genoa, and Pisa with the crusader states, the Levant, and the Maghreb also implied a strong infiltration of the new economic concepts and culture. That these contacts had a different quality and had not much to do with religion is shown by the fact that, even after the last Christians left Syria and Palestine, these interchanges and economic presence became even stronger.

Already in the twelfth century, the Christian rulers of Palestine and the chivalric Orders had come to depend on the supply and transport services of the maritime republics of Amalfi, Genoa, Venice, and Pisa. The crusades and the permanent flow of pilgrims to the holy shrines of Palestine would have been unthinkable without such transport services. The branches and colonies of these Italian cities soon obtained exemptions from tax and custom and won extraterritorial privileges and their own jurisdictions. Their consuls and representatives in Tyre, Jaffa, Acre, Caesarea, and Beirut soon became extremely influential factors in Latin Syria and Palestine.

A good indication of this change of spirit and culture was the fruitless effort of Pope Gregory X in 1272 to instigate a new crusade. His call found hardly any echo in the West, a development that had dangerous consequences for the reputation and situation of the chivalric Orders. This is shown when a general council was convened in Lyons in 1274 to discuss the political, ideological, and theological status of the Hospitallers and Templars. It soon challenged the very existence of these chivalric Orders. The official and unofficial causes which some bishops and feudal lords presented to move the pope to dissolve the Orders or to unify them in one institution were multifaceted. The central reason was certainly the exemption of the Orders from the jurisdiction and authority of the local bishops and princes. It was only natural that many feudal lords and princes very much resented that the Hospitallers and Templars in the German empire, France, Aragon, Castille, and Italy had gained huge territories in the twelfth and thirteenth centuries whose taxes and revenues were then lost to the former lords. A special reason for the bishops' envy was the right of the Orders to collect money, pittances, and charity in their territories. The right of the chaplains of the Orders to conduct Christian funerals for excommunicated people also created conflicts. The latter point appeared to the representatives of the bishops a massive and dangerous interference in ecclesiastical and episcopal jurisdiction.

The permanent tension and visible rivalry between the Templars and the Hospitallers of course played in the hands of those who pressed

The Holy Land and Middle East, a detail from Abbé Vertot's (1655–1735) Histoire des Chevaliers... *(1726).*
National Museum of Archaeology Library.
See also map on page 29.

Camar
Salef
R. de Sequin
le fl. Cidnus
PRINCIPAUTÉ
Mont
Negro
Alexandrete
ou Scanderone
D'ANTIOCHE
GOLFE DE LAYAZZO
Antioche
Chateau
de Harem
Alep
Port de St. Simeon
Cap St. André
Nicosie
Famagouste
ISLE DE CHYPRE
Episcopia
Limisso
Laodicée de Syrie
Biblis
Fleuve Oronte
Margath
Tortose cidevant
Rapha
COMTE DE
Crac ou Arac aux Hosp.
Trypoly
TRIPOLY
Gebile
Riv. d'Adonis
ou Thamiras
Barut ou Beryte
Sidon
ou Sayette
Damas
RRANÉE
Tyr
Beaufort
Thoron
Cesarée de P
St. Jean d'Acre
ou Ptolemaïde
Zabulon
Chateau des Pelerins
ou Pierre encise
Nazareth
Mt. Thabor
ROYAUME
Busseret ou B
Cesarée de Palestine
Sebaste ou Samarie
Arsur Cte.
Jaffa ou Joppe Cte.
Yblin
Lidda
Rama
Gué de Jacob
DE JERUSALEM
Jerusalem
Bethlehem
Betanie
Jerico
M. Olivet
Ascalon Cte.
Gaza
JUDEE
Bersabée ou
Gibrin
Darom
Bouche du Tanis
Mont Royal Seigneurie
nommée aussi Crac ou Ar
cydevant la Pierre du De
Larisse
Bilbeis
autrefois Peluse

the pope to take away the old privileges and exemptions from the chivalric Orders. It certainly helped that grand masters of the Templars and the Hospitallers were personally present at the council of Lyons. By pointing out their still valid role in protecting pilgrims and fighting the infidels they aimed to prevent any direct actions against them. The representatives of the Hospitallers furthermore stressed the utility of their Order by presenting their important role in the caring after the sick and poor. An important reason why the pope and the leaders of the West refrained from taking direct actions against the huge property and lands of the Orders for the moment were the high costs of the fight against the growing pressure of the infidels in the Levant.

What, however, was apparent was a growing antipathy against the chivalric Orders. It did not take long for Philip IV of France successfully to press Pope Clement V to act against the Templars. In 1312 the council of Vienne dissolved the Templars, who, after the loss of the Holy Land, had moved back from the borders of Christian-Muslim fighting. It was therefore much easier now to accuse them of uselessness, idolatry, and heresy. The greed of Philip IV in the end led to the killing of many Templars and the annihilation of the institution.

Grand Master Guillaume de Villaret and his Hospitallers arrive at Limassol, Cyprus in 1291. Expelled from Tolomaide (Acre), they still held the castles of Crac and Margat in Syria.
Lionello Spada (1576–1622) fresco, Ambassadors' Room, Grand Master's Palace, Valletta.

Rhodes – the new headquarters

Such a disaster was avoided by the Order because of one main reason. A few years before (1306–09) – after a short interlude in Cyprus – the knights had conquered the island of Rhodes, establishing their headquarters in the city of Rhodes. This was perhaps the decisive move which ensured their ideological, military, and political survival, together with some deft diplomatic work in Rome and Paris. A papal bull of 2 May 1313 transferred most of the Templars' property to the Hospitallers.

The island of Rhodes was attacked by Grand Master Fulques de Villaret in 1307. After a two-year campaign the island surrendered in August 1309.
Lionello Spada (1576–1622) fresco, Ambassadors' Room, Grand Master's Palace, Valletta.

Pope Clement V stood firm on the side of the Hospitallers. In a bull of 5 September 1307, he confirmed the acquisition of Rhodes and stressed the merits of the knights of St John in spreading the Latin-Christian doctrine and their 'noble' intentions to expel all schismatics and infidels from Rhodes. The status of the Hospitallers seemed to have been fully cemented when, on 17 December 1307, Clement confirmed all rights and exemptions of the Hospitallers and asked all prelates to respect their prerogatives and to protect them from all attacks. On 17 April 1309 the exemption of the knights from the episcopal jurisdiction was re-confirmed.

The conquest of Rhodes and the move of the convent there demonstrated to the public the ever-growing importance of the military aspect of the institution.

It fits in the picture of this internal restructuring of the Order which, in the late thirteenth and early fourteenth centuries, stopped running many hospitals in central Europe. This must have lead to diminishing the flow of indulgences and pittances but the balance of the institution moved towards the military side. Many historians have explained this as an effect of the growing Muslim threat to the west. However, looking at the general contemporary ideological and social changes in the west, there may have been other reasons. The emergence of the new bourgeois class had lead to a sort of 'aristocratization' of the nobility which started to concentrate on 'heroic' military duties, just as the noble members of the Order moved away from the old concept of the caring of the sick. More and more they were freed from charity duties. A late thirteenth-century privilege by German King Rudolf of Hapsburg praises the military spirit of the knights of St John but does not mention their charity work. Of course, the multi-faceted charity work of the institution survived but it did not remain the Order's central *raison d'être* any more. The general picture of the institution in the fourteenth century was composed of knightly virtues, military bravery, and the old monastic-like organization.

While the hospitals of the Order in the west started to disappear, a prestigious huge new hospital was erected at their new headquarters

The Hospitallers are ousted from Tolomaide (Acre) by the Mamelukes in 1291.
Lionello Spada (1576–1622) fresco, Pages' Room, Grand Master's Palace, Valletta.

at Rhodes, equipped with the most comfortable and modern rooms and services. Throughout its history the Order kept this tradition to build prestigious hospitals at its headquarters, symbolizing the institution's roots. In Jerusalem, as in Acre, Limassol, Rhodes, and finally in Malta, the Hospitallers managed to impress with huge and most modern hospitals. By the fifteenth century the central hospital was reserved for the sick while ordinary pilgrims were looked after in a *hospitium*.

New orientations

After the move to Acre, then the most important Christian port in the Holy Land, the Order influenced life in this city so much that the place soon was called in French 'St Jean d'Acre'. After long preparations, in 1291 the Mamelukes conquered this last Christian outpost in Palestine. In 1285 the Hospitallers had lost the fortress of Margat, their former headquarters and subsequently the knights – like the Templars – had to rely on the goodwill of the Latin-Christian king of Cyprus, Henry II of the house of Lusignan. Henry allowed the Hospitallers to take up their headquarters in Limassol for a limited amount of time, but they soon realized the consequences of the loss of the Holy Land for the institution. Thanks to the energetic policy of Grand Master Fulque de Villaret, the Order soon changed from a mainly land-based chivalric institution into a maritime power.

Was the move from Palestine to Cyprus and finally to Rhodes and the political implications of these moves a form of decline? In Syria and Palestine the knights of St John had basked in the limelight of western attention, so to say in the focus of world politics, the centre of Christian, Jewish, and Muslim interests, and the nerve centre of western and eastern economic exchanges. The island of Rhodes

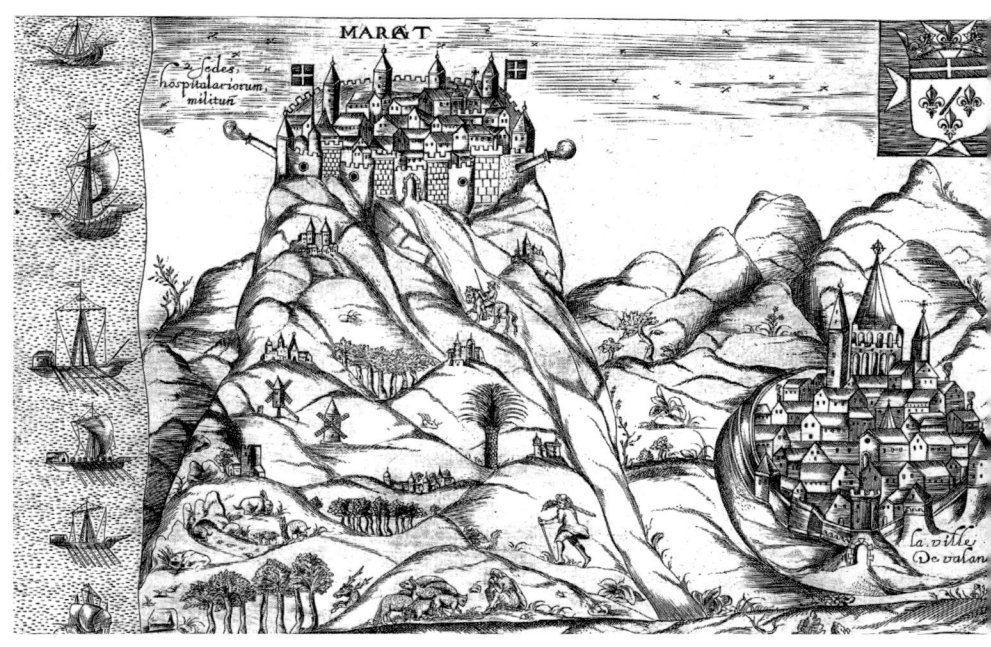

Margat Castle in a 17th-century engraving by Henry Raignauld. The flags of the Order fly over the towering fortification overlooking the Mediterranean Sea. (Jewish National Library)

– formerly the possession of the moribund Byzantine empire only gained western attention and became an important intermediary stop-over to Constantinople and Palestine after the Order took over. The Hospitallers began to receive huge attention again after they converted Rhodes in a highly esteemed Christian bulwark against the Mameluke or Ottoman expansion. Treaties and alliances with the Genoese *condottiere* Vignolo de Vignoli and Pope Clement V brought the Hospitallers new military, logistic, and legal security. The aim of the Order's policy was very clear to see: while the Templars and the Teutonic knights had withdrawn from the Muslim frontier, its establishment at Rhodes would keep the Order in geographical and spiritual contact with its roots and history. The tradition of the perpetual fight against the Saracens and Mamelukes had to be kept alive. As the documents show very clearly, there was a constant and close exchange with the Roman *Curia*. A papal bull of 5 September 1306 consented to the 'liberation' of Rhodes from the 'yoke' of the infidels, that is the schismatic Greeks under Byzantine Emperor Anastasius II.

With the new task to protect the pilgrim ships and to fight the infidels on the maritime field, the knights of St John at least maintained the façade of their *raison d'être*. For

Just a year after the conquest of Rhodes, the island was attacked in 1310. Duke Amadeo V (Spada mistakenly wrote Amadeo Quarto – fourth) came to the rescue of Grand Master Fulques de Villaret and his Hospitallers.
Lionello Spada (1576-1622) fresco, Ambassadors' Room, Grand Master's Palace, Valletta.

Grand Master Philibert de Naillac (1396–1421) needed to fortify the stronghold on the tiny island of Kos, situated in the middle of the bay of Bodrum, Turkey. German knight-architect Heinrich Schlegelholt built the present castle at Bodrum, Turkey in 1402. The fortification became known as St Peter's Castle.

the next 500 years this maritime aspect would become the backbone of the Order's organization and identity. This aspect would contribute to the Order's survival as it changed from medieval to early modern concepts of government and rule. The other two major chivalric Orders, the Templars and the Teutonic Order, opted for different directions. While the Templars fell victim to French King Philip IV in 1312/14, the Teutonic Order was transferred from the Mediterranean scene to the eastern borders of the German empire to colonize and convert the Slavs. Its anachronistic structure, however, prevented the institution from achieving lasting success. After hefty defeats in the fourteenth and fifteenth centuries, the Teutonic knights withdrew to the German mainland and lingered on as a political insignificant principality with its headquarters in Mergentheim.

On 15 August 1309 the Hospitallers and their auxiliary troops seized the city of Rhodes, and then conquered some more nearby islands in the Dodecanese and the fortress of St Peter at Bodrum on the Asian mainland. In terms of land and maritime infrastructure and population, the situation of Rhodes was quite promising. Although partly depopulated because of Seljuk attacks, the city of Rhodes had a well-built harbour, a cosmopolitan structure of Latin-Christian and Greek-Orthodox people and merchants. Compared to Palestine, the hinterland was much more fertile and

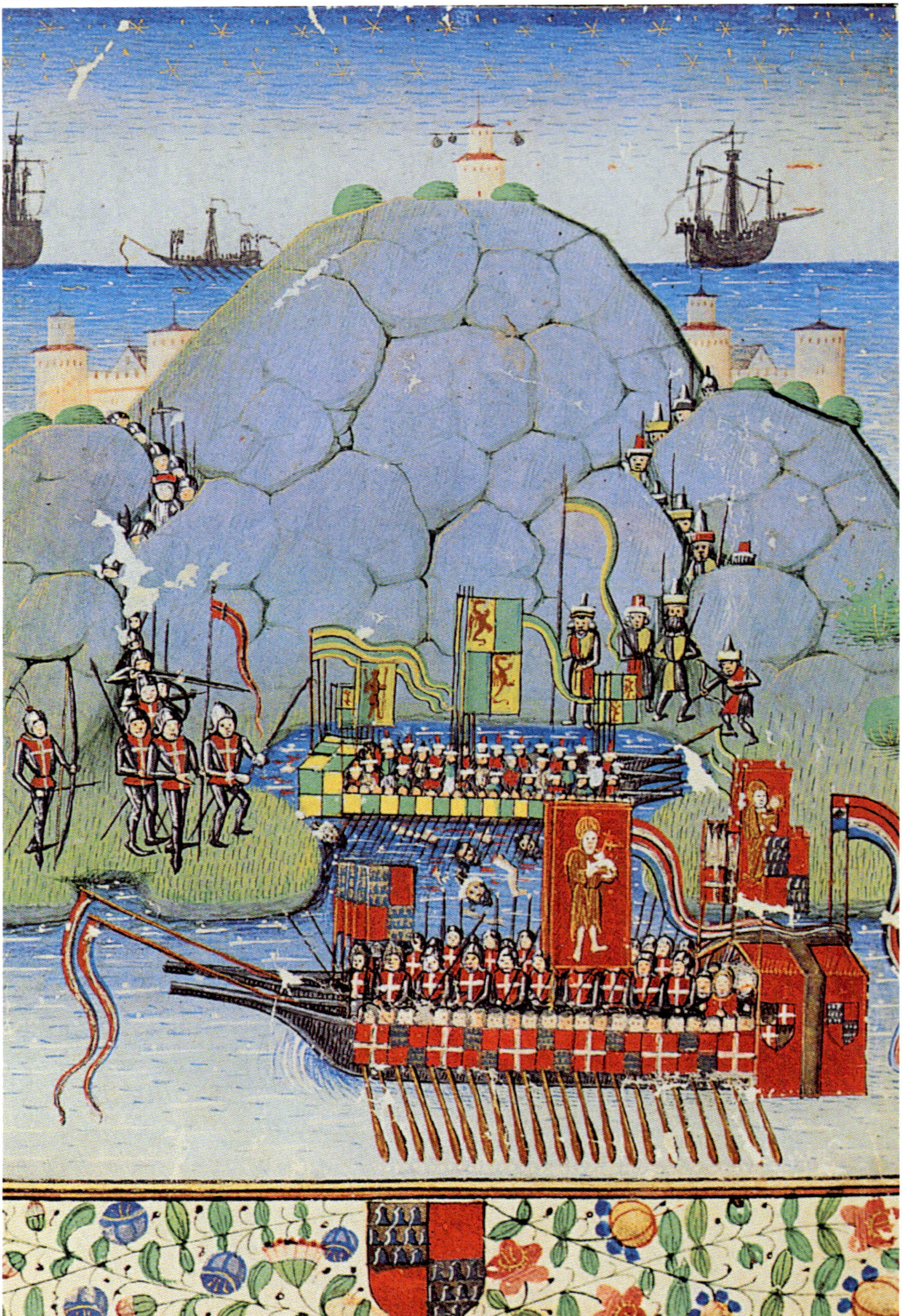

easier to cultivate. Geographically the island was situated on important west–east and north–south sea routes between Constantinople, Jaffa, and Alexandria. After the Order converted Rhodes into a safe haven, more and more ships from Genoa, Venice, Bari, Ragusa, Otranto, Barcelona, Valencia started calling on the way to Constantinople, Famagusta, Aleppo, Jaffa, Acre, and Alexandria. With this dynamic integration in the trade net and the security guaranteed by the Order, the population of Rhodes doubled from c.10,000 in 1310 to 20,000 in 1522. With the loss of Palestine, the Order lost some of its *raison d'être* and the previous showering with privileges, prerogatives, donations, and pittances ceased, but the ecclesiastic and autonomous status of the Hospitallers had been established enough to guarantee their sovereignty.

The decline of donations forced the Order to buy land to establish new commanderies. In the fifteenth century, the Hospitallers clearly adapted to the changing economic situations starting from Flanders and Italy, replacing an economy based on exchange of natural products into one based on money. Until then the Hospitallers had concentrated on acquiring land, but now more and more leasing contracts and annuity rents start to be documented with the Order not refraining from taking interest. Yet the Order's budget continued to show debts, a situation partly caused by the huge expenses for the upkeep of fortresses, ships, and military equipment as well as decreasing payments from many commanders. The Order compensated for these losses by the income of raids and the legendary *corso*. The more than 200 years of sovereign rule over Rhodes strengthened this military and aristocratic orientation. This internal structural re-shaping happened without spectacular events and moments. The spectacular events came through the successful nautical operations against the infidels and the successful halt to Muslim expansion.

The Hospitallers re-structuring from a monastic, charitable organization into a military-aristocratic Order with strong princely and sovereign ambitions must have also changed relations with the Holy See. According to the historian Hans Prutz, by the fourteenth century the Hospitallers as an institution had moved away from national or political borders and also from the universal church. What was not to oversee was that with the loss of Acre in 1291 and the dwindling crusading spirit the time of expansion of the Order had had its days. As the donations ceased to come, new lands could only be acquired by buying

Two galleys of the knights of St John commanded by George de Bosredon blockade 3 Turkish galleys, c.1460. The heads of the defeated Turks float in the bay between the two ships, whilst the knights display banners dedicated to St John and St Mary.
Illumination from the Book of Hours, *c.1475 for Pierre de Bosredon, the Hospitaller, Prior of Champagne. Pierpont Morgan Library, New York Glazier 55, f. 140^v.*

which made the establishment of new commanderies more difficult. The last big acquisition of land dated to 1312 and 1313 when most of the Templars' possessions were handed over to the Hospitallers.

In the fifteenth century the Order could not do but adapt to the new economic changes which were mainly brought from Flanders and Northern and Central Italy and slowly replaced the natural economy by the monetary system. Previously the knights had mainly concentrated on the acquisition of land but now the documents show that the Order was turning more to paying contracts which guaranteed them interest in cash. Despite of this late medieval 'modernization', the Order sank more and more in debts, partly as a result of the fact that many commanders were not paying their responsions in time or at all to the treasury. The Order had to make up its deficit by their naval exploits and by corsairing. In the fifteenth century there were moments when the convent at Rhodes was hardly able to take immediate and full control over all its possessions and commanderies in Europe.

The cleft between pretension and reality got progressively wider and wider and could not be eliminated even by strict measures. The impoverishment of the noble classes in many regions of Late Medieval Europe strongly decreased the number of prospective new noble

Main gates of the Collacchio *on Rhodes. The Hospitallers lived in this area behind high walls that isolated them from the other quarters of the city.*

Survival Methods 49

Street of the Knights in old Rhodes town. The street has been completely restored beautifully and is lined by the buildings of the hospitallers inside the Collacchio.

members for the Order. The entrance fee, the *passaggio*, into the Order was seen to be too high for these groups, and the functions and posts became concentrated in the hands of a few competent and energetic members, which sometimes resulted in a slow-down of the administrative process. This lack of internal control and obedience of the old statutes led to some langues – especially the Italian and the French – accepting bastard sons of high nobles, although this was strictly forbidden by the rules. The exception in this loosening of the statutes was the German langue which in the sixteenth century continued to refuse freshly ennobled persons (the *Briefadel*) and extended the proofs of nobility from 4 to 16 ancestors of noble Christian blood. With the exception of the

Rhodes and Malta

The presence of the Order in Rhodes formed the institution's concept and policy decisively. Most of the features which were developed in Rhodes also were applied on Malta. In these Mediterranean co-ordinates of policy the role of the increasing pressure of the Ottomans and their satellites played a most important part. In Rhodes the Order developed into a naval power, established the corso, and gave a clear signal to stay at the frontline of the Christian fight against the Muslim world. The protection of the pilgrim traffic to Palestine and the possibility of continuing the struggle against the infidels at sea kept, at least officially, a modicum of raison d'être of the Order alive. These functions also allowed the knights to identify themselves with the old statutes of the Order. In the long run the change into a maritime power and the decision to remain at the frontier of the Christian-Muslim border would be the reason why the Order would survive for another five centuries. It also explains why the knights kept their generally independent status and military power during the stormy transition from Late medieval to early modern Times. Even when, with the expulsion from Palestine, the legitimatization of the existence of the Hospitallers might have appeared doubtful and, in fact, the showering of privileges, prerogatives, donations, and letters of protection ceased, the autonomous position of the Order and its internal structure and substance were too solid and firm to be questioned. Its sovereignty over Rhodes and later over Malta was hardly ever questioned by the Latin Church or western powers.

langues of France, Auvergne, and Provence, in the fifteenth and sixteenth centuries the number of the commanderies and of clerics in the Order dwindled.

Especially in the towns the Mendicant Orders had displaced the Hospitallers in offering spiritual services. After the loss of Palestine, the administration of the Order faced various problems to solve the internal ideological crisis. Quite a few knights did not accept the restructuring and new orientation which took place with the moves to Cyprus and to Rhodes. They saw no real connection between the new maritime-orientated institution and the brethren's original task and vow to protect the shrines of the Holy Land and they refused to fulfil their military service at Rhodes. This ignoring to military service at Rhodes, the focusing on worldly careers by many brethren, the turning away from the old ideas by some commanders who often declined to pay responsions led to the calling of seven general chapters just in the 27 years of rule by Grand Master Helion de Villeneuve (1319–46).

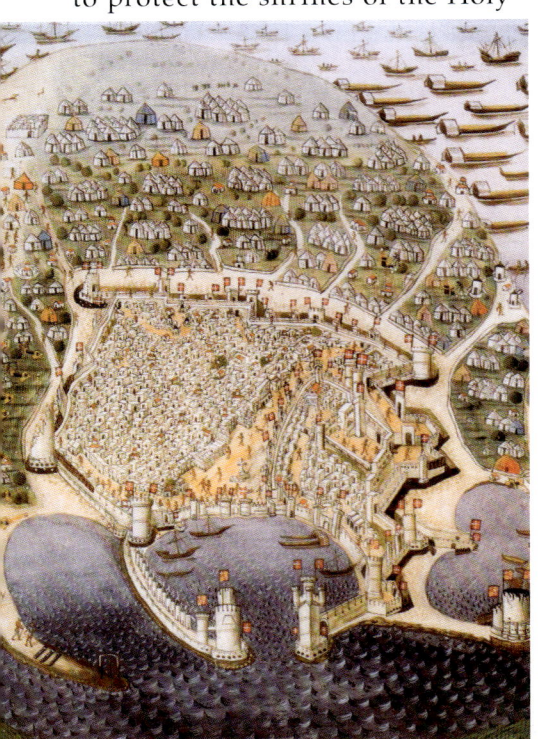

As a consequences of these consultations, in 1329 a decree was issued to stipulate that only knights who had fulfilled a certain amount of time of service in the administration or military of the Order could be bestowed with offices in the Order and given commanderies. The peak of disorder was reached between 1385 and 1395 when a rival 'grand master', Ricardo Caracciolo, was residing in Rome. This bizarre situation was partly the result of rivalry in the *Curia* and Papal State which also resulted in the election of several rival popes. Despite of these turbulences, the ties between the knights and the Holy See in general remained firm. As a special favour, in 1409 Grand Master Philibert de Naillac was granted the protection of the council of Pisa a tradition which survives to the present. Grand masters still enjoy the honour of keeping the keys of the Sistine Chapel where cardinals gather to elect a new pope.

The town of Rhodes and its harbour at its zenith (compare with opposite). Guillaume Caoursin, Bibliotheque Nationale de Paris. MS Lat.6076, f.37v.

Under Ottoman pressure

The situation of the Order in the island of Rhodes – and the knights were fully aware – was very closely knit with the entire situation in the Levant and the Oriental countries. The Order's naval campaigns – sometimes carried out with other southern European powers – like the temporary conquest of the harbour town of Smyrna in 1344, the attack on Alexandria in 1365, the actions against Nicopolis in 1396, and even more the heroic defence of Rhodes against the Ottomans in 1480 and 1522 found a huge echo in the West. In the fifteenth century the energetic expansion of the Ottoman empire moved the Hospitallers back into the limelight of world politics. To understand this complex situation which contributed to the final fall of Rhodes in late December 1522 to Suleiman II one has to see from outside a Eurocentric point of view. The relations of the knights of St John with the Ottomans after the fall of Constantinople in 1453 ranged from an acute and massive military threat in the times of Mehmet II (1451–81) – with the first siege of Rhodes in 1480 – to some cautious diplomatic approaches under Bayezid II (1481–1512) – with the handing over of the relics of St John. Later under Selim I (1512–20) and Suleiman II (1520–66), there were hostile confrontations again which culminated in the conquest of Rhodes.

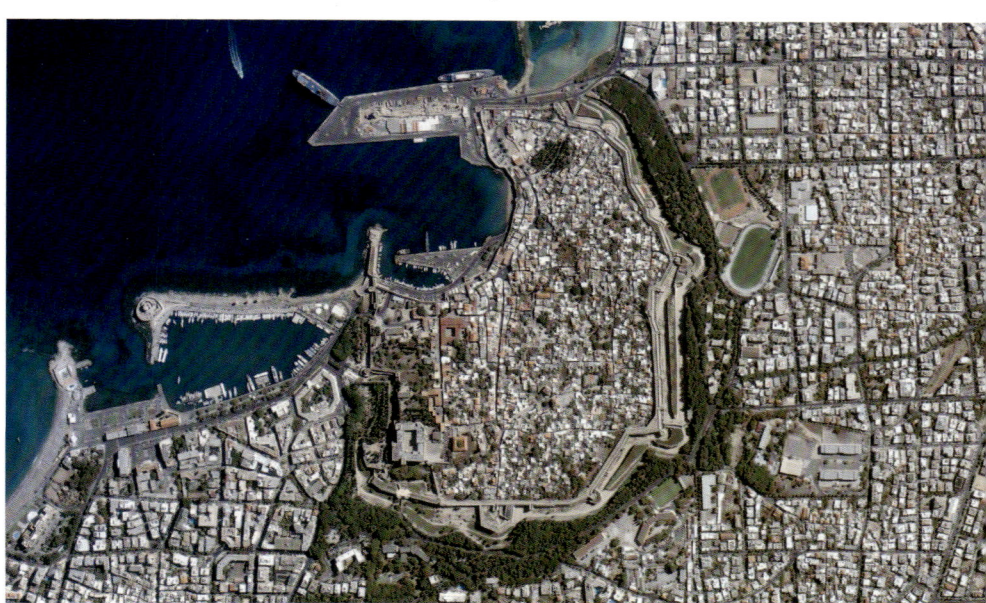

A satellite image of the city of Rhodes. The walls surrounding the medieval town are clearly visible. The palace of the grand masters can be seen left bottom corner of the medieval city. The Collachio *is next to it.*

*The Flemish Guillaume Caoursin chronicled Rhodian history and the siege of Rhodes of 1480.
Bibliotheque Nationale de Paris: MS Lat. 6067, f. 79v.*

In the wider picture Suleiman II's (the Magnificent) attack on Rhodes in June 1522 was the logical consequence of an Ottoman Mediterranean expansion policy. Previously the Ottomans conquered Syria (1516) and Egypt (1517), fought against the Mamelukes, established Alexandria as a prosperous Ottoman seaport, and defeated the Persians. This rapid expansion in the 1520s and 1530s reached a peak with the siege of Vienna in 1529 and was helped by the political situation in Europe with the antagonism between the French and the Hapsburgs and the Lutheran challenge to the Catholic Church. The major part of the wars between French King Francis I and Emperor Charles V in the 1520s was fought in North Italy. A temporary end only came in 1529 when in the peace treaty of Cambrai Francis renounced his claims over Italy. In view of this political situation Pope Leo X's plans for a unified Christian action against the increasing Ottoman threat must have appeared illusionary, just as it was a mirage to think of a joint effort by the Latin Christian powers to relieve the knights of St John during the six-month Ottoman siege of Rhodes.

That Ottoman pressure after Mehmet II's siege of Rhodes in 1480 had relaxed under Bayezid II was mainly due to an internal crisis in the Ottoman empire. The re-organizer of Shiite Persia, Shah Ismail I, had encouraged religiously motivated uprisings and rebellions in Anatolia. After Bayezid resigned from power, Sultan Selim I consolidated the empire internally and resumed an aggressive expansionist policy. After dealing with the rebellious Turkmenes, Selim conquered Palestine, Egypt, and Arabia, which, for the next centuries, formed the political frontiers and spheres of influence of the Ottoman empire. On 24 August 1516 Selim decisively defeated the Mameluke Sultan Kansuk Ghani at Mardach Dâbik and integrated his lands into his empire. In the same year Syria and Palestine came under Ottoman power. In 1517 there was the annexation of Egypt and Hedscha's which brought the holy shrines of Mecca and Medina respectively into the sphere of the empire. This was an inestimable asset for the spiritual legitimatizion of Ottoman power.

At that time it must have become clear that the long-term aim was the control of the entire Eastern Mediterranean Basin, a region of great economic and strategic importance. The west must have been aware of these aims at least since 1516 when Algiers fell under the dominance of the Ottomans. The solid protection of these new acquisitions and a strong naval presence and economic profit could only be secured by safe maritime routes. The unceasing attacks by the knights against Muslim shipping was an obvious disturbance and obstacle. This situation would also later lead to many tensions during the Hospitallers' rule over Malta. Therefore, it was only too clear that a second attack on Rhodes was a question of time.

In 1521 Sultan Selim's successor, Suleiman II, had started the military actions of his long rule on the Balkans by attacking Belgrade. But this only was meant to protect his flank before commencing his ambitious Mediterranean undertakings. Already in the autumn of 1517, when

The attack on Rhodes of 1480 by Mehmet II, from the Stabilimenta Rhodiorum Militum *(the earliest statutes and regulations of the Order) by Guillaume Caoursin. Woodcut, printed in Ulm in 1495.*

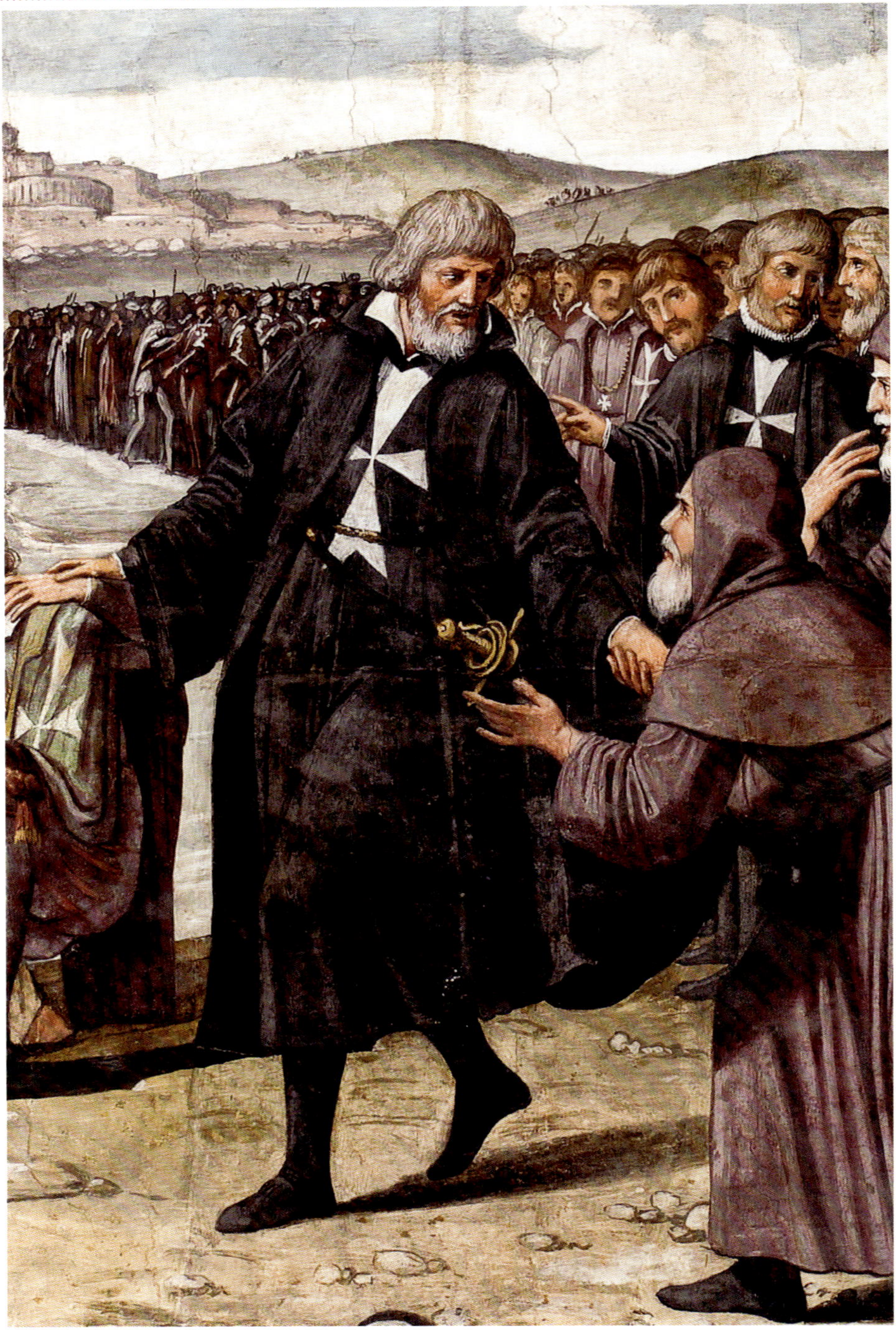

the Ottoman fleet on its way back after the successful expedition in the Levant and North Africa, had paraded near Rhodes and informed Grand Master Fabrizio del Caretto of their latest successes, the knights must have been aware that their island now would be the next victim. In the years after 1518 the fortifications were strengthened and augmented and the grand master started a hectic correspondence with European princes and powers to secure support. With a few exceptions these calls for support, however, proved rather disappointing. Still in 1520 the galleys of the Order achieved a widely noticed victory over the fleet of the corsair Muslih ad-Dihn who then stood in the service of the Ottomans.

By 10 June 1522, when Grand Master Philippe de Villiers de L'Isle-Adam received Suleiman's final demand to surrender the islands and possessions of the Order in the Aegean Sea with the promise of a free withdrawal, it was clear that the 7,000 defenders could not expect real support from the Christian powers. The ongoing conflict between the French and the Hapsburgs occupied the maritime forces of Genoa and Venice, the only powers which could have guaranteed a quick and effective support for the knights.

Grand Master Philippe de Villiers de L'Isle-Adam and his Hospitallers leave Rhodes on 1 January 1523 with the honours of war.
Lionello Spada (1576–1622) fresco, Ambassadors' Room, Grand Master's Palace, Valletta.

Genoa's siding with the Hapsburgs and the Spanish – mainly because of the lucrative participation in the Spanish overseas trade – finally helped the Hapsburgs to defeat the French. The Venetians' alliance with the French was too fragile and short-lived to bring useful results. In fact, between France and Venice there had been too great a rivalry about their ambitious Levantine and Oriental trade to form a well-functioning and long-lasting alliance. For King Francis I and many members of the French court maintaining good contacts with the Ottomans appeared as the most effective and powerful weapon.

This situation, of course, was known very well by Suleiman when, on 13 June 1522, he handed over to the grand master the declaration of war. In total the Ottoman forces numbered over 50,000 men. The Order had just 600 knights, 4,500 soldiers, and the local militia. On 24 June Suleiman landed his troops and the assault started. Despite heavy Ottoman losses, by early December Suleiman knew that the town of Rhodes would very soon fall. The defending troops were reduced to 1,500 men and powder, munitions, and victuals were running out. Without relief and after exhausting all available military sources, on 25 December 1522 the last bastion of Rhodes fell. On the last day of the year, the surrender was officially put into practice. Two days later the surviving members of the Order and a part of the Rhodiot population left the island.

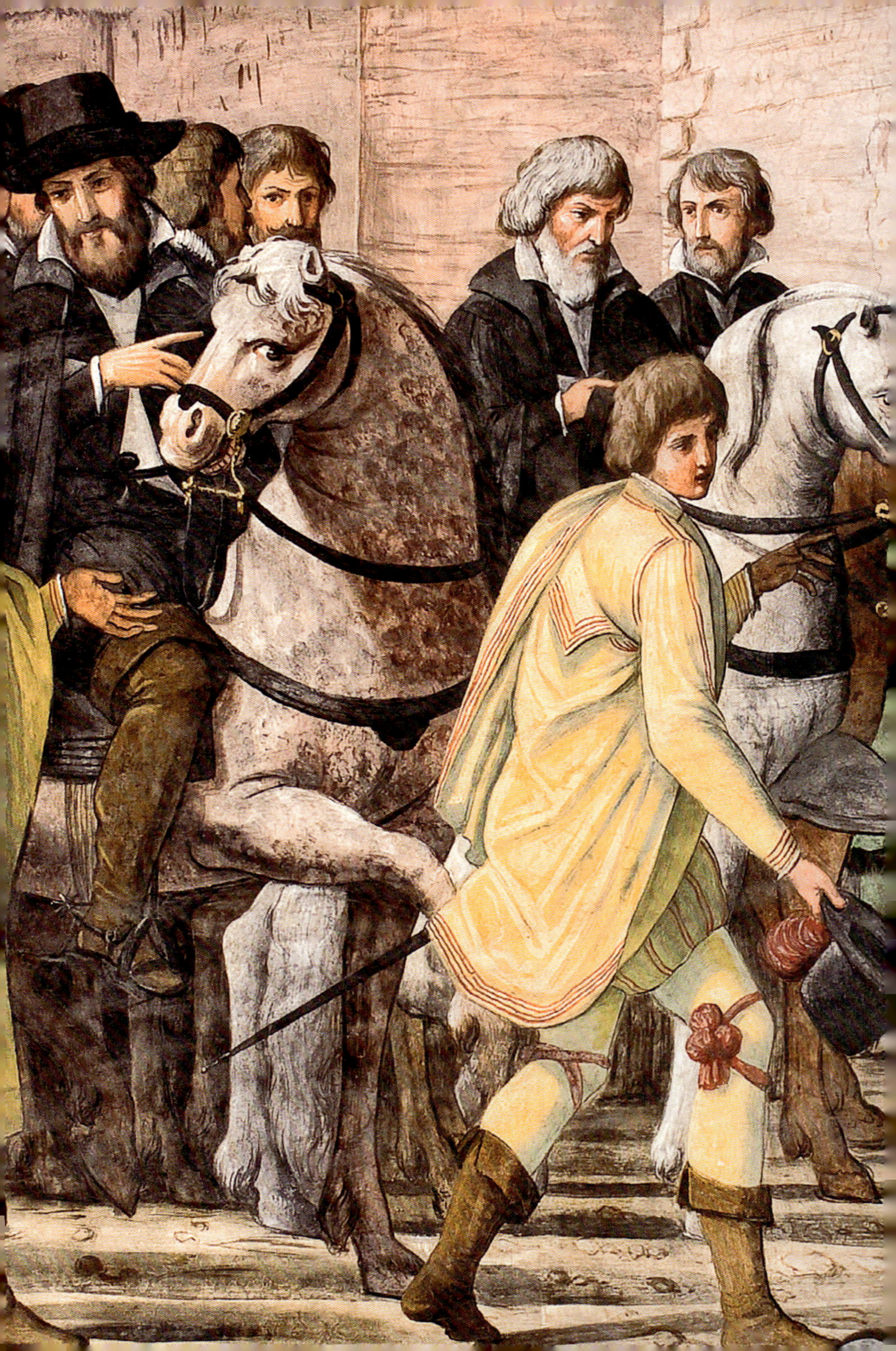

Although the Order suffered some losses of income and indulgences in the European mainland dwindled, the institution managed to keep its prestigious status in late medieval times. By the 15th century, the internal structure and the division into the langues had been fully established and was kept like that until the late 18th century.

Chapter 3

On the Road to Malta

**The Order and its rule:
Power, statutes, and organization**

It is necessary to look at the international scene for a better understanding of the Order's complex structure on the eve of its move to Malta. In the thirteenth century the Hospitallers were estimated to own no less than 19,000 *manoirs* of land spread over Europe. Each *manoir* brought an income which was enough to maintain and equip a knight. The Order then had 1,000 commanderies. It is obvious that such a vast organization could not be ruled and administered from Jerusalem or, later, from Rhodes or Malta only. The beginning of the presence of the institution in Europe had been their foundations for hospitals in the provinces of southern France, namely on the intersections of the important pilgrim roads. In 1113 a hospital of the brotherhood is documented at the French

*Grand Master L'Isle Adam (central figure with white beard and hair) and his convent arrive at the city of Viterbo (central Italy) in 1524.
Lionello Spada (1576–1622) fresco, Ambassadors' Room, Grand Master's Palace, Valletta.*

port town of St Gilles, from which foundation the langue of Provence would later emerge. By the first half of the thirteenth century, with the grand priories of France and Auvergne, the bases for the three oldest langues of the Order had been formed. The chapter-general which gathered in 1206 in the fortress of Margat, presided over by Grand Master Alfonso of Portugal, made up the basic and necessary regulations for the administrative and legal structure of the new Europe-wide institution.

Margat Castle, is also known as Marqab from the Arabic Qalaat al-Marqab (قلعة المرقب), *'Castle of the Watchtower'). It is near what is now Baniyas, Syria. The castle, built of basalt stone, is located on a hill formed by an extinct volcano on the road between Tripoli and Latakia, about 500 metres above sea level, overlooking the Mediterranean Sea.*

But it was not until 1294 that an administrative body was formed out of seven 'langues': Provence, Auvergne, France, Italy, Aragon, England, and Germany. In 1331 a chapter-general held in Montpellier confirmed this structure. In 1462 the langue of Castille was formed after it split from Aragon and the final set-up of eight langues was established. Each langue was divided into grand priories made up of a varying number of bailiwicks. The etymology of the term 'bailiwick' shows the strong French influence when the Hospitallers formed its internal hierarchy and structure in the thirteenth century. Originally *bailli* (in Italian *balí*) meant an administrator of royal domains. In high medieval times a *bailli* was a judge appointed by the French king who had plenipotentiary powers.

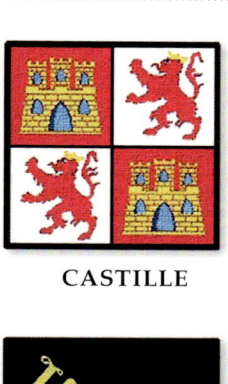

CASTILLE	GERMANY
ENGLAND	ARAGON
ITALY	FRANCE
AUVERGNE	PROVENCE

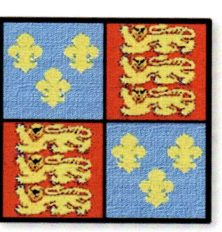

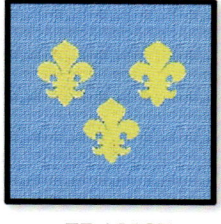

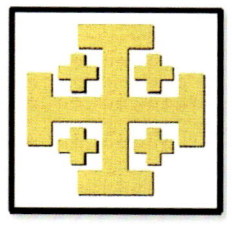

Already some years before, chapter-generals from 1428 and 1445 had confirmed that the langues should be headed by conventual-baillis or *piliers*. These had to reside at the convent of the Order in their langue's auberge, which practically meant that langues had their own 'department minister' at the Order's residence. The eight provinces or *langues* of the Order were divided into grand priories. Only the langue of Auvergne consisted of just one grand priory. Provence was divided into the grand priories of St Gilles and Toulouse; France into Aquitaine, France, and Champagne; Italy into Lombardy, Rome, Venice, Pisa, Capua, Barletta, and Messina; Aragon into Catalonia and Navarre, and the chastellany of Ampost; Castille into Leon and Portugal; England into Ireland and England

The coat of arms of the eight 'langues' of the Order. Seven were formed in 1294, whilst the langue of Castille was formed in 1462 after a schism from the langue of Aragon.

itself; and Germany into Bohemia, Hungary, Dacia (Scandinavia), Germany, and the bailiwick of Brandenburg.

The lowest administrative unit of this hierarchy was the commanderies, managed by commanders. Its function was clearly defined in the statutes: '... our commanderies have to be administered most faithfully and every year a fixed part of their income must be transferred to the Order's treasury... .' The bestowal of a commandery depended on the number of years which the knight had already been a member of the Order. But there were also other criteria: participation in military actions (since Rhodes there had been obligations to participate in the 'caravans' – the naval campaigns of the galleys) and the time the knight had spent at the convent. The distribution of commanderies – and in the period of absolutism this happened quite often – could also be done directly by the grand master (*ex gratia magistrale*) or the grand prior (*ex gratia priorale*). Although it is beyond the frame of this book to discuss in detail how the organization adapted to the political changes in Early Modern Europe, it might be added that when the Hospitallers were in the Holy Land the Order incorporated a branch of sisters who lived according to the rules of the canonesses of St Augustine. These sisters were headed by a prioress who was directly subjected to the grand master. After the Order left

The acceptance of a Hierosolymite Sister into the Order.
Statuta Hospitalis Hierusalem.
[Ed. Giovanni Battista Rondinelli].
Romae: ex typographia Titi & Pauli de Dianis, 1588.

Palestine, we find these sisters also in Aragon, England, Bohemia, and Germany, but in the fifteenth century this female branch had been reduced to a few sisters.

From the commanderies' revenues at first a third part, from the late medieval period onwards a fifth part, had to be sent to the convent. This money was called 'responsions'. To control the regular payment of the responsions the office of preceptor was created in 1357. The reduction of the responsions to a fifth of the profit clearly indicates how the Hospitallers changed from an institution determined by the vow of personal poverty into an aristocratic chivalric Order. Obviously to pay less responsions must have made it more attractive to be a knight of St John in late medieval times when the old enthusiasm and crusading spirit had gone. Now the commandery was mainly perceived as a means of providing for the knights. All the profit above what had to be paid as responsions and for the upkeep of the commandery fell to the commander.

When this 'supra-national' hierarchic administration with its mixed concept of resorts and centralization was developed it was a quite 'modern' adaptation to the needs and profile of the Order. The heads of the langues, the conventual baillis or piliers, had to reside at the main residence of the Order. Together with the grand master and the present grand crosses they formed the grand council of the Order. In the thirteenth and fourteenth centuries a clear profile of the respective department emerged. This structure survived until the end of the Order's rule in Malta.

The administrative division into the provinces of Provence, Auvergne, Italy, England, and Aragon seems to have been on its way during the magistracy of Raymond de Puy in the mid-twelfth century. As head of the oldest and most distinguished langue the conventual bailli of Provence held the office of *Grand Praeceptor*, who administered the finances and the treasury. The conventual bailli of Auvergne held the post of *Grand Marshal* and was responsible for the foot troops of the Order, an office that had lost its former importance after the move to Rhodes and its new-found maritime vocation. The head of the French langue was the *Hospitalier* and he supervised all the hospitals and charitable work of the Order. The *Grand Conservator* from the langue of Aragon looked after the internal affairs, while the English *Turcopolier* was the head of the cavalry and

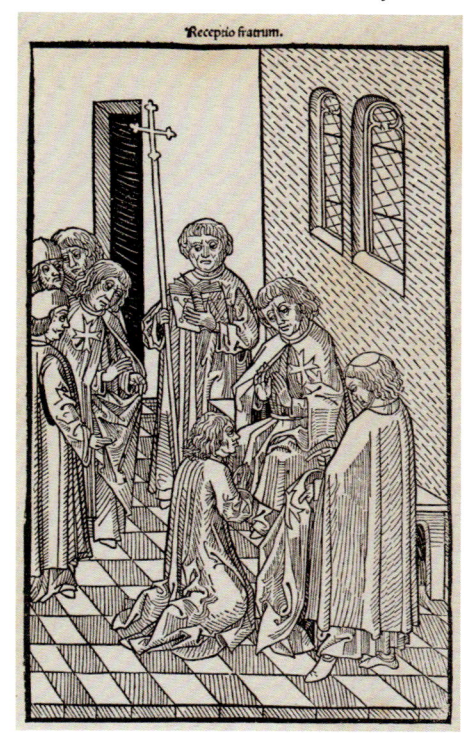

The acceptance of a postulant into the Order from the Stabilimenta Rhodiorum Militum *(the earliest statutes and regulations of the Order) by Guillaume Caoursin. Woodcut printed in Ulm in 1495.*
National Library of Malta.

Consilium.

auxiliary troops. The German grand bailli was responsible for the fortifications. The post of admiral, created after the loss of Palestine when the Order turned into a naval power, was bestowed upon the head of the Italian langue. When the langue of Castille was established in 1462 the chapter-general presided over by Grand Master Zacosta decided that the head of this langue, the *Chancellor*, should take care of the foreign policy.

The grand master, the highest office of the Order, was elected for life. In his decisions he was answerable to the council and the chapter-general. As prince he drew all the revenues from Rhodes and later from Malta. These revenues were customs duties, a share in the prizes and booty taken by corsairs, and the left property of the chaplains of the Order. As the only worldly prince, he was allowed to carry the title 'Eminence'. The official full *intitulatio* read: *Frater N.N. Dei gratia sacrae domus hospitalis sancti Joannis Hierosolimitani et militaris ordinis, sancti sepulchri dominici, magister humilis pauperumque Jesu Christi custos.*

Although he had authority over all members of the Order, his orders and actions had to obey the statutes of the institution. Otherwise the so-called *sguardio* could be called in action and request him to account for his actions. In his administration and decisions, he was assisted by the *consiglio* which, since 1462, consisted of the eight conventual *balís*, the *prior della chiesa* as the highest cleric in the Order, the seneschal, and the treasurer. The *consiglio compito* or grand council, consisting of these dignitaries plus two knights from each langue, acted as a certain instance of appeal. The *sguardio* was responsible to settle criminal cases. The chapter-general had jurisdictional powers and, when it was convened, it stood above all other bodies of the Order. It was generally convened where the Order had its residence. The chapter-general, composed of members of all eight langues, even had the right to call the grand master and other highest dignitaries of the Order to account. To document the authority of the chapter-general, all its members had to vacate their posts and offices temporarily when the negotiations started.

Each langue chose two of its members as representatives. The chapter-general decided over the confirmation, abolition, or change of the regulations and statutes, financial decisions, fixing of responsions, and the formulation and confirmation of new laws. That official rules were not always obeyed in the course of everyday business can be seen in the practice of the chapter-general

The Grand Council in session from the Stabilimenta Rhodiorum Militum (the earliest statutes and regulations of the Order) by Guillaume Caoursin. Woodcut printed in Ulm in 1495. National Library of Malta

itself. Quite often the limit of the maximum duration of the chapter-general of 15 days was overstepped. In the seventeenth century, the maximum time of five years between the convening of chapter-generals was ignored. Reflecting the dwindling power of the parliaments, diets, and summits of the classes in the period of Absolutism, the chapter-general was not convened in Malta between 1631 and 1776 at all. The Archives of the Order in Valletta possess most of the proceedings of the chapter-general between 1330 and 1776 (AOM MSS. 279–315).

The Order's aristocratization, which went together with its militarization, was also documented in the statutes of the thirteenth and fourteenth centuries. It found its clearest reflections when, in 1354, the chapter-general in Rhodes decided that serving brothers (*Fratres servientes*) could not be made knights any more. This group of non-nobles, which in their charitable and military roles formed the backbone of the internal structure and ideological profile of the institution in the twelfth century, decisively lost ground in the councils of the Hospitallers. Until the fourteenth century, a knight only needed proof of a legitimate noble birth to be enrolled as a knight or as a *miles conventualis*. The fifteenth century witnessed a clear tendency towards 'deeper' aristocratization. This is documented by the fact that the langue of Italy now demanded four

The 1776 chapter-general summoned by Emanuel de Rohan.
Detail frontispiece from Codice de Rohan, *National Library of Malta*

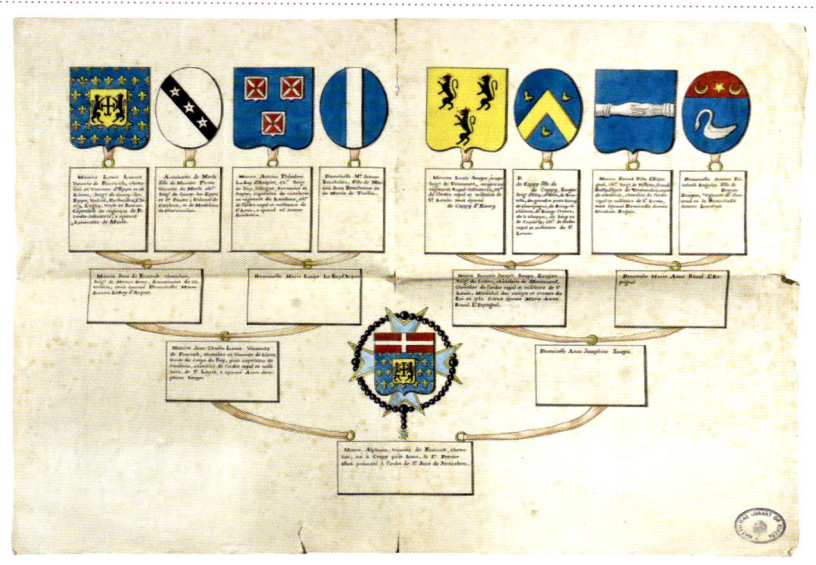

A late 19th-century document from the National Library of Malta showing a proof of nobility with four 'quarterings'.

generations of noble ancestors, the Spanish and French langues eight, and the German even sixteen.

In elections and councils the clerical members of the Order had the same rights as the knights. Jurisdictionally they came under the prior of the conventual church. The stricter aristocratization had been a reaction to the increasing movement of ennoblement of the civic members and officers at the courts of Europe and the phenomenon that more and more rich patricians and merchants were getting ennobled. With the extension of the proofs of nobility the Order kept its exclusivity. The relatively high admission fee, the *passagio*, mainly limited the membership to sons of well-off families. Around 100 European noble families had the right to enrol their sons already at a tender age. Around the age of twelve, these boys were sent as pages to Malta to the court of the grand master. These families had to pay a certain annual sum for the living expenses of their children, besides the passage. This extra sum was to be paid until the young knight was found suitable to take over a commandery or was provided with a prestigious office.

Individuals like the architect Pietro Paolo Floriani and the painters Mattia Preti and Michelangelo Merisi da Caravaggio could be bestowed with the honour of a knight of grace by a decision of the grand master or the chapter-general for their merits in the Order. But, even after the move to Malta in 1530, the professed knights remained the backbone of the Order. Their members came from the langues of Provence, Auvergne, France, Italy, Aragon, Castille (with Leon and Portugal),

Germany, and England. However, the English langue after 1542 was reduced to a mere titular existence when Henry VIII confiscated its possessions. As in earlier centuries, the three French langues retained their strong influence. Over half of the professed knights came from the French langues which, in the sixteenth century, included about 270 commanderies.

Acceptance as a professed knight needed a legitimate noble birth. A novice had to spend at least one year at the convent in Rhodes or Malta. On his eighteenth year, he could take the vow of his religious profession. To be promoted to a lucrative position in the Order and to get a commandery, he had to stay four more years in Malta.

Either personally or by sending an able replacement, a knight had to undertake at least four caravans. These celebrated caravans were tours of duty on the ships of the Order against Muslim shipping or raids on Muslim territory. In general every professed knight had to spend at least five years in Malta. Once enrolled in the Order, a professed knight could only leave through death or by the highest dispensation – for example, from the pope.

The interest of European noble families to enrol their second- or third-born sons in the Order remained until the end of the eighteenth century. One could choose to join in search of a political career or social prestige, while others did so out of religious zeal or lust for adventure. Especially in France, with its system of primogeniture inheritance,

Dress code of members of the Hospitaller Order of Malta from Bernardo Giustiniani's Historie Cronologiche dell' Origine degli Ordini Militari *published in Venice in 1692*

the Order must have appeared an attractive institution to provide posts and commanderies for the second- or third-born sons of the middle or lower nobility. When a professed knight died four-fifths of his inheritance went to the Order as the *spoglio*.

That this structure of the Order survived for so many centuries is indeed surprising. Without an extensive and profound education and training of the members for their respective positions and careers, everything had more or less the character of a permanent improvization, as the French historian Claire Éliane Engel says, whether this was as a sailor, an officer, a diplomat, or a nurse: all that was needed was goodwill, and some words of advice from the senior members.

From Rhodes to Malta – aspects of a continuation

As in Rhodes, life in Malta was overshadowed by the trauma of the loss of the Order's original *raison d'être*, the protection of the pilgrims and the holy shrines of Palestine. With the fall of Jerusalem in 1187 and then with the surrender of Acre in 1291, its core vow could not be fulfilled any more. 'The international organization of the Order' – the historian Jonathan Riley-Smith concluded – 'was the creation of the twelfth century that was already out of date in political terms by the thirteenth.' In the fourteenth century, when several plans for new crusades were set forth, a reconquest of Palestine, might have still appeared possible for some members of the Order. Certainly after the fall of Constantinople to the Ottomans in 1453 and the loss of Rhodes in 1522, even the last member of the Order must have lost hope of returning to Jerusalem one day. The special concept of the caravans and the *corso* has to be understood as a manifestation that some of the ideology of the *Milites Christi* and of the crusades still survived. These well-organized cruises against the trade, ships, and ports of the Mamelukes, Ottomans, Egyptians, and later North Africans were a 'compensation' for the crusades. It is significant that these 'caper crusades' received a tremendous attention in Christian Europe. These mythical exploits contributed substantially to make

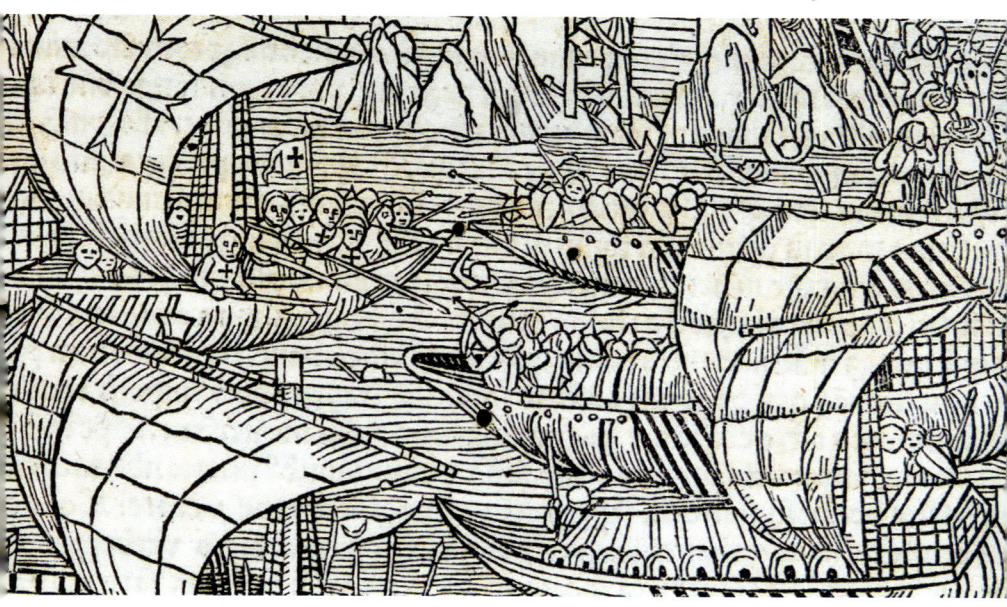

Ships of the Order attack Muslim ships. Stabilimenta Rhodiorum Militum (the earliest statutes and regulations of the Order) by Guillaume Caoursin. Woodcut printed in Ulm in 1495. National Library of Malta.

a membership in the Order attractive. In the sixteenth and seventeenth centuries many French, German, and Italian non-members of the Order longed to volunteer for these caravans.

For the modern historian they furthermore show the state of mind of Christian Europe which from time to time still was dreaming of better days of an *unitas Christiana*. The hard facts of the political truth however were less idealistic and rather prosaic. Despite of the ideological aspects it was a matter of fact that the Order since the fifteenth century needed the *corso* for its economic survival. Especially for Malta's economy the *corso* and later even more so corsairing developed into a most important moment. Therefore, it was disastrous twice over when, in the eighteenth century, the Ottoman empire became fully integrated in Western diplomacy and treatises and therefore its trade could not be attacked. Firstly the Order lost an important part of its income; secondly, its last political and military *raison d'être* was taken away. This important aspect of the Order's activities will be described in a separate chapter in greater detail.

After Suleiman had guaranteed to the members of the Order and to those Rhodiots who wanted to leave free departure, the ships of the Hospitallers left Rhodes on 1 January 1523. As soon as Grand Master L'Isle Adam arrived in Messina, negotiations started with Ettore Pignatelli, duke of Monteleone and viceroy of Sicily, and with Pope Hadrian VI about a new permanent residence for the Order. Already then Malta was discussed as a possible site. Research has not yet established if the Order then had precise geographical, historical, and military documents at its disposal with the necessary information about Malta. That already in late medieval times, the islands – then part of the Aragonese empire – because of their geographical location and maritime position were regarded as a good base for naval expeditions against the North African coast and the Levant is proven by several documents. Regarding the attacks of Malta-based pirates in the early sixteenth century in the Central Mediterranean, the contemporary Venetian diarist Marino Sanuto gives several examples. Already in his crusading plans and proposals written around 1300, the Mallorquin visionary Ramon Lull had praised Rhodes and Malta because of their positions and good ports as excellent bases for naval activities against the infidels. Only recently it has been found out that in April 1523 there was already a plan for the Order to pay 100,000 ducats to Emperor Charles V for the island of Malta. In his function as king of Spain (Charles I), the emperor was feudal lord over Malta.

Opposite page: A painting at the Maritime Museum of Malta showing a naval battle between the Order's navy and a Turkish galleon. Dated 25 June 1709.

Overleaf: The Mediterranean, a detail from Abbé Vertot's (1655–1735) Histoire des Chevaliers... *(1726). National Museum of Archaeology Library.*

THE CORSO 69

PRESA DELLA CAP.^A DI TRIPOLI UNA
TARTANA AL CAPO S. MARIA DALLE GAL.^{RE}
E NAVI DELLA S. R. SOTO IL COMADO DE
IlL.^{MO} S.^{IG}.BAGLIO FLEVRIGNY GOVERN. GEN.LE
25 GIUGNO 1709

E U R
FRANCE
Plaisance
Parme
Boulogne
CROATIE
GOLFE DE VENISE
DALMA
Genes
Nice
Ville franche
Toulon
Florence
TOSCANE
Piombin
Marseille
Calvi
Calle de Giralatte
Elbe
Giglio
Pto Ercole
Cita-vechia
Orvicte
Aquila
Layazzo
S. Bonifacce
CORSE
Rome
Gayete
POUILLE
Barce lone
Isles Baleares
Cumes
Naples
Salerne
CALABRE
Golfe de Bayes
Melphe
SARDAGNE
Majorque
Ivica
Cagliari
M E R
Drepana
Melazzo
I. Favignana
Palerme
SICILE
Messine
Bone
Ruines de Carthage
Catane
Isles de
Bugie
Cap Matafu
Alger
Alcaraz
Cercelle
Tunis
C. Bon
Panta larée
Augusta
Siracuse
Linoso
C. Passaro
ROYAU DE TUNIS
Lampedouse
Goze
la Valete
ROYAUME D'ALGER
Monaster
ISLE DE MALTE
Cumelieres
Medine
Oran
Tremisen
Cairoan
Sousa
Africa ou Mehedia
TREMISEN
ROYAU. DE CAIROAN
Calibie Fort
Seches de Querqueni
Isle de Gelves
Canal de Cantara
Tripoli
Tour d'Alcaide
la Rochete
la Zoare
Langir
Adabus
Seches de Palo
Tajora
Gienzor
Almaya
Mont Atlas
ROYAUME DE TRIPOL
Mont Atlas
A F R I C

Abbé de Vertot's Map of the Mediterranean

The palace of popes at Viterbo. Clement VII established the Hospitaller convent in the city, 40 kilometres north of Rome. Here, from January 1524, the Order had its magisterial palace, a conventual church, a hospital, and the auberges for the langues.

Although the Order found that 'the island was not defended enough to withstand an armada of 50 or 100 galleys', the grand master authorized his envoys Don Diego de Toledo and Frà Gabriele Tadino to negotiate further with Charles V. It soon became apparent that Charles V besides Malta also wanted to enfeof the fortress of Tripoli in North Africa. For the Order it was clear that if they accepted Malta and Tripoli, they would become much more involved in European politics than when they were in Rhodes. It was not so much the obligation to respect the privileges which the house of Aragon had granted to the Maltese as the difficult task to defend the North African fortress town of Tripoli which temporarily halted negotiations. During this period of uncertainty, on 13 July 1524 the Order sent a commission composed of one member of each of the eight langues to Malta, Gozo, and Tripoli. The viceroy of Sicily ordered the Maltese *Capitano d'armi* Girolamo Campo to provide the commission with all necessary information about the islands. Unfortunately the original report of the commission seems to have been lost. But the gist of the report, given by Giacomo Bosio, shows that the commissioners mainly focused on the maritime, economic, topographical, and military profile of the islands. In the late sixteenth century Bosio quotes the 1524 commissioners report on the possibilities of building a main fortress on the island on the site where Valletta was to rise in 1566.

The report makes it clear that Malta – and even more so when its population was augmented by thousands of Hospitallers, their serfs and soldiers, and the Rhodiots travelling with them – was heavily dependant on Sicily for its provisions. Malta could only grow enough food for four months for its population. What also made life difficult in Malta was the constant danger of raids by corsairs and pirates from North Africa. For many knights life in isolated Malta appeared to be 'truly hard and almost intolerable, mostly in summer'. Despite all these disadvantages, Malta's perfect natural ports and strategic position seemed to make it a better place for settling the convent and main residence than the geographically more distant and more difficult to defend North African town of Tripoli.

It was also apparent that a decision was pressing. A further exile on the European continent would have the Order dragged deeper in intra-European conflicts and would have destabilized the integrative power of the Order's substance and its cosmopolitan structure. In the meantime the Order had carried out a veritable odyssey which led the convent from Messina to Civitavecchia (August 1523), Viterbo (January 1524), Corneto (June 1527), Villefranche (October 1527), and Nice (November 1527). The offer of Nice as headquarters was wisely turned down as it would certainly have directly involved the Order in deadly European conflicts. Some knights proposed re-conquering Rhodes but, after some intelligence from their agents in the Eastern Mediterranean, this also was turned down. By May 1527 the decision finally fell on Malta. On 19 May a chapter-general accepted to take over Malta, Gozo and Tripoli. In 1529 the convent moved again southwards and, before settling in Malta, resided for a while in Augusta (August 1529) and Syracuse (October 1529).

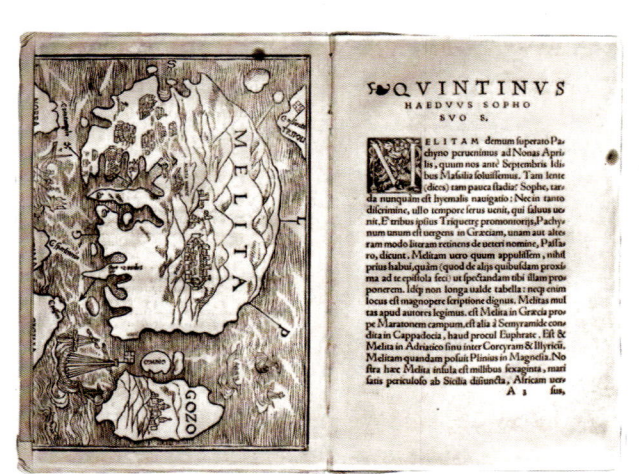

Left: Jean Quintin (1500–61) arrived in Malta with the convent in 1530. He published this map in the first published description of Malta in 1536, Insvlae Melitea Descriptio ex Comentariis Rervm Quotidianarvm.

Overleaf: The deed of donation of Malta, Gozo, and Tripoli (North Africa) by Charles V. The deed was signed at Castelfranco on 23 March 1530.

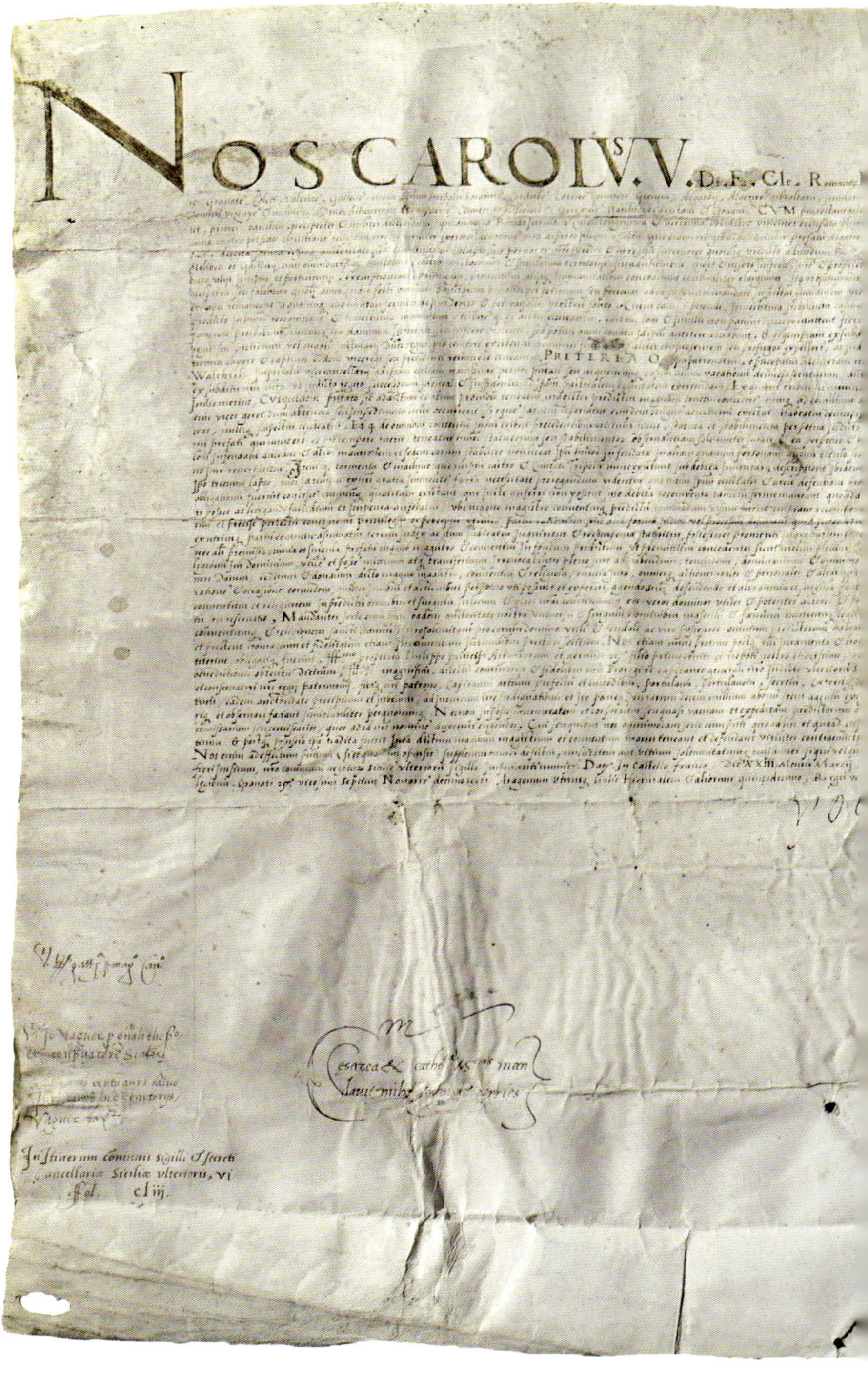
NOS CAROLVS. V. D. F. Cl. R

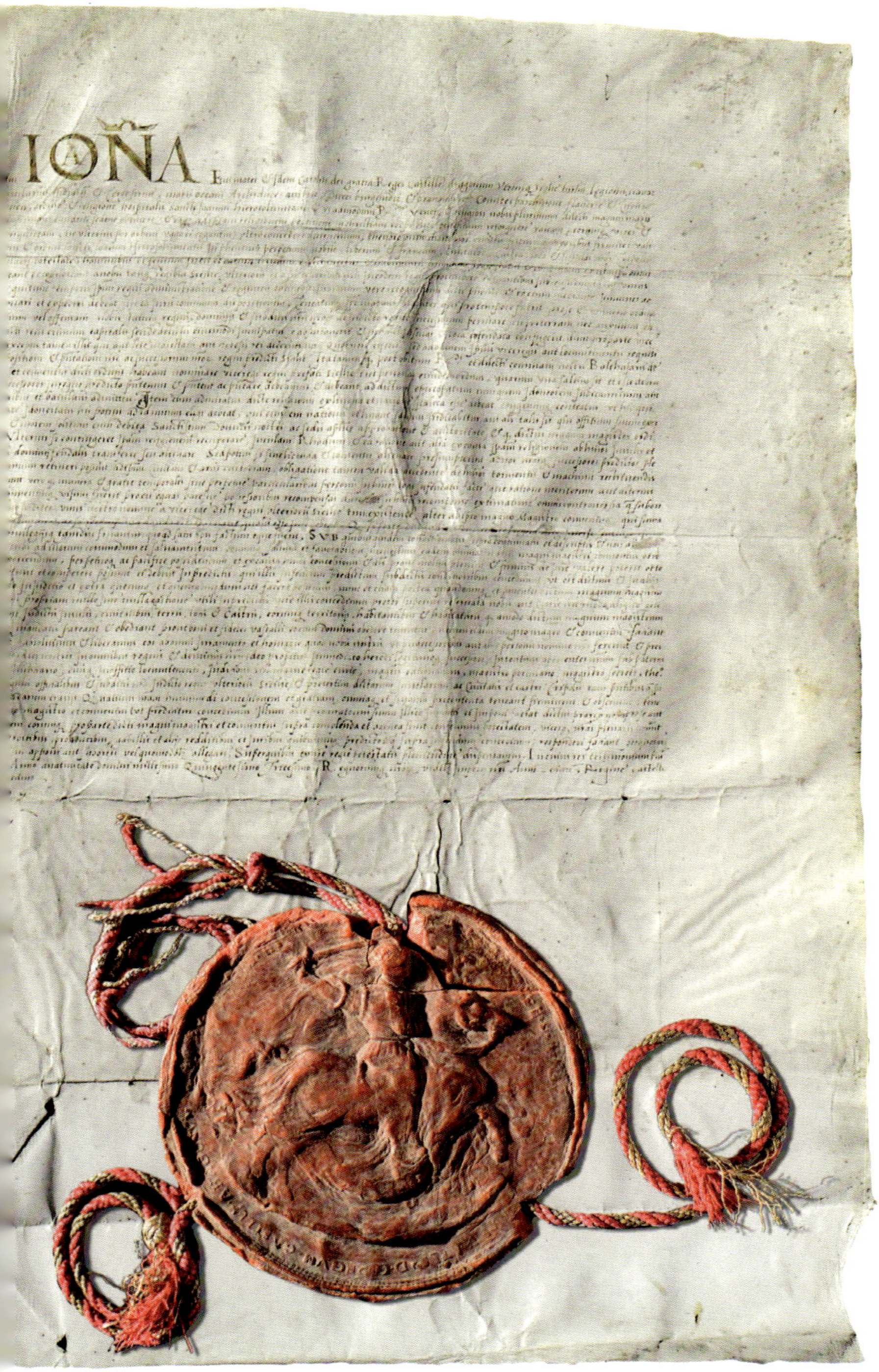
IOÑA

76 THE ORDER AND ITS RULE

On 24 March 1530, at Castelfranco, the Order of St John was invested with Malta, Gozo, and Tripoli 'in perpetual, noble, full, and free enfeoffment'. The donation deed exempted them from military service and guaranteed the knights full freedom to continue to live according to their statutes and their historic mission. As a symbolic act and confirmation of the enfeoffment, the Order had to present every year a falcon to Charles in his function as king of Sicily. On 25 April the Order's representatives ratified the document and on 7 May 1530 Pope Clement VII ratified the deed. Charles V kept the *dominio diretto* over Malta, Gozo, and Tripoli and the *gius patronato* over the local Church. Therefore the Order never gained full sovereignty over their new possessions. When, for example, on 27 July 1530 Grand Master L'Isle Adam asked Charles V for the right to mint the Order's own coins, this was at first refused.

Although the Order, in the sixteenth and seventeenth centuries, came more and more to adopt the attributes and attitudes of a sovereign power, in terms of state law it was only a fief-holder of Malta for the crown of Aragon and later of the kingdom of the Two Sicilies. When, for example, in the autumn of 1798 Lord Nelson sent a British corps under Sir Alexander Ball to Malta to support the Maltese rebels against the French, he did this after a request by the king of the Two Sicilies, Ferdinand IV. *De jure* Hospitaller Malta had the status of vassal of the crown of Sicily. If the Order were to move elsewhere, the Maltese islands and Tripoli would return to the direct possession of the house of Aragon or the crown of Sicily.

The situation in Malta was different than the one in Rhodes as the new possessions came to the Order not by conquest and papal guarantee but by enfeoffment through the king of Spain. This also meant that the viceroys of Sicily kept some prerogatives, especially their recommendation in the election of the bishops. In reality the rule of the grand masters was rather ambivalent. On the one hand, they swore to respect the rights of the Maltese, the council of the *universitas* of Mdina – the old capital of the island – while, on the other hand, they actually interfered very much in local affairs by introducing new taxes, laws, and law-courts, and establishing a new *universitas* at Birgu. Just as power came to be concentrated in the hands of the princes in the Absolutist Europe, also in Malta there was a tendency to centralize power in the hands of the grand master.

The meeting of Clement VII with Charles V at the Sala di Clemente VII. *Painting (detail) by Giorgio Vasari, at Palazzo Vecchio at Florence. These two men were crucial for the Order and with their help the Religion acquired a new home in Malta.*

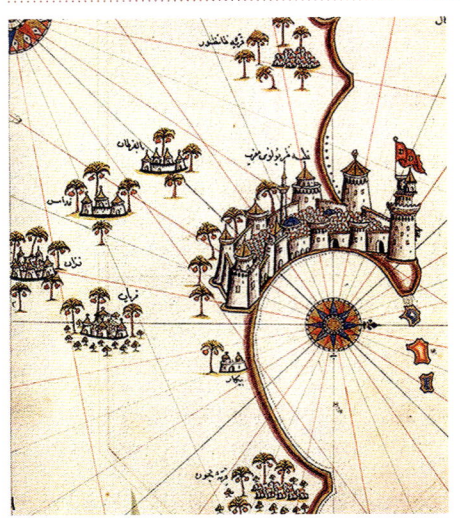

Tripoli (Libya) from the Kitab-ı Bahriye (باتك ط - باهر ي), *Book of Navigation, by Piri Reis done between 1524 and 1525. The book contains portolan charts with detailed information on ports and coastlines.*
National Library of France.

That the Order, immediately after settling in Malta, continued its glorious tradition of corsairing and trade in Muslim slaves was part of an economic, political, and ideological programme. In fact the resumption of the *corso* and corsairing breached L'Isle Adam's promise to Suleiman in Rhodes never to undertake these activities again. The resumption of the *corso* was a clear signal to Christian Europe that the Order still stood firm in its tradition of an 'eternal' fight against the infidels. The very slow progress on the fortifications of Birgu and Isla (Senglea) up to 1565 might have indicated that the Order had not yet fully accepted to stay in Malta and still dreamed of returning to Rhodes. Certainly the Birgu fortifications then could not compete with the monumental bulwarks of Rhodes. In this connection one might also interpret the proposals by the future Grand Master Jean de Valette – then governor of Tripoli – in 1546 and in 1548 – to transfer the headquarters of the Order from Malta to the North African town. On the one hand, this proposal was born out of the idea that the limited troops then present at Tripoli could not long resist the Muslim enemy. On the other hand, it was also thought that at Tripoli, with its hinterland, the Order could supply its needs and escape dependence on Sicily or on Spain, as well as to keep farther away from intra-European crises and conflicts. After all Valette was a Frenchman and not many French knights felt easy with the increasing close ties of the Order to the Spanish hemisphere. For obvious reasons, Spanish Grand Master Juan de Homedes did not want to hear much about this idea. Partly, as a result of this decision, in 1551 Tripoli was lost after being besieged by Murad Agà, one of the many Christian renegades in the Ottoman empire and North Africa.

Militarily the Order in general always complied in participating in the Spanish campaigns against the North African beys. So the Order's contingents joined the Spanish forces in their attacks on Tunis (1535), Djerba, Algiers (1541), the actions of the Holy League against the Ottomans (1570/71/72), and in the Spanish fights against the English in the gulf of Cadiz.

The decision for Malta – and its global implications

Despite the complicated and long drawn-out process of decision-making, for the kings of Spain and their viceroys in Sicily it was certainly an advantage for the knights to settle in Malta. There the knights would relieve the Sicilian and Spanish treasury from having to invest in more fortifications and garrisoning more troops on the south-east border of Sicily, while better naval protection could be expected against the constant threat of North African corsairs and pirates. Certainly the

Though built on top of a number of older buildings (including a Roman public bath), much of the earliest defensive structures of 'Assaraya al-Hamra' (the Red Castle) are attributed to the knights of St John.

Hapsburgs longed to see the Catholic Order on its territory and therefore must have opposed the plans of Francis I for the Order to settle in Nice. Of course the Order was expected also to oppose the numerous corsairs from the nearby Barbary Coast. Malta furthermore was a link between Sicily and the newly conquered Spanish possessions on the North African coast. In political and ideological terms, the Order and Spain had many similar aspects and the presence of the Hospitallers in Malta was not seen a threat to the political and administrative authority of the viceroyalty of Sicily.

It soon became obvious that Charles V was only willing to cede Malta to the knights if they also took over the fortress of Tripoli. The Hospitallers clearly understood that taking over of Malta and Tripoli

meant a greater involvement in European politics and the complicated balance of power in the west than during their rule over Rhodes. It was not so much the obligation to respect the privileges which the house of Aragon had ceded to the Maltese – which Charles V expressly reminded the Order in November 1524 – but the obligation to be responsible also for the defence of Tripoli which lead to the long drawn-out discussion.

From the beginning the Hospitallers were aware how much Malta depended on Sicilian supplies. In the 1520s Malta could only grow grain and raise animals to feed the local population for four months of the year. With a growth of population and the increasing presence of soldiers, sailors, and military personnel, this dependency on foreign imports would increase even more, while they had to be on permanent alert for piratical raids. Overall life in sterile Malta was not all too comfortable, especially in the unbearably hot summer months. A sure plus were the excellent and spacious natural harbours and the manageable coastline. The much bigger burden was the geographically distant and difficult-to-defend Tripoli. Already before the Hospitallers settled in Malta the island had – in spite of its mostly Semitic populations – a clear political, economic, and cultural orientation towards Latin-Christian western Europe, especially towards

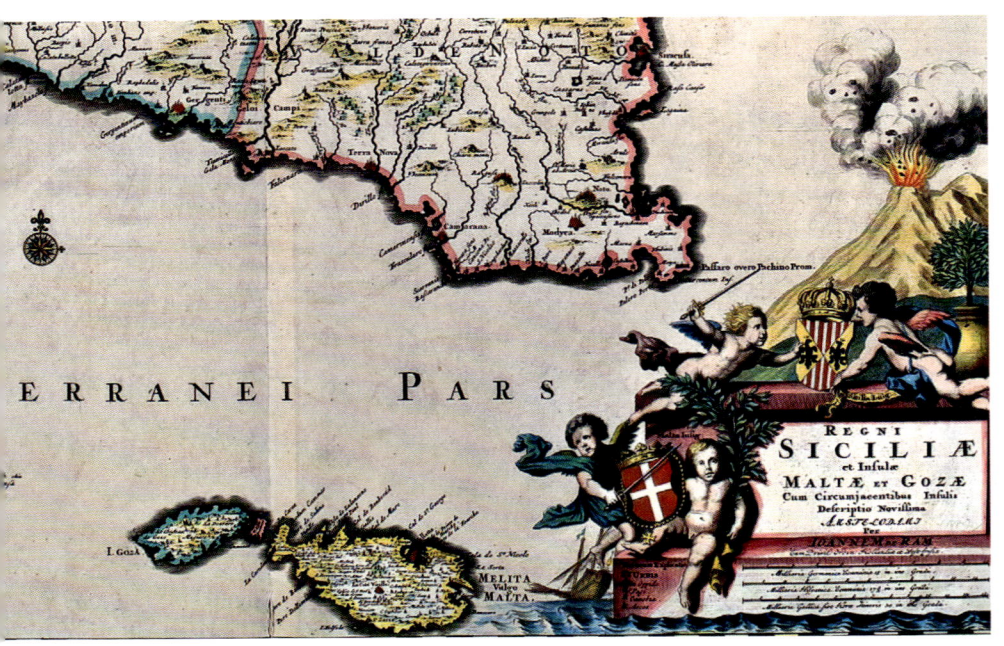

A detail from a 17th-century Dutch map showing the proximity of the Maltese archipelago to Sicily and the connections between the two.

A 17th-century narrative painting of a naval battle between the Order's galleys and Turkish vessels off the coast of Alexandria.
Malta Maritime Museum.

the Aragonese empire with its Italian lands. Fernand Braudel sums up Malta's position as 'Italy's maritime front against the Turkish threat'. For the crown of Aragon, before the island was given to the Order, Malta had a triple function, 'to provide a naval base for the Spanish fleets, to offer resistance to Turkish armadas, and to defend its own territory against pirate attacks'.

This strategic interpretation of Malta therefore corresponded closely with the concept according to which Emperor Charles V handed over the Maltese islands and Tripoli to the Order. With the town and fortress of Tripoli and the Maltese archipelago in the hands of a staunch and active chivalric Order and Sicily and the south of Italy in direct Spanish hands, the Sicily channel would divide the Mediterranean into two basins – at least so it was hoped.

But there was also another – most interesting – aspect to be considered. Preferring the obvious idea to instrumentalize the Hospitallers as a Spanish bulwark against Ottoman expansion, historians have until now paid only scant attention to another emerging political phenomenon. At least since 1525, the Spanish court had been receiving alarming intelligence from France that Francis I of France was more and more seeking contacts with the Ottoman empire. By doing so he hoped to escape the encirclement of France by the Hapsburgs – then ruling in Spain and the German empire. On the other hand the secret French-Ottoman negotiations threatened deeply Charles V's vision of the Hapsburgs as protectors of the *Unitas Christiana* and also the safety of the Spanish territories. The installation of a staunch Catholic chivalric Order in Tripoli and Malta, that is in the central axis of the Mediterranean, can be interpreted as a clever effort to prevent any joining of Ottoman and French navies. In the next decades these French-Ottoman approaches were to become closer and closer. In 1535, and again in 1553 peace treaties were signed between France and the Sublime Porte. France, indeed, welcomed any Ottoman attacks on the Spanish territories in Southern Italy and Sicily.

There were, in fact, many secret agreements that if the Ottomans conquered the South Italian ports they would be allowed to raid the towns and to enslave the populations, before handing the conquered lands over to the French. Although these plans were never achieved, the central Mediterranean remained in the focus of bitter Spanish-Ottoman conflicts for the rest of the sixteenth century, often involving also Venice and Genoa. Of course, the

The Siege of Algiers in 1541. British Museum. The valour of the knights of Malta was not forgotten, and the spot where they made their stand is still called 'The Grave of the Knights' (قبر الفرسان).

Hospitallers knew about the French 'aspect' of the emperor's offer to take over Malta and Tripoli but, lacking other options, they had to accept.

This alliance between Charles V and the knights persisted. The achievements of Cortés and Pizarro in Central and South America respectively and the establishment of the Spanish in the New World and the Portuguese in Africa and India changed the focus of world politics. Although economic power, in particular, gradually shifted from the Mediterranean to the lands overseas, Charles still looked at the Mediterranean as a major field of interest. As the great protectors of the Roman Catholic faith, the Hapsburgs styled themselves as defenders of Europe against the evils of Islam. That the knights played an important role in this concept was only natural. Charles frequently requested the co-operation of the Order's fleet for Spanish attacks on North Africa. In 1535 his operation at La Goletta against Kheiredin Barbarossa was supported by the full fleet of the Order. In 1541 the Order's galley squadron joined the Spanish expeditionary force against Algiers.

That the Order did not choose places like Nice or Viterbo as it had been suggested but preferred the remote Maltese islands and therewith kept its role as a permanent fighter against the infidels, would turn out to be a most favourable decision. In remote Malta, the Order did not become directly involved in the developments and upheavals of European politics and could keep – at least for two more centuries – its *raison d'être* as *miles christianae*.

The main gate of Viterbo saw the departure of Grand Master L'Isle Adam and his convent in 1527. The plague had taken over the city. The convent moved to nearby Corneto and then to Nice before arriving at Malta in October 1530.

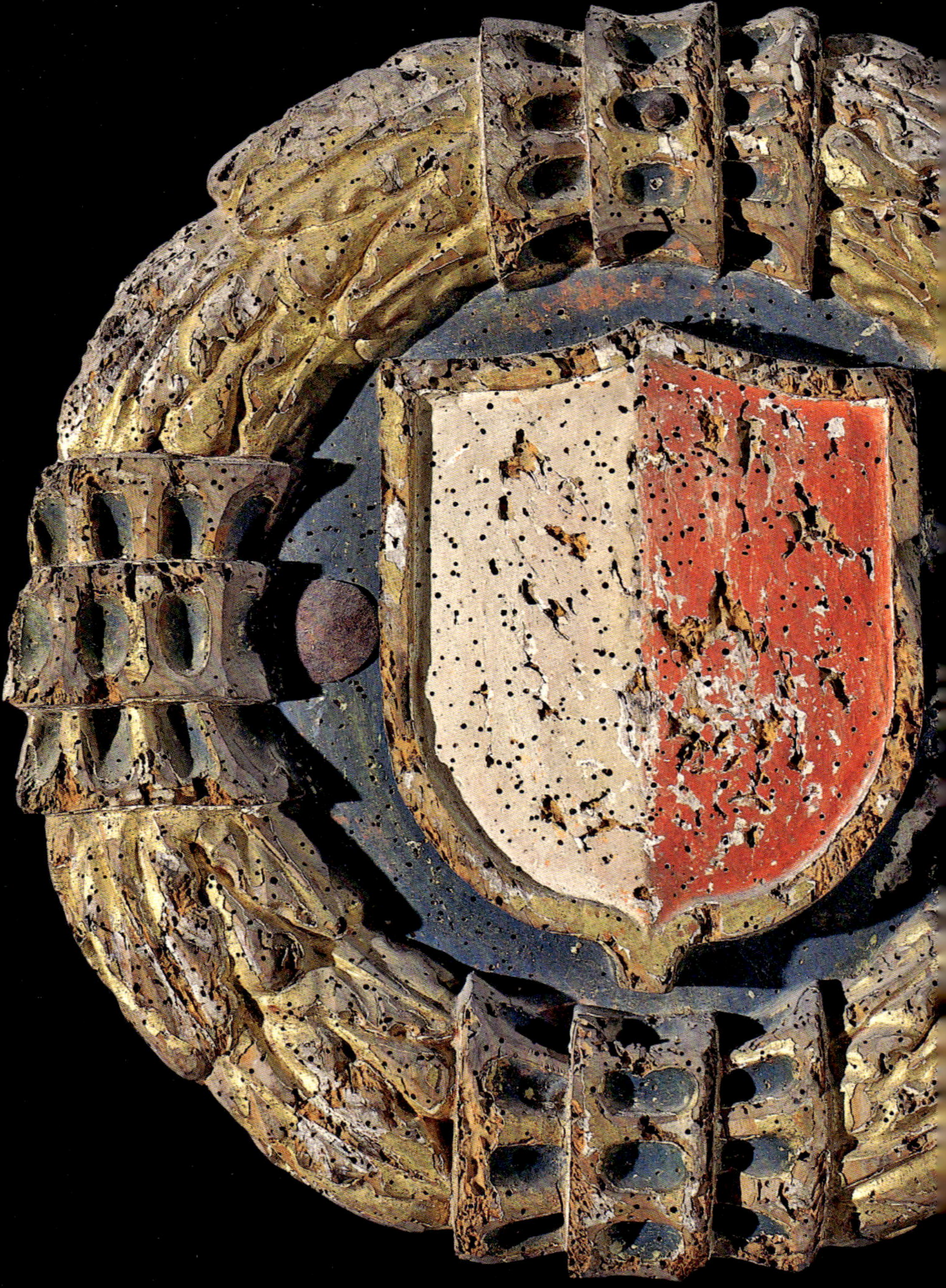

Although the forced move from Rhodes to Malta meant a drastic change of the geopolitical environment, the Order kept its old structure and policy. To establish its convent at the border of Christian Europe was a clear signal that the institution was set to continue its fight against the infidels.

CHAPTER 4

THE HOSPITALLERS IN MALTA
A DIFFICULT BEGINNING

**Malta and Sicily:
the legal and social background**

The establishment of the Order in Malta was not received enthusiastically by the local population. In particular, the ruling classes and the *universitas* of Mdina rightly feared a diminution of their power. At least since the 'Monroy-affair' in the early fifteenth century, it had been most clear that the Maltese wished fervently never to be separated from the dominion of Sicily. Only the lower classes might have welcomed the Order as another source of income and a protection against the seemingly never-ending corsair raids on the coasts. What also changed the face of Malta drastically was the decision of the Order to establish its headquarters not in the old capital of Mdina but in the *Castrum Maris*

Until the knights arrived Mdina was the capital of the archipelago and the residency of the Maltese aristocracy. A wooden coat of arms of the local governing organ called the Universitas *is now housed at the Cathedral Museum, Mdina.*

at the harbour. The formal possession of the sovereignty of the Maltese islands took place on 13 November 1530 when L'Isle Adam was welcomed in Mdina by the *capitano delle verga* and the jurats of the *universitas*. L'Isle Adam swore to 'observe and command the observance of all the privileges and concessions granted to the Islands by the Invincible Kings of Aragon and Sicily'.

Although the Order in the course of the sixteenth and seventeenth centuries more and more showed the attributes of a sovereign ruler, in terms of state law it was a fiefholder of the crown of Aragon. The symbolic documentation of this status was the yearly sending of a falcon to the viceroy of Sicily. If the Order were to move to another residence instead, these possessions would return to the crown of Sicily or of Aragon.

Fort St Angelo from Willem Schellinkx: Journey to the South 1664–65. *This view of the fort, before the 17th-century reconstruction of the bastions, gives us a clue of how the* Castrum Maris *could have looked like when the Order arrived in Malta.*

This situation in Malta resembled somewhat that in Rhodes. When, in 1454, Grand Master Jean de Lastic had refused to pay taxes to the sultans, he had declared: '*Haec insula mea non est; Papae ego, ut domino tuo, subitus sum.*' As another consequence of this legal situation, the viceroys of Sicily or the kings of Spain were involved in the appointment of the bishops of Malta and the priors of the conventual church of the Order.

An arrangement with the local authorities appeared more difficult. A Maltese delegation, led by Ingeraldo Inguanez and Antonio

Bonello, protested to the viceroy of Sicily, pointing out that the 1428 decree where the Maltese against payment of 20,000 florins, were guaranteed once again that their island would never be separated from the royal *demesne* of Sicily, that is, direct royal government, was ignored. In fact a royal charter proclaimed that the Maltese commune was to remain a demanial town, that is, ruled directly by the king and his officials in Palermo. Until then the internal situation in Malta had been clear: The *universitas* was dominated and controlled by an élite group of landowners comprising the higher clergy, the land-owning gentry, notaries, and lawyers. The Maltese islands had enjoyed a certain measure of autonomy in their status as demanial towns of the kingdom of Sicily. Both Malta and Gozo had their own *universitares* or local municipal governments which administered justice, regulated the markets and public health, and raised taxes.

Theory and facts often did not agree. On the one hand the grand masters swore to respect the rights of the Maltese and of the council, the Mdina *universitas*, while on the other hand, they tried their best to cut down its power and influence by introducing new taxes, laws and law courts. To counterbalance the influence of the old Maltese nobility in Mdina there was even another *universitas* established in Birgu.

Legally the Order now faced a different situation in Malta when compared to the times in Rhodes. The Maltese islands were not conquered and held through the consent and guarantee of the Holy See but given by the king of Spain as a fief. This implied that the viceroys of Sicily, as the direct representatives of the crown of Aragon (and Spain), had the right to interfere in several aspects of ruling and administering the three islands. These situations sometimes led to clashes and tension.

Although Malta is considerably smaller than Rhodes, the Hospitallers still could not guarantee full security to all the inhabitants of the archipelago. Although to a lesser degree

A detail from the 1536 map in Insvlae Melitea Descriptio ex Comentariis Rervm Quotidianarvm, *Jean Quintin's (1500–61) description of the islands.* Civitas *refers to Mdina. On this map the area of the old town is exaggerated.*

than before 1530, the islands were still objects of attacks by Ottoman fleets and Barbary Coast corsairs in the sixteenth and seventeenth centuries. In April 1540 the fleet of the notorious corsair Dragut – also known as Turgut Reis – attacked Gozo but did not conquer the *castello*. In 1551 Gozo was sacked by the forces of Sinan Pasha, Salih Pasha, and Dragut. A few days before they had unsuccessfully besieged Birgu, Fort St Angelo, and Mdina. In October 1583 Gozo was again raided by North-African corsairs, and many inhabitants were enslaved. In 1614 an armada of 60 Ottoman ships and 5,000 soldiers attacked Marsascala and Żejtun. Obviously the knights – much more concerned with the wider picture than establishing internal harmony with the local population and authorities – had to concentrate on external affairs.

Sieges and heroes

The Orders arrival propelled Malta into the limelight of Mediterranean and European awareness. In 1551 Malta came in the direct focus of international action when the Turks, helped by North African forces, launched an heavy attack on Malta and Gozo and subsequently seized Tripoli. The events started in July 1551 when Dragut and Sultan Suleiman the Magnificent's general Sinan Pasha – a Sicilian renegade – landed in Malta with a large contingent. It was feared originally that

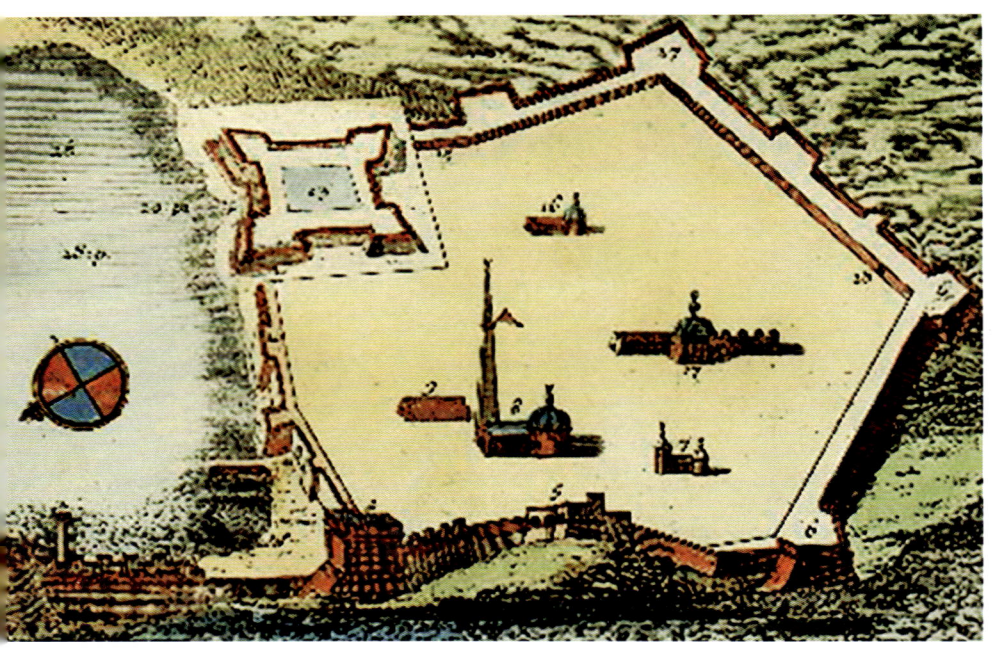

A coloured plan of the fortifications of Tripoli. The knights' castle on the top left protected the coastline of the walled city. From the Peter Kiewit Institute Library.

A copy of an inscription dated 1579 indicates Bernardo DeOpuo's house in the Gozo Citadel. The original is in the Archaeology Museum, a hundred metres down the road.
Legend has it that DeOpuo, a soldier of fortune, at the arrival of the Turks into the narrow streets of the Gozo citadel, killed his wife and daughters rather than allow them to be hauled into slavery. He was killed soon after, fiercely fighting the invaders.

the main assault would be directed towards Mdina. As a precautionary measure it was ordered that all the Rabat buildings which could be used by the attackers were to be pulled own. Sinan Pasha had landed at St Paul's Bay from where he attacked Mdina then under the command of the erudite French knight Nicolas Durand de Villegagnon, whose decisive role in the defence of the city is recalled in the name of the main street. Mdina did not surrender. Even the Order's forts at the *Porto Grande* proved to be too strong to attack. So the invaders turned to Gozo. The poorly manned Gozo *castello* could just withstand the attack for three days. Nearly all of the islands' inhabitants – about 5,000 – were carried away into slavery. The following month the Muslim forces attacked Hospitaller Tripoli, whose precarious defences and lack of support did not make it too difficult for Dragut and Sinan Pasha to take. In a few weeks the governor of Tripoli, Gaspard de Vallier, surrendered and Sultan Suleiman installed Dragut as pasha of Tripoli.

Unfortunately the grand master, the Spaniard Juan de Homedes, was not one to face such events with nerve and courage. On learning of the Muslims' intentions to attack Tripoli, he had asked the French ambassador August D'Aramont, who then just had called at Malta, to set sail for Tripoli to try to prevent the surrender of the fortress. So on 2 August 1551, late in the night, D'Aramont left for Tripoli, arriving

IMAGO SVLEYMANNI TVRCΞRVM IMP. IN ORIENTE, VNICI SELIMY FILII, QVI AN. DO. M D XX. PATRI IN IMPERIO SVCCESSIT: QVO ETI:
AM ANNO CAROLVS V. MAXÆMYLIANI CÆSARIS NEPOS AQVISGRANI IN OCCIDENTE CORONATVS EST CHRISTIANI IMP. A MELCHIO:
RE LORICHS FLENSBVRGENSI, HOLSATIO, ANTIQVITATIS STVDIOSISS, CONSTANTINOPOLI, AN.MDLIX, MEN. FEB, DIE XV, VERISSIME EXPRESSA.

just in time to witness its surrender. He could only manage to free the governor and some senior French knights. On Sunday 23, D'Aramont and some of the knights returned to Malta. The French group reported what had happened and – somewhat unjustifiably – Homedes blamed Vallier and the French knights for the loss of Tripoli and threw them into prison.

The Great Siege, however, was still to come. The news that Suleiman the Magnificent was preparing to attack Malta with a huge armada filtered into the west in early 1563. By the summer of 1564 Grand Master Valette knew for certain, through his agents in Constantinople, that the attack was imminent. All knights were called to convent and strategies of defence discussed with the viceroy of Sicily, Don Garcia de Toledo. Suleiman assigned the command of the fleet to Pialí Pasha, his son-in law and the land-forces to the experienced Mustapha Pasha, who was strongly recommended to discuss the strategy of attack with the experienced Corsair Dragut. The soldier Francesco Balbi di Correggio, a reliable chronicler of the Great Siege, estimated that the Ottoman fleet with more than 190 vessels carried 28,000 fighting men, including an élite force of 6,300 Janissaries and 6,000 volunteers. The forces of the Hospitallers consisted of some 6,100 combatants: 3,000 of them were Maltese, 500 knights, 500 galley soldiers, 200 Sicilian and Greek familiars of the Order, and 600 Spanish and Italian infantry soldiers.

In the spring of 1565 a great part of the population of Malta, old and infirm people and children, were evacuated to Sicily. The evacuation was still in progress when, on 18 May 1565, the Ottoman armada appeared off Marsaxlokk and then moved on to Ġnejna Bay. But on 19 May they were back in Marsaxlokk and started landing their troops. After a few skirmishes Grand Master Valette decided to concentrate most of his troops in the fortified enclaves of Birgu, Forts St Angelo, St Michael, and St Elmo. That the Ottomans ignored to attack the old weakly fortified capital of Mdina and the island of Gozo can be explained by the fact that time was pressing. The key to conquering Malta was Birgu and Fort St Angelo and this had to be concluded by autumn for the fleets to retire to their home bases. There was some friction between the Ottoman leaders Mustapha Pasha and Pialí Pasha where to attack first. Finally it was decided to concentrate on taking Fort St Elmo first, which would give them access to the Grand Harbour.

On 24 May the Ottomans moved their heavy artillery from the fleet to the Sceberras peninsula where

*Portrait by Melchior Lorck (1526–88), of Suleiman I (Ottoman Turkish: نامیلس) the tenth and longest-reigning sultan of the Ottoman empire, from 1520 to 1566. He is known in the west as Suleiman the Magnificent and in the East, as the Lawmaker (Arabic: یناقلا), because of his complete reconstruction of the Ottoman legal system.
Woodcut, Statens Museum for Kunst, Copenhagen.*

they raised a parapet and a battery, one opposite of Fort St Michael and another opposite Fort St Angelo. Another platform was built on the highest point of the Sceberras hill to fire on Fort St Elmo. In the meantime the grand master had welcomed the Knight Pierre de Massuez Vercoyran with 400 soldiers from Messina. In total now there were some 900 men troops to defend Fort St Elmo. On 25 May the bombardment of the fort began. The knights still managed to maintain communications and exchange of fighting men between Birgu and Fort St Elmo.

In the panel of the Fall of St Elmo in the cycle of frescoes at the Sala del Gran Consiglio *at the Grand Master's Palace, d'Aleccio painted Dragut after he had been wounded (detail).*

In the same cycle at the palace, in the panel showing the whole siege, d'Aleccio painted the attack on St Elmo and the defence of the fort by the knights and Maltese.

On 2 June Dragut arrived with 15 vessels and 2,500 volunteers from Tripoli and Algiers and took over the attacks on Fort St Elmo. On 5 June the attackers launched direct assaults but still they were halted by the defenders. On 14 June the Muslims suffered a setback when the aga of the Janissaries (the chief officer) was killed in the trenches below the fort. Things got worse when, on 18 June, Dragut was mortally wounded and he died five days later. With him the attackers lost their possibly most competent leader. In the meantime the Ottoman artillery and Piali's ships had managed to stop St Elmo from being provided with munitions, food, and fresh fighting men from Birgu. This meant

THE EPIC GREAT SIEGE 93

that the fort had sooner, rather than later, to surrender. On 23 June the last assault was launched and, after a brave defence, nearly all Christian defenders were killed.

Mustapha Pasha and Pialí Pasha now decided to concentrate on Senglea and Fort St Michael and by the first week of July begun large-scale attacks, opening fire on St Angelo, St Michael, and Birgu from Mount Sceberras, Mount Salvatore, Corradino Heights, and Gallows' Point. With the constant bombardment the attackers hoped not only to pound the defences into pieces but also to demoralize the defenders. This hope, however, proved vain. Even the great assault on 2 August failed. On 7 August the Ottomans attacked Birgu and Senglea simultaneously. They were

A battery of 20 cannon fire away at Birgu and Fort St Angelo from heights of Ponta di San Salvatore, now Bighi. Matteo Perez d'Aleccio, detail from the Bombardment of the Post of Castille panel.

OVERLEAF: Matteo Perez D'Allecio's graphic depiction of the Great Siege showing simultaneously the most important events in progress.

A: The Castle of St Angelo, with the Great Chain connected to Spur of Isola.
B. The Borgo, with the bridge leading to Isola.
C. Bormla, where there were two great guns firing on Fort St Angelo.
D: Isola, where the palisades of wooden stakes prevented the Turkish craft from reaching the shore.
E: Santa Margarita, where six cannon and a basilisk bombarded St Michael and the post of the knights of Provence.
F: The Belvedere which was the camp of Mustafa Pasha and his corps of guards.
G: The Mandra, with 3 cannon bombarding the bastion of St Michael.

H: The heights of Corradino with 13 cannon in three emplacements bombarding the curtain wall of Isola.
I: Assault craft being transported overland from Marsamxett for the seaborne assault on Isola.
K: Two batteries of 6 cannon bombarding Isola and part of the Borgo.
L: A battery of 5 cannon bombarding St Angelo.
M: Two batteries, one of 14 and the other of 10 cannon, bombarding St Elmo.
N: St Elmo, with the ravelin, siege battery, and trenches built by the Turks.
O: Kalkara, where there were 2 cannon firing on the Post of the knights of Castille.

P: San Salvatore, where there are more than 16 cannon, 2 basilisks, and 2 murlacchi.
Q: The bay where many great ships disembarked artillery for San Salvatore.
R: Gallows' Point.
S: Dragut Point, where 4 cannon were placed to bombard Fort St Elmo.
T: The harbour of Marsamxett where the Turkish armada lay after the fall of St Elmo.
V: The little island in the harbour of Marsamxett.
X: The place where it is possible to ford the water to reach the little island.
Top: The chain constructed by the Turk. **Bottom right:** Paulo Miccio's vineyard.

94 The Hospitallers in Malta

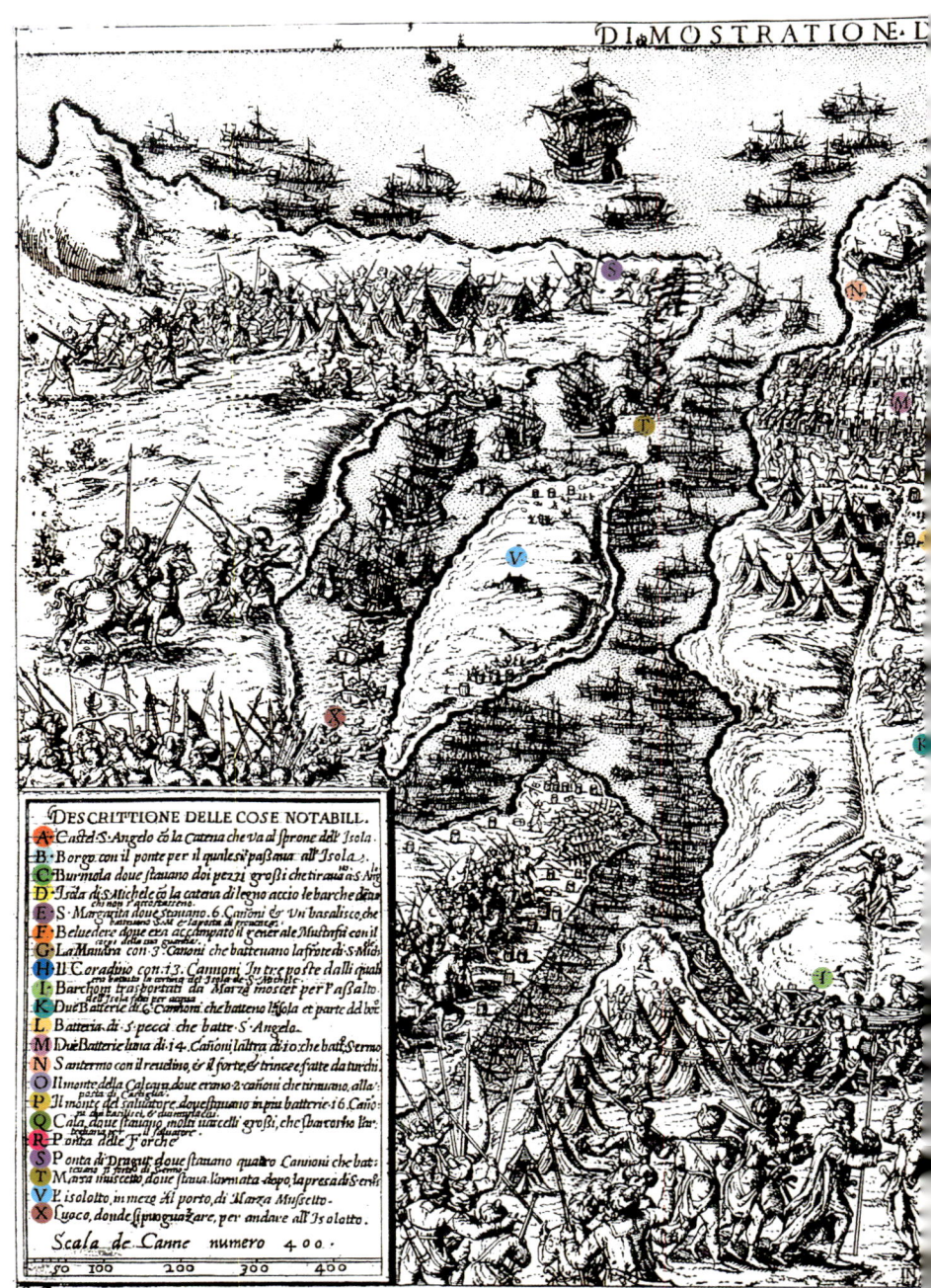

The Epic Great Siege

96   THE HOSPITALLERS IN MALTA

TURKISH CAMP ON DRAGUT POINT

TURKISH ARMADA IN MARSAMXETT HARBOUR

TURKISH TRENCH

TURKISH CAMP ON MOUNT SCEBERRAS

TURKISH ARTILLERY ON MOUNT SCEBERRAS

15 JULY 1565
ASSAULT ON SENGLEA BY LAND AND SEA

OTTOMAN TURKS
JANISSARIES: 5,000
LAYALARS: 2,500
SAPHIS: 7,000
HEAVY ARTILLERY: 45,000 ROUNDS
LEVIES: 4,000
ALGERIANS: 10,000

KNIGHTS OF ST JOHN
KNIGHTS: 600
MALTESE: 4,000
MEN-AT-ARMS AND MERCENARIES: 7,200
REINFORCEMENTS:
50 KNIGHTS AND 600 SPANISH INFANTRY

MAIN CLASHES

EARLY MORNI
ALGERIAN TRO
MOVE IN FRO
MARSA, BREA
THROUGH THE W
DEFENCES A
ATTACK SENG

MARSA BASIN

THE EPIC GREAT SIEGE 97

halted at Birgu but managed to breach the walls of Senglea. The town seemed to have been lost when, after a whole day's fighting, news came in that a Christian relief force had attacked the Ottomans in their rear at Marsa. Mustapha ordered a retreat, only to find that this news was false. The attacks continued for the whole of August.

It was obvious that, sooner or later, the defenders had to surrender because of lack of supplies. On the other hand, the Ottomans were pressed by time. While Mustapha Pasha opted to spend the winter in

Malta, Pialí Pasha, fearing for the safety of the fleet, objected. If Malta did not surrender by mid-September, he intended to sail the fleet back to its bases in Turkey. Things, however, turned out differently when, on 6 September, the long-awaited Spanish relief force under Viceroy Don Garcia de Toledo reached the Gozo channel. This *Grande Soccorso* was composed of 28 vessels and galleys with 10,000 soldiers. The Spanish ships anchored at Armier from where the troops proceeded under Ascanio de la Corna to Mdina. In the meantime the Ottomans had abandoned their camps at Sceberras peninsula and Marsa, with some retreating to Marsamxett. Most of the fleet had moved to St Paul's Bay. Quick assessing the situation, Mustapha Pasha decided against a general retreat and to attack the

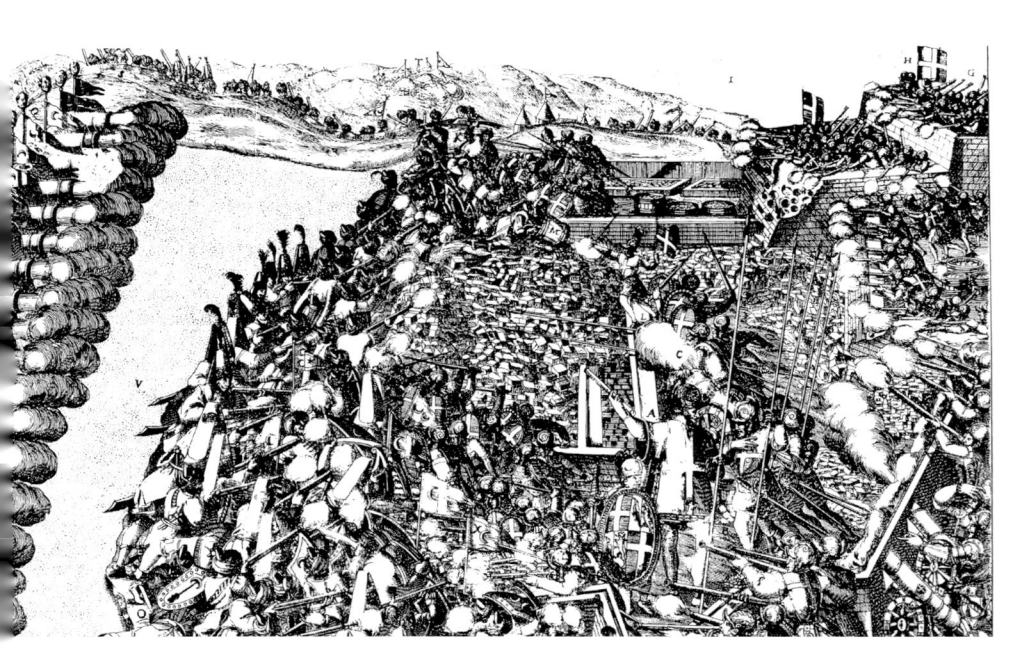

The engraving of Matteo Perez d'Aleccio depicting the assault upon the Post of Castille showing the heroic stance taken by the grand master to defend the post at all costs.
Private collection.

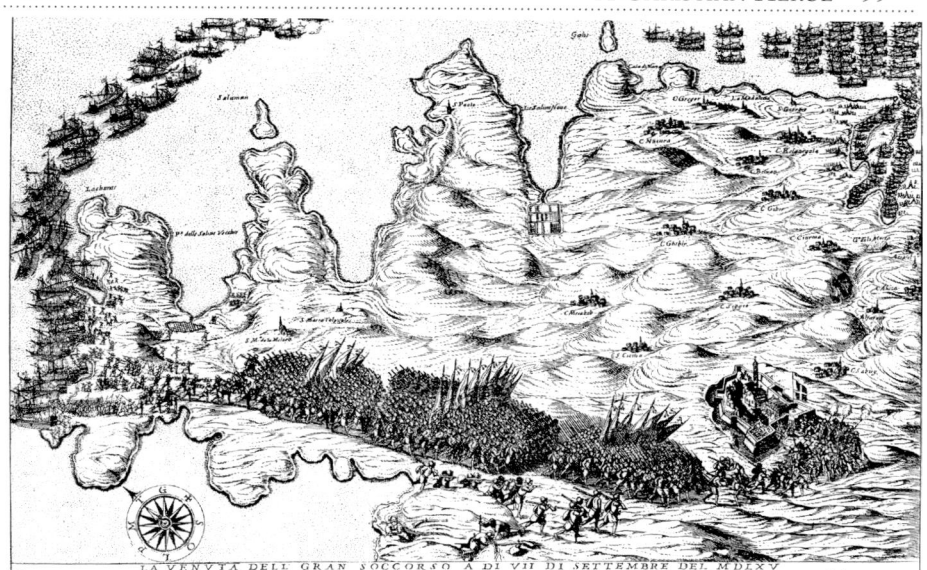

The etching done by Antonio Francesco Lucini in 1631 of the arrival of the Grande Soccorso on 7 September. Lucini published, in Bologna, a precise copy of Matteo Perez d'Aleccio's original engravings of 1585. Private collection.

Spanish relief forces. This however proved a disaster and the Ottoman contingents were heavily defeated by the fresh Spanish troops and the troops from Mdina and the Maltese militia near Naxxar. The Muslim soldiers moved back to St Paul's Bay and on 8 September the remains of the once impressive Ottoman armada set sail to retreat to their bases. The military and political importance of the Turkish defeat of 1565 was, and still is, very much overestimated by historians and commentators. It did not have any grave consequences on Turkish politics or its naval strength. Indeed only a few years later, the Turks conquered the Venetian possession of Cyprus. Despite of the disasters of Malta (1565) and Lepanto (1571), the Ottoman fleet remained powerful enough to threaten the Western and Central Mediterranean. Politically the status quo in the Mediterranean remained more or less the same until the early eighteenth century, there raged 'the whole scale of war and peace, enmity and alliance, and the intermediate forms of contact', as the Dutch historian Alexander H. de Groot has written.

The main importance of the Great Siege and the heroic defence of the island under Grand Master Jean de Valette was psychological *'Rien n'est plus connû que le siège de Malte,'* ('nothing is so well known as the siege of Malta') Voltaire wrote in the mid-eighteenth century. Indeed the Turkish siege of Malta between May and September 1565

The portrait of Grand Master Jean de Valette as he defends the Post of Castille during the Great Siege. Matteo Perez d'Aleccio, detail from the Assault upon the Post of Castille panel, Sala del Gran Consiglio *at the Grand Master's Palace.*

under Mustapha Pasha, Pialí Pasha, and Dragut became one of the most known events in Early Modern History. Together with the Turkish attack on Vienna of 1683, it was the most famous siege in the sixteenth and seventeenth centuries. Malta was literally placed on the European map when after the siege a flood of Latin, French, Italian, Spanish, and German descriptions of the events of 1565 were published and the allure of the mythic knights' state spread beyond Catholic frontiers. Although Valette believed that the Turks would launch a new attack in 1566 Suleiman now concentrated on the Balkans, during which campaign he died on 7 September 1566 near the fortress town of Szigetvár.

Undoubtedly the best-known hero of the Great Siege as well as the most popular of the 28 grand masters who ruled in 268 years over Malta is Grand Master Valette. The legendary grand master was born on 4 February 1495 at the castle of Labro in the province of Rouergue. In 1515 Valette was received as a professed knight in the langue of Provence of the Order. He was in Rhodes when the island was attacked and he too went through the eight-year odyssey that finally brought the Order to Malta. In 1534 he was given command of the galley *San Giovanni Battista*. A few years later an incident occurred which resulted in Valette's imprisonment. No exact details have survived but Grand Master

Homedes decided that, because of his 'aggressive behaviour', Valette was to be imprisoned for some months in Gozo.

Before his governorship of Tripoli another event happened which was to contribute to Valette's fame. In 1541 his galliot was captured near the Barbary Coast and, for a full year, he survived the hardships of a galley slave before he was released through an exchange of prisoners. From then on he made rapid progress in the Order. Before his appointment as governor of Tripoli, Valette had served as one of the three *agozzini reali* responsible for the fortifications of the Order. When his spell as governor of Tripoli came to an end in 1549, Valette returned to Malta. In the summer of 1551 he participated in the successful defence of Malta against Sinan Pasha and Dragut. In 1554 he was appointed to the prestigious post of captain general of the galleys of the Order, and subsequently *Balí* of Langò and grand prior of St Gilles.

When Jean de la Sengle died, Jean de Valette was elected grand master on 21 August 1557. Clearly the central event of his rule was the siege of 1565, which not only put Malta in the limelight of European awareness and brought tremendous glory and esteem for the knights but also changed the Order's attitude towards the tiny and rocky island. After the siege Malta became their island also in spirit and the thoughts that it was only a temporary residence came to an end.

After the siege Valette and the knights were showered with honour and gifts from European monarchs and leaders. Valette even refused to accept a cardinal's hat offered to him by Pope Pius IV. The pragmatic grand master used this situation of unique European sympathy in another way and, with the guarantee of papal and Spanish funds, planned the building of a new fortress city on Mount Sceberras which should carry his name, La Valletta. Time was pressing as Valette expected

The sword of the grand masters of the Order of St John, known as the 'Sword of the Religion' and the matching dagger. These weapons were sent to de Valette by Philip II of Spain as a token of admiration towards the grand master after the successful defence of Malta during the Great Siege.

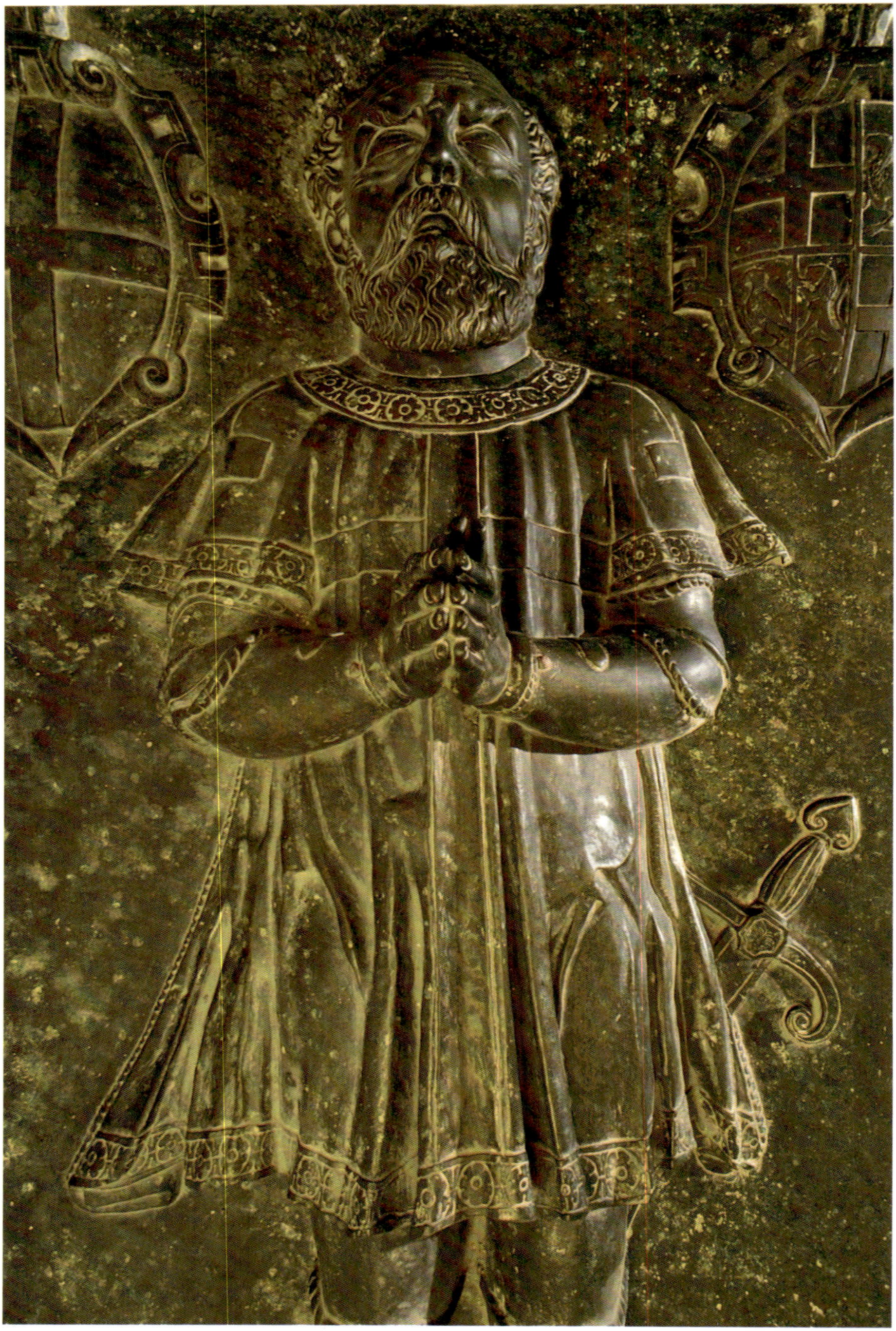

a new Turkish attack in the summer of 1566. The chief architect was Francesco Laparelli, ably supported by the Maltese Girolamo Cassar. On 28 March 1566 the foundation stone was laid. In relatively short time the city took shape and by 1574 the headquarters of the Order moved there from Birgu. Valette did not live long enough to witness all this. He passed away on 21 August 1568 and was buried in the church of Our Lady of Victory. After the new conventual church of St John was finished, his body was laid to rest in a sarcophagus in its crypt. Still, amongst the Maltese population he was not such loved. In fact his person was connected with the knights' government turning to injustice and arrogance towards the local population.

The *corso* – backbone of a society and state
Could it be that in the fourteenth century when in Christian Europe still were plans of new crusades many members of the Order believed in a realistic chance to return to Palestine this hope totally faded when in

The cover of the sarcophagus holding the body of Grand Master de Valette now in the crypt of St John's Co-Cathedral. It is believed that the face of the bronze effigy of the sarcophagus was done from a death mask of the grand master. The Latin inscription on his tomb states: Here lies De Valette,/ Worthy of eternal honour,/ He who was once the scourge of Africa and Asia,/ And the shield of Europe,/ Whence he expelled the barbarians by his Holy Arms,/ Is the first to be buried in this beloved city,/ Whose founder he was.

1453 Byzantine Constantinople fell to the Ottomans. With the loss of Rhodes in 1522, the Hospitallers even were driven out of the Eastern Mediterranean and lost total contact with the geographical hemisphere of their roots.

The concept of the caravans and the *corso* remained as the visible symbol and manifestation of the idea of the *milites christi* and the crusades against the infidels. This concept had been perfected during the Order's rule over Rhodes and was brought over to Malta. The Hospitallers *corso* against Mameluke and Ottoman shipping and ports were seen as a sort of compensation for the crusades and found a deep echo in all Latin-Christian countries. It remained attractive until the eighteenth century. With the development of printing, these naval exploits of the Order circulated in thousands of *relationi*, reports, and pamphlets. For the general public they provided proof that the Order was still alive and reality, especially in the early sixteenth century, when the Ottoman threat seemed to increase constantly.

But the *corso* also played another very important role for the Hospitallers; especially during their residence in Malta the *corso* was the essential backbone of the local economy and an essential source of income for the treasury. It not only meant a steady influx of treasures, merchandise, and cash but also slaves. The political development of the eighteenth century with its special treaties and alliances made it impossible for the Order to conduct an effective *corso* and the economic as well as the ideological and political consequences on the Order were disastrous.

In terms of the *corso*, the move from Rhodes to Malta did not bring about any interruptions or changes. Already in the second half of the fifteenth century military reasons and financial temptations had contributed to an increase of corsairing under the red-and-white flag of the Hospitallers. The swift and fast ships of the Rhodiot corsairs operated without the bureaucracy and logistic necessities of the galley fleet and temporarily played havoc to Muslim

An engraving showing the capture of the corsair Simain Rais by the Order in 1585. It took four of the Order's galleon to capture and intercept the notorious pirate.

During the Great Siege, the knights left floating next to St Angelo a large Turkish galleon said to be one of the biggest prizes of a corso *before the siege.*

shipping along the maritime lifeline between Constantinople and Alexandria. It was not only private entrepreneurs who sailed under the Order's flag, but the Hospitallers too adapted some of their vessels to the new tactics the 1490s.

In 1499 all Christian corsairs operating from Rhodes were made to carry out their business under the supremacy of the Order. In subsequent years this increasing corsairing business even formed a special 'Rhodian personality', as the historian Anthony T. Luttrell put it. For the Ottoman empire and Muslim trade the situation became more and more intolerable. Immediately after the arrival in Malta the Hospitallers resumed their nautical activities.

A FLEET WITH A STATE   105

Already in 1531 the ships of the Order were cruising in Levantine waters looking for prizes. The resumption of corsairing was an open violation of Grand Master L'Isle Adam's promise to Suleiman never to fight against the Ottoman empire anymore when the knights were granted safe conduct on leaving Rhodes. Even more than in Rhodes, corsairing, trade in Muslim slaves, and the profit from incoming wealth became the most important shaping forces of Hospitaller and, therefore, Maltese society. Besides the economic and political aspects, there was of course also the ideological dimension. The tradition of the perpetual fight against the infidels could be shown nowhere better than in the maritime victories over Muslim shipping. This propaganda was also meant as a signal to justify the huge possessions and property the Order had all over Europe.

European contemporaries were well aware of the maritime profile of the Order of Malta. In 1636 the Saxonian nobleman Georg Christoff von Neitzschitz observed: 'It is the duty of the galleys of Malta to cruise the sea to fight the corsairs and pirates.' By then the *guerre de corse* had become an important aspect of Maltese identity and glory. Myth and reality of the *corso*, however, did not always correspond. The fact is that the *guerre de course*, corsairing, piracy, and the slave trade formed

The capture of the Algerian 22-gun ship, named Bechir Hoggia, *off Capo Passero by galleys of the Order in January 1647. Tapestry Chamber, Grand Master's Palace.*

an even more decisive aspect of the economy of Hospitaller Malta than of Rhodes. We already have mentioned that the institution of the *corso* was intrinsically connected with the structure of the Order. Every novice had to participate at least at four caravans. Each caravan in general lasted six months. Alternatively sometimes these maritime tours could be undertaken on board of one of the many corsair ships that flew the Order's flag. To understand better the character and purpose of the *guerre de course*, one might quote the instructions by Grand Master Cassière on 17 September 1578 to the captain of the galley *San Giovanni*: 'We want you ... to search all vessels of Ragusa and all Turkish vessels, and also those which are headed for Ancona, provided they are not Venetians, and finding on board Turks, Moors, Jews, and other Infidels, you will seize them, together with all their goods; you will, however, pay the Christians their freight changes.'

From the beginning of the Hospitallers' rule over Malta, corsairing run by members of the Order and the Order's control of Christian ships carrying Muslim cargoes caused tensions and conflicts with European powers. One example is the tense relations between Malta and Venice. When the corsair and knight Filippo Mazza although he had been warned several times by Venice

The Capitana *or flagship of the Order, illustration from* Malta bil Ghzejer Tahha u li Ghadda min Ghaliha *by P.P. Castagna, 1865.*

Grand Master Jean l'Evesque de la Cassière (1502 – 21 December 1581) was elected on 30 January 1572 to succeed Pietro del Monte as grand master. Engraved by Laurent Cars from The History of the Knights of Malta, *by Abbé Vertot, 1728.*

to stop his corsairing activities in the Adriatic, continued his activities until he was captured and beheaded by Venetian forces in 1534. After it had been informed about the numerous attacks on Venetian and Muslim ships carrying Venetian cargo by the knight Giustino Giustiniani, in 1552 Venice sharply protested to Grand Master Homedes. The grand master was asked to compensate all the losses and to punish Giustiniani. Already in 1536 the *Serenissima* had tried to keep the Order's ships and corsairs out of the Adriatic and requested support from the pope. In 1553 the legitimacy of the Venetian requests was confirmed by Pope Julius III.

When the Order would not refrain from sailing its corsairing vessels in the Adriatic and from disturbing the Venetian trade, Venice would respond by confiscating the property, goods, and money of the priory of Venice. These threats, however, rarely worked. At the end of the sixteenth and in the beginning of the seventeenth century, under Grand Masters La Cassière, Verdalle, and Wignacourt, the activity of the Order's fleet and of Malta-based corsairs increased again. This was not the result of a reinforced anti-Muslim policy or by a temporarily rekindling of the 'crusading spirit'. The reasons were rather material-istic. The religious wars in France and the Spanish-Dutch conflicts had stopped the responsions from some priories from flowing in on a regular basis and these financial losses had to be made up somehow.

Already some decades earlier the revenues from England, some Protestant lands of the German empire, Denmark, and Sweden had been lost. Therefore the economic aspect of the *corso* became even more important for the Order than before; in times of emergency its ships were also keen to provide Malta with grain or wheat. Being a Catholic or even a Christian was very often not enough in itself to remain unmolested. The German eyewitness Georg Christoph von Neitzschitz in 1636 observed:

If the knights of Malta attack a Turkish vessel and – which happens very often – find travelling Christians on it, they rob them of every thing that they possess. These Christians just get away with their lives and freedom. But Turks not only lose all their property, but also their lives or freedom.

Two of the main corridors of the Grand Master's Palace have lunette paintings commemorating the capture of Turkish sultana *and other* vascelli. *Here the 80–cannon* Sultana Benghen *falls into the hands of the Order in 1700.*

Contemporary historians of the Order like Salvatore Imbroll, Heinrich Pantaleon, Pierre Boissat, Juan Agostin de Funes, and Giacomo Bosio, however, still declare the *guerre de course* of the Order's fleet and the excursions of the corsairs flying the Order's or grand master's flag as part of the ideological and spiritual mission of the Hospitallers in their 'just' crusade. In this official picture the *corso* appeared without its economic and financial context. It is described as a platform of Christian chivalric bravery and as a symbol of a God-pleasing and 'justified' war. The innumerable pamphlets and leaflets celebrating the knights' naval successes should not to be seen as proof of a Christian-military identity and efficiency but as documents of the economic dimension of the *corso*. So, for example, Bartolomeo dal Pozzo reports for August 1577 about a long cruise of the Order's galleys in Levantine waters which brought a tremendous booty of expensive cloth and 300 slaves. In 1589 in one caravan the Order's galleys captured 260 slaves, 4,000 golden *sultanini*, and more than 100 rolls of precious brocaded cloth. Just the sale of the booty from middle-sized Venetian galleon *Toniella* – captured in the Gulf of Antalya in 1575 – brought a prize of 15,000 *scudi*.

Although the successes of the Order's naval campaigns were described and glorified in numerous pamphlets throughout the sixteenth, the seventeenth, and the eighteenth centuries, their military significance was, and still is, very much overestimated. However, on the level of ideology, religious antagonism, and emotional charge, the sacking and raiding of coastal villages and the seizing of prizes meant a lot. In practical terms, this lucrative preying on Muslim trade was essential for the Order's treasury and for Malta's economy in general. In fact a great part of the Maltese workforce depended directly or indirectly on corsairing, which was seen as a commercial activity and did not have a bad reputation. It was an international phenomenon carried out by businessmen-investors and protected by statesmen. It blossomed on a large scale when the major hostilities in the Mediterranean ceased to exist after Lepanto. The end of conflict between great states brought to the forefront of the sea's history that secondary form of war: corsairing and piracy.

The bagnio, *or slave prison, was established within the city of Valletta. The slaves were placed in it when not employed at sea. Whilst kept in the* bagnio, *the prisoners were used in the docks or on the repair of the fortifications. The prison used to be at the corner between St Christopher and St Ursula Streets overlooking the Lower Baracca gardens.*
The bagnio *is the big building seen in the centre of this detail from a painting of Valletta, c.1600, now at the Museum of Fine Arts, Valletta.*

Joseph Muscat, a noted Maltese maritime historian, describes the milieu:

'Malta became a rendezvous for corsairs; knights and adventures operated in the Levant with impunity. Numerous corsairs from other countries organized their ships which they armed in search of Muslim prizes. In the seventeenth century the Barbary Regencies, especially those of Tripoli, Tunis, and Algiers, attained a high degree of efficiency in running their corso business. Indeed the seventeenth century was definitely marked with a craze for the corso business.'

Another lunette with a battle scene from the main corridors of the Grand Master's Palace, Valletta.
The panting commemorates the capture of a galley from Algiers known as La Gran Gazela *close to the island of Lampedusa. The attack on the 24 March 1729 was carried out by the ship* San Vincenzo *under its commander F. Scipione Deaulx.*

What was essentially required was a busy marketplace where the prizes and goods could be quickly disposed of. With the knights, Malta had a significant number of clients who consumed every type of luxury goods and a large amount of consumables.

In the seventeenth century Malta was fully integrated in the great trade and exchange network that came about when, in addition to the French, the Genoese, the Ragusans, and the Venetians, the Dutch and the English entered the Mediterranean. Corsairing required more than licences and a functional system of law; it also needed skilled labour, carpenters, shipbuilders, gun-founders, caulkers, and a thousand-and-one other tradesmen. Also essential was a supply of galley slaves, well-trained sailors, and men willing to sign up for adventures at sea. In the late sixteenth century, and

A painting by an unknown artist from the Museum of Fine Arts of Grand Master Aloph de Wignacourt (1601–22). The suit of armour in the painting is Wignacourt's parade armour bought from Milan in about 1602.

The painting used to be hung in the Palace Armoury. An identical copy now hangs in the Ambassador's Room in the Grand Master's Palace.

especially since the times of Grand Master Aloph de Wignacourt who saw himself as a sort of *condottiere*, Malta became fully equipped for this business, especially after 1605 when a *Tribunale degli Armamenti* was set up, made up of five commissioners, chosen by the grand master to regulate all corsairing business on the island. However, to avoid its jurisdiction and restrictions, in the seventeenth century many corsairs chose to sail under the grand master's flag instead of the Order's. The 'official' glorified picture of the island of the 'heroic' knights of St John was not disturbed by the disasters in Central Europe. The Thirty Years War (1618–48) between the Catholic League (headed by the Hapsburg emperors) and the Protestant Union (with Danish King Christian IV and Swedish King Gustav Adolf as its main leaders) began in 1618 because of confessional reasons.

That the Order, especially after 1650, attracted a great number of noble volunteers might also be the result of the end of the Thirty Years War and the reduction of armies on the continent. It was also caused by the fact that under the Grand Masters Nicolas Cotoner (1663–80) and Gregorio Carafa (1680–90) the fleet of the Order reached its peak in quality and quantity. In this period the activities of the Malta-based corsairs reached its climax. Between 1660 and 1680 the grand masters issued no fewer than 98 licences for corsairs sailing under the Order's flag. The restrictions, which officially forced the corsairs

The Order's fleet under the command of Balí Jacques François Chambray captured the Turkish Admiral Ali-Mehmet in the waters of Damietta on 16 August 1732. Grand Master's Palace, Valletta.

from Malta to stay away from the Eastern Mediterranean, were very often ignored. The wars of Candia and the Morea – where the fleet of the knights frequently participated on the side of the Venetians – offered ideal training for European naval officers and volunteers.

There were many famous protagonists of the *corso*. One legendary figure was *Balí* Jacques François Chambray (1687–1758). Like his compatriot, the French admiral *Balí* Pierre André de Suffren de St Tropez, Chambray was one of the last famous naval heroes of the Order. His military life is a paradigmatic example of a naval career in the Order. His link with the Maltese islands is especially manifest in the imposing fortress which still bears his name on top of the hill that overlooks Mġarr harbour, at Gozo. Appointed a captain in 1723, Chambray made considerable prizes even during his first campaigns. He is especially remembered for the capture of the *patrona* of Tripoli. Between 1723 and 1735 Chambray undertook 55 campaigns during which he distinguished himself as one of the bravest and most competent naval leaders of his time. In 1727 he received the commandery of Virecourt (Lorraine). One of the many highlights of his naval career was the capture of Turkish Admiral Ali-Mehmet near Damietta in 1732, the year after he had been promoted lieutenant general. Because of his merits, in 1733 he received the *commanderie magistrale* of Metz and made a grand cross of the Order. Various examples document how the activity of the knights and the Maltese corsairs was very often counterproductive to Christian-Muslim trade and the safe passages from the west to the east. The lucrative trade between France, England, Venice, and other European states with the Levant finally brought about restrictions in the Maltese *corso* in the late seventeenth century. Throughout the sixteenth century, Venice, Genoa, and France had already complained against the attacks by Maltese corsairs. The knights had to accept that the relationships of England, Holland, France, Genoa, and Venice with the Ottomans were characterized by a sense of pragmatism which also led to a strong criticism of the

Fort Chambray in Għajnsielem, Gozo, was built with the Balí's fortune from his corso campaigns.

BALÍ JACQUES FRANÇOIS CHAMBRAY

Alleged portrait of the young Chambray at the Museum of Fine Arts, Valletta.

Like his compatriot the French admiral Balí Pierre André de Suffren de St Tropez, Balí Jacques François Chambrai (1687–1758) was one of the last famous naval heroes of the Order. His link with Malta is especially manifest in the imposing fortress which still bears his name on top of a hill overlooking Mgarr harbour at Gozo. It was the Order's last major military work in Malta. Chambray entered the Order at a very young age and in 1699 he came to Malta as a page of Grand Master Perellos y Roccaful. He served in the French army between 1702 and 1705, in which year he returned to Malta to undertake his caravans in the Order's navy where he soon showed his naval talents. In 1707 he participated in the battle of Oran where he was injured. Chambray held his first important post in 1722 when he was appointed major general of Gozo and Comino. In 1723 he was appointed captain. Already during his first campaigns Chambray had taken considerable prizes, one of the most outstanding being the capture of the patrona of Tripoli. Between 1723 and 1735 Chambary undertook 55 campaigns during which he distinguished himself as one of the bravest and most competent naval leaders of his time. In 1727 he had received the commandery of Virecourt (Lorraine). One of the numerous highlights of his naval career was the capture of the Turkish admiral Ali-Mehmet near Damietta in 1732. In the previous year Chambray had been promoted lieutenant general. After his retirement from the Order's navy, he held the post of lieutenant general of the defences.

Order, especially when its caravans or corsairs molested or threatened their trade. This is shown by various examples. At the end of 1591, when there were definite indications that Malta would once again be invaded by the Ottomans, Philip II of Spain ordered the viceroy of Sicily to prepare a relief force in case the island was attacked. The attitude of some other Christian states was, however, entirely different. Venice and England were especially annoyed about the activities of the Order's fleet and the Maltese corsairs against Muslim trade and showed understanding for any Ottoman measures against the Order. In his *'Relazione dell'Impero Ottomano'*, the Venetian Lorenzo Bernardo wrote in 1592: *'Because the constant damage which the galleys of the ... Maltese are wreaking up to the Dardanelles [and] Constantinople,*

Sometimes, the attack on an enemy galleon ended with the sinking of one of the ships. Here, on 21 October 1714, the galleon il Sole d'Oro d'Algieri *is sunk by Commendatore Frà Adriano di Langon. Grand Master's Palace, Valletta.*

the Turks are overwrought with them and desire revenge, awaiting merely the right occasion, having threatened Malta publicly .... Yet I believe they shall finally realize their intent, since they cannot any more tolerate such damage and caution.'

Very often the Order's ships did not limit themselves to Muslim vessels but also confiscated 'suspicious' Christian cargo ships. Throughout the sixteenth and seventeenth century, there is an abundance of references of sometimes dangerous, sometimes peaceful, encounters between Dutch, English, Danish, Venetian, Ragusan, and Genoese ships with Maltese corsairs or warships of the Order in the waters of the Levant, although the latter were expressly forbidden to venture there. The more European powers like Venice, France, and England, and later even Denmark and Holland, integrated the metropolises of the Ottoman empire and North Africa into their economic network, the more the activities of the knights and the Maltese corsairs were seen as a disturbance. In fact, the grand masters soon had to agree on geographical limitations where the ships of the Order could prowl.

From 1647 onwards, the knights and the Maltese corsairs were forbidden from seizing prizes within ten miles from the ports of Acre and Jaffa. This was the result of the pressure brought about by the Franciscan friars who, as custodians of the Christian shrines in the Holy Land, they were afraid that continuous attacks on Muslim ships would provoke revenge on the numerous European pilgrims who were visiting Palestine again following the success of the Counter Reformation. In 1673 the Roman *Curia* forced the Order to respect the lives and property of Christian Greeks, both by its fleet and by the Maltese corsairs.

In the eighteenth century, the effects of the winds of change could be clearly seen. The warning to the Order had been loud and clear and could hardly have been missed: '*Réformez-vous; sinon, nous vous réformerons*' ('If you don't reform your institution we will reform you'). These were the words said by Count Kaunitz, chancellor of the Holy German Empress Maria Theresa, to *Balí* Colloredo, *chargé d'affaires* of the Order at the court of Vienna. Obviously the era of agreement and understanding between the centuries-old chivalric Order and the states of *Ancien Régime* Europe was approaching its end. As a result of intensified economic links – especially by France – with Turkey and the Barbary States and

Grand Master Antonio Manoel de Vilhena's flag flies over the bowsprit of an attacking warship of the Order during the capture of the Turkish Admiral Ali-Mehmet near Damietta in 1732. Detail from lunette painting at the Grand Master's Palace.

treaties between the European states and the Sublime Porte, the Order lost its main enemy.

The main threat for Hospitaller Malta and its conservative structure and traditions came with the global shift of politics and society in the eighteenth century. Already at the beginning of that century, it had become obvious that, because of the economic arrangements of the Mediterranean powers and of England with the Sublime Porte, the neutral principality of the knights had its days counted. The treaty of Karlowitz (26.i.1699) between Austria, Venice, Poland, and the Ottoman empire stipulated that the Order should limit the geographical 'fishing grounds' of the famous 'caravans' and the activities of corsairs sailing under its flag and that of the grand master because of Venetian, English, Dutch, and French complaints. Not to harm international relations and trade, for example, most of the waters of the Levant were declared out-of-bounds. The whole situation had started to change at the beginning of the eighteenth century when the big European powers, such as France, England, and Spain, started to increase control over the Mediterranean basin. The general change in the balance of Mediterranean power and the decline of the Order itself reduced the caravans of the knights to mere spectacles and training cruises.

The Sublime Porte was the name of the open court of the sultan, led by the grand vizier. It got its name from the gate to the headquarters of the grand vizier in Topkapi Palace in Istanbul, where the sultan greeted foreign ambassadors.

A full galley model from the Order's nautical school was used to illustrate to new sailors the way to rig the ship. Now at the Maritime Museum in Vittoriosa.

To avoid any danger and not to interrupt commercial relations, the knights even communicated the destination of their warships before they departed to the Barbary States. Ovide Doublet, from 1782 Grand Master Rohan's secretary for French affairs, wrote in similar terms: *'I have heard captains of galleys boast that they did not want to attack Barbary Corsairs .... in order to spare themselves the expenses and inconvenience of quarantine.'* So, by the middle of the eighteenth century, during the rule of Grand Master Pinto the backbone of the Order, its fleet, had degenerated to an ornament. Diplomatic and military careers were not based any more on military experience and bravery in the Mediterranean battlefields. Malta and the state of the knights became an object of curiosity and romantic chivalry. While the Order's fleet reduced its activities, the corsairs of Malta, however, kept on going. Since the intervention of France and England had made the Eastern Mediterranean a forbidden zone, they concentrated their activities on vessels from Tunisia, Tripoli, and Morocco.

In discussing the Order's naval activities, one has to mention its main vehicle: the galley. Used in the Mediterranean since classical times, the galley was the famous backbone of the Order's navy in the

COMBATTIMETO DELLA NAVE S. GIORGIO CON
I TRE VASCELLI DI TUNIS, E PRESA D'UNO D'ESSI
IL PORCO SPINO, FATTA DAL COMENDATORE
D'ALLOGNY LA GROIS NEL CANALE DI MAL-
TA, LI 23. MAGGIO. 1721.

sixteenth and seventeenth centuries. In European eyes, the galleys of the Order became more than war machines; they were seen as symbols of the Order's virtues and bravery. Although the Order had other types of vessels to its disposal, chebecs, brigantines, frigates, and later the *vaxxells* or third rate, at least until the early eighteenth century the main naval component of the Order's fleet operating from Malta, as it had been in Rhodes, was the galley. During the apex of the Order's *corso* in the second half of the seventeenth century, the galley squadron numbered seven or sometimes eight galleys. Even when third rates were introduced in 1704, the galley squadron was not abolished but slowly reduced to a stable four in number of full-size galleys. The last naval engagement came in early June 1798 just a few days before the surrender to Napoleon. Generally the war season began in spring, when the *corso* started and the galleys moved out of their winter shelter in Augusta or Messina. On several occasions the Order's fleet teamed up with other Christian naval forces.

To keep up with the changing necessities of maritime military activities, in 1704 Grand Master Perellos commissioned the third rate squadron. In Maltese these ships were called *vaxxell*, in Italian *vascello*. Equipped with three square-rigged masts and a bowsprit sail, a *vaxxel* mounted from 56 to 69 guns. The Order normally had three *vaxxeli* and a 40-gun frigate mounted, together with other types of vessels. The brigantine has rightly been described as the workhorse of the Mediterranean as it was to be found all along its coasts. In Malta, brigantines operated between the fifteenth and nineteenth centuries. It was lateen-rigged but had to 14 benches on each side and was used by Maltese corsairs as well as by merchants. Crewed by between 17 and 23 men, in the eighteenth century the Maltese brigantines mostly operated on the Western Mediterranean and Lisbon routes, most of the time hugging the coasts for logistic and security reasons. The brigantine also took the main share of the traffic between Malta and Sicily.

The chebec was a very fast three-masted lateen-rigged vessel that proved its great value as a comparatively low-cost corsairing vessel. Of quite obscure origin, the chebec came into its own in the latter part of the eighteenth century when the fact that it did not need a large crew made it particularly attractive to small and large navies alike. It was also invaluable to ship cargo in a limited time and could also operate regularly during the winter season.

Another detail from one of the lunettes in the main corridors of the Grand Master's Palace, Valletta.
This painting commemorates the naval battle in the Malta Channel between three ships from Tunis and the vascello *San Giorgio on 23 May 1721.*

Therefore it was a favourite vessel with both Muslim and Christian navies. Thanks to its shallow draft, it could approach shores and beaches, which was very useful in creeping on unsuspecting victims and also in escaping larger pursuers who would be wary of following it too close to land. The Order introduced the chebec in 1743 in its small but highly efficient navy, following the examples of several other Mediterranean navies. The Barbary Coast corsairs had long seen the usefulness of the vessel, while Spain started building chebecs early in the eighteenth century. The first chebec was built in Malta in 1743. It was estimated to cost 2,000 *scudí* monthly to run, but could be armed for the *corso* as well as used to transport merchandise as required. Chebecs could also prove their worth in accompanying the Order's squadrons by carrying fast scouting missions and also to transport supplies in a short time.

The chebec (xebec) was one of the fastest ships of its era. It was a typical ship of North African countries, frequenting the ports of Algiers, Tunis, and Tripoli. The chebec was armed with 24 cannon. The French and Spanish both copied the North African ship design for its speed.
Photo by Dr Michael Czytko.

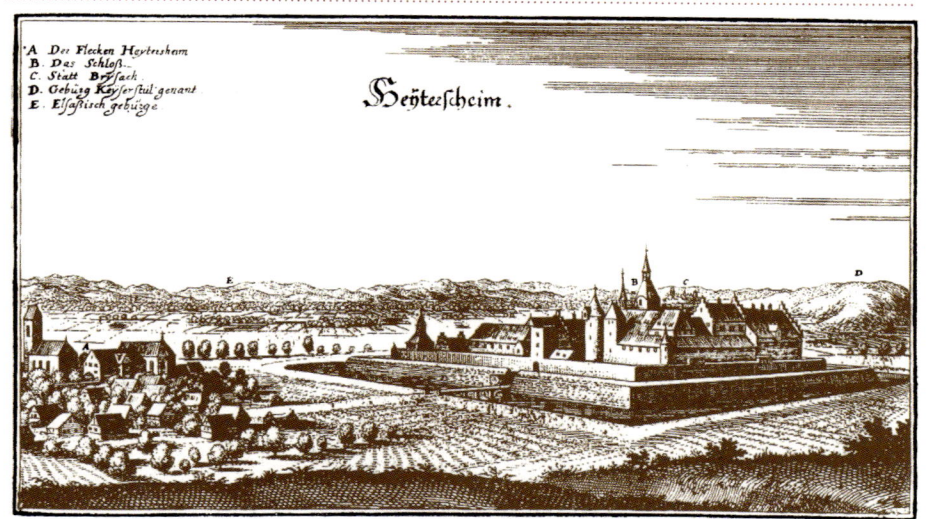

Upheavals and changes

The sixteenth century is very often described as the great epoch of political and intellectual transition. A cosmopolitan institution like the Order could not remain unaffected. But, even before the dramatic events of the early sixteenth century in Central Europe, the Order had felt the winds of change. In the fifteenth century princes had rather aggressively tried to extend their power and dominions at the cost of cities, vassals, and ecclesiastical and chivalric Orders. In fact, at times, despite its old privileges and rights, the Order of St John had been forced to sell some possessions and lands.

With the loss of Rhodes and the turbulent times that followed as the convent moved through several cities of Italy and France, the government of the Order could not control the situation in the single priories as strictly as usual. Several forces, especially in Germany, took advantage of this situation. Princely ambitions, greed to lay hands on the Order's possessions, as well as the rise of Protestantism all took their toll. At first the Order's headquarters seemed to rather underrate all this. While the effects of Protestantism and rebellion against the Catholic Church were not much felt in the territories of the grand priory of Bohemia-Austria, the lands in central and northern Germany were severely hit. But the problems had already started earlier with the economic and political crisis of the fifteenth century in some parts of Germany, although the

A 17th-century engraving of the castle of Heitersheim, in the town of Heitersheim in southern Germany. Since 1428 Heitersheim was the seat of the grand prior of Germany. It is still called the Malteserstadt (Maltese City) with the eight-pointed cross as its coat of arms.

Reformation worsened the situation for the German grand priory. As the historian Walter G. Rödel has found out in his extensive study of the visitation reports of the German grand priory, there were only 40 professed knights in 1495 in its territory existing, but by 1540 this number had dwindled to 26. In 1495 there were still 322 chaplains of the Order in the grand priory, but in 1540 this number had fallen down to 132, while there were only 16 sisters of the Order left. In total there were 105 houses and commanderies of the Order (exclusive of the Dutch commanderies) in the grand priory in 1495, but the upheavals and changes of the Reformation caused the loss of 28 of them. In 1495 there had been 151 parish churches incorporated in the grand priory, and just 50 in 1540. In 1495 the total number of the members of the grand priory were 363 (excepting the members of the bailiwick of Brandenburg and those living in the Netherlands, and the sisters of the Order – of whom there are no exact figures); by 1540 this total number had dwindled to 176. Obviously this decrease meant less responsions to be paid to Malta.

Lutheranism provided the princes with a good instrument to seize many possessions of the Order in their domains and to declare the old Hospitallers' privileges as void. After the loss of Rhodes the convent seemed to have been too occupied with other problems, mainly finding a new home, to be more active in Germany and to try to halt these developments. The German grand prior and the local *balís* were more or less left to their own devices, but only after the convent had settled in Malta were things sorted out and the old order and working process restored. In May 1530 Charles V issued a letter of protection to help the Order regain its sequestrated German possessions. But this came much too late. The wheel of history certainly could not be moved back and it inevitably rolled faster and faster forward. When in 1540 there was an order for general visitations of the German commanderies, many things had already taken a rather bad turn for the German grand priory. Quite a few commanders, especially in the bailiwick of Brandenburg, had become Protestants, while others had become rather indifferent to the zeal and vows of the Order.

Such visitations had a precise fixed form. In late medieval times they generally resembled the pattern stipulated later in the book of statutes from 1584. Normally these visitations were carried out every five years. During a visit, besides the member of the Order entrusted with the visitation by the grand magistracy or grand priory, there would be a notary present and, sometimes, some witnesses. The reports described exactly the property and income of the commandery while the books and accounts were carefully audited. A report was then drafted, a copy of which was deposited in the archives of the grand priory.

Spanish Grand Master Ramón Perellos y Roccaful 1697–1720. Portrait from San Anton Palace by an unknown artist.

In 1707 Grand Master Perellos y Roccaful issued a new *Instrumentum visitationis* which had to be obeyed. To order a visitation and to receive the cash of the responses were, however, two different things.

The situation *cujus regio, ejus religio*, meaning that the ruling sovereign of a country could decide about the confession of his subjects, created by the treaty of Augsburg in 1555 had disastrous consequences for several German Hospitaller commanderies. Again the bailiwick of Brandenburg was a special case. In the sixteenth century the bailiwick experienced deep changes and upheavals. In 1527 a German grand prior confirmed the appointment of a *Herrenmeister* for the last time. With the division of the inheritance of Brandenburg in 1535, Viscount Hans von Küstrin (1535–71) became the new overlord of the bailiwick. At various times this energetic viscount interfered in the internal affairs of the Hospitallers and tried to influence the elections of new *Herrenmeister*. In 1538 he converted to Lutheranism. Already in the years before some commanders of the bailiwick had become Protestant. It is, for example, documented that in 1543 the commanders of Lagow, Nemerow, and Schivelbein were married. The ever-active Küstrin finally took over the most important duties of the *Herrenmeister* while the latter more or less only concentrated on internal administration. By the late 1540s most of the Brandenburgian

The Marquis of Brandenburg (detail). From the Theatrum Orbis Terrarum sive Tabula veteris Geographiae *(c.1570), in folio. Engraved by Wieriex, after Gérard de Jode.*

knights had become Protestants. To avoid clashes with the dukes of Mecklenburg and Brandenburg, the convent in Malta could not take direct actions like the immediate expulsion of these knights. That might have led the sovereigns and rulers to annex and sequestrate the Hospitaller possessions in their territory forever. By 1545, the bailiwick of Brandenburg under *Herrenmeister* Joachim von Arnim had officially converted to Protestantism. Not to lose these possessions, after some negotiations, the convent in Malta agreed that the knights of Brandenburg could remain members of the Order and keep their status. To avoid the bailiwick of Brandenburg from being completely separated from the Order, the provincial chapter of the German grand priory at Speyer in 1551 officially agreed that the married and Lutheran commanders could keep their commanderies and functions. So the members of the bailiwick still kept paying their responsions to Malta. What could not be avoided was that the richly endowed churches and patronages of the Order in Brandenburg nearly lost their importance completely and many of them were given away. This development in Brandenburg cannot be seen separately from the turns of global history. Even the Teutonic Order in Brandenburg then had converted to Lutheranism.

Maybe the best symbol of how much the princes interfered in the affairs of the Order was that, from 1610 onwards, the office of the *Herrenmeister* was mainly filled by a member of the house of Hohenzollern, the dynasty which ruled over Brandenburg and Prussia. This had already been more or less agreed upon in 1594. In 1610

Friedrich, Viscount zu Brandenburg, became the first *Herrenmeister* from the princely house of Hohenzollern. In 1602 Grand Master Aloph de Wignacourt appointed a Catholic titular-*balí* of Brandenburg with residence in Malta in the hope of moving the bailiwick back into the haven of Catholicism. But it was all in vain as this titular-*balí* was more or less ignored by the members of the bailiwick. As a result the existence of this Protestant branch of the Order was more or less tolerated.

While the bailiwick of Brandenburg remained within the Order, other possessions were irrevocably lost, as was the case with the Dutch commanderies of the German grand priory, most of which were lost by the early seventeenth century. In 1619 the bailiwick of Utrecht more or less ceased to exist. These events also concerned the possessions of the grand prior of Germany which, in the early sixteenth century, officially had the commanderies of Utrecht, Arnheim, Cologne, Bubikon, Heimbach, and Heitersheim at his disposal for his income. As a consequence of the Reformation, in Sweden (1527), in Norway (1532), and in Denmark (1536), the Order's possessions were sequestrated and incorporated into the lands of the crown. Even when the priory ceased to exist, the title of prior of Dacia was kept as a dignatary without territory. One of its prominent holders was the erudite Christian von Osterhausen, author of several books on the Order's legislation, structure and history.

Other parts of the German langue more or less completely had disappeared from the map in the sixteenth century. Early in that century the priory of Hungary had ceased to exist when the Ottomans conquered its territory. The title of prior of Hungary was kept as a titular-dignity. Such priors kept on participating at the meetings of the council until the Order left Malta in 1798. Sometimes the title was held by a distinguished member of the langue of Italy, at other times by a member of the langue of Provence. For example, in 1562 the famous architect Gabrio Serbelloni held this title. In 1594 Antonio Bertucci tried in vain to restore the priory of Hungary when the Hapsburg armies had temporarily pushed back the Turks. A few years later tensions arose between the Italian and German langues over who was to hold the title of prior of Hungary. In a bull of 4 March 1600 Pope Clement VIII decided that the title should belong to the German langue; so from 1604 the prior of Germany and that of Bohemia alternated in carrying this title.

The Order's property in England had already been sequestrated in the early 1540s by King Henry VIII. In the 1530s the relations between the English crown and the Order had turned sour because of Henry's attitude to matters of property and the power of the Church in general. In 1534 he had claimed part of the money which the Church in England used to pay to the pope, before splitting with the pope. In 1538 a demand

> Henry by the grace of God, King of England and France, Defender of the Faith, and Lord of Ireland, to the Rev. Father in Christ, Philip Villiers de L'Isle Adam, Grand Master of the Order of Jerusalem.
>
> Our most dear friend
>
> Greeting :
>
> The venerable and religious men, Sir Thomas Docreus, Prior of St John's in this kingdom, and Sir W. Weston of your convent, Turcoplerius, have lately delivered to us the epistle of your Reverence, and when we had read it, they laid before us the commission which they had in charge, with so much prudence and address, and recommended to us the condition, well being, and honour of their Order with so much zeal and affection, that they have much increased the good will, which of ourselves we feel towards the Order, and have made us more eager in advancing all its affairs, so that we very much hope to declare by our actions the affection which we feel towards this Older.
>
> And that we might give some proof of this our disposition, we have written at great length to His Imperial Majesty, in favour of maintaining the occupation of Malta, and we have given orders to our envoys there to help forward this affair as much as they are able. The other matters, indeed, your Reverence will learn more in detail from the letters of the said Prior.
>
> From our Palace at Richmond, Eighth day of January, 1523 (sic.),
>
> Your good friend,
> HENRY REX.

that the English Hospitallers should support his forces in the defence of Calais was refused by the Order. In the same year Henry's quest for absolute power went so far as to demand that all new English knights of St John should swear allegiance to the king like all other English subjects. Of course the Order did not agree with that. A milestone was set in April 1540 when Henry officially confiscated all the Order's property in England, a development which fitted very well in the noxious economic patterns of Henry's policies and his concept of the supremacy of royal power over the church. At the same time he had secularized the religious convents and the monasteries in England. Most of the Order's possessions in England were granted to Henry's favourites. This confiscation of the Order's English property

A letter written in 1523 by King Henry VIII to Grand Master Villiers de L'Isle Adam supporting the grant of Malta by Emperor Charles V to the Order of St John (Archives of the Order at the MNL, translated by Winthrop and Vella).

meant that the English langue would in the long run factually cease to exist. Still according to the Order's statutes, the English langue did not disappear but lay dormant. Later attempts by the English and the Order to re-establish the langue failed. In 1782 the English langue and the newly erected Bavarian grand priory were unified as the Anglo-Bavarian langue.

Opposite page: Detail of The Family of Henry VIII, *at Hampton Court Palace, c.1545. Pictured here are Prince Edward, left, Henry VIII, and Jane Seymour.*

ENGLISH INTRUSION 127

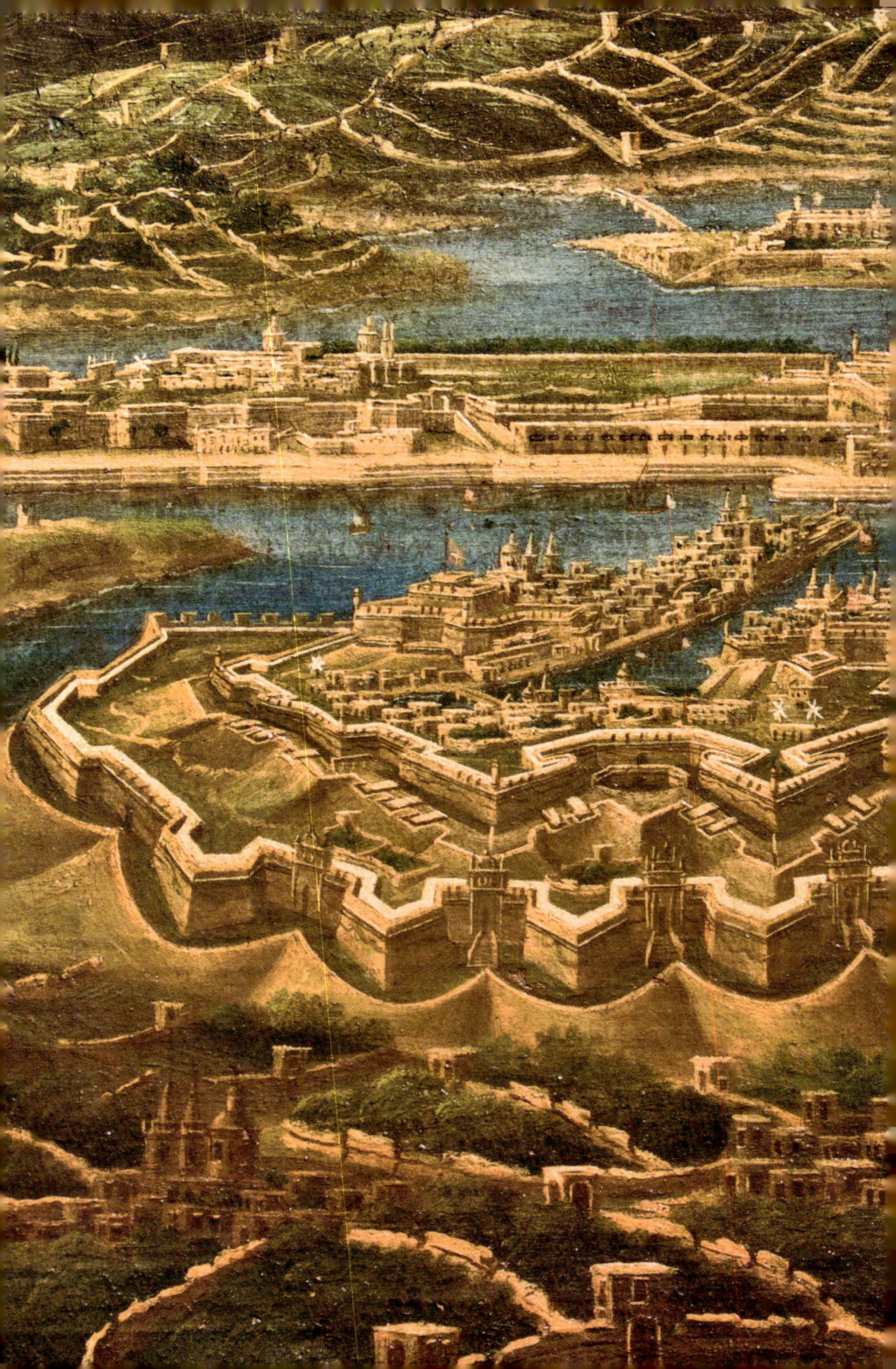

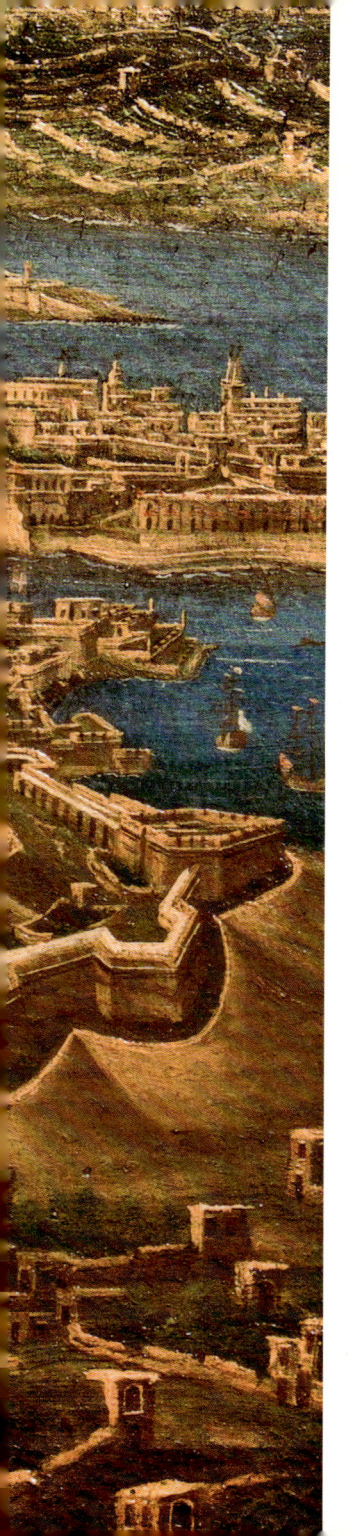

In the 16th century, the Mediterranean was divided into the two hemispheres of the 'Super Powers', Spain (the western part) and the Ottoman Empire (the eastern part). Hospitaller Malta was used by the Spanish Hapsburgs as a bulwark against Ottoman expansion. Malta's strategic position in the very centre between East and West also promised to block a much-feared unification of the French and Ottoman forces.

CHAPTER 5

THE GLOBAL PICTURE AND THE MEDITERRANEAN ENVIRONMENT

Before the Order had settled in Malta – in spite of the largely Semitic character of its population – the island was politically, economically, and culturally clearly orientated towards Latin-Christian Western Europe, especially towards the territory of Aragon, the coast of Western Spain, and Sicily. Fernand Braudel defines the military and strategic situation of Malta as 'Italy's maritime front against the Turkish threat'. Before the knights, Aragonese Malta had three main functions; 'to provide a naval base for the Spanish fleets, to offer resistance to Turkish armadas, and to defend its own territory against pirate attacks'. While the loss of Rhodes, the rise of Protestantism in Europe, and the subsequent losses of property and influence in the sixteenth century had brought considerable setbacks and problems for the Order in the

The Cottonera Lines in the late 18th century, from a detail of an anonymous oil on canvas from the Museo dell'Accademia di Cortona Veduta della Isola di Malta *(View of the Maltese Islands).*

seventeenth century, there came a last flicker of splendour. The glory and attractiveness of Hospitaller Malta had peaked in the second half of the seventeenth century, thanks very much to the efforts of Grand Master Nicolas Cotoner, under whom Malta changed to the 'baroque' island we know today. Despite this baroque glory, Cotoner's reign also was a true reflection of Malta's fragile situation. The island was still dependant for its provisions on Sicily and other countries and an embargo – caused by political reasons or by epidemics – would cause havoc.

The Order's fleet and privateering in Malta peaked during the rule of Grand Masters Rafael (1660–63) and Nicolas Cotoner (1663–80) and Gregorio Carafa (1680–90). Nicolas Cotoner's most ambitious project was the 'Cotonera lines' which were designed to protect the land approaches to the fortified peninsulas of Senglea and Birgu. For this huge project he had requested the advice of the papal military engineer, Count Valperga, and levied a tax on immovable property which, in 1673, was commuted to the issuing of licences and the granting monopolies on imports such as leather, tobacco, or paper. Another important moment in his magistracy was the institution of the medical school at the *Sacra Infermeria*. It was during his magistracy that Mattia Preti completed his monumental painting of the vault of the conventual church of St John's, to which Cotoner also contributed considerably towards its baroque embellishment.

When Spain joined in the war that France was waging in the Netherlands, this started years of great difficulties for Hospitaller Malta. The Order became directly involved in 1674 when Messina with French help rose up against its Spanish overlords and the Sicilian viceroy asked Grand Master Cotoner to send the Order's galleys to help put down the insurrection. Cotoner agreed only that the ships of the Order could carry troops and munitions but that they should refrain from taking an active part in the fighting. As a result of a clash with the navy's commander-in-chief Spinola, Cotoner recalled the ships and the viceroy retaliated by suspending all commerce between Sicily and Malta. This decision caused great problems in Malta and led to considerable famine and tension.

Even more disastrous was an outbreak of the plague in December 1675. By August 1676, between 8,000 and 11,500 inhabitants had died out of a population of *c.*60,000. Another great setback came in 1679 when the Brancati merchants of Naples, the Order's agents for collecting the revenues from its estates in Castille and Aragon and France, went bankrupt. All their remaining money was seized by Naples.

In the reconstruction on the opposite page Mattia Preti explains the work on the ceiling of the conventual church of the Order to Grand Master Nicolas Cotoner. Until this period the interior of the church was quite bare.

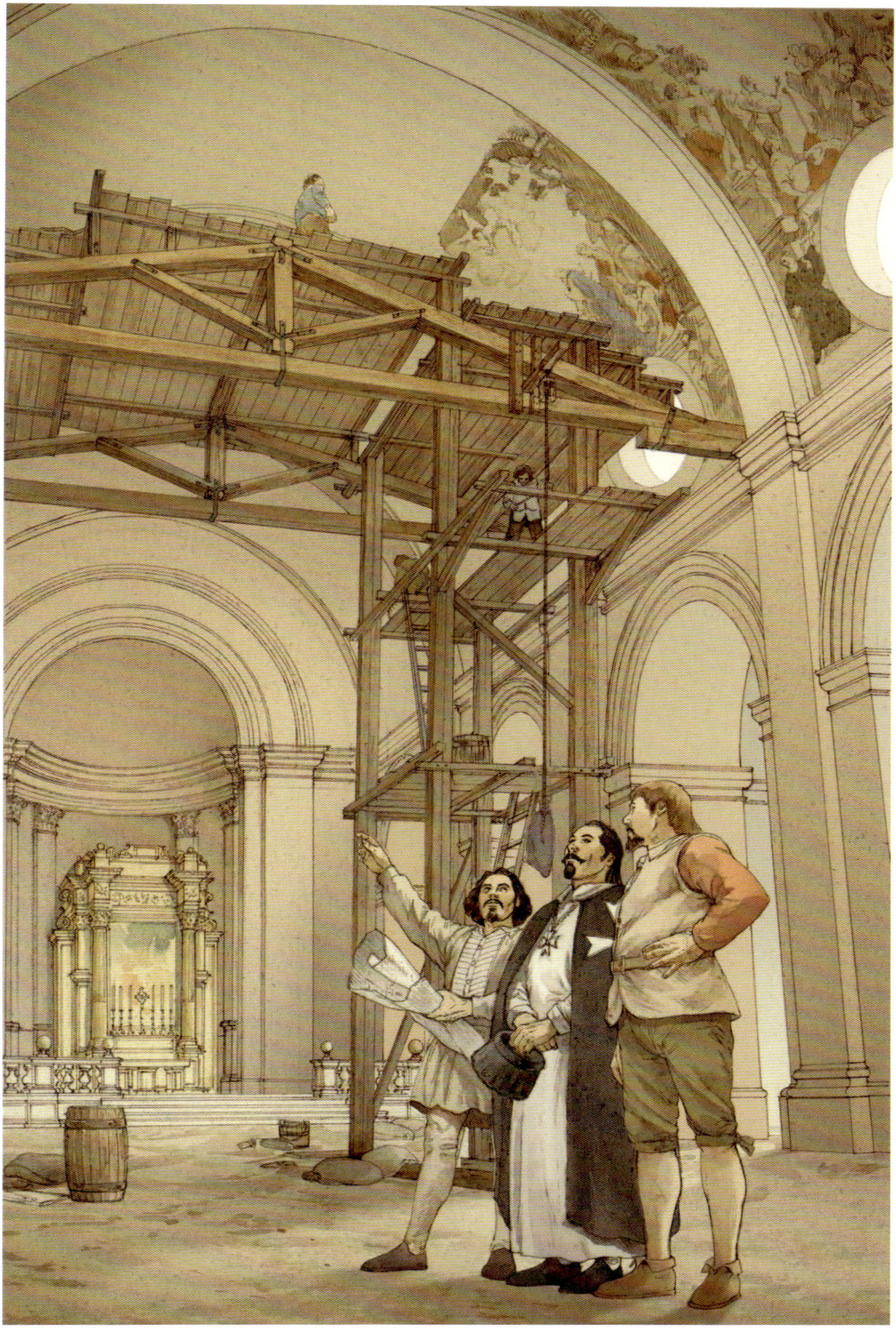

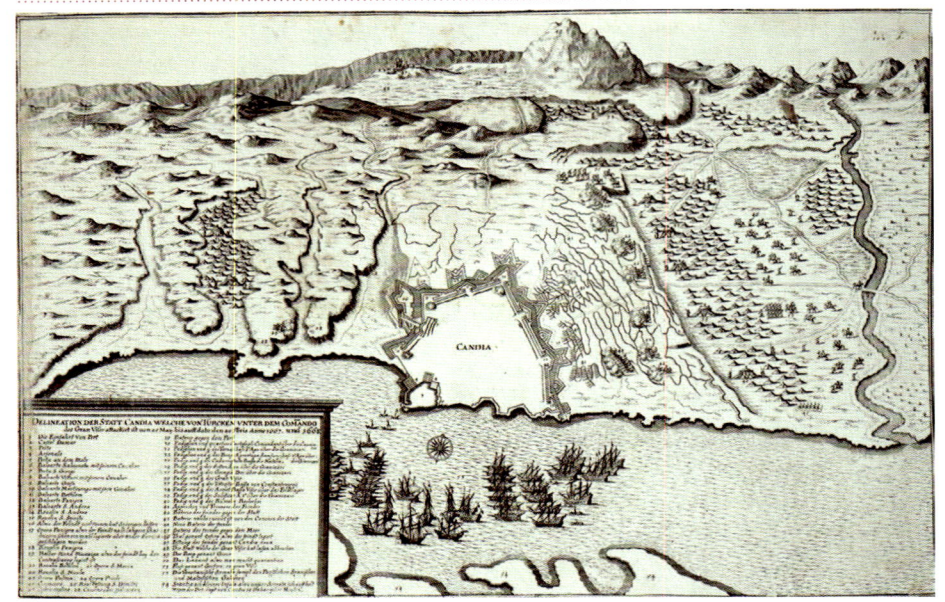

This was also the time when the Catholic Counter-Reformation propaganda kept publicizing and celebrating the 'triumphs' of spectacular conversions from Islam to Christianity. Some famous cases took place in Malta and had far-reaching political consequences. In 1651, Captain General *Balì* Frà Baldassare Demandolx, had captured a Moroccan vessel with '*Mehmed Bin Thesì, tenuto per figlio del Sultano del Marocco*' on board. Educated in Malta, this 'son of the sultan of Morocco' was baptized and given the name of Baldassare Diego and later joined the Jesuits. His patron was the Portuguese Knight Diego de Melo. Another celebrated case was that of the so-called Padre Ottomano. This mysterious character, allegedly the first-born son of Sultan Ibrahim, was captured when the knights of Malta seized a giant galleon on 28 September 1644. This gave the sultan the pretext to declare war on Venice whom he accused of collaborating with the knights. The result was the bloody war of Candia and the loss of Venetian Crete to the Ottomans. The captured boy finally became a Dominican friar known as Padre Ottomano. After much-publicized sojourns in Naples, Rome, and Paris, he also participated in one of the Christian campaigns of the war of Candia. But the great scheme to install him as a pretender to the throne of Sultan Mehmet IV and so fuel a rebellion in the Ottoman

A German map of the last stage of the Siege of Candia 1667–68. It illustrates the city's trace italienne *(star fort) fortifications, and the proximity of the Ottoman siege trenches, especially in the north-western sector (right), to the walls. The extensive camps of the besiegers are seen further right. Private Collection*

empire failed. In the quest for a crusade – a subject which came up time and time again in the sixteenth and seventeenth century – Malta and the Order of St John always kept playing prominent roles. The spiritual and intellectual dimensions of the fear – not to say phobia – of Ottoman attacks in the Christian countries of south and south-east Europe still formed an essential part of the seventeenth-century *Zeitgeist* and culture. As the Dutch historian de Groot writes, 'The purpose of so many "fanciful" sermons and writings was to keep alive a strong sense of threat in the public opinion of Christian Europe, irrespectively of the actual extent of Ottoman power at any one point in time. In this way, fancy may be said to have created fact.'

Modern historians claim that the power and attacking potential of the Ottomans was overestimated at that time, but for those then living in the Christian Mediterranean border countries or near the Austro-Hungarian border and facing the seemingly ever-expanding Ottoman empire, this fear was certainly a solid reality. The cultural historian Edward W. Said comments: 'The rigorous Christian picture of Islam was intensified in innumerable ways, including – during the Middle Ages and ... the Renaissance – a large variety of poetry, learned controversy, and popular superstition. By this time the Near Orient had been all but incorporated in the common world-picture of Latin Christianity.' Especially in Malta, Southern Italy, Sicily, and along the Mediterranean coast of Spain, the popular attitude was strongly anti-Ottoman and most of the population was very receptive for poetical propaganda against the infidels and all sorts of fictitious tales or true reports of Christian successes against the Ottoman 'Anti-Christ'.

In the sixteenth century the 'Catholic' affairs in the Mediterranean had been determined by Spain. With the rebellion of the

Court painter Antoine Favray (1706–98) left for Constantinople after 17 years in Malta. This oil on canvas Interior with Orientals *is now in the collection of the Mdina Cathedral Museum.*

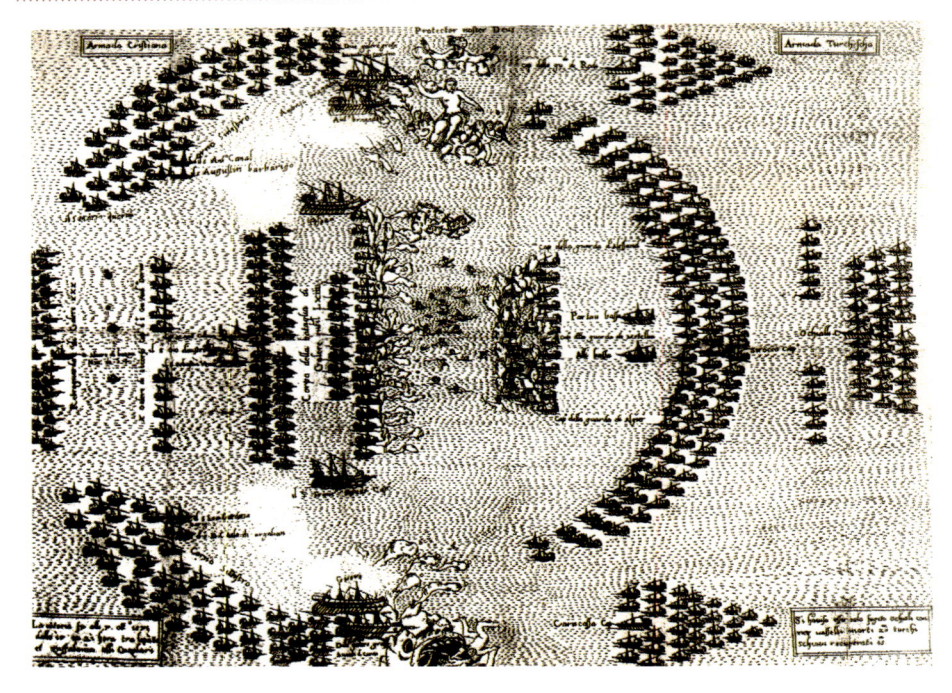

converted Moors, the Moriscos, in 1568; the subsequent wars in Granada in 1569/70; and the threat of Ottoman assistance to the Moriscos, Spain became once more fully absorbed by Mediterranean matters. Although new and potent quarrels were emerging in northern Europe, Spain concentrated on the south and east again. The Holy League promoted by Venice and Pius V now started to make progress and in May 1571 Spain, Tuscany, Venice, Malta, Genoa, and the Papal State formally agreed to join forces. Spain was given command of the planned campaign which was entrusted to Don Juan of Austria, while Philip II of Spain had to pay for most of the men and the equipment. On 7 October 1571 208 Christian and 230 Muslim galleys

The battle lines at Lepanto, from a contemporary engraving held at the Museo Storico Navale di Venezia (Venice Naval Museum).

clashed in the Gulf of Lepanto and the Christians won a glorious victory destroying or capturing all but 30 Turkish galleys and losing only ten. Despite this victory, the Christian powers failed to check the Ottomans who, just a year later, were able to put another mighty fleet to sea.

Even though the huge amount of contemporary propagandistic literature, sermons, reports, and triumphant celebrations might suggest otherwise, the Ottoman defeats at Malta in 1565 and Lepanto in 1571 had no long-term effects on their military power and naval presence in the Mediterranean. The Ottoman fleet recovered relatively soon while the squadrons of the North African beylerbeys remained as efficient as ever. The threat against Christian coastal regions remained a very real one. The slow decline of the Ottoman empire was caused mainly by economic reasons and its own internal structures and cannot be connected with one single military event. As already pointed out, for the Order and for the entire Christian world, the importance of the Great Siege of Malta of 1565 was primarily psychological and propagandistic but it failed to create a unified Christian effort to fight the Ottomans. The antagonism between the French and Hapsburgs and the consequences of Lutheranism were too deep to allow Christian fraternization. The so-called 'Holy League' whose forces won the day at Lepanto was not a direct effect of the Great Siege. As the war of Candia shows, the concept of a 'Holy League' was even more difficult to put into practice in the mid-seventeenth century. This failed attempt to gather a strong Christian League caused the fall of Crete and the constant support of the Order's naval squadron could not do much to stop its loss.

Even after the Great Siege and Lepanto and well through the seventeenth century, there was permanent fear of Muslim raids on the Christian coasts of the Mediterranean. In April 1566 an Ottoman contingent conquered the island of Chios, then in possession of the Genoese. In 1571 Venice lost Cyprus to the Ottomans. In 1576 an Ottoman fleet attacked

THE BATTLE OF LEPANTO

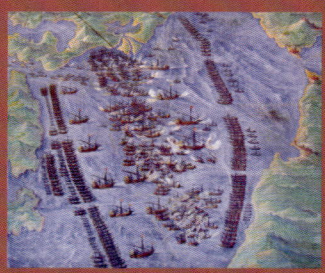

The battle of Lepanto, at the *Galleria delle Carte Geografiche* (Gallery of the Geographical Maps) in the Vatican Museums.

As in many other battles and naval campaigns of the Mediterranean Christian powers against Muslim shipping, the Order's fleet also participated in the campaigns of the Holy League (Spain, Venice, Genoa, the Papal State, Tuscany) against Sultan Selim II in the early 1570s. The climax of these campaigns was the naval battle in the Gulf of Lepanto (Greek Naupaktos). The Christian fleet was lead by Don Juan de Austria, half-brother of Spanish King Philipp II and illegitimate son of Emperor Charles V. The two fleets (230 warships on the Turkish side, 208 on the Christian) came upon one another on 7 October 1571 at the entrance to the Gulf of Lepanto in which the Christian fleet succeeded in trapping their adversary. The finer tactical skills by its leaders, the superior fire power of the artillery, and the ordnance of the Spanish galleys contributed to a resounding Christian victory. Only 30 Ottoman galleys under the command of Uluch Ali escaped. The Maltese galley squadron which participated in the battle was composed by the Capitana, *the flagship; the* Padrona *(Santa Maria della Vittoria); the* San Giovanni; *and the* Sant'Anna. *They stood under the command of Captain-General Jean François St. Clement.*

136   the Mediterranean environment

the coast of Palermo. In 1588 the coast of Valencia was raided. In 1588 and 1591 Reggio di Calabria and various coastal towns of Sicily and Calabria were attacked. Between 1592 and 1594 corsairs from Bizerta and Ottoman contingents raided the coasts of Calabria and Sicily. In 1614 Malta was hit again. In the course of a Turkish manoeuvre of active defence against a Spanish fleet gathered at Messina, 80 Ottoman ships attacked the southern coast of Malta and carried away 1,000 locals off into slavery.

All this corresponded with a general change of political realities in the central Mediterranean. In 1574 Tunis had become a definite vassal of the sultan, while after 1576 the Ottoman influence and pressure on Morocco kept increasing. Braudel comments that: 'Christian Spain, victorious but ill at ease, lived in terror of Turkish intervention, which was indeed discussed at Istanbul. Spain consistently, both before and after 1568, over-estimated the threat from Islam.' Indeed it was only in the seventeenth century that the power of the Ottoman fleet decreased. In 1571 at Lepanto the Ottomans and their allies could gather 230 galleys. In the early seventeenth century they, however, only had 50 galleys at their disposal, although this number could be increased by the fleets of their North African allies and vassals. But Lepanto also marked the end of the epoch of huge Ottoman-Christian naval clashes. The main threat to Christian shipping in the central and western Mediterranean now came from the small but very flexible and efficient squadrons of Algiers, Tripoli, and Tunis. The division of the North African region into these three provinces ruled by a sort of general governor (*beylerbey pasha*) was put into practice by the Sublime Porte in 1577. Morocco remained an independent kingdom. Very often the forces of North African beys and corsairs were used as instruments of Ottoman policy. In the early seventeenth century, Algiers possessed six galleys and 60 warships of different categories; Tunis six galleys and 14 warships; and Tripoli just three galleys. Very often not a few of the crews of these vessels were Spanish, Italian, English, and Dutch renegades.

Historians have concluded that Ottoman naval power continued to dwindle in the late seventeenth century. This decrease in efficiency was not so much a question of the number of warships but of outdated techniques. This diminished power could be seen when, in the war of the Morea, the Venetian, papal, Maltese, and Florentine contingents finally forced the sultan to surrender major ports in Dalmatia and the Morea. This is surely true, but a few years before, during the war of Candia (1645–69), the Ottoman army and fleet had shown that it was

A detail from Grand Master Gregorio Carafa's (1680–90) marble monument in St John's Co-Cathedral depicting the Battle of the Dardanelles, 1656 in which Carafa was one of the leaders against the Ottoman fleet.

still superior to those of most other Mediterranean states.

Still one has to point out that the belief of clear-cut borders between the Christian and Muslim worlds is naïve and anything but true. The Dutch historian de Groot comments: *The quality of Ottoman culture and society in North Africa, characterized by a great openness to western Christian influence, further strengthened the defensive and offensive powers of the 'Barbary Regencies'. These western outposts of the Ottoman Empire offer a unique example in early modern times of political realism and supremely pragmatic attitude towards the vexing problem of how to maintain relations between States ruled on the basis of Islamic law and the non-Islamic world, the 'House of War' in traditional Muslim legal usage.*

Thanks to this *modus vivendi* between the beylerbeys and France, the Netherlands, and England the military threat – except for corsairing – gradually ceased after 1600.

From now on, the nature of the relationship between Algiers, Tunis, and Tripoli on the one hand and the major western seapowers on the other began to experience a gradual change of proportion. The increasing frequency with which peace treaties were concluded provides sufficient evidence that relations were being built on firmer ground. The idea of

The torture practised by the Ottoman Turks was infamous all over the Mediterranean. The torments were meant to inflict the most horrific pain on the poor victims without killing them. Similar tortures were also used by the Inquisition. 16th-century etching, Private collection.

The extent of the Ottoman Empire in c.1600. Although Malta was under the control of their sworn enemies, the knights, the position of the island proved an important port of call to the empire.

the Barbary states as threat began slowly to diminish, to be replaced with the need to maintain peaceful friendly relations between trading partners and of discreet military relations. By adopting western-style diplomacy, the Barbary states were again the forerunners of modernization within the Ottoman world as they had done earlier with the adoption of western armaments and shipbuilding.

But, besides politics and economy, there was also another level of the relations between Christians and Muslims which has to be taken into consideration: culture. Even Hospitaller Malta played an important role in this matter. In fact it came to the bizarre situation that the island of the knights and the sworn enemies of Islam in some aspects became a bridgehead of interchanges between the two great Mediterranean cultures and religions. This was due to Malta's geographical and strategic position and its development as an important port of call for shipping, as well as because the local population spoke, and still speak, a Semitic tongue. Maltese priests and intellectuals like Leonardo Abela and Domenico Magri were used by the Roman curia for important missions and functions in connection with Oriental countries and rose to important ecclesiastical offices. In the 1630s a school for Arabic was finally established in Malta, but the idea of Malta as a bridgehead between the Christian

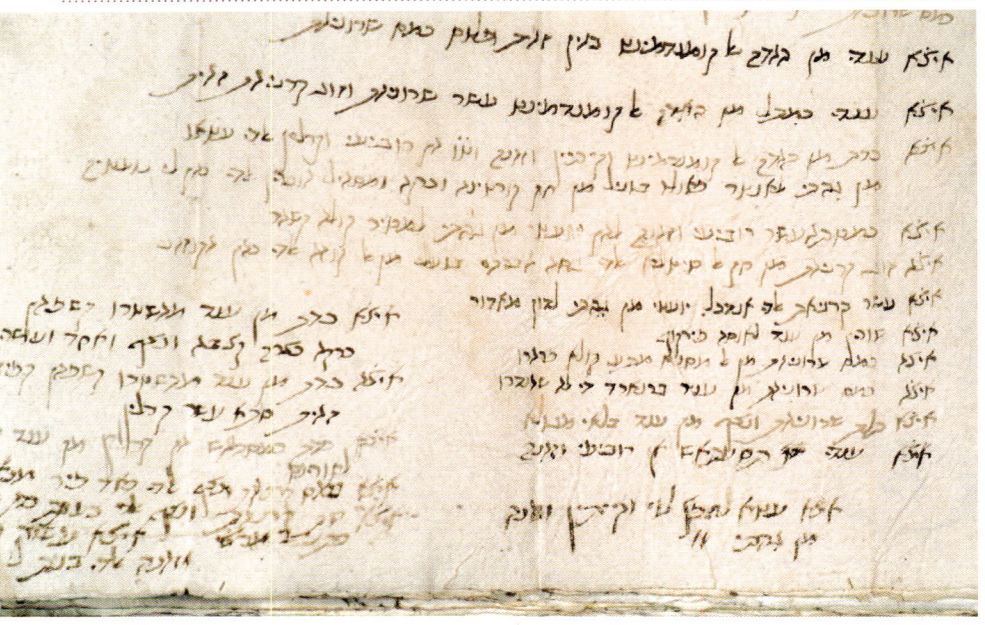

A document from the Mdina Cathedral Archives written in Judeo-Arabic. These documents are examples of vernacular Arabic writing recording business deals. Mdina Cathedral Museum Misc. 36.

and Muslim worlds had started years before. Ignatius of Loyola had the vision of using the Spanish Moriscos and the Maltese as the spearhead for missionary work in North Africa and the Levant because of their knowledge of a Semitic language. Since 1554 the founder of the Society of Jesus had planned to establish a Jesuit college at Malta to further this aim. A Jesuit college was finally founded in Malta in 1592. Of course, even the presence of thousands of Muslim or Jewish slaves, brought to Malta by the caravans of the Order and the Maltese corsairs, had an impact.

In the framework of European politics, however, this was the period when the Mediterranean's importance was eclipsing.

The historians Braudel, Setton, Duby, Aymard, Fontenay, Hess, and others have described and analysed in great detail how, in the sixteenth and seventeenth centuries, the Mediterranean suffered a political and economic decline and the centre of interest shifted towards the Atlantic and Pacific oceans. With the new option of direct trade with India and Asia via the sea route round the Cape of Good Hope and the opening of the New World in the sixteenth and seventeenth centuries, the economic heart of Europe moved from Italy and the Mediterranean to the new economic super-powers England and the Netherlands. Of course, even France, Portugal, and Spain had their share and for them the central and eastern Mediterranean became regions of secondary importance. Maybe the most significant and symbolic event took place in October 1503 when news reached Venice that three Portuguese ships had carried 3,000 *quintali* pepper from India to Portugal via the sea route round the Cape of Good Hope. This quantity was equivalent to the amount of pepper which the Venetians received through their trade with the Levant in one year. The contemporary Venetian diarist Girolamo Priuli commented that 'Nobles and merchants ... were stunned by the news, which left them little hope of resuming their trade, and they were in a bad mood.'

This development is also supported by the fact that the Mediterranean was hardly the scene of big naval battles any more after the 1580s. The great battles between Spain, England, and France were now fought in the Atlantic or Pacific oceans. Maybe the best example of this decline – but not entirely representative of other economic more active and prosperous regions – is the Kingdom of the Two Sicilies.

For Malta, Sicily and Southern Italy remained most important as sources of food and many other essential goods and also as main reference points for culture and education. So Malta was also concerned when, because of restrictive policies and the conservative power of the Catholic Church, the regions of the Kingdom of the Two Sicilies were hardly touched by the innovations of North Italian humanism and the liberalization of trade; intellectually and economically it sank far behind central and north European standards. In terms of pragmatic politics, legislative structure, and liberality, the republic of Venice could then be classified as the opposite of the Kingdom of the Two Sicilies.

The Kingdom of the Two Sicilies resulted from the reunification in 1442 of the Kingdom of Sicily with the Kingdom of Naples by King Alfonso V of Aragon (1396–1458).
Statue in the façade of the Royal Palace of Naples.

At the end of the seventeenth century, Venice was seen by many Europeans as a paradigm of an exemplary well-governed state with a wise constitution. Only in the eighteenth century did this admiration shift from Venice to England. Even the wider environment of Hospitaller Malta was afflicted by these important developments. Besides Italy, it had been especially the former world power of Spain whose slow technological, economic, and political decline could be felt in the Mediterranean. Trade, political influence, and the network of international contacts and processes of exchange in the Mediterranean in the seventeenth and eighteenth centuries were decided and determined by England, the Netherlands, and France. Still some Mediterranean powers – like Genoa, not the least because its indirect participation in the Spanish and Portuguese overseas trade – remained solid economic forces. Michel Fontenay sums up the situation around 1600:

At this date, while Genoa, at the height of its financial fortune, was the arbiter of European exchanges, while Marseilles had just experienced an astonishing commercial boom in the Levant, while Leghorn, hardly born, witnessed an exceptional growth, and while Ragusa commanded the most powerful commercial fleet ever seen in the Mediterranean, Venice was still a very large imperium *.... That this Mediterranean prosperity was fragile and threatened would be amply proved by its subsequent decline.*

Still one should not underestimate the importance of the Mediterranean. In the sixteenth and seventeenth centuries, trade in the Mediterranean grew so much that they could not do without English, Flemish, French and Dutch transport ships. Until the turn of the sixteenth century, the Mediterranean remained Europe's biggest transshipment region for exports and import. Still in 1660 only 10 per cent of the English exports went to East- and West-India while half of their exports went to the Mediterranean. Massive changes only came about in the second half of the seventeenth century. Between 1700 and 1790 English exports to the Mediterranean dwindled from 23 to 6 per cent, while the exports to India, the Far East, and America increased from 12 to 49 per cent. Similar figures exist for contemporary French trade.

With these tendencies of 'peripheralization' and the 'slow down of the rhythm', there was also the 'problem' of the established political and economic structures. This situation was especially apparent in Spain and its territories in the Mediterranean. In contrast to central and northern Europe, hardly any decay of the feudal structures and medieval order could be observed in the southern regions in the sixteenth and seventeenth centuries. With the exception of Northern Italy and the port cities of southern France, the Christian regions of the Mediterranean remained tied in feudal and conservative structures and therefore had old and very often anachronistic forms of production and distribution. The effects were inevitable and the same for many regions:

They remained fettered by frozen structures which favoured a conservative mentality. Faced with the dynamism of the North, they betrayed clear signs of uncompetitiveness. Their production costs were inflated with relatively high wages and by the hypertrophy of indirect taxation which permitted the dominant aristocracy to burden producers and consumers with the weight of urban splendour and monarchical glory.

The economic development in the Mediterranean had different social and political consequences according to the different countries' participation in the process. It was mainly France, the Netherlands, and England who profited from it and gained new levels of power and influence. As Hospitaller Malta still was very much tied to Sicily and Spain and as a great part of its members came from Mediterranean countries, the Order was economically, intellectually, and politically affected by this too. In this context historians speak of a phenomenon of 'refeudalization'.

Hospitaller Malta was influenced by these political and intellectual developments on different levels. Besides Italy and France, Spain had

Grand Master Martin Garzes (1595–1601), castellan of Emposta, of the langue of Aragon. San Anton Palace.

very close ties with the state of the knights. Many leading seventeenth-century exponents of the Order came from the Spanish hemisphere, such as Grand Masters Garzes, Vasconcellos, and the Cotoner brothers. This orientation towards Catholic Spain – a country which under Philip III and Philip IV was visibly in technological, economic, and political decline – must have also had its effects on the position of Malta in the fragile balance of the Mediterranean.

Most stock-owners in Spain, Southern Italy, and Sicily were either members of the old aristocracy or newly ennobled individuals and did not invest in modern ways of production and did not risk to invest money in private commercial shares. Instead the money from their lands and taxes were used to buy iconographical manifestations of power, namely palaces, art, and splendid representation. Another important factor which drew away money from the modern branches of economy was the strong presence of the Catholic Church and religious Orders in these southern countries. The tremendous riches of the church therefore also was 'dead' capital and did not flow in the 'modern' enterprises and economy. After 1580 also in Hospitaller Malta the Dutch and English presence in the Mediterranean was felt more and more. Malta's ports and markets started getting attractive for these countries.

The Order itself – always in need of modern equipment for its forces and fleet – used this occasion to establish new and more heterogeneous trading connections. Surely the need was felt to be more independent from the one-sided ties with Sicily and Southern Italy, but Malta never escaped from its dependence on the Sicilian *tratte*. In the sixteenth and seventeenth centuries Malta cautiously opened up towards other sides but, at least up to the end of the rule of Nicolas Cotoner in 1680, the state of the Order remained under the solid political and intellectual influence of the Hapsburgs.

Although in the eighteenth century the Order was mainly ruled by Spanish and Portuguese grand masters like Perellos y Roccaful, Manoel de Vilhena, Ramon Despuig, Manoel Pinto de Fonseca, and Francisco Ximenes de Texada, an increasing contact with and the influence of the French Bourbons could be noticed.

Very often French politics clearly influenced the decisions made in Malta. A great part of the members of the Order anyhow still came from the three French-speaking langues. Under the long rule of Louis XV, France developed into the Order's main protector, as can be seen by the very close relations of Portuguese Grand Master Pinto with the French king. As an outcome of these ties, for example, on 12 July 1765 the parliament in Paris granted all Maltese living in France the same rights like the French, including dealing in French property. On the other hand, all French citizens living in Malta were given the same rights as the locals. The beginning of a *'Lettre Patentes du Roi'* printed in Paris in 1765 stresses that the inhabitants of the islands should be considered as citizens of France to all intents and purposes. Also Malta's role as a training centre for French naval officers should not be underestimated. Historian Alain Blondy notes that, for the French government, the Order was 'an educational convent and naval training centre for young noblemen'. As gesture of this special alliance, in August 1765 Louis XV donated to the Order three relics of high devotional value: a rib of King Louis the Holy, and

*Grand Master Nicolas Cotoner
(1663–80) showing with pride the
plans for the fortifications that were
later named after him.
Grand Master's Palace, Valletta.*

fragments of the skulls of the martyrs St Valerian and St Innocent taken from the sequestrated possessions of the Jesuits in Rue de Fer at the Faubourg St Germain.

As a rather 'profane' manifestation of the close ties between the French Royal House and the Hospitallers, there was Louis XV's offer to transfer to the Order extensive possessions, including special prerogatives and exemptions in Guyana in South America.

Although the Knight Gautier Valabre was already prepared to travel to South America to examine, the particular state and economic possibilities of these possessions made the council of the Order refuse the French king's offer. This negative answer might have been caused by the Order's bad experience with its colonial experience in the Caribbean in the mid-seventeenth century.

Even in the matter of class, society, and politics, the Order had to acknowledge the general developments in contemporary Europe. The seventeenth century saw the nobility being integrated into the absolutistic administration of the state and the absorbing of the nobles into the rules and conventions of the royal court. The once independent economic and social status of the nobles was reduced more and more in favour of the absolutistic state. Many European princes gradually forced the nobles to 'retire' from social reality and activity and thus isolated their old social values. Still in the eighteenth century the European nobility tried to uphold the façade of their class as the true and powerful exponents of the new and the old order. The reality was, however, different.

Especially in the epoch of Absolutism with its tendencies to force

Some males who were not heirs apparent of European aristocratic families decided to become knights of St John. Some even started as pages to the grand master. Their elegant costumes were noted by many visitors to 18th-century Valletta.

Right and opposite page, unknown artist: H.J. Vinkhuijzen's Collection of Uniforms and Regimental Regalia: Illustrations of military uniforms of Knights of Malta, 1048–1799. The New York Public Library.

Right: Page to the grand master holding the 'Sword of the Religion' (see page 101) on Victory Day.

Left: Two knights in their conventual habit.

noblemen into the strict ties and patterns of service in the sovereign's military, centralized administration or at court, and because of the impoverishment of many old noble families, membership in the Order became an attractive and prestigious alternative, a sort of compensation for the lost glory, independence, and power. In the eyes of some critical contemporaries of the age of reason and utility, it even looked as an escape from reality. In this respect, the Order underwent a similar development like the Teutonic Order after the loss of its Prussian and Baltic lands. The once so active and politically important Teutonic Order had become a rather passive institution used by the Catholic nobility of the empire to provide their younger sons with lucrative positions.

The Order's international character and political ties never allowed it to remain distant from the latest political and intellectual tendencies in Central Europe. In fact, tendencies of absolute rule are documented in the increasingly autocratic rule by the grand masters. From the 1650s onwards the grand masters longed for a strong iconographical presentation of their own personal glory and a baroque attitude to preserve this glory for eternity in art and architecture. Especially because they could not have dynastical ambitions, the grand masters' aimed to preserve their names and glory through military exploits, foundations, and extensive building programmes. The grand masters – like the kings of Aragon before – had the right to bestow on Maltese subjects titles of nobility and land.

A full-length portrait by French painter Charles A.P. van Loo (1719–95) of the young Louis XV in the Ambassador's Room at the Grand Master's Palace.

Just as class councils had their powers nibbled away in Absolutistic Europe, even in Malta the chapter-generals of the Order ceased to be convoked between 1631 and 1776. At the same time, it was the ambition of the grand masters to revalue their titles in concert with the European rulers. Previously the grand master had stood on the same level as a cardinal-deacon and held the titles of an *Altezza Serenissima* and Eminence. He was addressed by the French king as *Mon Cousin*. In a diploma of 20 March 1607, Emperor Rudolph II bestowed upon the grand master the rank of an imperial prince and confirmed the title of *Altezza Serenissima* which was also confirmed in a diploma by Emperor Ferdinand II on 16 July 1620. The title of imperial prince had been already bestowed upon the grand prior of Germany, Georg Schilling von Cannstatt, by Charles V in 1548 in occasion of the German diet at Augsburg. In a bull of 10 June 1630 Pope Urban VIII bestowed upon the grand master the title *Eminenza*. In 1631 the chapter-general of the Order left it up to the grand master which title to choose. Finally the title *Eminenza* was accepted. When Pinto was elected grand master in 1741, he claimed the title *Altezza Eminentissima* and *Principe*.

A full-length portrait of Grand Master Manoel Pinto de Fonseca (1681–1773) by Pierre Bernard dated 1740. Grand Master's Palace, main corridor.

P. Bernard pinxit

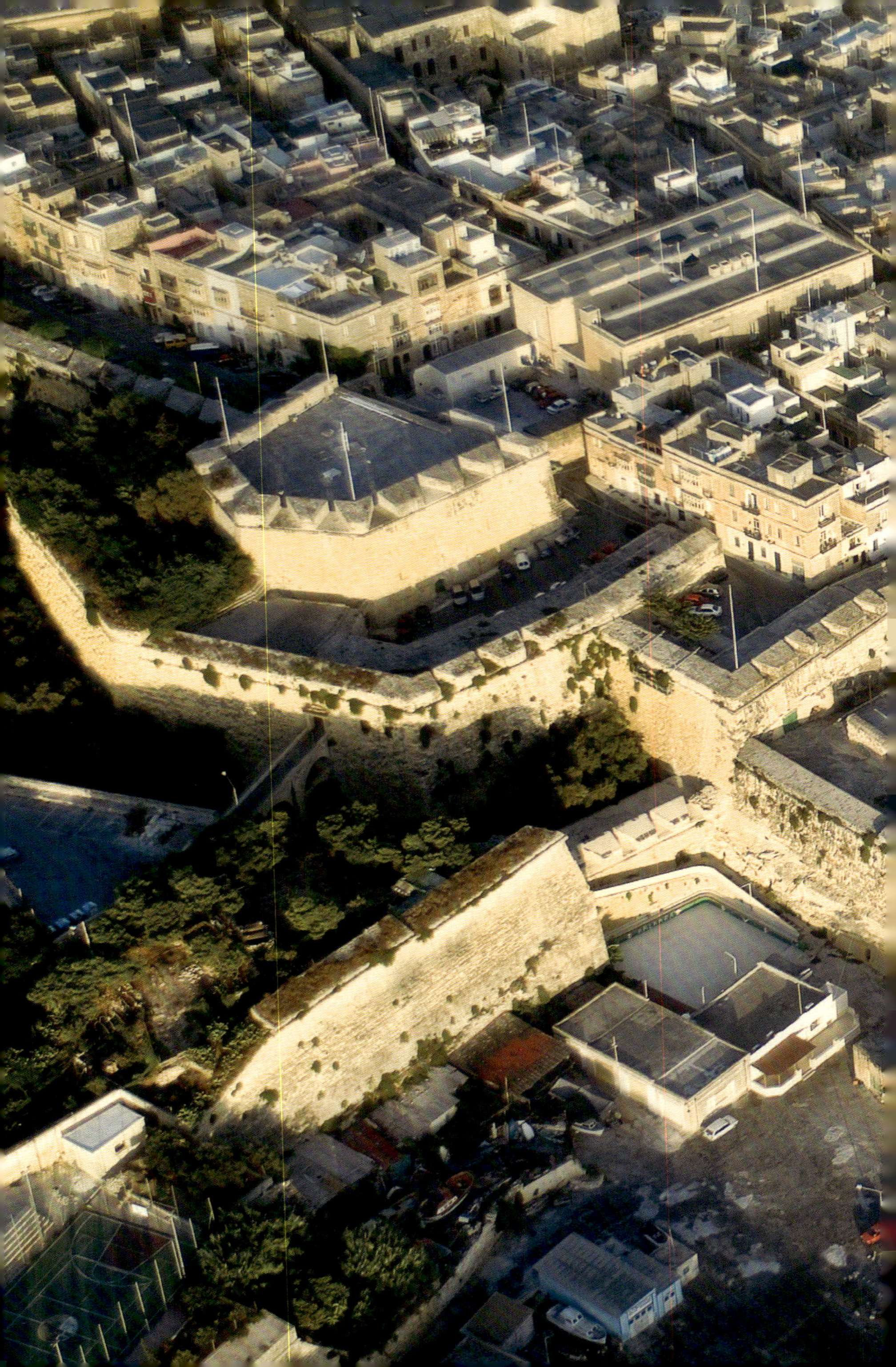

The arrival of the Order and especially the building of the new capital of Valletta meant the end of the medieval times in Malta. New ideas, new artistic styles, and a huge demand of workforce of all sort changed the profile of the island considerably. That the Order chose to establish its convent at the Porto Grande *signalled the dynamization of the maritime profile of Malta.*

Chapter 6

Malta and the impact of the rule of the Hospitallers

Social and demographic changes

The Order's rule had drastic direct and indirect effects on Maltese society. The coming of the Order led to a development of the vital sea-links which in turn meant a relative neglect for the hinterland. The structure and maritime orientation of the Order made it clear that its capital had to be located near the harbour. In fact the Order first took up residence in Birgu and the old *castrum maris,* subsequently called Fort St Angelo. Later it built the prestigious new fortress city of Valletta on the Mount Sceberras between Marsamxett harbour and the *Porto Grande*. The constant threat of corsair raids on the coastal area before 1530 had made it necessary for the capital of the island to be sited in a safe place in the hinterland. The military power

An aerial photograph of the Post of Castile overlooking Kalkara Creek. The large building in the top centre of the photo was the knight's armoury in Birgu. Next to it is the Cavalier of St James.

of the Order was now too strong to allow Muslim corsairs to attack the harbour conurbation. This concentration of the manpower resources of the Order on Malta meant that there was a great risk of losing the weakly manned fortress of Tripoli, which is what indeed happened in 1551. While Malta became relatively safer in the sixteenth century, the situation in Gozo remained perilous. Throughout the sixteenth century the knights were not very interested in fortifying Gozo. The effects of this was shown in 1551 when a combined force of Dragut and Pialí Pasha could not conquer Birgu but only took two days to capture the Gozo *castello*. In the following hundred years or so, the few remaining locals and the newcomers from Malta and Sicily were concentrated in Rabat. Only in the second half of the seventeenth century did the Gozitans feel safe enough to establish new villages in the countryside.

In Rhodes as well as in Malta, the presence of the Hospitallers contributed substantially to a heterogeneous profile of the local population. When the Order went to Rhodes, it had brought over many Christians from Palestine and Cyprus, many of Italian, Provençal, and Catalan descendance, together with some Maronites. In the fourteenth and fifteenth centuries, Rhodes became a popular place of refuge for Greeks and Jews from former Byzantine lands now occupied by the Ottomans.

The magisterial palace inside the castrum maris, *Fort St Angelo. Before the arrival of the Order this was the castellan's residence. Grand Master L'Isle Adam converted it into his palace and household.*

The plan of Fortizza di Gozo *in folio 15 of Matteo Perez d'Aleccio's set of engravings of the Great Siege published in Rome in 1585. The plan shows the medieval walls of the old citadel with a proposal to rebuild the land-front of the castle. The plan was never realized. Private collection.*

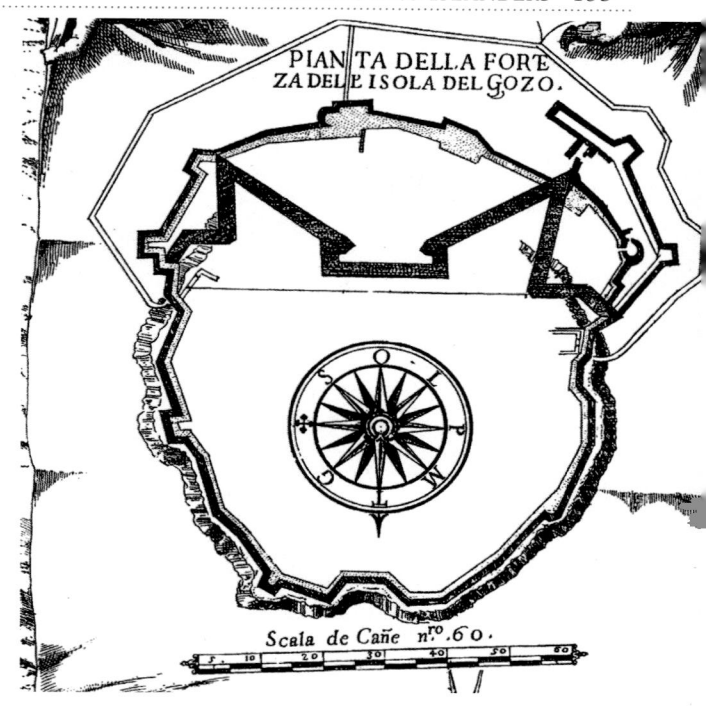

There was also a permanent influx of Muslim slaves captured in course of the caravans of the knights as well as many Christians from all Mediterranean regions who were freed by the naval forces of the Hospitallers. The merchants at Rhodes were mostly Greeks, together with Italians and a few Catalans. Very soon after the conquest of Rhodes, the population agreed to acknowledge the superiority of the pope in Rome although Greek Orthodox believers were allowed to keep their liturgical rites. The language of the church of Rhodes remained Greek, while the Greek metropolite kept his ecclesiastic properties and income. The grand master had the right to appoint Greek priests or to cancel their appointment. He was also entitled to fill Greek monasteries and churches with clerics and priests. Since the Hospitallers took over, Rhodes had two 'bishops', two cathedrals, and two sorts of clergy, Latin and Greek-Orthodox. According to a regulation from 1474, the grand master chose the new metropolite from two or three candidates proposed by the Greek-Orthodox church. The Latin bishop had to confirm this appointment. The Greek-Orthodox metropolite had a suffragan status to the Latin archbishop and had to take an oath to pay obedience to the Latin Church.

As in Rhodes in the early fourteenth century, when the Hospitallers moved to Malta in 1530 the local society was heterogenized and internationalized. At Rhodes the city of Rhodes with its port developed into

Borgo S. Angelo

the centre of power and commerce, while in Malta it was the town of Birgu, situated directly at the impressive and spacious *Porto Grande* which became the Order's new headquarters. Besides the old-established Maltese and Aragonese families, the town was now populated with the group of Greek merchants and craftsmen, seamen, officers, lawyers, and priests who had come from Rhodes. Together with newcomers from Sicily and Italy, the former Rhodiots supplied the Order with their manpower and crafts, namely sailors, soldiers, craftsmen, and more refined specialists like silver- and goldsmiths, doctors, lawyers, priests, and officers. This brought a dynamic change compared to the previous situation, as is described by the Maltese historian Stanley Fiorini:

In 1524 the Order sent an eight-man commission of knights and they described the Borgo *as a small defenceless town in the* Porto Grande, *with some old houses mostly in poor condition, next to the* castrum maris *(Fort St Angelo). A detail from an engraving of the Borgo 1565. Fort St Angelo collection.*

The mainstays of the Maltese economy before 1530 were agriculture and corsairing. The great majority of working people, other than the few score professionals – the lawyers, doctors, notaries, and priests – the few hundred craftsmen, and the seafarers in harbourside Birgu, were all agricultural workers. They worked their own land or that leased to them by the Mdina fief-holders and other larger estate owners.

Immediately after their arrival, the Greek immigrants were exempted from the jurisdiction and the pastoral service of the Maltese clergy, an exemption which survived throughout the sixteenth century. An assimilation of the new Greek residents with the locals was a very slow process. In 1575 there were still three Greek parishes in Birgu. In 1587 the Order was still paying 833 *scudí* every year to persons in need in Messina and Syracuse who had come from Rhodes.

This cosmopolitan atmosphere and heterogeneous ethnic profile with its mercantile character, however, was limited to Birgu and the *Porto Grande* area. The old capital of Mdina (*Città Notabile*), situated in the very centre of the island, kept its exclusive aristocratic and feudal character and remained the seat of the clergy. The *universitas* was preserved. The administrative and jurisdictional structures which the Hospitallers established in Birgu were – with very few exceptions – the same ones that had existed in Rhodes. The decisions of the councils were still presented as *Pragmaticae Rhodiae*.

The organization of Maltese society after 1530 cannot be understood without a closer view at the structure of the state of the Hospitallers in Rhodes. As they had done in Rhodes, the Hospitallers tried to organize the local society and population in Malta according to the patterns of military and maritime utility. A special emphasis was laid on the maritime aspect. Besides the few hundred knights, the Order needed a supply of well-trained mariners and sailors as well as mercenaries. There was also a local

The coat of arms of the Mdina Universitas *from the old door of the Medieval cathedral.*

militia: after 1776 Grand Master Rohan added the Regiment of Malta and the Regiment of *Chasseurs* of Militia.

There was also a steady supply of arms and military goods, while the upkeep of the extensive network of fortifications required a huge number of workmen and specialists. Rhodiot, and later Maltese, society had to be organized and instrumentalized to conform with these military and economic needs and concepts. A solid ideological and spiritual framework was also needed. Contrary to the situation in Rhodes, in Malta there was at least confessional harmony between the local population and the knights. All of them were Roman Catholic. The chaplain of the Order and *uditore* to Grand Master L'Isle Adam, Jean Quintin D'Autun, who arrived in Malta a few months before the main contingent of the Order in 1530, was very pleased to note a deep devotion

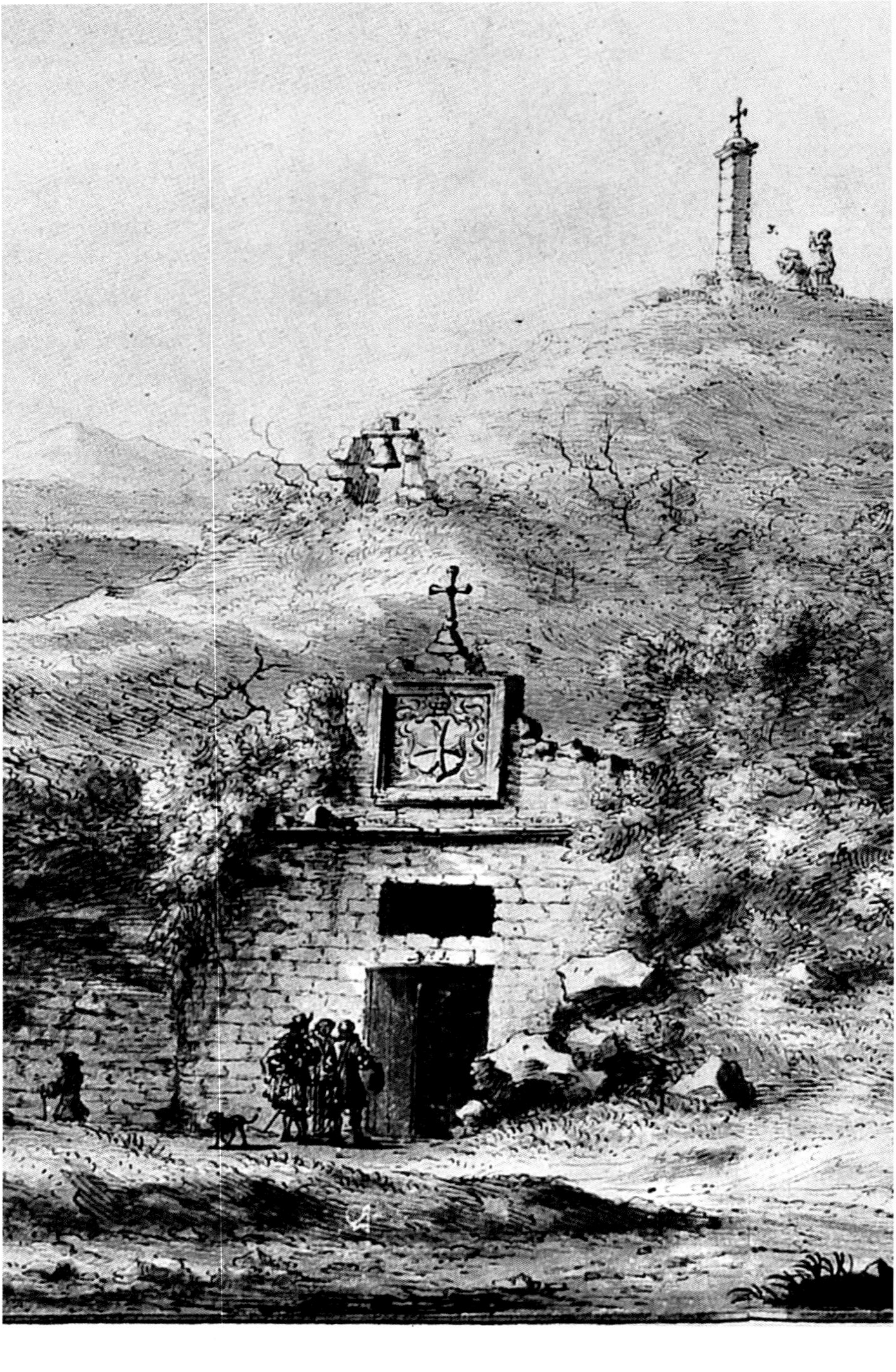

of the local population towards the Catholic faith: 'The local people are very religious ... there is a special cult of St Paul who is worshipped all over the island.'

Despite the knights' intention to keep their military and administrative structure, still they had to make efforts to adapt to the prevailing situation in Malta, where the powerful local clergy created not a few problems. The anger of the Maltese nobility that their island had been – against the several expressed declarations of the representatives of the crown of Aragon in the fourteenth and fifteenth centuries – dismembered again from the domain of Sicily and enfeoffed once more to a foreign lord meant further tension. The local clergy was, moreover, unwilling to accept competition to their centuries-old authority and jurisdiction. In theory the Order was quite conscious of the nature of the old rights of the Maltese. As we will see later on the reality, however, very often was different.

Because of the geographical position of Malta and the internal structure of the Order, the State of the Hospitallers was immediately affected by the slightest development in the Mediterranean or the smallest shift of the international balance of power. In the seventeenth and eighteenth centuries, the State of the Order was a nerve centre of international diplomacy and exchanges in the Mediterranean. Nearly every European State or principality had its *chargé d'affaires* (who had to be a member of the Order), representative, or consul in Malta. The growing cosmopolitan and multinational character of sections of the population is explained by the naval and military needs of the Order. Another cause of these demographic and social changes was the constant influx of foreign workmen, craftsmen, specialists, engineers, merchants, and artisans, especially after the building of the new fortress city of Valletta commenced in 1566. The prestigious private residences of the knights also employed a good number of foreigners.

'Cold' demographic numbers document these developments and this prosperity. The commissioners' report of 1524 mentions 20,000 inhabitants in Malta and 5,000 in Gozo. In the late sixteenth century Malta had four cities, Mdina (*Città vecchia*), Birgu (*Il Borgo*), Senglea (*L'Isla*), and Valletta (*Città nuova*), and about 60 villages (*casali*). In 1571 the Order moved to Valletta which became the centre of the island's political and cultural life. The demographic concentration on Valletta is visible by 1590, when the new city already had 4,000 inhabitants, as much as Birgu and Senglea together. By 1614

The site of St Paul's Grotto in Rabat, Malta adapted from Willem Schellinx's Viaggio al Sud *1664–65. The Maltese cult for St Paul was already strong at the arrival of the Order in Malta. The site of the grotto is marked clearly in many maps of the island drawn for the knights.*

Valletta had over 10,000 inhabitants. In 1574 the apostolic delegate Mgr Pietro Dusina reported to Rome that there were 29,000 people living in Malta and Gozo. In 1600 Diego Quadra estimated the population to be about 32,000. If one considers that Malta after 1590 was severely hit by outbreaks of the bubonic plague and by waves of famine which decreased the population by 35 per cent, the increase was tremendous, especially when one compares numbers with contemporary Central Europe. In 1617 the population rose to 43,000, double the figure of the period of plague and famine in 1590/91. In 1633 59,923 people lived in Malta and Gozo, not counting the 621 members of the Order and the 4,430 foreigners – soldiers, sailors, craftsmen, and slaves – resident on the island. The member of the Order and historian Bartolomeo dal Pozzo who wrote two generations later estimated that, out of these *c.*60,000 persons, only 51,750 fell under the grand master's jurisdiction. These numbers kept increasing in the seventeenth and eighteenth centuries; when the Order's rule came to an end in 1798 the islands had a population of not less than 100,000.

In the seventeenth century the situation in the *Porto Grande* conurbation, with the new capital of Valletta as its centre, changed the whole structure of the island. It is, however, not true that the old capital Mdina started being called *Città Vecchia* or *Notabile* only after the building of Valletta (*Città Nuova*). To distinguish the old capital from the new residence at Birgu (1530–71), Grand Master La Sengle coined the name *Città Vecchia* in 1554.

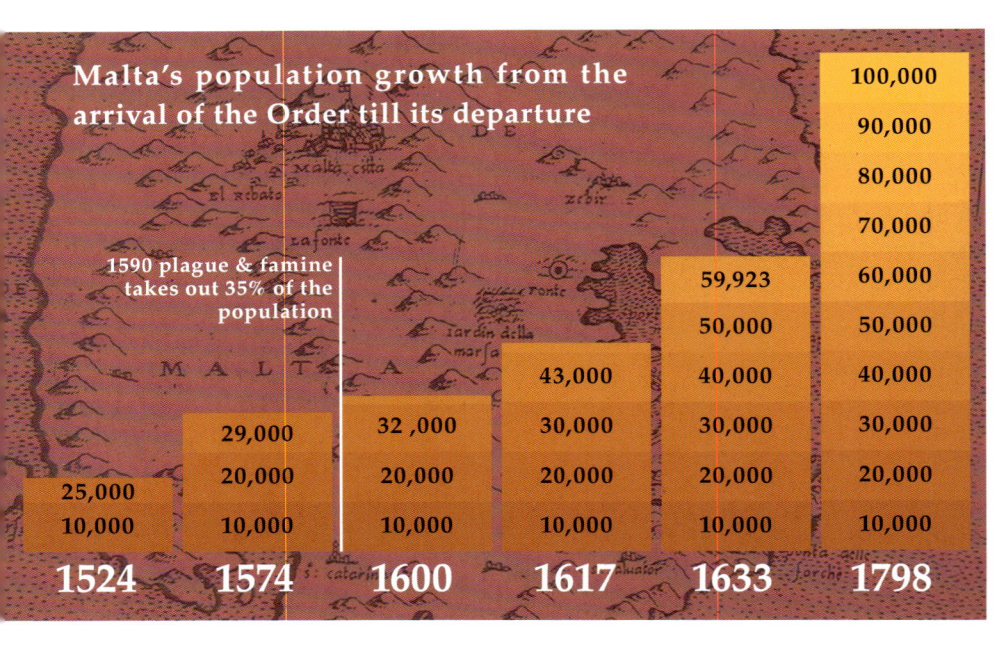

Malta's population growth from the arrival of the Order till its departure

Year	Population
1524	25,000
1574	29,000
1600	32,000
1617	43,000
1633	59,923
1798	100,000

1590 plague & famine takes out 35% of the population

A detail from a 1719 German map of Malta. The extended urban area opposite Valletta across the Porto Grande *consisted of the three cities of Vittoriosa, Cospicua, and Senglea within the Margerita Lines.*
Heritage Malta collection.

Later the Order changed the names of, Birgu into *Vittoriosa*, Bormla into Cospicua, Qormi into *Città Pinto*, Żebbuġ into *Città Rohan*, Żejtun into *Città Beland*, Siġġiewi into *Città Ferdinand*, and Żabbar into *Città Hompesch*. Except *Vittoriosa* and *Cospicua*, these names reverted to the old forms after the Order left Malta.

The late sixteenth century witnessed the radical transformation of the Sceberras peninsula. The building of Valletta was not just an architectonical and strategic event but also a symbol and allegory of the Order's steadfastness and strength.

Laparelli's and Cassar's, and later Floriani's, Grunenbergh's, and Valperga's works turned the *Porto Grande* conurbation into an area which strikes a balance between the landscape and the seascape through the ingenious utilization of its geographical features. Although it was planned years before, Grand Master Valette's building of the new city complemented the Order's initial development to create safe haven for its fleet. This sheltering function for its famous fleet – the backbone of the Hospitallers' force – was the essential reason for the Order to establish itself on the islands. The building of Senglea and later the Cottonera fortifications and Fort Ricasoli to complement the existing urban area of Birgu was an ingenious development over a natural inlet between two peninsulas. In the late sixteenth and the entire seventeenth century, many famous architects and exorbitant financial efforts contributed to fortify the outer flanks of both peninsulas to create a defendable geographic space, including an inlet that could be closed off by a heavy chain.

Although there were no confessional differences between the Order and the population in Malta, the jurisdictional situation in Malta was much more complicated. Ecclesiastically Malta was composed of a conglomerate of Latin-Christian religious Orders, brotherhoods, and influential parishes which were not willing to give up their positions and prerogatives even under the Order. Before 1530, the local bishop hardly had resided in Malta; after 1530 he was permanently present on the island. With the exception of the Maltese Baldassare Cagliares, the bishop was always a foreigner and generally a member of the Order.

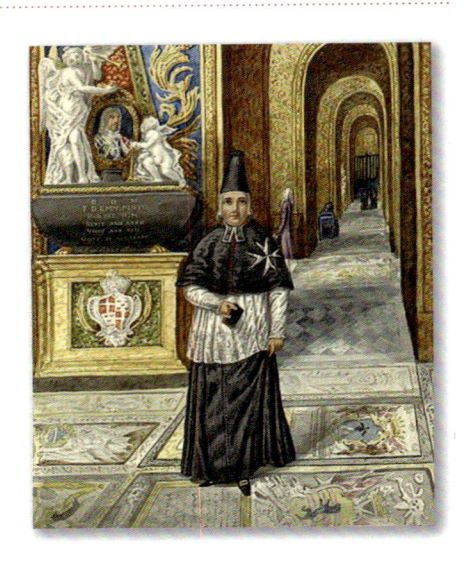

Top and opposite page, unknown artist: From H.J. Vinkhuijzen's collection: Illustrations of military uniforms of Knights of Malta, 1048–1799. The New York Public Library Archives. Chaplains

The enfeoffment of Malta had stipulated that the viceroy of Sicily had the right to choose from the candidates proposed to him by the grand master. After 1574, with the arrival of the papal delegate Pietro Dusina, the office of bishop and inquisitor were separated for the first time. The inquisitor was always a foreigner, mainly a person of trust from the circle of the Roman *Curia*. As representative of the *Curia*, the inquisitor had his own jurisdiction. Although the bishop was generally a member of the Order, when he acted in his official capacity he very often tended to follow the advice of the higher Maltese clerical dignitaries and quite often his policies went contrary to

GRAND MASTER, INQUISITOR AND BISHOP

at the conventual church of St John's, top; in the chapel of langue of France, top opposite; chapel of the langue of Castille, Leon, and Portugal, bottom opposite in the grand master's crypt.

the Order's aims and risked open conflicts. The Order itself had its own clergy and conventual church in Birgu and in Valletta after 1574. All members of the Order were exempted from the jurisdiction and the courts of the bishop. On the other hand, the many clerics in Malta were exempted from the grand master's jurisdiction and fell only under the bishop. The inquisitor's household and officials were similarly independent of the grand master, and were only subject to the inquisitor or the Holy See. The archives of the Order are full of accounts of conflicts and clashes with the bishop and the inquisitor. The latter remained at Birgu even after the building of Valletta.

The new global changes also brought inevitable internal changes. The effects tested the integrity and

THE ORDER, THE CHURCH, AND THE INQUISITION

The ecclesiastical-jurisdictional situation in Malta during the rule of the Order of St John was a complicated one. With the exception of the Maltese Baldassare Cagliares, the bishop was generally a foreigner and member of the Order. The enfeoffment of Malta to the Order had stipulated that the viceroy of Sicily had the right to choose from the candidates proposed to him by the grand master. The office of inquisitor in Malta, with powers delegated to it directly by the Congregation of the Holy Office, dated back to 1561. From 1574 onwards the prelate occupying this office became known as inquisitor general. After 1574 with the arrival of the papal delegate Pietro Dusina, the office of bishop and inquisitor were separated. His jurisdiction extended over all the inhabitants in the Maltese islands, including the members of the Order. Although the bishop had in most cases been a member of the Order, he very often tended to the opinion of the higher dignitaries of the Maltese clergy in his decisions. The bishop, therefore, quite often followed a policy contrary to the aims of the Order and risked open conflicts. The Order itself had its own clergy and conventual church in Birgu and, after 1574, in the newly built fortress city of Valletta. All members of the Order were exempted from the jurisdiction and the courts of the bishop. On the other hand, there was also a great number of clerics exempted from the grand master's jurisdiction and fell only under the bishop. Also the inquisitor's retinue and the officials were independent from the grand master's jurisdiction but subject only to the inquisitor or to the Holy See.

The Inquisitor of Malta Fabio Chigi later became Pope Alexander VII (1655–67)
Portrait by Gian Battista Gaulli (il Baciccio) (1639–1709).

internal stability of the Order. In the mid-sixteenth century, Lutheranism also spread to Malta. Bishops Domenico Cubelles and Martin Royas investigated various cases and confiscated property of rich Maltese who fled to Sicily or France. This new threat to Roman Catholicism and the various clashes between the authorities of the Order and the bishop of Malta, as well as the fear of Protestant infiltration, brought further changes. The Roman Inquisition, as distinct both from the old medieval version and from the Spanish version, had been instituted by the pope with the bull *Licet at Initio* on 21 July 1542 but it was officially introduced in Malta in October 1561. The first inquisitors were the bishops of Malta; but in July 1574, Pope Gregory XIII appointed Mgr Pietro Dusina as inquisitor with a separate jurisdiction from the bishops'. The inquisitor was vested with several functions: as inquisitor he was responsible for the custody of the Faith, while as apostolic delegate he was the official representative of the pope in Malta. From the very start, the inquisitor's authority was very much despised by the members of the Order. The office of the inquisitor came to an end with Napoleon's conquest of Malta. Two seventeenth-century inquisitors who served in Malta later became popes: Fabio Chigi became Alexander VII and Antonio Pignatelli, Innocent XII. Their examples were proof that the assignment of an inquisitor for Malta was regarded as a stepping-stone in an ecclesiastical career.

Sometimes the inquisitors had to act as intermediaries. In the late 1630s, serious problems had arisen when the grand master had raised taxes and Inquisitor Fabio Chigi had to mediate between the Maltese and the Order. Throughout his stay in Malta, Chigi was instrumental in helping the financing of the ongoing building of the fortifications. He was also involved in the conflicts between the Italian langue and Cardinal Antonio Barberini (junior) in 1634, when the pope bestowed upon the latter the Order's priorate in Rome. Other conflicts arose when the Spanish knights protested against the bestowing of grand crosses to certain French noblemen. The most serious of the clashes between the knights and the Jesuits led to the Jesuits' temporary expulsion in 1639. The deeper reason for this tension was that many knights thought the Jesuits had too much influence on the grand master. Chigi could not do much about the matter. As with so many other inquisitors, throughout his term in Malta Chigi had to witness continuous troubles regarding ecclesiastical jurisdiction and that of the Order as the lord over the Maltese islands.

Antonio Pignatelli's years in Malta after 1646 were marked by serious famine and poverty among the local population caused by a dearth in Sicily which used to provide the islands with all types of food provisions. Inquisitor Pignatelli himself wrote to Rome to plead on behalf of the Maltese but received no positive answer. Acting on his own responsibility as the head of the *Reverenda Fabbrica* of St Peter which had in custody the pious legacies of the diocese of Malta, he offered its moneys for food provisions until the situation improved when the money had to be returned. The jurisdictional situation in the microcosm of Malta and

Frescoes of the coat of arms of the inquisitors that served in Malta in the main hall of the piano nobile *of the Inquisitor's Palace in Vittoriosa.*

Gozo must have made uneasy times for the grand master. Clerics were only subject to the bishop, and those in the service of the inquisition only subject to the inquisitor. When the tribunal of the Congregation of the *Reverenda Fabbrica* was installed in 1628 another small group of persons became exempted from the civil and ecclesiastical jurisdiction. Another point of tension was that the pope still was the nominal spiritual head of the Order. How much the pope could interfere in the matters of the Order was shown in 1631 when a chapter-general was convened at the express wish of Pope Urban VIII. This chapter – the last until Grand Master Rohan summoned another one in 1776 – aimed to legislate various reforms in the ways and customs within the Order.

The relationship between the Order and the Maltese was not always an easy one either. Very often it was members of the local Maltese clergy who figured as the intellectual exponents of secret or open protest. A well-known example was the parish priest of Birkirkara Dun Filippo Borg who in the early seventeenth century compiled a report who blamed even the hero of the Great Siege Grand Master Valette as being unscrupulous and harsh against the rights of the Maltese.

Opposite page: The full-length portrait of Grand Master de Valette by painter Antoine Favray (1706–98). Grand Master's Palace, Valletta.

New economic perspectives

Although separated by more than 60 miles of sea and after 1530 by political and administrative systems, Malta and Sicily remained very strongly linked. Especially in the sixteenth century these links were basic for the economic and political survival of Hospitaller Malta. Just to quote possibly the most famous example. It was yet again from Sicily that the Spanish relief forces set sail for besieged Malta in the late summer of 1565. The civil population was often induced to take refuge in the domains of the viceroy of Sicily whenever the Maltese archipelago was threatened by Ottoman forces. Although, in the late sixteenth century, the – French – grand masters embarked on a process to loosen the ties with Sicily and – not the least for economic reasons – moved on to give a more cosmopolitan profile to the territory, many political institutions continued to nurture close ties with Spanish Sicily.

Commercial links also remained very strong. Malta kept its consuls and representatives in the principal Sicilian towns therewith securing a regular supply of commodities and food. The Sicilian merchants had their representatives in Malta. Messina, Pozzallo, and Licata remained the ports of departure for most of Malta's imported grain. Many important links were established by the Order itself which form important features of the historical process of early modern Malta. Many of the Order's galleys and vessels were built in Messina which was

LINKS OF TRADE 165

also one of the most important priories of the Order, with over ten wealthy and prestigious commanderies. Many high-ranking members of the Order owned property in Sicily.

Socially and economically, in the last decades of the sixteenth century Malta transited from Medieval to Early Modern Times. This was mainly caused by the tremendous influx of foreign goods and workmen as well as the new policies of the grand masters, namely to open up Malta to foreign markets. A deeper reason was to loosen the age-old dependency on provisions from Sicily. It has already been noted that, up to the 1570s, the Maltese society and economy were almost exclusively linked to the Spanish and Italian hemisphere. After 1570 the two new 'superpowers' in world trade, England and the Netherlands, appeared in the Mediterranean. Additionally Malta became involved in the traditional strong Ottoman–French relations and the ongoing Anglo-Spanish conflict. Maltese archives provide enough evidence of the increasing presence of French, English, and Dutch tradesmen. A milestone was set in 1697 when Grand Master Perellos set up the *Consolato del Mare* (Mercantile Tribunal) to deal exclusively with maritime commerce for the benefit of ship-owners, shareholders, and insurance people. The Malta *Consolato del Mare* followed the same norms of the *Consolati* of Barcelona and Messina.

Malta in the time of the Order produced cotton, a small quantity of grain, and an even smaller quantity of wine. Except cotton, the demand for more goods had to be satisfied from

Grand Master Ramón Perellos y Roccaful 1697–1720, Tapestry detail from the grand master's gioia *to the conventual church of St John's. Museum St John's Co-Cathedral.*

Sicily. The grain from Sicily was stored in granaries near the grand masters' palace in Valletta. It was partly because of this shortage of food that the six galleys of the Order with its crews wintered every year in Messina or Syracuse. The Gozitans were obliged to send their grain to Valletta. Most of the meat came from Sicily. Besides the limited resources of locally produced food, there was another disadvantage: the scarcity of wood. The Swabian merchant Samuel Kiechel observed in the late sixteenth century: 'Except for some cypress trees, there are hardly any trees on the whole island. The ovens where bread is baked are heated by the excrements of horses and donkeys. These excrements are dried by the sun and then burnt.' To compensate for this, wood was imported from Spain but this was more or less exclusively used for palaces, churches, and houses in Valletta.

Most of the cotton produced in Malta was sold directly to Sicily to be trafficked on the international market, as can be confirmed, for example, by an analysis of the arrival of goods at Palermo (*Responsali; Registri della Secrezia di Palermo*) between 1600 and 1605. Maltese cotton was especially popular to make high-quality sails. To a certain extent a similar trade must have also taken place in cumin which was shipped from Malta on small vessels to Messina and Palermo to be trafficked in international directions. That, long before the sixteenth century there was a local production of spun cotton, coarse cloth, linen, and even silk is well documented. The more costly products, such as fine linen, brocade, velvet, and damask, were imported frome France, Sicily, and Majorca. Textiles came from Valencia, London, Bruges, Florence,

The last windmill still standing on St Michael demi-bastion Valletta in a 19th-century photograph. Built by Fondazione Cotoner in 1674.

and Flanders. After 1580 the import of tapestry, furniture, and gold and silver items increased considerably in spite of the efforts of the grand masters to halt tendencies to extreme luxury and who forbade knights to import silver plates worth more than 600 marks' each. Still in 1600 Malta was not yet a place where much currency and variety of foreign coins circulated.

The drying of grapes to make raisins, the production of honey, the growing of barley, flax, pepper, melons, pomegranates, lemons, olives, oranges, almonds, figs, dates, and other type of fruits were mainly

A gold coin minted during the magistry of Adrien de Wignacourt (1690–97). In 1695 the grand master introduced a new gold denomination, the four zecchini coin. On the obverse St John is presenting the flag of the Order to the grand master.

Scenes from the equitorial jungles were introduced to Malta through the Gobelin Tapestries which were presented to the Order by Grand Master Perellos y Roccaful (1697–1720)

meant for the local market. In fact, from the 1580s onwards, local fruit production did not have seemed to have been enough to satisfy the needs of the increasing population of the Three Cities and Valletta any more.

Besides imports, the Maltese fishermen also supplied the local market with all type of fish. Also popular was the catching of the sea turtles in the channel between Malta and Sicily. The meat of these animals was sold to be eaten.

Late-sixteenth-century Malta with the building of Valletta, its various projects of new fortifications, and as residence for hundreds of the sons of the European aristocracy had much more needs than could

LINKS OF TRADE

be satisfied by Sicily only: iron, cloths, copper wire, nails, armour of all kinds, tools, and, of course, all types of luxury goods for the private use of the knights. In many respects the structure of the import of specialized goods and luxury goods for Malta in the 1580s could not be very different from the one of Sicily which imported cloth from England and Flanders, canvas from Holland, skins, iron, wood, paper, wool, tin, copper, leather, marble, linen, furniture, pictures, books, silk, Venetian glass, soap and nails from Venice, Leghorn, and Genoa.

Traditionally Sicily supplied Malta with wheat, wine, meat, vegetables, oil, spices, firewood, wax, and sugar. Spain sent over draperies; Venice, timber; and France, metal and munitions. This now started

Ġnien is-Sultan (the Grand Master's Garden) on the outskirts of Rabat, Malta. This fertile area yielded good-quality olives from the many trees which were planted here.

THE GRAND MASTER'S *GIOIA*

Every new grand master, within five years of his election, was expected to make a donation from his privy purse to the conventual church of St John. Very often the gioia or donation took the form of sacred vestments or works of art for the embellishment of the church. Perhaps the best known of these donations are the Flemish tapestries presented by Spanish Grand Master Ramon Perellos y Roccaful. The Flemish tapestries at St John's form the largest complete collection in the world. The set consisting of 29 pieces was ordered from the Brussels atelier of Judecos de Vos for 40,000 scudí and was based on cartoons by Peter Paul Rubens. The entire set consists of 14 large scenes depicting the life of Christ and allegories and 14 panels representing the Virgin Mary, Christ the Saviour, and the Apostles. It reached Malta by 1701. Later Perellos also donated a set of Gobelin tapestries to the magisterial palace. The last set of vestments and furnishings which the church of St John received from the grand masters was that donated by French Grand Master Emanuel Rohan Polduc. Rohan's gioia was made of cloth of silver delicately embroidered with flowers and with the donor's armorial bearings, and consisted of chasuble, five dalmatics, nine copes, and four altar frontals.

to change gradually. Some of these goods, mostly ironware and cloth, were now trafficked by the English and Dutch. That the Order already at the beginning of its residence in Malta had discussed an eventual freer trade is confirmed by a papal brief of 1 October 1530 when Clement VII granted it the right to trade 'freely with the Infidel in foodstuffs, that is, grain, fodder, vegetables, wine, oil, and other provisions; and to this effect, to sell to the said Infidels in or outside Malta, even in countries of the same Infidels, tin and bronze in small quantities and provided these will not be used for artillery purposes'. Another aspect which inevitably must drive Malta more and more in strongest dependency to foreign markets was the ever-increasing population, especially at the urban area round the Grand Harbour. In around 1590 Valletta had already about 4,000 inhabitants, while the Grand Harbour area was home to about 10,000 souls, including knights and their slaves and ship crews. By 1614 the number of inhabitants in Valletta had more than doubled.

Because of its importance, the English and Dutch approach to Malta and to the Mediterranean in general must be described in some more detail. In September 1581 a letter patent by Queen Elizabeth was granted to a 'Company of Merchants to the Levant' which prospered from the beginning and in the 1580s and 1590s was making profits of up to 300 per cent. Malta was considered as one stepping stone to the Levant. In 1582 the Order granted a safe-conduct to the English. In the following years the British ships brought over saltpetre, gunpowder, tin, steel, iron, copper, canvas, iron balls for shot, millstones, wood for ship-building, and coal. The studies by Andrew P. Vella, Alexander Bonnici, and Carmel Cassar, based on the archives of the Inquisition, give clear evidence how in the late 1570s and early 1580s the increasing number of English ship-owners, merchants, and sailors in Malta caused suspicion and interrogations by these authorities. That around 1600 the first English consul William Watts was appointed, was just a logical step.

There was also a considerable trade in armour, military instruments, and tools from South Germany and Austria to Sicily and Malta, but this was carried out by Venice and Genoa or by the Dutch. Very often Dutch ships transported German goods such as cinnabar, amber, copper wire, and iron to Italy and the Levant. To meet Dutch trading vessels in the Malta channel in the early 1600s was a common practice. With the fall of Antwerp, sacked in 1576, and the subsequent blocking of the Schelde for shipping, Flemish trade started to decline considerably. But the days of Venetian and Genoese glory were still not over. In fact the early seventeenth century was the great age of the revival of Genoese finance. Deeply connected with this political and economic transition was a change in culture and infrastructure. Malta was on the road of internationalization.

Filippo Paladini's frescoed frieze at the banqueting hall of Verdala castle describes the highlights of the life of Grand Master Hughues Loubenx de Verdalle (1582–95). Here the grand master receives congratulations for his election from Pope Gregory XIII. In 1587 he was nominated cardinal by Pope Sixtus V.

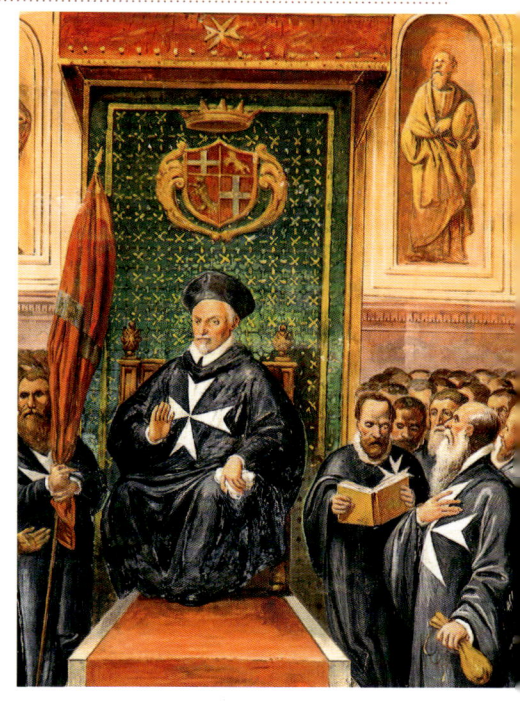

The building of Valletta from 1566 onwards was essential for absorbing European manpower and new ideas. Especially under the rule of the erudite French Grand Master Hugue Loubenx de Verdalle, the ambition and funds of the knights as well as their demands based on the idea of the Counter Reformation proved very fruitful for artistic commissions in Malta. The majority of these commissions were given for 'official' works, that is for churches or residences and palaces of high dignitaries and clerics. But even then a situation can be noticed where more and more knights in Malta and the local aristocracy were refining their taste and approach to art and started to commission works of art primarily for domestic 'use'.

In fact, the knights and their retinues preserved their original lifestyle and demands unchanged in Malta. This did not just mean that they brought their tailors, chefs, and craftsmen to Malta, but they also imported luxury goods of all type. The French compiler Pierre D'Avity who consulted the works of the sixteenth-century Andalusian scholar and traveller Luis Marmol y Carvajal and some French knights, wrote: 'With regards to the foreigners in Malta, every nationality prefers their very own style of fashion.' The knights and institutions of the Order were essential for a thriving trade in basic supplies as well as luxury goods. A famous example is the huge trade in ice for the Order's requirements and for

One of the huge water cisterns under Casa Rocca Piccola. The house had three cisterns. During World War Two the two larger wells were converted into bomb shelters, thus the central column and reinforced concrete platform.

wider local consumption. Most of it arrived direct from Mount Etna. In the second part of the seventeenth century, Don Diego Pappalardo, a conventual chaplain of the Order, had a monopoly of the ice-trade. Until the building of an aqueduct from Rabat to Valletta in the early seventeenth century, there was no sweet water in the new capital so everyone had to build a cistern. All building stones were taken direct from the place where the house was being built. That is the reason why every house in Valletta has a cellar. It was common knowledge that the Order was one of the 'big buyers of galley slaves'. The meeting point for slave dealers was *Piazza S. Giorgio* opposite the grand master's palace. Prices for slaves could vary from 30 to 300 crowns.

Contrary to the more and more prosperous region of the Grand Harbour, the old capital of Mdina experienced a decline. There was no real commerce and enterprise in Mdina and Rabat. The Mdina nobility was more or less driven to 'splendid isolation'. In Rabat there was the church of St Paul with its grotto whose miraculous stone was held in high esteem against poisoning. In around 1600 this became a considerable business and in Valletta there were craftsmen whose only job was to work this 'miraculous' stone into cups, dishes, and medals for export. At the end of the sixteenth century those items of folk medicine known as Maltese 'snake tongues', *Terra Melitensis* or *Terra di S. Paolo* were exported all over Europe in huge quantities and many witnesses reported that they saw ships being loaded daily with such items. In fact there were 'two' Malta's. The increasing prosperous conurbation of the *Porto Grande* with its cosmopolitan atmosphere and the *Malta rurale* more or less still untouched by the dynamic integration of Malta in the European and Mediterranean context.

All this reflects how, in the 1580s, Malta went through the crucial transition towards the patterns of Early Modern times which were essentially based on opening economic links and relations. The building of Valletta moved Hospitaller Malta away from its previous limitations and heavy dependency on Sicily and the Spanish hemisphere. This partly coincided and was partly caused and dynamized by the appearance of English and Dutch traders in the Mediterranean. This development found ready response in the open-minded and refined French grand master Hugues Loubenx de Verdalle who – despite the suspiciousness of the Roman inquisition against the influx of Northerners and new ideas – put Malta on a track towards a new 'de-Sicilianized' and cosmopolitan profile. The new forms of economic links and the new balance of power and economy in the Mediterranean were instrumental for this to happen.

In the 268-year-long rule of the Order, Malta changed radically from an almost completely agricultural society with a population dispersed in small villages over the island into

The Grotto of St Paul in Rabat, Malta. The limestone Terra di S. Paolo *excavated from this grotto was used all over Europe as an antidote against snake bites. It was even worn inside glass amulets to protect the bearer from poisonous snakes. Another legend said that the rock cut out of the grotto would conveniently grow out again during the night.*

174 The Rule of the Hospitallers

a society where 40 per cent lived in the prosperous harbour conurbation. Most of the Maltese and foreigners who lived in the harbour area made their living by the 'industry' of corsairing and privateering and by supplying the Order's navy. In the seventeenth century this became the most lucrative business on the island.

In the new emerging world of European capitalism and non-ecclesiastical and politically controlled enterprise, it was the 'physical' and geographical position of Malta and its resources and markets which came to matter. The term 'Bulwark of Europe' or the island of the 'heroic' knights was left to clerics, politicians, and historians. Generally speaking, on the one side there was still the ideal picture of the famous chivalric Order – in a way representing the dream of an armed *comunitas christiana* at a time when Christian Europe was torn apart in different religious and political factions. On the other side – and this is presented by the predecessors of a modern 'capitalistic' Europe – there is a vision of a society based on trade without military and religious frontiers. In this respect, the main *raison d'être* of the Order must have appeared as 'medieval' and anachronistic, not to say harmful for progress.

Naviglio del Secolo XVII.
The ships of the Order in the 17th century. Adapted from an illustration by Fra Opizio Guidotti.
National Library of Malta.

Behind the scene

Besides the official glorious picture of Malta as the brave shield of Europe which was distributed in so many descriptions and accounts as well as visually promoted in art, maps, and engravings, there was an unofficial – maybe more realistic – side as well. From the start Hospitaller Malta could never develop into a place of European unity and a refuge of Roman Catholic harmony in troubled times, as it was imagined by many. The effects of a politically divided Europe, the traditional conflict between the Hapsburg empire and the French crown, and the new movements of Lutheranism and Calvinism were also felt in remote Malta. That the Order in Malta was far from being a unity is apparent in various instances. From the beginning of the establishment in Malta the Order went through much internal hardship and discord. The members of the Order, hailing from different, sometimes belligerent, countries at times put their national interests before everything else. In the sixteenth and seventeenth century there was an especially strong tension between the three French langues, Auvergne, and Provence and the two langues from the Iberian peninsula, Castille and Aragon. The commanderies and priories of the Order all over Europe linked Malta with the European mainland and left no space – neither politically, nor economically and culturally – to escape. When, after 1530, the lands of Brandenburg in the German empire became Protestant, even the local bailiwick of the Order followed suit, but remained part of the Order by special dispensation. Much worse was the effect of English politics when in 1540 Henry VIII confiscated the Order's property and the English langue became dormant.

But there were also some massive internal problems. Already in the seventeenth century, there was an obvious discrepancy between the statutes of the Order and how many knights were actually behaving. Officially the term of the 'Bulwark of Europe' for Malta was well deserved until the seventeenth century, when the knights retained a solid internal attitude towards their institution and its ideology. Before the winds of change of the enlightenment and the new national state concepts, the Order was more or less not hit by the *crise de la conaissance européenne*. Throughout the seventeenth century, there was hardly any tendency to reformism and personal ideological doubts. In 1689, for example, the knight Jean-Baptiste de Cany wrote two over 600-page-long manuscript volumes about *'Réflessions d'un chevalier de Malte sur la grandeur et les devoirs de son état'* (NLM, Library MS. 324), in which he

The frontispiece of the third edition of Giacomo Bosio's Historia della Santa Religione et illustrissima militia dei Cavalieri di San Giovanni di Gerusalemme, *Rome, 1594.*

Symbols of the values of the Order; 17th-century engraving, from the book Giouco D'Armi Dei Sovrani e Degli Stati d'Europa, *penned by the Jesuit priest Claude-Oronce Fine de Brianville in 1659, and translated into Italian by Bernardo Giustiniano in 1725. This book, at the National Library, was specifically dedicated to Grand Master Manoel de Vilhena.*

represented the gist of the concept of the Order as still the same as that in high medieval times, with a mission to serve the poor, carry out works of mercy, and to serve and defend the faith. *Pauvreté*, *obéisme*, and *chasteté* were still its main pillars. What was new was the adaptation of some aspects of the new concept of the refined seventeenth-century *honnête homme*: prudence, justice, temperance, and *mépris de la douleur*. The ideology and *raison d'être* of the Order still had the old goal to 'carry out the vengeance of the Lord against the persecutors of his Church'. Some young knights continued to live according to these standards. Returning from a caravan, the Chevalier Gabriel de la Ferté (1644–1702) wrote to his parents:

'It is rather difficult not to get sick during these naval campaigns .... but when one thinks that they are undertaken for the sake of God one feels consoled and compensated for all these hardships.' One of the last exponents of this fighting spirit of a *soldat du Christ* and the strong antagonism against the Muslim world was the *Balí* de Chambray. In his *Mémoires*, he wrote: 'In the lands of the infidels the term "honour" does not exist.'

Behind the curtain, however, it was very often different. Concerning the difficulty of Grand Master Lascaris in taming the life style of the young conventual chaplains of the Order, Inquisitor Fabio Chigi wrote to Rome in 1636: 'Instead of obeying to the rules of their

A guva, *an underground prison cell, used to hold errant knights. This one is in Fort St Angelo, Birgu, just opposite the chapel of the Nativity of Our Lady. This* guva, *practically an oval hole in the ground, 3.3 by 4.2 m and 3.4 m deep, has its walls decorated with graffiti. The earliest one is by Frà Jeronimo Palan, dated 7 August 1532.*

religion and their statutes ... a good number of these knights go out at night and lead a life of bad habits and bad vices.' Besides the increasing libertarian life style of the knights, Malta in the seventeenth century became one of the major places for violence, fraud, and imposture south of Naples. This followed the great influx of men from all over Europe after the Great Siege and the building of Valletta. One major reason of violence, however, was the mostly young knights who lived on the island. An impressive number of knights were imprisoned in Fort St Angelo at various times and there were regular clashes between foreigners and locals or between soldiers of the Order and foreigners.

Besides these personal clashes, there was also tension on the public level, namely the conflicts between the different jurisdictional powers of the grand master, the bishop, and the inquisition who all had individual powers over their subjects. The bitterest fights were between the Order and the inquisition. The inquisitor was vested with several functions: he was responsible for the custody of the Faith while, as apostolic delegate, he was the official representative of the pope in Malta. The knights soon came to regard the inquisitor as an intruder in their country. Besides the common quarrels between the langues of the Order and officials, there were regular clashes with the inquisition. A good example for the attitude of the knights against the inquisition is a comment by Grand Hospitaller de Boccage: 'Who can answer for the just indignation of a high-spirited company of warriors of illustrious birth, against the usurpation of their liberties and privileges by a stranger sent here solely for jurisdiction over heresy.' The aggression of the knights was not only directed against the inquisitor. In 1639 it came to a conflict with the Jesuits. Except the prominent members Fr. Sebastiano Salelles and Fr. Theoderich Bech, all Jesuits were exiled to Scicli in Sicily. Grand Master Lascaris had to obey the majority of the knights in this affair.

Because of the complicated jurisdictional and political situation Malta became drenched in a situation of denunciation and blackmail. In its function to control the state of faith the inquisition not only turned its eye on the members of the Order but also on the bishop. In 1646 Inquisitor Pannelini wrote to Rome to complain about the way how Bishop Balaguer acted his office:

The clerici *never serve in his churches .... They live* alla Francese *or* all'Lombardi, *they carry weapons, have children, are masons, tavern-keepers, butchers, but cannot do guard service (for the island defence, under the command of the Religion) because they keep no horses, and they refuse to pay customs and taxes ... This mode of life and behavior of Mgr Balaguer, has constrained the Prince (grand master) to abhor him and the Religon to loathe him as a monstrosity, and the people too detest him.*

What was also a taboo to mention in most of the published works was the tension between the Order and the Maltese. A manuscript 'Relazione di Malta' written around 1660 preserved in the 'Fondo Barberini Latino' of the Biblioteca Vaticana (Biblioteca Vaticana, Fondo Barberini Latino, MS. 5353) lists some reasons for this tension and gives valuable insight into the attitude of the Maltese against the Order:

The Maltese accuse the knights of treating them like slaves and not like subjects. They damage their honour and even the grand master does not interfere much in this bad situation. He more or less just follows what the grand crosses tell him and does not interest himself how the situation of his subjects really is ... Therefore many Maltese suffer and have lost their hope that the situation one day will improve and that in future they will be respected as citizens.

In the sixteenth and seventeenth century, these tensions were intensified in periods of famine.

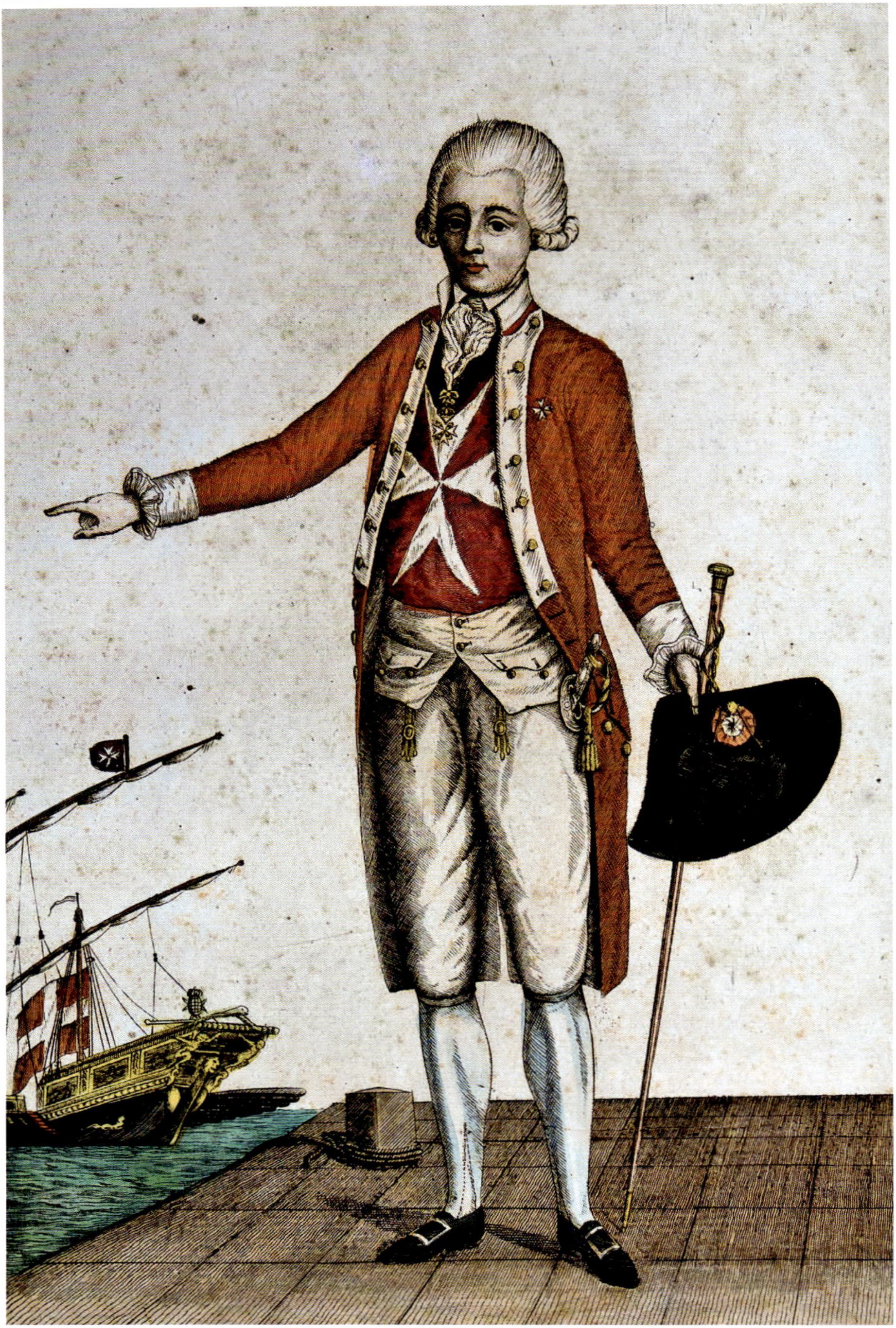

New cultural horizons

The urban concentration on the harbour also changed the intellectual and cultural life. Until the middle of the sixteenth century, it was the Mdina grammar school and the teachers of the monastic convents in Mdina and Rabat which influenced the upbringing of the intellectual *elité*. The arrival of the Order opened the door to an influx of foreign know-how and intellectuals. Malta opened up to international movements and influences. Most of the Maltese intellectuals and men of letters – very often members of the clergy or religious orders – had received their final education in Catania, Naples, or Rome. Some Maltese scholars as Giovanni Myriti and Giovanni Francesco Buonamico were even trained in French, Dutch and German universities. A most successful career of a Maltese abroad in the eighteenth century was that of Joseph Barth who was appointed surgeon to Empress Maria Theresa and her son Emperor Joseph II.

There are many indications how Malta underwent an intensively dynamic transformation after the Great Siege and the economic developments which followed. The Grand Harbour area developed towards Mediterranean and European cosmopolitanism. That meant wider artistic prospects and increasing refinement. It was a big step from the impression Jean Quintin D'Autun had of Birgu in the 1530s ('Apart from the city and some houses in the suburb, one would take all the rest for African huts') and the cosmopolitan and multifaceted conurbation of the Grand Harbour of the late seventeenth century. The previously provincial artistic milieu of the islands – heavily deriving from Sicilian and Aragonese sources – was deeply transformed in the late sixteenth century. One of the main driving forces behind this development was the building of Valletta, with its subsequent influx of foreign craftsmen and artists. This was mirrored in the increasing mobility and outlook and in the absorption of foreign artistic talent and new ideas. Indeed, at the beginning of the seventeenth century, Malta had become fully integrated in European culture and heritage, and recognized as such.

After the Great Siege, financial aid from Philip II of Spain and the pope realized Master de Valette's dream of building a new fortified city on a promontory with an important harbour on either side. Lack of funds had not allowed the plans of eminent architects like Bartolomeo Genga to materialize earlier. By 1571 the convent of the Order could move from Birgu to Valletta. The chief

A captain-general of the galleys; c.1790. An illustration from Libr. MS. 1165 by Francesco Zimelli (1748-1803) Malta National Library.

architect of the whole project was the Italian Francesco Laparelli. In subsequent decades this new city – both a symbol of the desire for a unified Christendom and a shield for Christian Europe – attracted the vivid interest of whole Europe. Famous architects like the Alsatian Daniel Specklin studied its concept.

Malta before the arrival of the Order lay firmly within the Sicilian and Aragonese artistic hemisphere. Until the mid-sixteenth century the impact of the Renaissance was hardly felt in Malta. The public and private patronage of the Order and its rich members changed this. Still, until the end of the sixteenth century, Malta could not attract any major European artist, with the exception of Matteo Perez d'Aleccio. The arrival of accomplished artists like Filippo Paladini, Michelangelo Merisi da Caravaggio, and, maybe, Lionello Spada during the reigns of Grand Masters Loubenx de Verdalle and Aloph de Wignacourt had particular reasons and can hardly be interpreted as the result of the attractive artistic scene on the island. Paladini came to Malta because he was an oarsman on a galley, while Caravaggio came because remote Malta promised him a temporary exile after a long list of criminal incidents in Rome and Naples and Grand Master Wignacourt too readily

Francesco Laparelli's Plan A of Valletta, June 1566. This was his first plan which concentrated on the fortifications. Accademia Etrusca, Cortona, Italy.

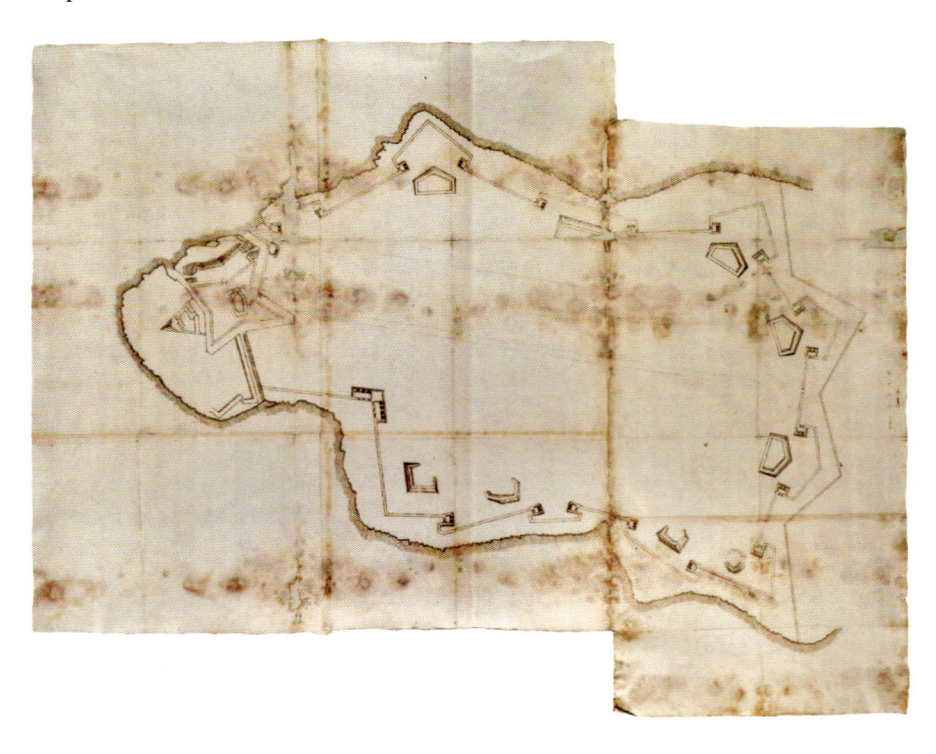

The Long Ward of the Sacra Infermeria, *is considered as the largest hall in Europe. The work on the hospital started in 1574 under architect Gerolamo Cassar (c.1520–92). The ward is 155 m long, 10.5 m wide, and more than 11 m high.*

responded to his desires to become a member of the Order. Lionello Spada was for a time a close follower of Caravaggio and his alleged coming to Malta might have been linked with the latter's sojourn on the island. Yet Caravaggio's impact on the local art scene was only temporary.

Much more influential was the arrival of the great Mattia Preti in 1661. It can truly be said that Preti's works introduced the art of the high baroque to Malta. Preti lived almost 40 years in Malta and carried out a tremendous *oeuvre*. Other important artists of the seventeenth century also came to Malta but had much shorter sojourns on the island. One was the friend of Murillo's and knight of St John Pedro Nuñez de Villavicencio, a very talented painter. Another well-known artist who then made it to Malta was the German 'Vasari', Joachim von Sandrart.

The climax of baroque splendour in Malta was reached under the vainglorious Spanish Grand Master Nicolas Cotoner (1663–80). In the second half of the seventeenth century the life style of the knights took a definite turn and their pretensions for glory and fame were best fulfilled. The ambitious 'Cottonera' fortification project was started, the conventual church of St John's was converted according to baroque patterns, and the *Sacra Infermeria* was embellished and enlarged to become the biggest hospital in the world. But, as if to recall the fragile structure of baroque splendour and fame and to crystallize the idea of *memento mori*,

Malta was struck by the most disastrous plague epidemic of its history in 1676 which caused the death of over 11,000 inhabitants and lead to a period of hunger and despair.

The interlink between the political and cultural developments can be shown by various examples. It is still difficult to have a balanced view of the real extent of the Ottoman threat to Europe and the Christian Mediterranean. Surely the Ottoman military power was overestimated but, for tiny Malta, the danger of an Ottoman attack remained clear and present until the eighteenth century. It determined the entire structure of the Order and had deep effects on town-planning and the organization of urban space on Malta. The building of Valletta and the ambitious projects of Grand Masters Rafael and Nicolas Cotoner in the seventeenth century provide ample proof. Throughout its rule in Malta, the Order called to the island the most highly reputed military engineers and architects to examine its fortifications and to develop concepts to make the island safer. Bartolomeo Genga, Francesco Laparelli, Pietro Paolo Floriani, Francesco Buonamici, and Count Antonio Maurizio Valperga are just a few well-known names who worked on these projects. In the eighteenth century, it was well-known civil architects of private residences, palaces and churches – like Romano Carapecchia and Stefano Ittar – who found a ready market in Malta. Still the Order did not cease updating the fortifications. In the mid-eighteenth century the fort above Gozo's harbour of Mġarr was built thanks to the private funding of the naval hero *Balí* Jacques François Chambray.

Besides Verdalle and the Cotoners, it was certainly Grand Master António Manoel de Vilhena who contributed most to the artistic shaping of the island. He brought the latest artistic fashions from Italy and Spain to Malta. The idea of building a fortress on the island in Marsamxett harbour to protect Valletta had been conceived at the end of the seventeenth century, but it was Vilhena who made it a reality. Other projects of his were the Vilhena palace (1730) in Mdina– now the Natural History Museum – and the Manoel Theatre (1732) in Valletta. An outstanding benefactor of the arts, Vilhena commissioned foreign as well as local artists, like Nicolò Nasoni, Pietro Paolo Troisi, and Enrico Arnaud to carry out important works. The religious Orders greatly benefitted from his munificence. Owing to his developments in Floriana, the suburb was called *Borgo Vilhena* for some time.

Opposite page: Mqabba – A plaque was placed in 1776 to commemorate a cemetery of the 1675 plague in front of the 15th- and 16th-century churches of St Basil and St Michael.

Right: Another façade remodelled by architect Romano Carapecchia was that of the first building of Valletta, Our Lady of Victories (1690).

During the rule of Vilhena's predecessor, Perellos y Roccaful, the eminent architect Romano Carapecchia moved from Rome to Malta and he went on to change the face of many Maltese urban spaces. He brought over the Late Roman type of Baroque which started to shape the silhouette and character of Valletta and some villages of the island. His façade of St Lawrence church at Vittoriosa (1691) soon became the model for many Maltese eighteenth-century churches. In 1706 he was promoted to the post of chief architect of the Order. He also designed the new façade of the church of Our Lady of Victories at Valletta (1690). Not all commissions came from the Order.

In 1738 Carapecchia designed a small palace in St Julian's for the rich Italian *Balí* Spinola. Important contributions were his rebuilding or remodelling of four of the chapels of the seven langues of the Order. Other significant works by Carapecchia where the nunnery of St Catherine and its adjoining church (1714), the Municipal Palace (*c*.1719–20), the annexes to St John's, and the Manoel Theatre, all in Valletta. He rebuilt the Franciscan priories in St Lucy Street and in Republic Street in Valletta (1733) and constructed the chapel of St Anthony of Padua in Fort Manoel (1725). The first of these commissions, the building of the chapel of St James with its elliptical plan, created a new form of church architecture in Malta.

In the 1720s the Italian painter and architect Nicolò Nasoni used Malta as a stepping-stone for a glorious career in Portugal. He mainly worked in the grand master's palace and the former treasury of the Order. While Nasoni only stayed a relatively short time on the island, after 1744 the French artist Antoine Favray made Malta his permanent home where, in over 40 years of

Frà Paolo Rafael Spinola, admiral of the fleet of the Order, built the original Spinola Palace in St Julian's in 1688. The façade was designed by Romano Carapecchia (1668–1738) in 1733 commissioned by the admiral's nephew.

Opposite page: The ceiling frescoes of the main hall of the Vecchia Cancelleria *(former treasury of the Order) in Piazza S. Giorgio. This is the work of Nicolò Nasoni, a painter from Siena who worked in Malta from 1723 to 1725.*

BAROQUE MALTA 187

The new Bibliotheca *designed by Stefano Ittar (1730–90) was the last major building project of the Order before the knights left Malta.*

residence, he had a deep influence on the local art scene. It might truly be said that it was him who introduced the French rococo style on Malta. He immediately established himself in Malta as a much appreciated artist and received commissions from the Order, the Church, and private persons. In subsequent years he adapted his French rococo training to his southern artistic environment and convention. Many of his paintings have local associations. Most of his fame rests on his numerous portraits of dignitaries of the Order. In 1751 Portuguese Grand Master Pinto de Fonseca received Favray as a *servant d'armes*. His *passaggio* for admission in the Order were the two semi-circular lunette paintings on the wall of the atrium to the oratory of St John's. Symbol of the absolutistic pretensions of Grand Master Pinto are Favray's full-length portraits of the Portuguese grand master.

The last important commissions by the Order in Malta were given to foreign artists. When the council decided to erect a new library in the early 1780s, it was the plan of the architect of Polish descendance Stefano Ittar that was chosen. The *Bibliotheca* in Valletta is a fully neo-classical building with monumental columns on its façade. The main hall measures about 5,600 square feet and it has five large windows. After Ittar's death in January 1790, the building was finished under the supervision of the Maltese architect Antonio Cachia.

Creating identities – religion and politics

Since high medieval times, the Catholic religion was inextricably intertwined with Malta's historical processes. With the help of the local clergy, especially the alleged presence of St Paul as described in the Acts of the Apostles (XXVII, XXVIII) became the root of Maltese identity. This process had already started in the fourteenth and fifteenth centuries. Indeed the dedication of the Mdina cathedral and other patronages show that St Paul's shipwreck on the island and his reputed foundation of the local Church headed by the first 'bishop', St Publius, meant a strong claim to a tradition dating back to well before the foundation of the Order. However, it needed the cosmopolitan and international Order to implement these traditions in the minds of Christian Europe. In the sixteenth century the Pauline Cult in Malta became deeply linked with the Maltese national identity. How soon the Order realized the potential religious, political, and cultural possibilities of the Pauline Cult is shown by its effort to incorporate St Paul's Grotto in Rabat in its own domains and administration. The grotto was believed to be the place where Paul was imprisoned in AD 60. In late medieval times it was turned into a modest place of worship and local pilgrimage. During the sixteenth century – when the establishment of the Order attracted more and more foreigners to Malta – the grotto was turned into an international devotional centre. Thanks to the efforts

Portrait of Juan de Venegas, by Pietro Erardi, St Paul's Collegiate Church, Rabat, Malta.

of the Andalusian Juan de Venegas, this international devotion reached a climax in the early seventeenth century. Venegas obtained many relics from Italy and Spain for the grotto and its adjacent church and was responsible for the erection of a college of chaplains to take care of the grotto.

The extraordinary national and international success of Venegas's activities can only be understood in connection with the movement of the Counter Reformation and the seventeenth-century *Zeitgeist*. A most significant part of the ecclesiastical programme of the Counter Reformation was the revival of the holy traditions of pilgrimages and their aims to rebuild or extend old monuments in the new baroque style, thereby practically creating new ones. Venegas's efforts to restore and subsequently build the churches of St Publius and St Paul are a visible proof of this movement. The apologetic and 'propagandistic' mission started by Venegas helped to make St Paul's Grotto a very impressive place of devotion. Duke Ferdinand of Mantua (1620) enriched the grotto with a fragment of the arm-bone of St Paul and the 1615 pastoral visitation of Bishop Baldassare Cagliares records five altars at the grotto.

In 1617 Grand Master Aloph de Wignacourt incorporated the grotto and the college into the domain of the Order. To have an important Pauline shrine under its dominion raised the prestige of the State of the Order as well. It was only logical that the grand masters should try to exploit this cult to further their own power, history, and glory. The support of the various grand masters for, and their many bequests to St Paul's Grotto make it evident that the Order kept on fostering the

The golden arm with the relic of the arm of St Paul at the collegiate church of St Paul in Rabat. The bone rests on a cubical gold plinth with the duke of Mantua's coat of arms inside a hexagonal crystal box.

Pauline Tradition also to further its own political ends. Shortly after Venegas had ceded the grotto with all its buildings to the Order, Wignacourt erected an institution for chaplains to look after the grotto. They resided in a *Collegio* just across the road from the grotto and Venegas was nominated as the first rector of this new institution. This extended baroque promotion of the Pauline Cult gave rise to an even wider 'utilization' of the places connected with St Paul. It was no coincidence that in the period of Venegas's activities in Malta the small chapel in St Paul's Bay (*Cala di S. Paolo*) was enlarged and adorned with precious works of art. Also the use of handbills to testify the authenticity of *Terra di S. Paolo* – earth from the grotto was a highly reputed antidote – seemed to have originated during the times of Venegas and might have been encouraged by himself. It is all too clear that the Order aimed to twin the Pauline Cult with that of St John the Baptist. Within a more global context, this political move was to run parallel with the fusion of Maltese identity with that of the Order. That more and more paintings showed St Paul and St John together documents how the Order fostered this fusion even visually and iconographically. Throughout the Order's rule, St Paul's shipwreck, preaching, and miracles in Malta were depicted in works of art on all media, from altarpieces to canvases, sculptures, drawings, engravings, silverware, and cartography.

Alessandro Algardi, Beheading of St Paul, *Museum of St Paul's Collegiate Church, Wignacourt College. Originally this magnificent bronze* tondo *was the centre piece of the antipendium of the altar of the chapel in St Paul's Grotto.*

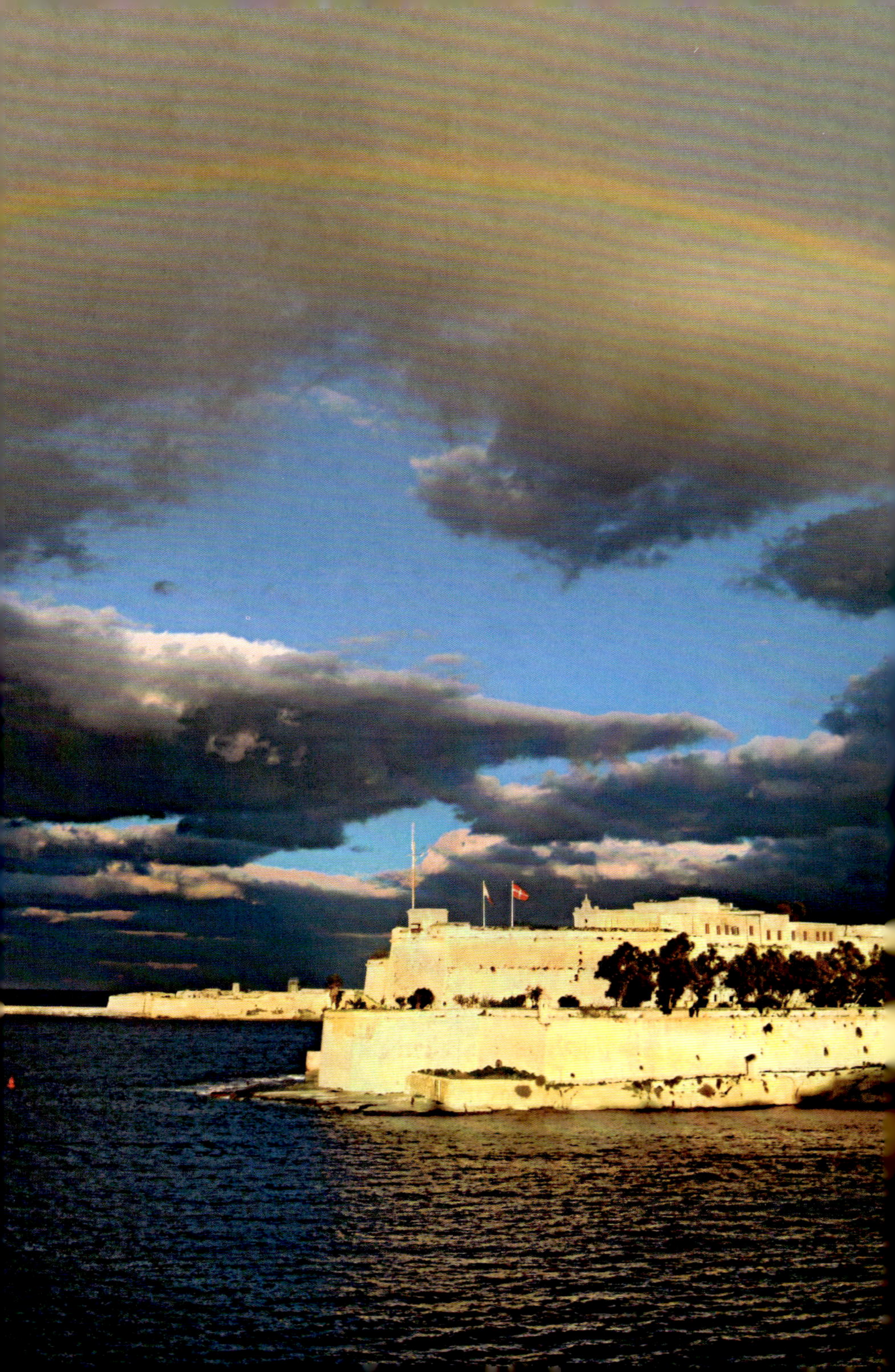

That, in the 18th century, the Ottoman empire more and more became 'tamed' and integrated into peace treaties with European powers made it difficult for the knights to keep its famous **corso** *alive. With the fading away of the old Muslim-Christian antagonism, a column of the knights* raison d'être *started to disappear.*

Chapter 7

The eighteenth century
last splendour and dark clouds

New horizons and a dangerous road

To understand the role of Hospitaller Malta in the eighteenth century, one has to focus on some more global political developments which had started in the second half of the seventeenth century. At the end of the seventeenth century, the era of smaller powers in Mediterranean drew to an end. In the eighteenth century, England and France and, to a certain extent, Austria and Spain did leave not much room for free political activities of the minor powers, such as Venice, Tuscany, and Malta. Although Maltese privateering and the Order's caravans continued in the eighteenth century, it was obvious that they had lost their traditional importance. By the 1750s, trade had become the predominant element in Maltese shipping.

Parts of the fortifications of the Three Cities dating back to the late medieval period and the 16th century certainly were outdated by 18th-century standards. In case of a siege these old walls could not withheld the new and drastically improved fire-power of the guns. Fort St Angelo was transformed into a modern fort during the 18th century.

The treaty of Karlowitz (1699) and the Spanish War of Succession (1701–14) marked a new era of Mediterranean history. The 13-year-long war was to have a very deep effect on the Order, not least in the change brought about in the traditional pattern of diplomatic power. The war not only split the continent, but also put the Order into the middle of a bitter fight between major backers of the brotherhood, Spain, France, and the Hapsburg empire. It was a most difficult task for the Hospitallers striving to keep their neutrality.

A portolan chart of the Mediterranean in 1563 by Portuguese cartographer Diogo Homem. Biblioteca Nazionale, Florence.

Spanish Grand Master Ramon Perellos y Roccaful reigned during these troubled times on the international scene which also experienced the evolution of the nation-state which went against the very structure of the Order. England and France emerged as the new superpowers and this would cause the Order to face new realities. In the subsequent decades the big nations like France, England, and, to a certain extent, Russia and Austria installed themselves as Mediterranean powers. It was no coincidence that the first Russian delegation reached Malta in 1698 during Perellos' magistracy. The most prominent member was the Russian field marshal and victor of the battle of Asov, Bojar

Boris Petrovich Sheremetev (Russian: Борис Петрович Шереметев) (1652-1719) was the first appointed Russian count (1706). A military leader and diplomat, he was the general-field-marshal during the Great Northern War. Painting at the Taleon Sheremetev Palace, St Petersburg.

Boris Petrovitch Sheremetev, who visited Malta in May of that year. But Perellos was too cautious to accept the proposal of a Russo-Maltese ally against the Ottomans as this would have involved the Order in the international struggle for European dominance. Perellos fully realized that, in this new political environment, the Order's policies against the Ottomans and the North African beylerbeys could not follow any more the old patterns of hostility. At that time the Ottoman empire and most of the North African states were widely integrated in a net of European treaties, contracts, and secret alliances owing to economic reasons. Contrary to what Grand Masters Carafa and Adrien de Wignacourt had done during the war of the Morea, Perellos hesitated to support the Venetians in their war against the Ottomans between 1714 and 1718. Yet Malta's policy of neutrality was a difficult task and complaints from the English as well as from the French and the Spanish sides were heard more than once.

Even as regards internal matters and reforms Perellos tried to keep the institution on the right track. The costly naval squadron was reduced to seven and the *Consolato del Mare* was founded while relations with some North African beys began to turn away from outright enmity. The Portuguese Vilhena (1722–36) was the grand master who took up this road of liberalization and opened contacts further. Some of the main achievements of his reign was the drawing up of the legislative code (*Leggi e costituzioni prammaticali*) in 1723 and the remarkable efforts he made to strengthen Maltese trade. He also cut custom duties. Especially important was the reduction of the tax on transhipment of cargo which boosted Malta's role as an important transit port. Already feeling the grip of the European super-powers, Vilhena opened up new diplomatic contacts with the North African beylerbeys and the Ottomans. Still one of the more exciting episodes of Maltese history during his rule was the planned Turkish attack on Malta in late June 1722. A real attack however never materialized. His achievements and prudent balance of politics led Pope Benedict XIII to grant Vilhena the stock and pilier. He was the first grand master to receive such a recognition.

In the subsequent decades the political stage in Europe as well as in the Mediterranean began to change for one main reason: the entry of Russia into European politics. The Order was affected by this too. In fact one of the keys for the destiny of the Order laid in Russia's hands. This certainly could not be foreseen at the beginning of a century still marked by a French hegemony in thought and culture. As already indicated, Perellos insisted on the strict neutrality of the Order and refused Czar Peter's proposal for a military alliance against the Turks. This attempt at approchment with Malta to gain support against the traditional Turkish enemy, however, opened an important path in Russo-Maltese relations which would last throughout the eighteenth century. Again and again – especially during the long reign of Czarina Catherine II – such proposals were made by Russia. Very often the Russian sovereigns wanted to use Malta's excellent harbours as a base against the Ottomans but, mainly due to the interventions of France and Spain, these plans never materialized. Even during the Russo-Turkish wars of the 1770s and 1780s, the Order never officially abandoned its policy of 'friendly' neutrality. Behind this façade, however, a large number of knights had since the 1760s favoured closer relations with Russia, the emerging European power. In fact there were several secret close contacts and well-prepared plans to support a Russian presence in the Mediterranean. That Malta began to play an important part in Russia's

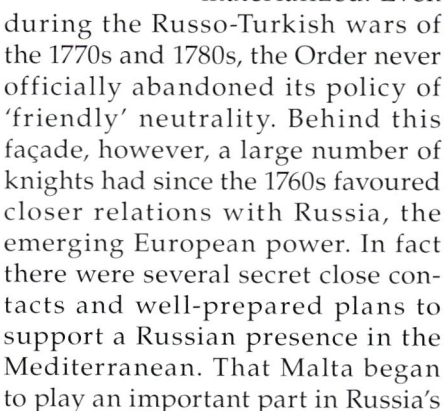

The statue of Vilhena by Pietro Paolo Troisi was inaugurated in 1736 and placed in the courtyard of Manoel Island. It is now situated at Floriana.

Mediterranean policies is reflected by the several so-called *chargés d'affaires*, envoys, and officers sent to the island.

Unfortunately, this was also the period when the Order was led by some figures whose competence was certainly inferior to their desire for power and majesty. Due to his importance for the Order's policies in the eighteenth century, a few words may be dedicated to Manoel Pinto de Fonseca. In Malta he is best known as the grand master who ruled longest (1741–73) and for his energetic personality. Hardly did any other grand master take greater pride in his majestic image. Politically Pinto was a follower of a concept of state and absolute power which was already outdated when he came into power.

From the very beginning of his magistracy, he had expressed his ambitions. As if to make up for the waning international importance of his tiny principality, Pinto crafted his majestic image on that of the absolute princes of the early eighteenth century. Since the late sixteenth century, the grand master's coat of arms had been surmounted by an open crown but Pinto now adopted the closed crown to underline that he alone was the Prince of Malta. Obviously he was most conscious of the concepts of cameralism and mercantilism. He tried to introduce new local industries, especially the silk industry. Mulberry trees were planted in the plain of Marsa and Sicilian workers were brought to teach the art of silk growing to the peasants. The grand master also encouraged tunny fishing. At the same moment he also halted prosperity by increasing taxation. Two milestones in his long rule were the expulsion of the Jesuits (April 1768) and the foundation of the university (1767/69).

A detail from Favray's full-portrait painting of Grand Master Pinto at St John's Co-Cathedral where Pinto is seen pointing to his sovereign crown.

Other events well-known in Pinto's magistracy were the crisis in Turco-Maltese relations because of the affair of the *Corona Ottomana* (1761) when Christian slaves captured a huge Turkish vessel and sailed it to Malta and the tensions between the Order and the Kingdom of Naples in the 1750s. The latter affair had shown in an exemplary form how far Pinto was ready to go to defend the sovereignty of his tiny principality. Basically the tension had started when young King Charles of Naples (later Charles III of Spain) had claimed the right, in view of the ancient feudal suzerainty of his crown over Malta, to interfere in the

198 Last Splendour and Dark clouds

ecclesiastical jurisdiction by appointing a *Regio Visitatore* to make, on his behalf as patron, a spiritual visitation of the diocese of Malta. Pinto refused and relations between Malta and Naples were broken. Even the essential flow of provisions from Sicily to Malta was halted. Pinto turned for help to Louis XV of France who intimated that he would assist the Order by force if necessary, in maintaining their rights against Naples.

In general Pinto always tried to remain on the best of terms with France – the most important protector of the affairs of the Order up to the French Revolution. In June 1765

Portuguese Grand Master Manoel Pinto de Fonseca (1741–73). 68th grand master of the Order.
Mosaic portrait from his mausoleum in St John's Co-Cathedral.

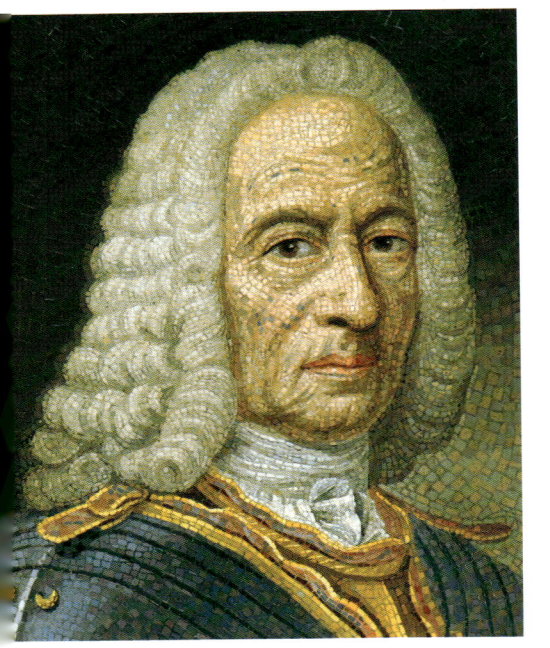

Aragonese Grand Master Francisco Ximenes de Texada (1773–75). The 69th grand master of the Order.
San Anton Palace, unknown artist.

King Louis XV had decreed that 'all inhabitants of the Islands under the domination of the Order of Malta shall be deemed to be nationals of the kingdom of France, where they are entitled to settle, acquire movable and immovable property ...'. The tensions with Naples and the subsequent interruption of provisions from Sicily had shown again the fragile nature of Hospitaller Malta. Pinto, in fact, kept all options open and even kept good contacts with the beys of Tripoli and Tunis and other North African states. For a while it was thought that Malta would be supplied with North African grain and wheat. Pinto's rule made him everything but popular among the local population and there were

INTERIOR PROBLEMS

French Grand Master Emmanuel de Rohan-Polduc (1775–97). The 70th grand master of the Order. Wignacourt Museum, unknown artist.

moments of tension and rumours of rebellion. His death in 1773 was received with satisfaction and joy. When Pinto died, the Treasury of the Order was in such a perilous state that his successors Ximenes de Texada and Rohan had to overhaul the whole financial system.

But the Order certainly was not only concerned with these Maltese internal affairs. On a global scale the rise of Russia to a major power in Europe was not only felt by its direct neighbours Poland, Prussia, and Austria. With the decline of the Ottoman empire, this also greatly affected the Mediterranean. For the cosmopolitan Order of St John with possessions all over Europe, this development was of the utmost importance. How less space for political moves the Order had is

GRAND MASTER XIMENES BURIAL PLACE

Detail from Charles Frederick de Brocktorff's illustration of St John's Crypt in c.1830

Spanish Grand Master Francisco Ximenes de Texada (1773–75) is buried in the crypt of St John beneath the pavement without a single line to mark the spot where he lies. This strange burial somewhat reflects and symbolizes his unpopularity with his subjects and with many members of the Order. After his predecessor Pinto de Fonseca had left a budget in deep debt for reasons of economy Ximenes de Texada decided to dismiss a number of officials and reduced the salaries of many others. He also increased the price of corn, and imposed limitations upon the pursuit of game.

A negative 'highlight' of his rule was the so called 'Rising of the Priests' in 1775. A group of Maltese led by some members of the local clergy rebelled against the Order and while most of the fleet of the Order was out at sea managed to seize Fort St Elmo. It was later maintained that this rebellion was instigated by the representative of Russia at Malta, the Marquis de Cavalcabo. However, no archival proof could be found for that yet. Ximenes de Texada convened the Sacrad Council and in a short time the rebels gave up.

shown when, in 1768, discussions were held in Malta about supporting the Russians in their fight against the Ottomans; very soon the grand master received a note from Louis XV expressing the French king's deep discontent with the Order's involvement with Russian plans. The French even threatened to confiscate the property of the three French langues should the knights insist in joining the Russian attack against the Ottomans, 'the most loyal of the French allies'. Pinto immediately obeyed the French wishes.

Even Pinto's successors, Francisco Ximenes de Texada and Emanuel Rohan de Polduc, did not have many options to move the Order out of French influence. The more than twenty years of rule by the latter marked a decisive period in the Order's history. Rohan's summoning of the chapter-general in November 1776 was a sign of good will to change the 'absolutistic' attitude of previous grand masters. It was, however, too late to make much difference in a situation in which the Order no longer had control of its own destiny but more or less depended entirely on the policies of the European powers. The 1776 chapter-general clearly showed the efforts to create better ties between the Order and the local population. It enacted the formation of the Regiment of Malta and of the Regiment of *Chasseurs* of Militia.

One of the last flickering of the old glory and reputation of the Order was its support of the victims of the 1783 earthquake in Southern Italy and Sicily. Other eminent moments in Rohan's rule were the building of Fort Tigné and the *Bibliotheca*, the latter being the last major building erected under the Order. In 1777 Rohan elevated the village of Żebbuġ to a city, which became officially known as *Città Rohan*. In 1776 the Order of St Anthony of Vienne was annexed to the Order of St John. On the political level, important episodes were the setting up of the Anglo-Bavarian langue in 1782 and, a sign of things to come, the conspiracy against the Order which led to the imprisonment of the Maltese scholar and patriot Mikiel Anton Vassalli.

Yet Rohan had tried from the beginning of his magistracy to tackle long-overdue legal and political reforms. It was he who, in 1784, instigated the *Diritto Municipale di Malta* commonly known as the *Codice Rohan*. Although it has been called by modern Maltese historians a monument of 'enlightenment' and a landmark in Malta's legal history, the *Codice Rohan* was still far away from the contemporary law reforms and liberalizations of, for example, Emperor Joseph II of Austria. In general 'the Enlightenment in Malta' was a rather limited affair. The torch of the 'century of Light' was carried by a few people, such as the advocate Gio Nicolò Muscat and the scholar Mikiel Anton Vassalli.

The frontispiece of the Codice Rohan; Del Diritto Municipale di Malta *(1784). National Library of Malta.*

Echoes of the Enlightenment 201

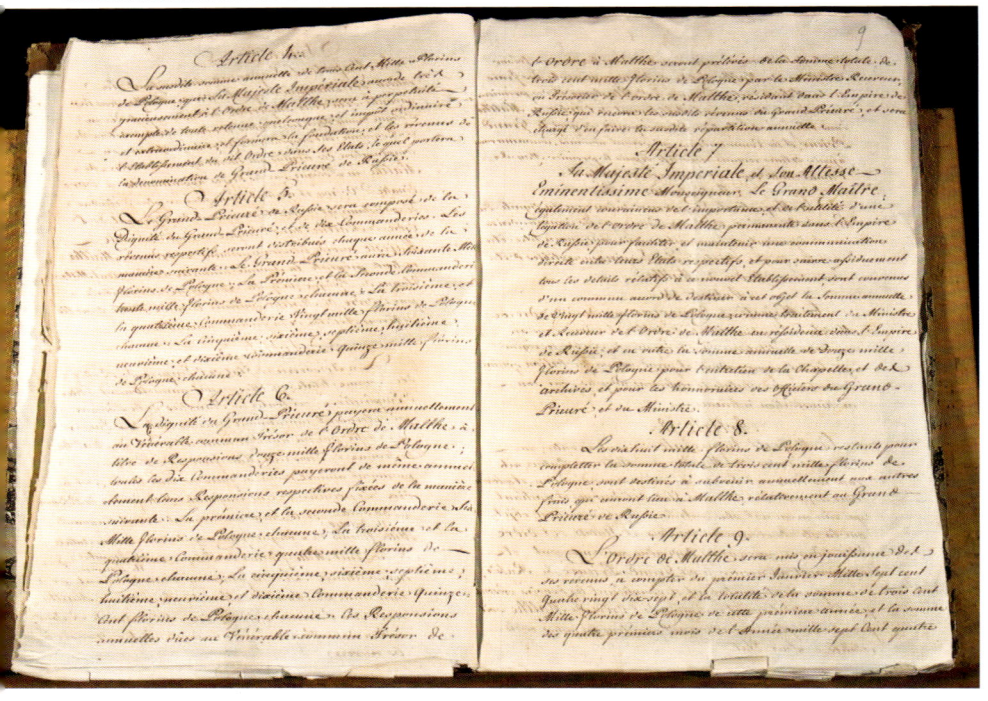

Convention of the establishment of a new Russian grand priory and its incorporation into the Anglo-Bavarian langue (AOM MS. 2196).

Vassalli's dedication of his dictionary *'alla nazione maltese'* is most indicative of the changes he dreamed of bringing about. This 'revolution' would only be brought about by a complete re-fashioning of the local mentalities and expectations, through education primarily conveyed through the vernacular. The events of the French Revolution had a great effect on the situation of the Order but a rather limited one on the ideas and mentalities of the local intellectuals and upper class.

Rohan's government also had very little in common with contemporary ideas of physiocracy and 'Josephinism'. Still Rohan's more liberal and modern ideas about clerical power brought tensions between the Order and the Roman Curia. But Rohan was not yet so 'advanced' as his Maltese *uditore* and legal advisor Gio Nicolò Muscat who rejected the idea of the Church as a perfect society and attributed to her only purely spiritual functions and values. Rohan was fully aware that Malta not was ready for a vision of an 'independent' country as dreamt by some of his contemporaries. That Rohan's rule was marked by a steadily increasing Maltese nationalism echoes the movement in various other European countries. The sustained attack on the privileges of the

Church in Malta had already started under Pinto's absolutistic rule. What gave permanent cause for clashes between the Order, the Church in Malta, and the pope was the paragraph in the *Diritto Municipale* that the government had the right to sanction or prohibit the execution of any legal instrument issued by foreign courts. In 1786 even those documents which concerned only religious matters were made subject to the examination of the authorities of the Order.

Internationally the tiny principality of Malta found itself embroiled in the upheavals which shook Europe after 1789. The French Revolution and its aftermath would bring the end of the European system of the *Ancien Régime* and in the long run also the end for the Order as the sovereign of Malta. In the eighteenth century most of the knights of St John were still recruited in France and also the larger part of the Order's revenues came from its six grand priories, four bailiwicks, 219 commanderies, and two religious communities in France. The end of all this came in August 1792 when the Tuilieres were attacked and Louis XVI sought refuge with the assembly. He was dethroned, and imprisoned along with his family, in the Temple, the palace of the grand prior of the Order in France. The Order's ambassador had escaped.

On 19 September 1792 the legislative assembly agreed to sequestrate and sell the Order's possessions in France. The proceeds of the sales were to go to the nation. These developments had disastrous effects on the Order's finances. In the following years, following the successes of the French armies, even many of the Order's lands in Spain and Italy were lost. The Order and many conservatives and refugees of the *Ancien Régime* in Europe looked towards Russia as the protector of the old system, traditions, and conservative values. 'Russia is now our diplomatic orient, and from her comes the light, faint it is true, and false, but seeing that it has lit up

Louis XVI of France (1754–93). He was guillotined on 21 January 1793.
Portrait by A.F. Callet (1741–1823)
Musée National du Château

the horizon, we must follow where it leads', wrote the Alsatian knight of the Order Charles Joseph Meyer de Knonau on 24 June 1792, struck by the mood and opinion of many nobles and *émigrés* not only in Malta. In fact the Order lost more than two-thirds of its income.

Indeed many knights in the 1790s looked to Russia mainly as the solution of their economic problems. To show that, despite of the political and intellectual changes, the Order still had a good presence in Europe in the eighteenth century, a few numbers should suffice. In 1789 the eight langues of the Order still had 22 grand priories, 19 bailiwicks, and 570 commanderies. In total there were 2,000 knights, 300 conventual chaplains and *servienti d'armi*, as well as 300 serving brothers. Just to compare: in 1788, the once so powerful Teutonic Order had a mere 11 bailiwicks with 96 knights and 71 clerics. In fact in the last years of the eighteenth century, the idea of unification of the Order of St John and the Teutonic knights was mooted.

Although he was pressed by a strong group within the Order, Rohan at first tried to avoid establishing too close contacts with the new emerging power of Russia. Yet some members of the French government believed that Malta was in danger of being seized by Catherine II and the French langues of being substituted by a Russian langue. Rohan's efforts to keep a balanced policy and neutrality was abandoned by his successor, the German Grand Master Hompesch.

Russian presence in the Mediterranean, and especially the obvious predominance over the Ottomans confirmed by the treaty of Küçük Kaynarca in 1773, caused a new political and strategic environment and problems of balance for the Order. Czarina Catherine tried hard to revive Black Sea trade and to connect it with the Mediterranean. As soon as her envoy Psaro arrived in Malta, he obtained an assurance from the representatives of the North African beys that no Barbary Coast corsair would attack ships sailing under the Russian flag. In the following years Russo-Maltese relations got closer and closer, and at the same time distrust of France and Spain increased. Both powers worked together against further Russian influence in the Mediterranean. In 1782 even Spain – for so long a bitter enemy of the Ottoman empire – concluded a peace treaty with Constantinople. In the concept of balance of power in the Mediterranean, the main preoccupation were no longer the Ottomans which were visibly in decline but the fear of the growing power of the Russians. Malta's and Naples' relations with Russia appeared more and more unpredictable and aroused strong suspicion in France, Spain, and England.

Opposite page: Czarina Catherine the Great, empress of Russia (1762–96) by Dimitri Gregoriovitch Levitzky (1735–1822). Ambassador's Room, Grand Master Palace, Valletta.

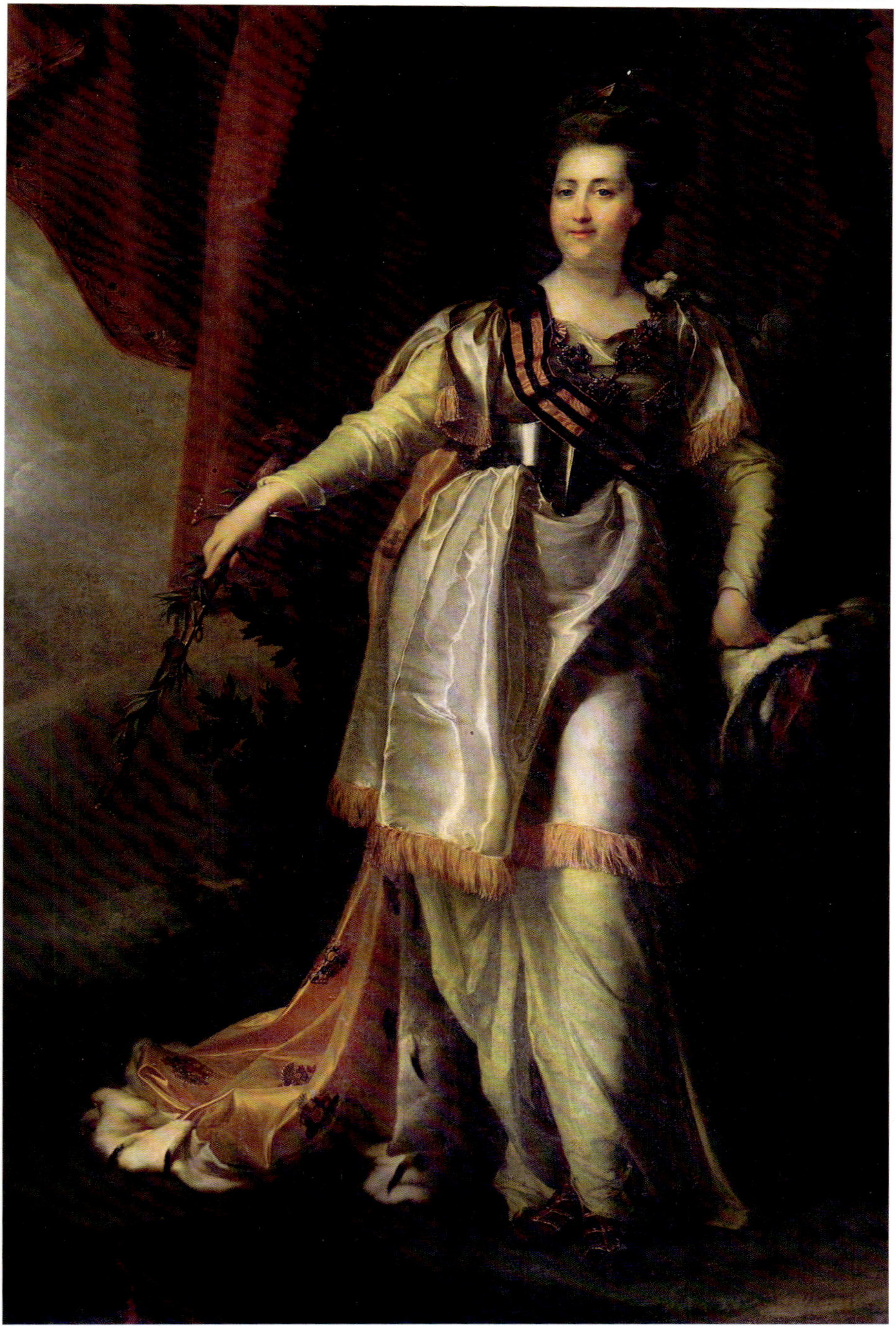

What became more and more obvious in the 1790s was that the Order did not remain hesitant any more in approaching Russia. This might have been due to the general political climate but it was also a result of the strong pro-Russian party within the Order. With the second partition of Poland (25 September 1793) most of the lands of the Polish priory passed under Russian control. The Knights Charles Joseph Meyer de Knonau and Joseph de Maisonneuve in 1793 were unsuccessfully sent as *chargés d'affaires* to St Petersburg to sort matters. On 14 April 1795 *Balí* Giulio Litta was nominated minister plenipotentiary of the Order to the imperial court of Russia and, on 7 August 1797, ambassador extraordinary of the Order in Russia. Russia acquired the duchy of Courland by the third partition of Poland and also annexed the remaining parts of the former territories of the Teutonic knights in Livonia, which had become Protestant during the Reformation. Especially the three Baltic provinces, called the 'German' provinces because of their cultural character and their representative institutions, provided the strongest link between old Russia and the Europe of the *Ancien Régime*. As a consequence of the second and third partitions of Poland in 1793 and 1795, the Order's grand priory on Polish territory and all its revenues – part of the Anglo-Bavarian langue – fell to Russia. Of course, it was in the Order's interest to ensure that it continued to benefit from its Polish revenues.

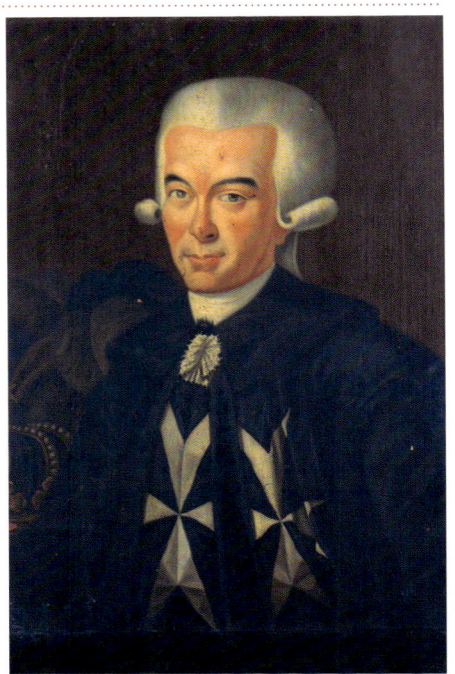

On 17 November 1796 Catherine II died and was succeeded by her son, the notorious Paul I, a character whose politics and intentions modern historians have still not fully explained. His short reign was characterized by a strong conservatism and censorship against the new liberal and democratic ideas. His antipathy towards France and Napoleon made him one of the last exponents of the principles of the European *Ancien Régime*. At first he joined Austria and Prussia in the war of the second coalition against France. After the French had left Malta in September 1800, Paul turned against Great Britain when it showed its ambition to keep the island in their possession. On 23 March 1801 he fell victim to a conspiracy led by Count Pahlen.

Right: Czar Paul I of Russia. National Library of Malta.

Left: Grand Master Hompesch. Wignacourt Museum, Rabat.

To what extent it was political *ratio* and calculated foresight (matters of strategic Mediterranean policies, symbolic loyalty to an Order which stood for the traditional values of the *Ancien Régime*) or just spontaneous irrationality and romantic sentiments which made Paul such a fervent defender of the Order, is hard to find out. The spiritual unifying idea is indicated by Baron Brünau: '*Emperor Paul regarded this institution as a novitiate from which the nobility of all the countries in Europe might learn lessons of loyalty and honour.*' The important political fact is that from the moment of his ascendance to the throne in 1796 the Order's affairs came to assume primary importance at the court of St Petersburg. This strong interest is first documented in Paul's handling of the Polish priory. When, with the second and third division of Poland, the Polish commanderies fell completely into Russian territory, a new solution was found. The grand priory of Poland and the six commanderies which 20 years earlier had been erected with the income from the lands of Ostrog were changed into a Russian grand priory with ten commanderies endowed with much higher responsions. Paul very readily let himself become involved in the internal and external affairs of the Order until finally, on 7 August 1797 – under the new German Grand Master Hompesch – the council agreed that Paul would be the new protector of the Order. After the surrender of Malta, Paul was proclaimed as the new grand master in November 1798 (27 October 1798 according to the Russian calendar) by the members of the Russian grand priory and some other knights who had taken refuge in St Petersburg.

Besides Paul another key figure of the period was Grand Master Hompesch, the last grand master to rule over Malta and certainly one of the heads of the Order with the weakest determination and zeal. Yet his short rule was one of the decisive milestones in Maltese history. It was Hompesch who ended the 268 years of rule of the Order and handed the islands over to the French. The end of the Order's rule over Malta was quite predictable but that it would come so suddenly and without a major resistance was, however, not foreseeable.

Ferdinand Joseph Hermann Anton von Hompesch had come to Malta in 1756 as a page to Grand Master Pinto. His family had their possessions in the Rhineland near the city of Coblenz. Hompesch was received in the Order when he was still 15 years old, thanks to a special dispensation obtained when the family agreed to quadruple the entry fee. This early entrance into the Order facilitated his subsequent career. Already in 1767 he was appointed councillor of the langue of Germany. In 1774 he was appointed commissioner for armaments, and the next year commissioner for fortifications. In 1787 he became *balí* of Brandenburg. In 1796 he was elected *grand balí* and therewith head of the German langue. Maybe his most important position and the one

Grand Master Ferdinand von Hompesh (1797–98).
Grand Master's Palace.

which formed his vision of politics was that of *chargè d'affaires* of the German emperor. Hompesch held this position for 22 years between 1775 until 1797. His election as grand master on 17 July 1797 was no surprise. The former Grand Master Rohan knew that it was most likely that a German should be his successor. The loss of the French property and the unstable situation on the Iberian peninsula made the Order drift towards the last bastions of the system of the *Ancien Régime*, the lands of the German empire and the new power of Russia.

End of an epoch

There were few episodes in the short reign of Hompesch so important as the acclamation of Czar Paul I as the Order's protector in August 1797. Hompesch ratified this acclamation in November 1797. This would later serve Napoleon as one of the main pretexts to justify his capture of Malta. The events of August and October were predated by a convention stipulated in January 1797 whereby the Russian czar decreed the establishment of a Russian priorate to be incorporated in the Anglo-Bavarian langue. Hompesch ratified this document in August 1797.

Hompesch's passivity during the French attack on Malta in June 1798 is still a mystery. Although he was well informed about Napoleon's plans by his plenipotentaries at the congresses of Rastatt and Campo Formio, he seems to have refused to believe the oncoming danger. He not even became suspicious when the French spy Henry Poussielgue visited Malta in December 1797 to carry out his investigations. Surely he must have counted on Austria's and Russia's protection in case of need.

Napoleon's arrival at Malta.
Coloured engraving, Fine Arts Museum Archives.

The French armada arrived on the coast of Malta on 9 June 1798 on its way to Egypt. The rest is well known. A launch from Napoleon's flagship *L'Orient* entered Grand Harbour with a message. The grand master was to be asked to admit the fleet to take water but the answer was in conformity with the Order's status as a neutral power: only four ships could enter at any one time. This gave the French the pretext to attack Malta which was met by chaos and uncertainty instead of an organized defence. Most of the French knights were not draw arms against their compatriots. The first French troops were landed at St Julian's Bay. Except from Fort Tigné, there was not much resistance and, by midday of 10 June, Napoleon's troops were in possession of the greater part of the Maltese countryside. In the meantime the French had also landed at Ramla Bay at Gozo under heavy fire from the hills but by the evening, they had captured Fort Chambray and the citadel.

The following day the French encircled Valletta and Floriana and it did not take long for Hompesch to surrender. On 12 June a convention was signed on board of the French flagship *L'Orient* in which the Order renounced all rights of sovereignty and ownership over the islands of Malta, Gozo, and Comino in favour of the French Republic. Another important article of the convention guaranteed the Maltese the right to continue to exercise the Catholic religion and to retain their property and privileges. No extraordinary taxes were to be levied. Hompesch, who refused to ratify the convention, sailed away on 17 June and proceeded to Trieste. He never received the compensations and annual pension he had been promised in the convention.

L'Orient *exploding in Aboukir, 1 August 1798 by Arnald George (1763–1841)*

After the surrender of Malta, Czar Paul I was proclaimed the new grand master of the Order on 27 October 1798 (Russian calendar) by the members of the Russian grand priory and some other knights who had taken refuge in St Petersburg. As the czar was not a Catholic and he was married to boot, this event must have appeared quite ridiculous to many contemporaries. Other factions of the Order and also Pope Pius VI as the nominal head of the Order, protested. In the general framework

Grand Master Giovanni Battista Tommasi (1803–05). Anonymous, Museum of the Etruscan Academy, Cortona, Italy.

of Russian politics at the end of the eighteenth century, this event did not come as a surprise at all. The historian Reinhard Wittram put the events in a global perspective:

In no other period of history, either before or since, was Russia so closely connected with the rest of Europe as she was during the Napoleonic era. That the Greek Orthodox Emperor, Paul I should become Grand Master of the Knights of Malta in 1798 was highly unusual but Russia's expansionist policies and the constant appeals for her intervention by the older European powers gave the framework of her foreign policy the capability to absorb even this.

Hompesch's numerous protests about the new developments in the Order and the taking of Malta remained largely unheard. After considerable pressure from Austria, Bavaria, Russia, and other powers on 6 July 1799 he addressed two letters, one to Paul I and the other to Emperor Franz II to inform them about his abdication as grand master.

But the thrilling period of Czar Paul would soon be over. In 1801 Paul died under mysterious circumstances and his son and successor, Alexander I, was too much of a rational character to continue his father's chivalric adventures. He refused the magistry of the Order and with the election of Giovanni Battista Tommasi as grand master the Order's headquarters moved back to the old scene of its exploits – the Mediterranean.

Considering the dynamism of the new forces of nationalism, anti-clericalism, and democracy, in the end the fall of Malta to one of the European major powers was inevitable. That it had to be the French under Napoleon who dared to drive the Order out of Malta was only a question of strategy and economics; in the end, it did not bother England or Russia so much that the Order was expelled but because they had lost an important strategic site in the Mediterranean. An epoch had come to its end. In a global context, the end of the Order's rule over Malta was another step in the move from the *Ancien Régime* to the new pre-imperialistic system. As the subsequent chapter will show, the Order kept paying the bill in the efforts of the European sovereigns to create 'modern' and secular states.

The surrender and deposition of arms by the French garrison based in the citadel of Gozo on 13 October 1798. The British Navy flag is already flying on the citadel and Sir Alexander Ball had already arrived on Gozo. Private collection.

New arrangements and a complicated resurrection

After Grand Master Hompesch's capitulation on 12 June 1798, the French took possession of Malta and Gozo. Napoleon himself left Malta a week later, leaving behind him 3,000 infantrymen and three companies of artillery under General Vaubois to garrison the island. At first Napoleon's troops had been widely welcomed by the Maltese but soon dissatisfaction with the anti-clerical French regime became widespread. On 2 September 1798 large groups of the Maltese population rose against the French. With the help of the British, the French were besieged in Valletta and the fortified area around the Grand Harbour for two years until they surrendered on 5 September 1800. When the French left, a Maltese delegation offered the islands to the British crown which took them under its protection.

As the 'election' of Czar Paul to the magistry kept dividing the Order and prejudicing its claim of independence, its hopes to regain Malta were very limited. The Russian approach must have automatically brought about the universal opposition of the Mediterranean powers as well as of the British. This development was completely ignored by Paul and, whatever his reasons were for accepting the title of grand master, even if he would have lived longer, there would have been very little hope of regaining Malta. His being both czar and grand master would have been an obstacle which Europe never have allowed the Order to regain sovereignty over Malta. On the other hand, having lost possession of Malta and with a Russian grand master and chapters general held in St Petersburg, the Order would soon have ended up as a 'private' Order of the Russian court. All this changed with Paul's assassination on 23 March 1801.

Five days later his son was enthroned as Alexander I. The new czar declared that he was taking the Order of St John under his imperial protection and he promised to try to reinstate it in all its rights, honours, immunities, and privileges. However, he refused to become grand master and appointed the *Balí* Field Marshal Count Nicholas Soltikov as provisional lieutenant. Later – if Austria and the Empire agreed – a chapter-general would be convoked and a new grand master elected. It is not known if Alexander was hoping to gain a certain Russian influence in the destiny of Malta and the Mediterranean by this moderate and neutral attitude. To make it clear: although Alexander refused the title of grand master, he kept the obligations stemming from being the protector of the Order. For a while, he was very interested that Malta would not be occupied either by England or France and he supported the return of Malta to the Order. This policy was shared by Count Worontzoff who became the new chancellor of the Russian empire in 1802. In the meantime *Balí* Soltikoff was ordered to remain lieutenant of the grand master with St Petersburg the seat of the Order. In a more global sense, Alexander's decision to refuse the title of the grand master and his

Il Maltin jassaltau l'Imdina occupata mil Francisi *(The Maltese attack French-occupied Mdina) from* Lis storia ta Malta bil gzejer tahha *(The history of Malta and its Islands) by P.P. Castagna (1888).*

IL MALTIN JASSALTAU L'IMDINA OCCUPATA MIL FRANCISI.

later decision to keep a distance from the affairs of the Order can be seen as an act of political pragmatism as well as 'spiritual' modernity. A newly-shaped Europe forged by the concept of national states would have prevented the Order from regaining its European possessions anyway. Paul's death, however, did not lead to an unification of the different factions and parties of the knights. This divide was clearly visible when Ferdinand von Hompesch tried again to revive his claims to the magistry but had lost the support of most of the remaining knights. When Hompesch heard of Paul's assassination, in May 1801 he wrote to the Austrian minister Thugut to promote his rehabilitation as grand master. He – Hompesch wrote – had only temporarily (sic) resigned in 1799 not to endanger the Russo-Austrian coalition. This situation was now obsolete and now Napoleon would not mind supporting his re-installation as grand master. The new czar, Alexander, would keep a friendly neutrality. That this was anything but the full truth was most obvious.

At first Hompesch's claim was supported by the new French government which hoped that the British would leave Malta again. After a few months, however, it was obvious that Hompesch was fighting a hopeless fight and soon even the French stopped supporting his case. Possibly the most influential supporter of the Order remained the papacy and the outcome of the Treaty of Amiens, concluded on 27 March 1802 and ratified on 18 April, definitely favoured the knights. Article 10 stipulated that Malta was to revert to the Order in full former sovereignty and that the new grand master should be elected by the general chapter to be held in Malta. The political environment forced some changes in the centennial institution. The future Order would not contain any French or English langues but a Maltese langue would be created. The independence of Malta would be guaranteed by France, Great Britain, Russia, Austria, Prussia, and Spain and the British would hand the island back to the Order within three months of the ratification of the Treaty. But paper and written agreements did not matter anymore so much when the new emerging super-powers were heading for the construction of their pre-imperialistic empires.

The general tendency amongst the Maltese were against a return of the Order and for the British. Especially the liberals and the merchant classes were considerably opposed to the Treaty of Amiens and in June 1802 a delegation of high-ranking Maltese submitted a petition to King George III asking for the protection by the British crown. The newly formed Maltese assembly formulated a new constitution which recognized the British king as sovereign lord on 15 June 1802.

First Declaration of Rights issued in Malta: 'Dichiarazione dei Diritti degli Abitanti di Malta e Gozo', *including the right to freedom of conscience under the rule of law. Marble plaque at Palazzo Parisio, Foreign Office, Valletta.*

DICHIARAZIONE
DEI DIRITTI DEGLI ABITANTI DELLE ISOLE MALTA E GOZO

MALTA 15 GIUGNO 1802

NOI MEMBRI DEL CONGRESSO DELLE ISOLA DI MALTA E GOZO, E LORO DIPENDENZE ELETTI PER LIBERO SUFFRAGIO DEL POPOLO DURANTE L'ASSEDIO, PER RAPPRESENTARLO NELL'IMPORTANTE AFFARE DI ASSICURARE I SUOI NATIVI DIRITTI E PRIVILEGJ (GODUTI DAI NOSTRI ANTENATI DA TEMPO IMMEMORABILE, E PER I QUALI, QUANDO FURONO USURPATI, ABBIAMO SPARSO IL NOSTRO SANGUE, PER RIACQUISTARLI) E DI STABILIRE UNA COSTITUZIONE DI GOVERNO, CHE ASSICURERÀ A NOI, ED AI NOSTRI DISCENDENTI IN PERPETUO LA FELICITÀ DELLA LIBERTÀ, E DEI DIRITTI DI UNA GIUSTA LEGGE, SOTTO LA PROTEZIONE E SOVRANITÀ DEL RE DI UN POPOLO LIBERO, S.M. IL RE DEGLI STATI UNITI DELLA GRAN BRETTAGNA ED IRLANDA, DOPO LUNGA E MATURA CONSIDERAZIONE, FACCIAMO LA PRESENTE DICHIARAZIONE, OBBLIGANDO NOI STESSI, ED I NOSTRI POSTERI PER SEMPRE, SOTTO CONDIZIONE, CHE IL NOSTRO OR RICONOSCIUTO PRINCIPE E SOVRANO DOVRÀ DA PARTE SUA ADEMPIRE, E MANTENERE INVIOLATA QUESTA CONVENZIONE CON NOI.

1. CHE IL RE DEGLI STATI UNITI DELLA GRAN BRETTAGNA ED IRLANDA E IL NOSTRO SOVRANO SIGNORE, AD I SUOI LEGITTMI SUCCESSORI SARANNO IN TUTTI I TEMPI AVVENIRE CONOSCIUTI COME NOSTRI LEGITTIMI SOVRANI.

2. CHE LA STESSA M.S. NON HA NESSUN DIRITTO DI CEDERE QUESTE ISOLE A NESSUNA POTENZA. CHE SE EGLI SCIEGLIE DI RITIRARE LA SUA PROTEZIONE, A DI ABBANDONARE LA SUA SOVRANITÀ, IL DRITTO DI ELLEGERE UN ALTRO SOVRANO, E DI GOVERNARE QUESTE ISOLE APPARTERRÀ A NOI, ED AGLI ABITANTI SOLAMENTE SENZA SOPRAINTENDENZA.

3. CHE I GOVERNATORI E RAPPRESENTANTI DI S.M. IN QUESTE ISOLE, E LORO DIPENDENZE SONO E SARANNO PER SEMPRE TENUTI DI OSSERVARE, E TENERE INVIOLATA LA COSTITUZIONE, CHE COLLA SANZIONE E RATIFICA DELLA STESSA REAL M. BRITTANICA, O SUI RAPPRESENTANTI, O PLENIPOTEZIARI SARÀ STATA STABILITA PER NOI, REGOLATA DAL GENERALE CONGRESSO ELETTO DAL POPOLO NELLA SEGUENTE CONFORMITÀ –

CITTÀ NOTABILE E CASAL DINGLI 14 MEMBRI – VALLETTA 12 – VITTORIOSA 4 – SENGLEA 4 – COSPICUA 4 –

CASALI – BIRCHIRCARA 5 MEMBRI – ATTARD 2 – LIA E BALZAN 3 – CURMI (ANCHE CITTÀ) 12 – NASCIARO 4 – GREGORIO 3 – MUSTA 5 – ZEBBUG (ANCHE CITTÀ) 8 – SIGGEUI 4 – LUCA 3 – GUDIA 1 – ZURRICO 4 – MICABIBA 2 – CRENDI 2 – ZABBAR 3 – TARSEN 2 – ASCIACH 1 – TOTALE MEMBRI 104.

4. CHE IL POPOLO DI MALTA E GOZO ED I SUOI RAPPRESENTANTI NEL CONSIGLIO POPOLARE RADUNATI, HANNO IL DRITTO DI MANDARE LETTERE, O DEPUTATI AI PIEDI DEL TRONO, PER RAPPRESENTARE E LAGNARSI DELLA VIOLAZIONE DEI DRITTI E PRIVILEGJ, O DEGLI ATTI CONTRARJ ALLA COSTITUZIONE DEL GOVERNO, O DELLO SPIRITO DELLA MEDESIMA.

5. CHE IL DRITTO DELLA LEGISLAZIONE E DI TASSAZIONE APPARTIENE AL CONSIGLIO POPOLARE, CON IL CONSENSO ED ASSENSO DEL RAPPRESENTANTE DI S.M., SENZA IL QUALE IL POPOLO NON SARÀ OBBLIGATO.

6. CHE S.M. IL RE E IL PROTETTORE DELLA NOSTRA SANTA RELIGIONE, ED È TENUTO DI DI SOSTENERLA E PROTEGGERLA COME PER LO PASSATI, E SENZA ALCUNA DIMINUZIONE DI QUEL CHE È STATO PRATICATO, DACCHÈ QUESTE ISOLE HANNO RICONOSCIUTO S.M. COME LORO SOVRANO SINO A QUESTO GIORNO, E CHE I RAPPRESENTANTI DI S.M. HANNO IL DRITTO DI PRETENDERE QUEGLI ONORI DI CHIESA, CHE SONO STATI SEMPRE DIMOSTRATI ALLE REGGENTI DI QUESTE ISOLE.

7. CHE NON SARÀ PERMESSA NESSUNA COMPETENZA IN MATERIE SPIRITUALI O TEMPORALI DI NESSUN ALTRO TEMPORALE SOVRANO IN QUESTE ISOLE, E CHE LA RIFERENZA DEGLI AFFARI SPIRITUALI SARÀ SOLAMENTE DEL PAPA, E DELLI RISPETTIVI GENERALI DEGLI ORDINI MONASTICI.

8. CHE GLI UOMINI LIBERI HANNO IL DRITTO DI SCEGLIERE LA LORO PROPRIA RELIGIONE. LA TOLLERANZA DI ALTRE RELIGIONI È PERTANTO STABILITA PER DIRITTO, MA NON È PERMESSO A NESSUNA SETTA DI MOLESTARE, INSULTARE, O DISTURBARE QUELLE DI ALTRE RELIGIOSE PROFESSIONI.

9. CHE NESSUN UOMO QUALUNQUE HA ALCUNA PERSONALE AUTORITÀ SOPRA LA VITA, PROPRIETÀ O LIBERTÀ DELL'ALTRO. IL POTERE RISIEDE SOLAMENTE NELLA LEGGE, ED IL RAFFRENAMENTO, E LA PUNIZIONE PUÒ ESSERE SOLAMENTE ESERCITATA IN OBBEDIENZA DELLE LEGGI.

SEGNATA DA TUTTI I RAPPRESENTANTI, DEPUTATI, E LUOGOTENENTI DEI VILLAGGI E CITTA.

CITTÀ VECCIA, RABATO, E CASAL DINGLI	EMMANUELE VITALE	ZABBAR	AGOSTINO SAID
ZEBBUG	NOTARO PIETRO BUTTIGIEG	TARSCIEN	GIUSEPPE MONTEBELLO
SIGGEUI	D. SALVATORE CURSO, PARROCO	LUCA	GIUSEPPE CASHA
MICABIBA	D. BARTOLOMEO GARAFFA, PARROCO	CURMI	STANISLAO GATT
CRENDI	GREGORIO MIFSUD	BIRCHIRCARA	VINCENZO BORG
ZURICO	D. FORTUNATO DALLI	GARGUR	CH GIOVANNI GAFA
SAFI	CH. GIUSEPPE ABDILLA	NAXXARO	CAV. PAOLO PARISIO
CHERCOP	ENERICO XERRI	MUSTA	D. FELICE CALLEJA, PARROCO
GUDIA	FILIPPO CASTAGNA	LIJA	SALVATORE GAFA
AXIACH	D. PIETRO MALLIA	BALZAN	GIUSEPPE FRENDO
ZEITUN	CAPO MAESTRO MICHELE CACHIA	ATTARD	NOTARO SAVERIO ZARB

In another illustration dated 1798, French flags fly over Valletta and Fort Manoel. British ships blockade the harbour. This view is from Trincera la Samra. *Museum of Fine Arts.*

As was to be expected, the British kept Malta against the conclusions of Amiens. Its strategic importance was too obvious to give the island away. That the French then did not retract from the Italian territory they had annexed, served as a welcome pretext for the British to keep Malta. The Order had other important issues to settle. Various princes and leaders were discussing the unification of the Teutonic Order and the Order of St John throughout 1802 and 1803. The German priory of the Hospitallers was very much in favour of this, as it still seemed that the Order would have the chance of regaining most of their German commanderies and Malta. The council of the Teutonic knights, however, hesitated, although even their Order had lost substantial possessions in the recent reshuffles in Europe.

All the efforts of the diplomats of the Order to re-establish their institution in Malta were in vain. However, various other proposals and plans were made for the Order to settle somewhere and take up its old activities. An interesting option was offered by King Gustav IV of Sweden who, in 1806, proposed that the Order should be given the island of Gotland as a permanent residence. The knights, however, refused as they feared that their claims on Malta would be lost forever; some European powers were rather sceptical about this proposal from the start.

In Malta itself the memories of the Order's rule were starting to fade and only a very few knights had remained on the island. The coming of the British did not mean that the Maltese now enjoyed the 'full rights' of a nation and *patria* as many had hoped. Soon the realities of the status of a 'colony' became visible. As the British government in Malta remained autocratic, political agitation would grow in the nineteenth

Grand Master Giovanni Battista Tommasi (1803–05).

Lieutenant Innico Maria Guevara-Suardo (1805–14).

century. The staunch Maltese patriots never stopped asserting their countrymen's right to re-establish the old *Consiglio Popolare*.

In the meantime even the Order had undergone changes and some sort of re-structuring. Without the support of the Holy See, Hompesch's star had sunk rapidly.

On 16 September 1802 the pope nominated *Balí* Bartolomeo Ruspoli as grand master and Hompesch once more resigned his claims to magistracy. The former grand master moved to Montpellier where he lived on an infrequently paid pension from the French and died on 12 May 1805. Tensions and uncertainties among the knights could be felt everywhere. The best example was the attitude of the new designated Grand Master *Balí* Ruspoli who was then living in London and was certainly gifted with farsightedness and political insight. Through his contacts with British leaders, he knew that there was hardly any hope that England would obey the stipulations of the Treaty of Amiens. He was also sceptical as to whether the extensive property which several European states had seized from the Order would be returned. All these negative perspectives made him decide not to accept the papal offer and he declined the magistracy.

On 9 February 1803 the seasoned former captain general of the Order's navy *Balí* Giovanni Battista Tommasi was nominated grand master. Tommasi accepted and moved again the Order's headquarters in the centre of the Mediterranean: to Catania. The last meeting of

Lieutenant Andrea di Giovanni e Centelles (1814–21).

Lieutenant Antoine Busca (1821–34).

the venerable council was held in St Petersburg – to where it has moved after the fall of Malta – on 17 November 1802 and the council was officially dissolved on 25 April 1803 passing its power to the new grand master and sending the insignia of the magistry to him in Catania. But until his unexpected death in June 1805 Tommasi could not achieve any progress in the efforts of the Order to regain its old principality. After his death, the tensions and confusion became even more visible when *Balí* Giuseppe Caracciolo's election as grand master was not accepted by Pius VII. The pope – and a group of malcontent knights – refused to accept Caracciolo as he was found to be too much pro-British. Pius instead declared as permanent the appointment of *Balí* Innico-Maria Guevara-Suardo as lieutenant of the magistry. That meant that for the next decades there was no grand master but a 'lieutenant' heading the institution.

Guevara-Suardo died in April 1814, that is a short time before the signing of the peace treaty of Paris of 30 May 1814, article seven of which incorporated Malta officially in the British empire. These bad news then did not seem to be the last word as the planning for the Congress of Vienna was already in the pipeline to settle the upheavals caused by Napoleon and to return Europe to calm waters. The Order placed its hopes in the oncoming gathering of diplomats and representatives of all Europe. Vienna seemed to be the last chance for the Order to regain lost ground. In the meantime the Sicilian

Balí Andrea di Giovanni e Centelles had been elected lieutenant of the magistry and confirmed by the pope. The Order's envoy at the congress of Vienna was Antonio Miari, who painted a much more positive picture of the institution than the bitter facts of reality would have permitted. He claimed that all its belongings in Sicily and Sardinia were still in the Order's possession, and that the duchy of Parma and the papal state had just restored the Order its old possessions and lands. Soon the old possessions in Lombardy and in Spain would also be returned.

The hard facts were different. As a result of the French Revolution, the three French langues had disappeared. In Spain, the king had made himself grand master of the Hospitallers in his country and had sequestrated all their possessions. With the conquest of North Italy by Napoleon, all local possessions of the Order had been sequestrated. The possessions in the south of Italy were sequestrated in 1811. The two Russian grand priories ceased to exist in 1811, following the decision of Czar Alexander to retake to State ownership the properties that his father had passed to the Order. So in 1811 only the grand priory of Bohemia-Austria remained functioning.

It was soon obvious that most of the representatives at the congress did not intend to support the Order's claim to regain Malta. Even worse, many diplomats found the affairs of the Order too 'complicated' and 'time-consuming' – as the Bavarian minister Montgelas put it – to be taken up seriously. Miari demanded that if there really was no way for the Order to regain Malta, it should be given another land to rule and to cover its duties and obligations. All European powers were to guarantee the Order's neutrality and independence, with England having to refund the Order for its lost property in Malta. The congress should insist that the single European sovereigns were to return the Order's property and lands they had confiscated. The future role and obligations of the Order were to be discussed and stipulated anew. England was amongst the leading opponents of these proposals and it soon was followed by some other States. After a short while there was a common agreement that the demands of the Order were not to be refused but, instead, slowly ignored. Even in later times Great Britain kept seeing the knights as a potential ally of the French and, therefore, a suspicious element to its Mediterranean naval hegemony.

That the disappointing outcome of the gathering in Vienna had an effect on the internal situation and composition of the old honourable institution was no surprise. The number of new knights making profession declined considerably and therefore the number of the confessed knights began to dwindle to insignificant dimensions, while more nobles started petitioning for the cross of devotion, setting a precedent for future times. The idea of a revival of the Order as a 'policeman of the Mediterranean' as, for

Klemens Wenzel von Metternich (1773–1859) by Thomas Lawrence (1769–1830). Kunsthistorisches Museum, Vienna.

example, suggested by the German diplomat and administrator Friedrich Herrmann in his study *'Ueber die Seeräuber im Mittelmeer und ihre Vertilgung'* published on the occasion of the congress of Vienna, must have appeared anachronistic. This was a concept of the times when the political theatre of the Mediterranean was composed of medium-sized powers which could or did not want to unite in joint military actions against the Barbary corsairs and the Barbary States. With the emergence of the super powers England and France – and also Russia – and their creation of spheres of influence and hegemony, there came also the end of the Barbary corsairs. In 1830 the French eliminated in Algiers the last centre that threatened Christian shipping. From then on there was no longer any reason for the proposals to restore the naval responsibilities of the Order of St John.

The restoration of the Order after the end of the Napoleonic era was a slow and difficult process. In 1825 the grand priory of Messina was suppressed, followed in 1834 by the grand priory of Portugal. Some positive feedback did come from the Austrian-Bohemian grand priory. That the Bohemian grand priory was still functioning was partly due to the protection by the powerful Austrian chancellor Klemens von Metternich, who would himself become a *balí* of honour and devotion of the Order. In 1818 at the congress of Aachen (Aix en Chapelle), Metternich had proposed

In 1831 the new headquarters of the Order were set up at Palazzo Malta *in Via dei Condotti, 68. In 1869, the palace and the other headquarters of the Order,* Villa Malta, *were granted extraterritoriality by Italy.*

the Order's case again on the international platform. Discussions were held to re-install the Order in the Mediterranean as a charitable institution as well as an international naval police, but nothing was concluded.

Andrea di Giovanni e Centelles died in Catania in 1821 and was succeeded as lieutenant of the magistry by the Milanese titular *Balí* of Armenia Antonio Busca, who had close ties with the Austrian chancellor, an important issue as Austria then, through dynastic connections and pure political interests, looking to dominate Northern and Central Italy. Thanks to Metternich's influence and papal permission, the Order's headquarters were established for some time at Ferrara in 1827. In 1831 the Order moved to Rome, to the palace of the grand prior of Rome on the Aventine Hill. A few years later the permanent headquarters were established in

Palazzo Malta on Via Condotti, formerly the residence of the Order's ambassador to the Holy See. It remains the Order's seat till the present day and it enjoys the right of extraterritoriality recognized by the Italian State. In 1839, the grand priory of Lombardy and Venice were re-established. Metternich, however, failed to convince Britain that the archives should be restored to the Order and that the Hospitallers should be compensated for the loss of Malta. When Metternich celebrated his eightieth birthday in 1852, the Order bestowed upon him the cross of devotion 'as thanks to him the Order of the Hospitallers could survive and keep its independence'.

In the meantime there had been two more lieutenants of the magistry: the Neapolitan Carlo Candida (1834–46) and the Austrian Philipp von Colloredo (1846–65). Even after Metternich's resignation as Austrian chancellor, the Order and especially the Bohemian grand priory kept its excellent contacts with the heads of the Austro-Hungarian empire. Emperor Franz Joseph, who had been made grand cross and honourable *balí* of the Order, acted as protector of the Hospitallers. Up to the end of the old Austrian-Hungarian empire in 1918 the Hungarian knights belonged to the priory of Bohemia. An independent Hungarian priory was never re-established.

But the Order had other powerful protectors. Through the pressure of the pope in 1816, the Roman grand priory was re-established. In 1839 even the grand priory of Naples was re-established. Despite these developments, the old days were irrevocably gone. This was shown when the pope was deposed in 1848 by a popular rebellion. In 1850 when the old situation was restored, the Order's head Philipp von Colloredo offered to form a military guard for the pope from among the brethren. Because of the old age of most of the professed knights and the insufficient numbers of younger members of honour and devotion, this guard would have had to be made up of paid mercenaries. The Holy See itself finally declined the offer. A military restoration of the Order was unthinkable. The only option was to go back to its roots and concentrate on its charitable and social aspects and medical services.

Even the internal structure of the Order had changed. The number of professed knights had dwindled drastically and the commanderies could certainly not be used to provide for the professed knights. The development of the national states had also to be taken into consideration for the establishment of new structures. So besides the still existing grand priories in the second half of the nineteenth century, the knights of devotion and knights of grace did not form langues but national associations.

For example, in 1859 a Rhinian-Westphalian Association of the Order of St John was founded and in 1867 an association of Silesian

The courtyard fountain at Palazzo Malta *in Via dei Condotti.*

knights of Malta. The foundation of similar institutions followed in 1871 in England, in 1877 in Italy, in 1885 in Spain, in 1891 in France, in 1899 in Portugal, in 1910 in the Netherlands, and in 1928 in the United States of America. In 1831 the attempt to revive the English langue under Prior Sir Robert Peat was acknowledged by the British crown but not by the Order. As a result an independent national 'Grand Priory of the Order of the Hospital of St John of Jerusalem in the British realm' was founded in 1871.

Even in Brandenburg-Prussia – where a unique Protestant bailiwick of the Order had existed since the sixteenth century – the Hospitallers were not completely forgotten. In 1812 Prussian King Friedrich Wilhelm III had founded a 'Royal-Prussian Order of St John' (*Königlich-Preussischer Johanniterorden*) in memory of the bailiwick and which admitted all former members of the bailiwick of Brandenburg. This Royal-Prussian Order of St John, however, had rather the character of a Court-Order. On 15 December 1852 the bailiwick was officially re-established and on 14 March 1853 the brother of the Prussian king, Prince Carl Alexander, was elected Herrenmeister. King Friedrich Wilhelm IV took over the patronage over the bailiwick and decreed that all members of the royal Prussian Order of St John could be received in it as knights of honour. The main aim of the bailiwick was charitable and social work. When the bailiwick was re-established in Sonnenburg in 1858, one of the first hospitals of the renewed Order was opened. In 1862 the bailiwick already ran 17 hospitals and numbered 155 knights of justice and 738 knights of grace.

Right: Balí *Giovanni-Battista Ceschi a Santa Croce (28 March 1879–24 January 1905) was the 74th grand master of the Order from 1931 to 1951.*

Opposite page: The façade of Villa Malta, *formerly the palace of the grand prior of Rome on the Aventine Hill in Rome. In 1765 architect and painter Giovan Battista Piranesi build the neo-classical façade and the adjoining* Piazza dei Cavalieri di Malta.

By now the charitable side of the Order had been established as its *raison d'être*. In 1855 an association of sisters of St John was established and when the Red Cross was founded in 1863, the Order sought good relations with this new institution. As a result in Vienna in 1866 – the Austria-Prussian War was raging – the Order founded its first military hospital. Negotiations were started with the Holy See about a return of the Hospitallers to the Holy Land and after long negotiations a hospital was built in Tantur in 1876. After 600 years, the Hospitallers returned to Palestine!

In the meantime the Order was lead again by a 'veritable' grand master. When the lieutenant of the magistry *Balí* Alessandro Borgia died in 1872, he was succeeded by *Balí* Giovanni-Battista Ceschi a Santa Croce. After long negotiations, an apostolic brief of 28 March 1879 conferred on Ceschi a Santa Croce the title of grand master once again. The revival of this office was confirmed by the Brief *Inclytum antiquitate originis* of Leo XIII in June 1888.

During the First World War, the Order performed inestimable charitable services through their military hospitals and providing for the sick and poor. Because of its sovereign status and independence from government finances, the Order could carry out its medical aid relief and charitable work very often freer from interference than the Red Cross. This sovereign status enables the Order then – and even now – to carry out projects beyond the scope of many other charitable organizations.

In these times of war and social upheavals, the Order was lead by the Austrian Grand Master Galeazzo von Thun und Hohenstein (1905–31), but it was his successor *Balí* Ludovico

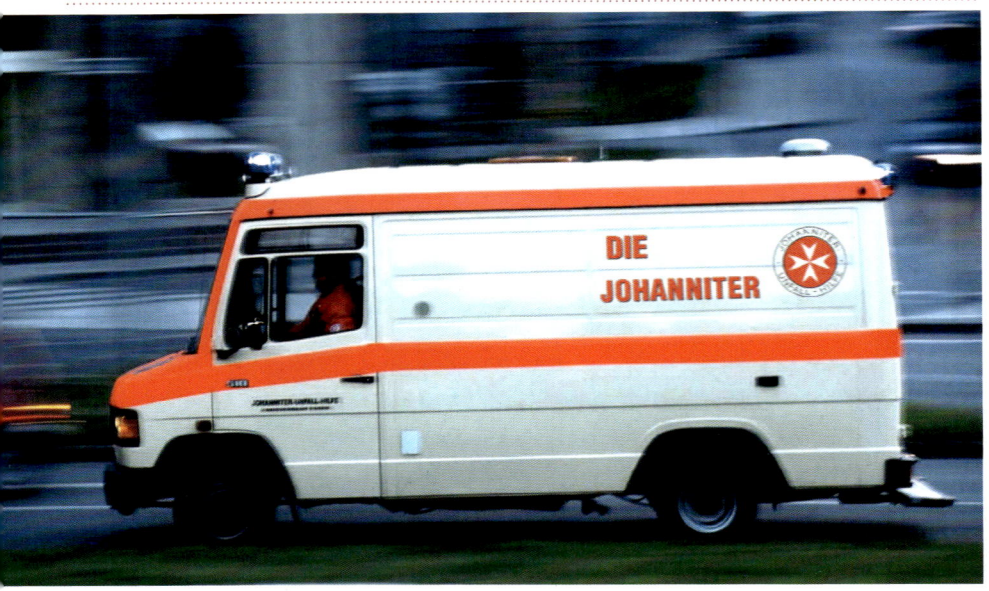

Chigi Albani della Rovere (1931–51) who faced even more serious challenges, mainly due to the rise of Fascism in Germany and Italy and the emergence of communist systems in Eastern Europe. Chigi Albani della Rovere showed his abilities not only in the fields of charitable and humanitarian work but also in the tricky grounds of international politics and diplomacy. For example, in 1933 he instituted the Missionary School of Medicine and Surgery to provide Catholic missions with trained medical personnel. Coping with the political challenges was much more difficult, especially in Hitler's Germany and, later, in the Communist East Europe.

The Catholic and Protestant branches of the Order continued their work even after the end of the German empire in 1918 – in the period of the 'Weimar Republic'.

Johanniter-Unfall-Hilfe (JUH; 'St John Accident Assistance'), commonly referred to as Die Johanniter, is a voluntary humanitarian organization affiliated with the Brandenburg bailiwick of the Order of St John, the German Protestant descendant of the Hospitaller. The organization has 22,000 active volunteers and around 1,500,000 registered members.

That the aged chancellor Paul von Hindenburg – a military hero of the First World War – was nominated commander of honour certainly helped to make the work easier but, when he died in 1934, times became more difficult. This was mainly due to the fact that the National Socialists under Hitler were suspicious about the international connections and aims of the German knights of St John and their loyalty to the dynasty of the Hohenzollern. More and more the members were forced to become members of Hitler's party, the NSDAP. As many German knights served as officers in Hitler's Wehrmacht, the Nazis for the time being refrained from dissolving the Order in Germany. This was planned for after the end of war. Not a few German knights of St John participated in the revolt and attempted assassination of Hitler on 20 July 1944. Eleven of them were executed.

The Bohemian grand priory experienced a new and bitter period when Austria was unified with Hitler's Germany in 1938 and the Order's possessions were sequestrated. To retain the status of the Order, an independent grand priory of Bohemia was quickly founded in Czechoslovakia but when a few months later Hitler's troops occupied that country even the possessions of the Bohemian grand priory were sequestrated. After the Second World War in 1945, the grand priory of Bohemia and the one of Austria were officially re-established. Yet, in other parts of the former German langue, things were rather bleak. When East Germany, Poland, Czechoslovakia, Hungary, Rumania, Bulgaria, Latvia, Estonia and Lithuania, and the Balkan countries fell into communist hands after the war, all possessions of the Order there were lost.

At first even the western powers forbade the German knights from taking up their charitable and social work again. After protests from knights in England, Sweden, and Switzerland, permission was granted again in 1949 under Herrenmeister Prince Oskar von Preussen. A change of regulations also meant that non-nobles could be received into the Order.

The well-known Johanniter-Unfall-Hilfe (ambulance service) was founded in 1952. Today associations in Austria, Hungary, France, Switzerland, and Finland also belong to the Protestant bailiwick of the Order. In 1961 at Nieder-Weisel, the only old commandery of the former German grand priory which could be re-acquired, an alliance-agreement of the Protestant branches of the Order was established. Besides the bailiwick of Brandenburg, there

Rudolf Christoph Freiherr von Gersdorff (1905–80) was a military officer in Germany's Weimar-period Reichswehr *and Nazi-period* Wehrmacht. *On 21 March 1943 he attempted to assassinate Adolf Hitler by a suicide bombing. He was the founding member of* Johanniter-Unfall-Hilfe *which he chaired from 1952 to 1963.*

Grand Master Angelo de Mojana di Cologna (1905, Milan – 18 January 1988, Rome) was grand master from 1962 to 1988.

participated the *Johanniterorden in Nederland*, the *Johanniterorden I Sverige*, and the 'Grand Priory in the British Realm of the Most Venerable Order of the Hospital of St John of Jerusalem'. Today the Protestant bailiwick of Brandenburg has over 3,000 members.

The autonomous and sovereign status of the Order in modern times was not unquestioned. In 1951 the conflict between the Order's role as a sovereign institution and its relation to the Holy See, its superior as a religious Order, was investigated by a commission by the Holy See. The pope's ultimate authority over the spiritual life of the first – and second – class brethren was, and remains, unanimously accepted. The situation with regards to the regulations of the lay members is a different matter.

After Chigi Albani della Rovere's death in 1951 – which was followed by the previously mentioned dispute between the Holy See and the Order as regards the nature of its sovereignty – the Order was governed by a lieutenant ad interim: Antonio Hercolani-Fava-Simonetti. In 1955 the pope approved the appointment of Ernesto Paternò Castello di Caraci as lieutenant of the magistry. In 1961 the re-working of the statutes of the Catholic Order of St John according to the canonical law was concluded. Under the provisions of international law, the Order maintains diplomatic relations, through accredited representatives, with the Holy See, on which, in its double nature, it depends as a religious Order, but of which, as a sovereign Order of chivalry, it is independent.

The 78th Grand Master, Fra Andrew Bertie who reigned from 11 April 1988 to 7 February 2008.
Palazzo Malta, *Rome.*

The institution was lead again by a grand master in 1962. This was the Milanese Angelo de Mojana di Cologna who in subsequent years furthered the Order's establishment as a sovereign diplomatic power and 'modernized' its relations with other States and associations worldwide. In 1988 he was succeeded by the British Andrew Willoughby Ninian Bertie, during whose term the Order was granted observer status in the United Nations, like the International Red Cross. Bertie died in March 2008 and was succeeded by the former British army officer and grand prior of England, Matthew Festing, the present grand master of the Sovereign Military Order of St John of Jerusalem. He still enjoys the precedence of a cardinal and therefore that of a royal prince, as well as the dignity of prince of the Holy Roman Empire. Formerly a reigning prince of Rhodes and then of Malta, the grand master is styled both eminence and highness, and is internationally recognized as a chief of state.

The life and activities of the Order are regulated by the constitutional charter approved by the Holy See, and the Code. The Code de Rohan, promulgated in the 1780s, retains its validity as a supplementary source of law, provided its provisions are applicable and are not contrary to the other sources of law. Juridical questions and problems of importance for the Order are dealt with by the consultative juridical council, which is appointed by the grand master with the consent of the sovereign council. To deal with cases outside the competence of canon law and ecclesiastical courts, the Order

Frà Matthew Festing, OBE, TD, DL, (born 30 November 1949) is the 79th prince and grand master. He is the second Englishman elected grand master since 1258.

has its own courts of law of first instance and courts of appeal, with the presidents, judges, promoters of justice, and auxiliaries being appointed by the grand master with the vote of the sovereign council. A board of auditors, elected by the general chapter, controls the income and the expenditures of the Order.

Today the *Sovrano Militare Ordine di Malta* consists of 6 grand priories, 3 sub-priories, and over 40 national associations in 37 countries with over 11,500 members, *c.*10,000 professional employees, and over 80,000 volunteer supporters. The headquarters of the Order in Rome has its governing body in the sovereign council which is presided over by the grand master and consists of the grand commander, the hospitaller, the chancellor, the receiver of the common treasure, and six councillors.

The SMOM – Sovereign Military Hospitaller Order of St John of Jerusalem, of Rhodes, and of Malta, also referred to as the Sovereign Military Order of Malta enjoys the status of a sovereign personality in international law and keeps diplomatic relations with over 100 countries. It has representatives at the European Council, UNESCO, the World Health Organization, the Red Cross, and other international institutions. The grand master is accorded the privileges of a foreign head of state in Italy, while the grand chancellor enjoys the privileges of a head of government.

The Order today carries out charitable work in more than 80 countries and runs over 70 hospitals, 13 homes for handicapped, 26 homes for old and homeless people, and more than 700 centres for first aid and social services. The institution also operates ambulance services and disaster relief agencies around the world.

Today there are many other organizations that style themselves with some variation or other of the name 'Order of St John' or 'Order of Malta'. They have no historical connection with the original Sovereign Military Order of Malta (SMOM). Only the Sovereign Military Order of Malta constitutes the sole unbroken continuation of the Order of the Hospital of St John recognized in the twelfth century. It has never ceased to be recognized by the community of nations as sovereign and independent of any civil power.

Diplomatic relations of the Sovereign Military Order of Malta

The background red represents bilateral diplomatic relations (104 countries) whilst orange represents other official relations (6 countries). The Order of Malta has also official relations at Ambassador level with the European Union and an observer status in the United Nations.

BILATERAL DIPLOMATIC RELATIONS

Europe
Albania
Austria
Belarus
Bosnia-Herzegovina
Bulgaria
Croatia
Czech Republic
Holy See
Hungary
Italy
Latvia
Liechtenstein
Lithuania
Macedonia
Malta
Moldova
Monaco*
Montenegro
Poland
Portugal
Romania
Russia, Fed. of *
San Marino
Serbia
Slovakia
Slovenia
Spain
Ukraine

The Americas
Antigua and Barbuda
Argentina
Bahamas, The
Belize
Bolivia
Brazil
Chile
Colombia
Costa Rica
Cuba
Dominican Republic
Ecuador
El Salvador
Guatemala
Guyana
Haiti
Honduras
Nicaragua
Panama
Paraguay
Peru
Saint Lucia
Saint Vincent & the Grenadines
Surinam
Uruguay
Venezuela

Asia
Afghanistan
Armenia
Cambodia
Georgia
Jordan
Kazakhstan
Lebanon
Philippines
Tajikistan
Thailand
Timor-Leste
Turkmenistan

Africa
Angola
Benin
Burkina Faso
Cameroon
Cape Verde
Central Africa
Chad
Comoros
Congo, Dem. Republic
Côte d'Ivoire
Republic of the
Egypt
Equatorial Guinea
Eritrea
Ethiopia
Gabon
Guinea
Guinea-Bissau
Kenya
Liberia
Madagascar
Mali
Mauritania
Mauritius
Morocco
Mozambique
Namibia
Niger
Sao Tome and Principe
Senegal
Seychelles
Sierra Leone
Somalia
Sudan
Togo

Oceania
Micronesia
Marshall Islands
Kiribati

* Relations maintained through a diplomatic special mission.

OFFICIAL RELATIONS
Belgium
France
Germany
Luxembourg
Switzerland
Canada

FRA FILIPPO VILLIERS L'ISLEADAMO XLIII.G.MAESTRO DELLA S.RELIG.GEROS.
FRA PIERINO DEL PONTE XLIV.GRAN MAESTRO DELLA S.RELIG.GEROSOL.
FRA DESIDERIO DI SANCTA GIALLA XLV.G.MAESTRO DELLA S.RELIG.GEROSOL.
FRA GIOVANNI D'UMEDES XLVI.G.MAESTRO DELLA S.RELIG.GEROS.
F.PIETRO DEL MONTE XLIX.GRAN MAESTRO DELLA S.RELIG.GEROSOL.
F.GIO.LAVESQVE DELLA CASSIERE L.G.MAESTRO DELLA S.RELIG.GEROSOL.
F.VGO DE LAVBENX VERDALA LI.GRAN MAESTRO CARDINALE DIACONO
FRA MARTINO GARZES LII.GRAN MAESTRO DELLA S.RELIG.GEROSOLIM.
FRA ANTONIO DE PAVLA LV.GRAN MESTRO DELLA S.RELIG.GEROSOLIM.
F.GIO.PAOLO LASCARIS CASTELLAR LVI.G.MAESTRO DELLA S.RELIG.GEROSOL.
FRA MARTINO DE REDIN LVII.GRAN MAESTRO DELLA S.RELIG.GEROSOL.
F.ANNETTO DE CLERMONT LVIII.G.MAESTRO DELLA S.RELIG.GEROSOL.
FRA GREGORIO CARAFFA LXI.GRAN MAESTRO DELLA S.RELIG.GEROSOL.
F.ADRIANO DE VVIGNACOVRT LXII.G.MAESTRO DELLA S.RELIG.GEROSOL.
FRA RAIMONDO PERELLOS LXIII.G.MAESTRO DELLA S.RELIG.GEROSOL.
FRA MARCANTONIO ZONDADARI LXIV.G.MAESTRO DELLA S.RELIG.GEROSOL.
FRA D.EMMANVELE PINTO LXVII.G.MAESTRO DELLA S.RELIG.GEROSOL.
FRA D.FRANCESCO XIMENES LXVIII.G.MAESTRO DELLA S.RELIG.GEROSOL.
FR.M.D.N.GIO.EM.ANUELE DE ROHAN LXVIIII.G.M. S.REL.GEROSOL.

The grand master, the highest office of the Order, was elected for life. As the only worldly prince, he was allowed to carry the title 'Eminence'. The official full intitulatio is: 'Frater N. N. Dei gratia sacrae domus hospitalis sancti Joannis Hierosolimitani et militaris ordinis, sancti sepulchri dominici, magister humilis pauperumque Jesu Christi custos.'

Chapter 8

Grand Masters of the Order of St John ruling over the Maltese islands

The Order was very fortunate that when its very existence as a sovereign and military power was threatened with the Ottoman pressure and the upheavals of Protestantism it was led by some very competent and able grand masters. Figures like L'Isle Adam and Valette managed not only to fight the exterior threats but also to keep up the inner spirit, zeal and determination of the Order. That this was no easy task is easy to comprehend when considering that the Order was composed of members of nearly all Christian Europe countries. Other grand masters like Homedes or Cassière showed less able to fight the divergenting forces and the challenges of new thoughts and new political developments in Europe. A highlight of disobedience was reached when the aged Jean Levesque de la Cassière was thrown into prison by his own members. It took the power of the Pope as the spiritual head of the knights of St John to restore order and to put the institution into calm waters again.

The grand masters that reigned over Malta portrayed in the engraving 'Chronology of the Grand Masters of the Hospital of the Sacred Military Religion of St John of Jerusalem and of the Order of the Holy Sepulchre now known as the Order of Malta'.

234 Grand Masters ruling over the Maltese islands

Philippe Villiers de L'Isle
Adam (1530–34)

Pierino del Ponte
(1534–35)

Didier de Saint Jaille
(1535–36)

Juan d'Homedes
(1536–53)

CLAUDE DE LA SENGLE
(1553–57)

JEAN PARISOT DE VALETTE
(1557–68)

PIETRO DEL MONTE
(1568–72)

JEAN L'EVÊSQUE DE LA
CASSIÈRE (1572–81)

Hughues Loubenx de Verdalle (1581–95)

Martino Garzes (1595–1601)

Alof de Wignacourt (1601–22)

Luis Mendez de Vasconcellos (1622–23)

Antoine de Paule
(1623–36)

Jean Paul Lascaris Castellar (1636–57)

Martin de Redin
(1657–60)

Annet Clermont de Chattes Gessan (1660)

Rafael Cotoner
(1660–63)

Nicolas Cotoner
(1663–80)

Gregorio Carafa
(1680–90)

Adrien de Wignacourt
(1690–97)

RAMON PERELLOS Y ROCCAFUL
(1697–1720)

MARC'ANTONIO ZONDADARI
(1720–22)

ANTONIO MANOEL DE VILHENA
(1722–36)

RAMON DESPUIG
(1736–41)

240 Grand Masters ruling over the Maltese islands

Manoel Pinto de Fonseca
(1741–73)

Francisco Ximenes de
Texada (1773–75)

Emmanuel de Rohan Polduc
(1775–97)

Ferdinand von Hompesch
(1797–98)

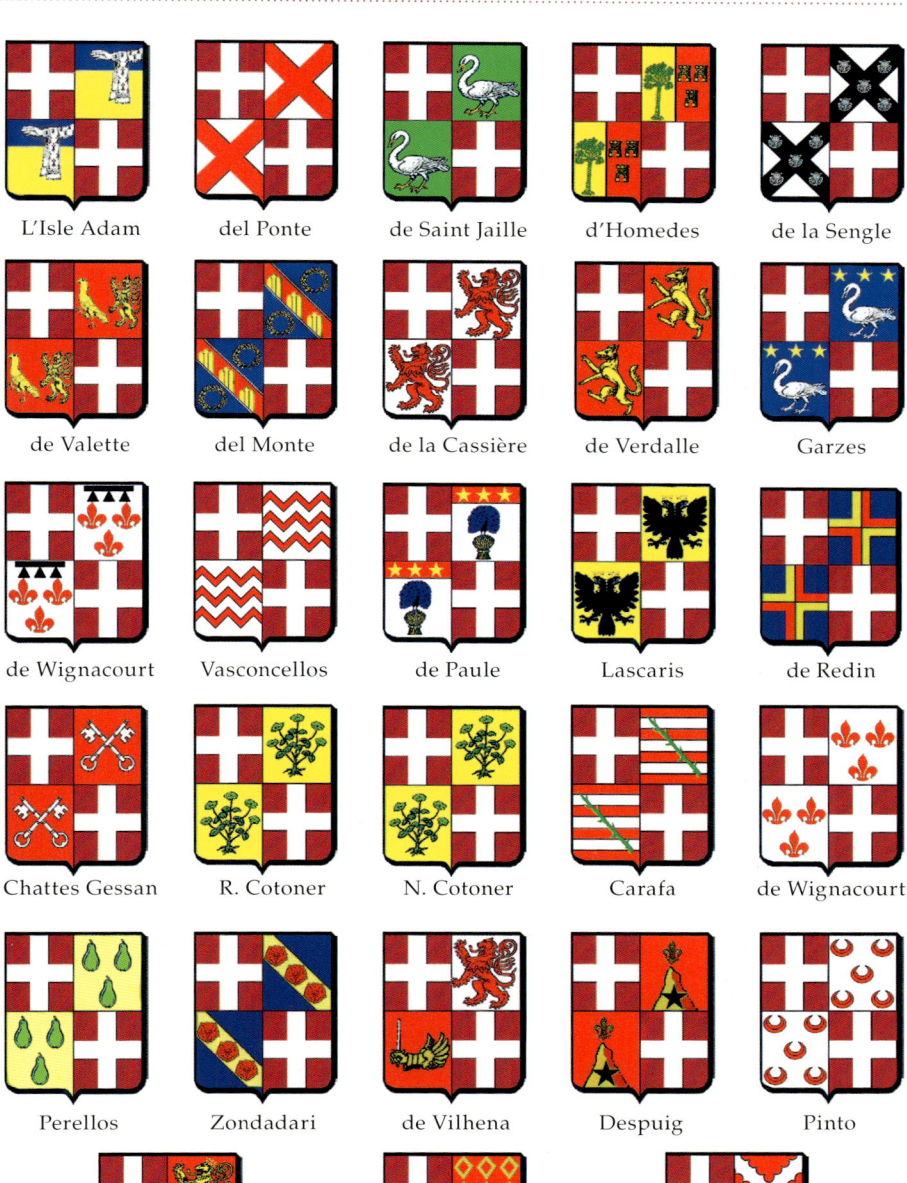

Grand Masters ruling over the Maltese islands 241

L'Isle Adam	del Ponte	de Saint Jaille	d'Homedes	de la Sengle
de Valette	del Monte	de la Cassière	de Verdalle	Garzes
de Wignacourt	Vasconcellos	de Paule	Lascaris	de Redin
Chattes Gessan	R. Cotoner	N. Cotoner	Carafa	de Wignacourt
Perellos	Zondadari	de Vilhena	Despuig	Pinto
 Ximenes	 de Rohan		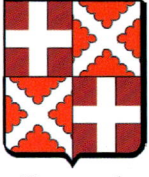 Hompesch	

242 The Order's Structure

Grand Master of the Order

Admiral of the Naval Forces

Marshal of the Armed Forces

Grand Balí of the Fortifications

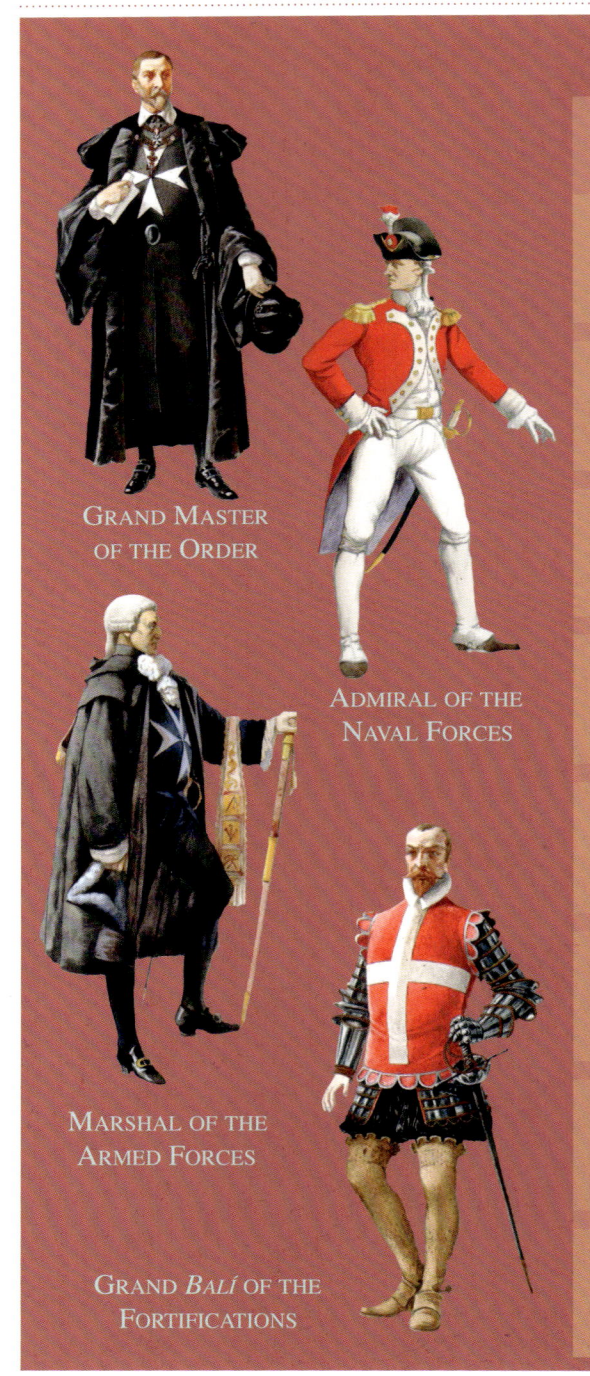

LEADING OFFICES

GRAND MASTER

Grand Commander
Financial Administrator

Marshall
Armed Forces

Hospitaller
Care of Sick & Poor

Admiral
Naval Forces

Grand Conservator
Supplies & Materials

Turcopilier
Cavalry

Grand Balí
Fortifications

Chancellor
Administration & Diploma

THE ORDER'S STRUCTURE

DIVISION OF COMPETENCES

PROVENCE	2 Priories 2 Bailiwicks 75 Commanderies	
AUVERGNE	1 Priory 1 Bailiwicks 54 Commanderies	
FRANCE	3 Priories 2 Bailiwicks 115 Commanderies	
ITALY	7 Priories 5 Bailiwicks 154 Commanderies	
ARAGON	3 Priories 6 Bailiwicks 112 Commanderies	
ENGLAND + BAVARIA + POLAND + RUSSIA	2 (3) Priories 1 Bailiwicks 32 Commanderies (dissolved 1540) 1782 Bavaria 28 Commanderies 1797 Russia 10 (98) Commanderies	
GERMANY	4 (5) Priories 1 Bailiwicks 67 Commanderies	
CASTILLE	1 Priory 2 Bailiwicks 31 Commanderies	

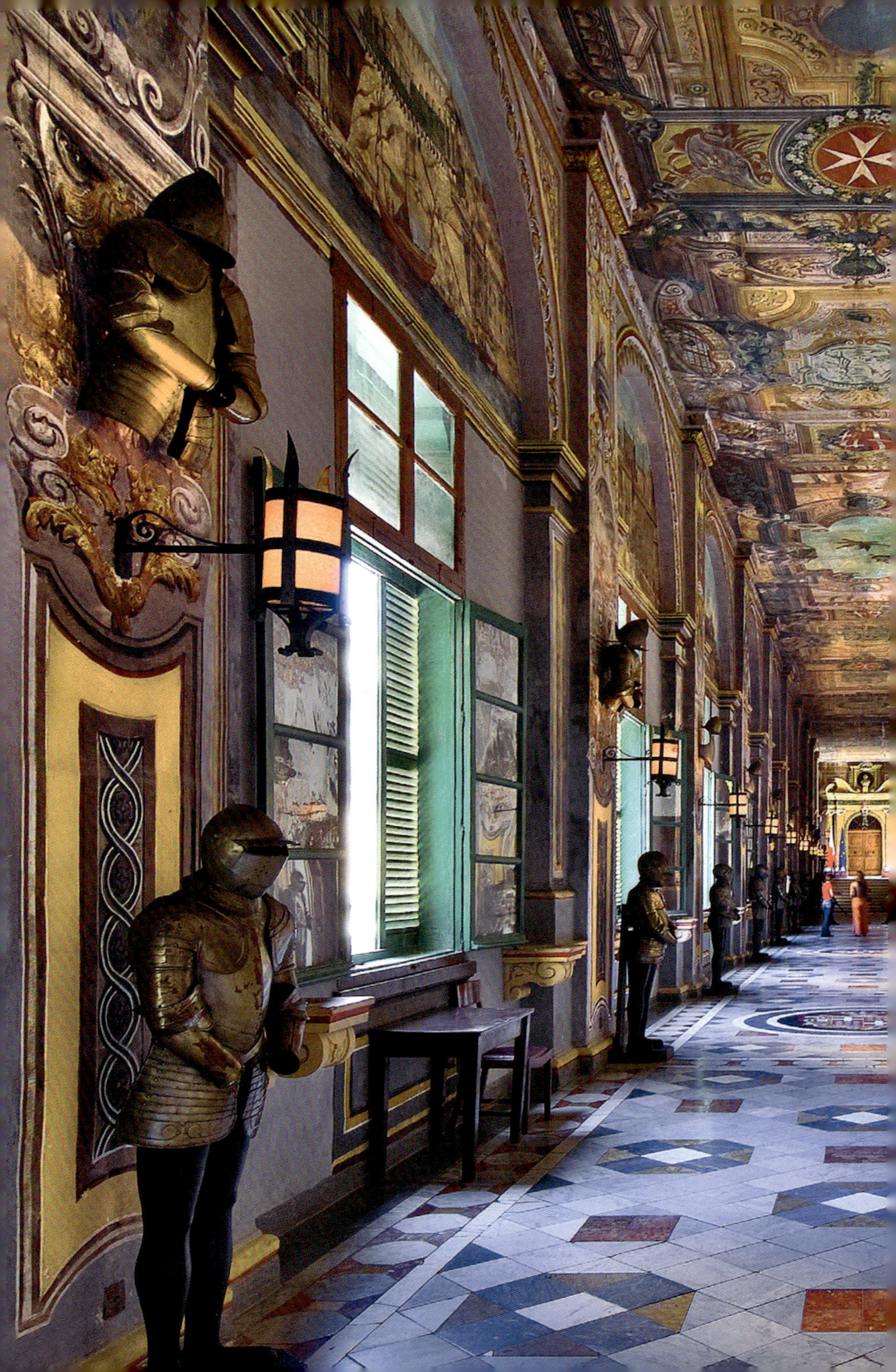

Lacking the possibility of establishing a dynasty and to leave heirs and successors many of the grand masters who ruled over Malta in the period of baroque and absolutism tried to establish a personal cult and imitate the splendour of the European princes. Art and architecture was the means to achieve this goal.

Chapter 9

THE SITES

The Order built some of the most prestigious architectural and artistic gems of the island of Malta. The history and development of these palaces, churches, and fortifications reflect the history of art and architecture in Malta, from the late gothic style to mannerism, baroque, and rococo. Their genesis and development was connected with some of the greatest names (Laparelli, Caravaggio, Preti, Favray, D`Aleccio, Nasoni) of architects and artists who worked on the island. At least since the epic Great Siege of 1565, Malta had carved its name in the European consciousness as a place of military strength and fortitude. Very often the name 'Malta' itself became synonymous with 'fortress' or 'bulwark of Christendom'. Its massive fortifications lent support that idea. The palaces of the grand masters and of some high-ranking knights, and the auberges, however, show another side of the picture. With the gradual shift of the Order's life-style in the seventeenth and eighteenth centuries, the architecture and embellishment of palaces and churches also changed.

Corridor in the Grand Master's Palace in Valletta. At least since the Cotoners, Nicholas and Rafael, in the late seventeenth century, the sombre austerity of the original architecture gave way to more elaborate, resplendent, and spectacular rhetorical imagery.

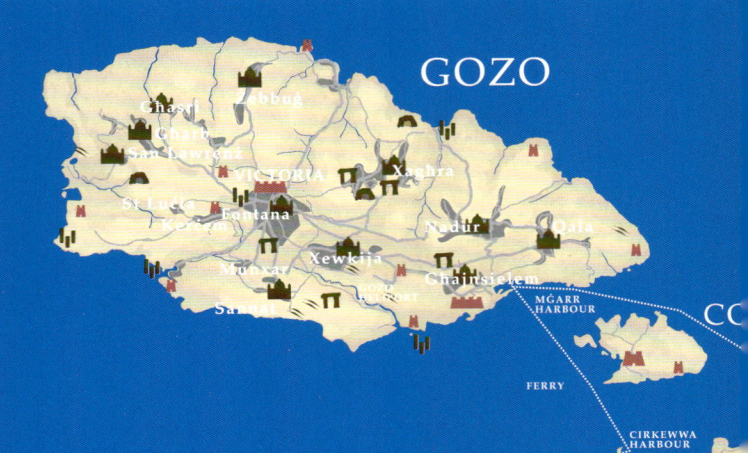

1. Valletta General .... page 248
2. St John's Co-Cathedral .... page 258
3. The Magisterial Palace............................ page 282
4. Fort St Elmo.. page 296
5. Fort St Angelo .... page 298
6. Fort St Michael .... page 304
7. Floriana .... page 306
8. The Cottonera Lines................................ page 308
9. Fort Ricasoli .... page 312
10. Verdala Palace.. page 318
11. The Palace and Gardens of San Anton.. page 324
12. Fort Manoel.. page 326
13. Fort Tigné .... page 328
14. The Gozo Castello..................................... page 330
15. Fort Chambray .... page 334
16. The Wignacourt Aqueduct .... page 336
16. The Coastline Fortifications................... page 338

LOCATION MAP 247

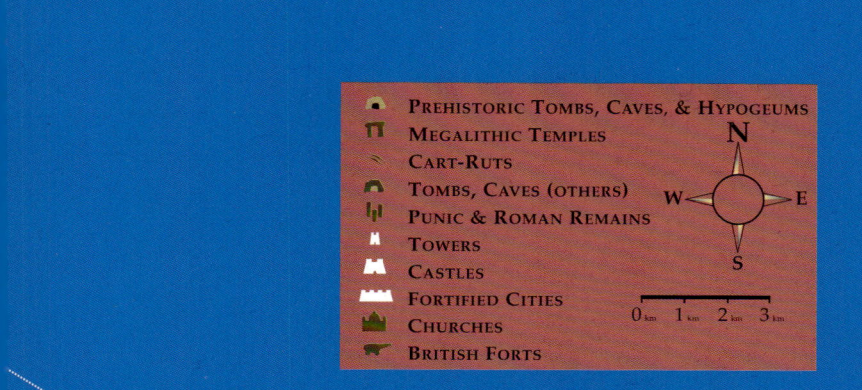

VALLETTA GENERAL
The *città nuova* – fortress city and work of art

Many eminent European architects and military engineers, such as Antonio Ferramolino, Baldassare Lanci, Pietro Pardo, Antonio Quinsani da Montalcino, and Bartolomeo Genga, were involved in the planning of a new city of the Order before 1565. Plans seemed to come to a final stage when, after the death of de la Sengle, Jean de Valette was elected grand master in 1557. He was more energetic in driving forward the decades-old plans to erect a new fortress city on Mount Sceberras. The only thing that had been done before was the erection of the small fortress of St Elmo in 1552. From the beginning of his magistracy, Valette – although facing a considerable lack of funds – tried to promote the project. In early 1558, the famous Cesena-born military engineer and architect Bartolomeo Genga arrived in Malta. Genga at first made plans for the reconstruction and re-building of the auberges in Birgu and drew up a plan for a new palace and residence for the grand master. Genga very strongly advised that a new fortress city should be built on Mount Sceberras and submitted a scheme in which the new town would cover all the peninsula and would therefore offer shelter for the population of Birgu and Isla. The grand master responded favourably to Genga's scheme and on 17 June 1558 the council agreed to develop Mount Sceberras. Things were made easier with the money which Grand Master Sengle and

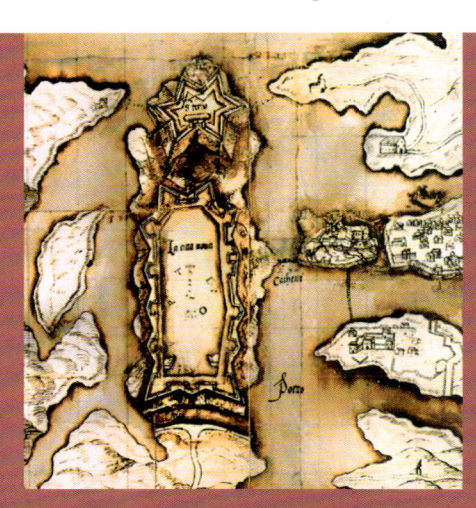

Bartolomeo Genga's plan (detail) for the new city to be build on Mount Sceberras, 1558, Albert Ganado Collection.

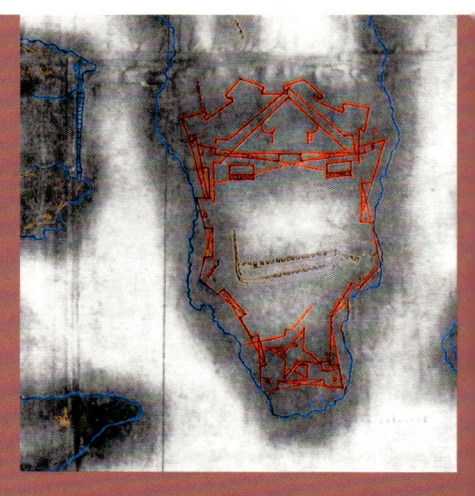

The 'Rocchi Drawing' (detail) depicts a series of suggestions for Mount Sceberras (here in red), Galleria degli Uffizi, Florence.

VALLETTA GENERAL   249

Orthographic photo of Valletta

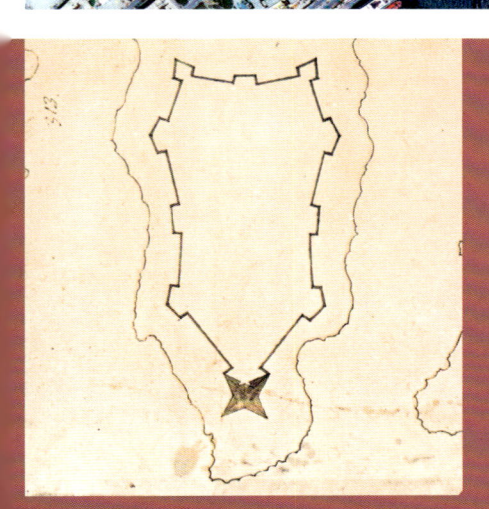

A pen drawing showing the walls of the new city attributed to Baldassare Lanci, 1562. Galleria degli Uffizi, Florence.

On this map (dated 1566) from the Laparelli Codex, Francesco Laparelli originally proposed a big fort on Mount Sceberras.

Diego de Toledo – a knight from a leading Spanish family– had left with their *spoglii*. Genga's scheme might have been identical with the anonymous drawing which was engraved in Rome in 1563 and published by Antonio Lafreri. Things came to an unexpected halt when Genga died suddenly in July 1558. Even the plans for a fortress city proposed in 1562 by Baldassare Lanci, the military engineer of the grand duke of Tuscany, did not materialize. Some modern architecture historians suggest that some of Genga's plans, such as those for the grand master's palace and some of the auberges, were later taken up by Maltese architect Gerolamo Cassar.

It was left to the architect and nobleman from Cortona Francesco Laparelli to put into practice the basic features of the city of Valletta.

After Genga's death, lack of funds had stalled this prestigious project. In July 1561 Grand Master Valette had asked Pope Pius IV for financial support. The papal bull *Salvatoris et Dominum* of October 1562 promised some support but nothing concrete materialized. During the final session of the Council of Trent, the Order again appealed to the Christian sovereigns for support, but things only moved when, after the epic Great Siege (May 1565–September 1565), Valette threatened to abandon Malta as he described the island's fortifications as being in ruins and the island more or less defenceless.

It was also rumoured that a new Turkish attack on Malta would come in 1566. The Christian sovereigns now reacted and Philip II of Spain and Pope Pius IV promised immediate financial help.

VALLETTA GENERAL 251

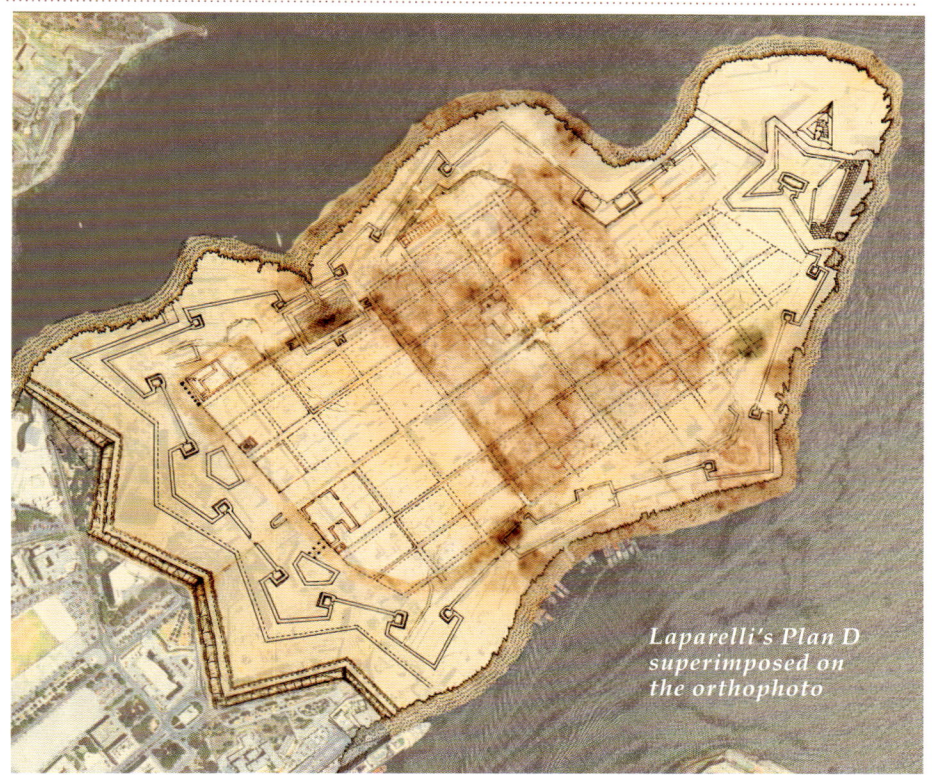

Laparelli's Plan D superimposed on the orthophoto

*Above: A sketch of Malta by Laparelli.
Right: A portrait of the architect from the book* Vita del Capitano Francesco Laparelli *by Filippo Venuti, Leghorn, 1761.
Both Accademia Etrusca di Cortona.*

*Left: One of the first printed maps of the harbour area, with Genga's plan, by Antonio Lafreri in 1563.
Chicago Newberry Library*

252　THE SITES　VALLETTA

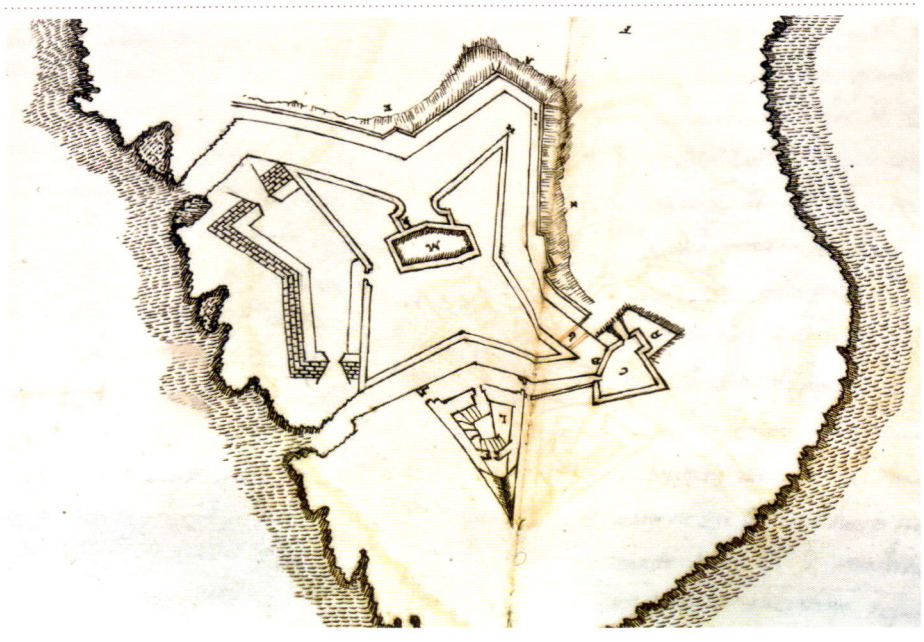

Another illustration from the Codex Laparelli showing a detailed plan of Fort St Elmo as the architect must have found it on his arrival to Malta in 1566. The fort had been restored after the Great Siege and Laparelli proposed to include the stronghold within the enceinte of Valletta unlike other proposed plans which separated the city from the fort. Laparelli Family Archives.

Fort St Elmo at the tip of Mount Sceberras suffered the full attack of the Ottoman army in May and June 1565. As long as the reinforcements from Birgu managed to get through, the defenders were able to maintain the fort. When the Turks encircled the entire position, Fort St Elmo was left isolated. Its fall then on 23 June was inevitable.

With financial support from King Philip II of Spain and the pope the knights could gather an expert group of architects and military engineers in Malta after 1566. These experts then constructed a line of defence which rated amongst the most modern of its sort in the Mediterranean.

Francesco Laparelli arrived in Malta on 28 December 1565 and, as time was pressing, he set to work immediately. The primary purpose of the *città nuova* was to be a 'shield for almost all of Christendom'. In his original plans, Laparelli had intended to adapt the streets to the contours of the Sceberras peninsula. His plans were intensively discussed by Valette, the viceroy of Sicily Don Garcia de Toledo, and Philip II who was the supreme feudal lord over the islands. In early March 1566 the eminent military engineer and prior of Hungary Gabrio Serbelloni – Laparelli's old teacher – arrived in Malta to heal the rift between Valette and Don Garcia de Toledo. Serbelloni was also commissioned by Philip II to examine the plans. In fact the present grid-iron plan of Valletta seemed to have been adopted on Serbelloni's advice. In early April Laparelli's revised plans were approved by the council of the Order. The first stone was laid by Valette on 28 March 1566 in the presence of the bishop of Malta and the leading members of the Order. In June Laparelli sent a detailed *discorso* about his designs and plans to the pope.

Before the building could start, great efforts had to be made to level parts of Mount Sceberras. The straightness of the streets of Valletta had less aesthetic than military reasons. If the enemy managed to enter the city, cannon and muskets could rake the streets. The main axis is the *Strada Reale* (today Republic Street). Six thousand men were deemed enough to defend Valletta.

The works were carried out with great speed with up to 8,000 men

For the excavation and building of the ditches and walls at the land front of the newly built fortress city of Valletta a workforce of several thousands was necessary. Excavation works like these were made easier because of the softness of the Maltese limestone.

Considering the vastness and ambition of the project the work on the fortifications of Valletta went ahead at an incredible rate. When Grand Master Valette died in the summer of 1568, many of the fortifications were well advanced.

254 THE SITES VALLETTA

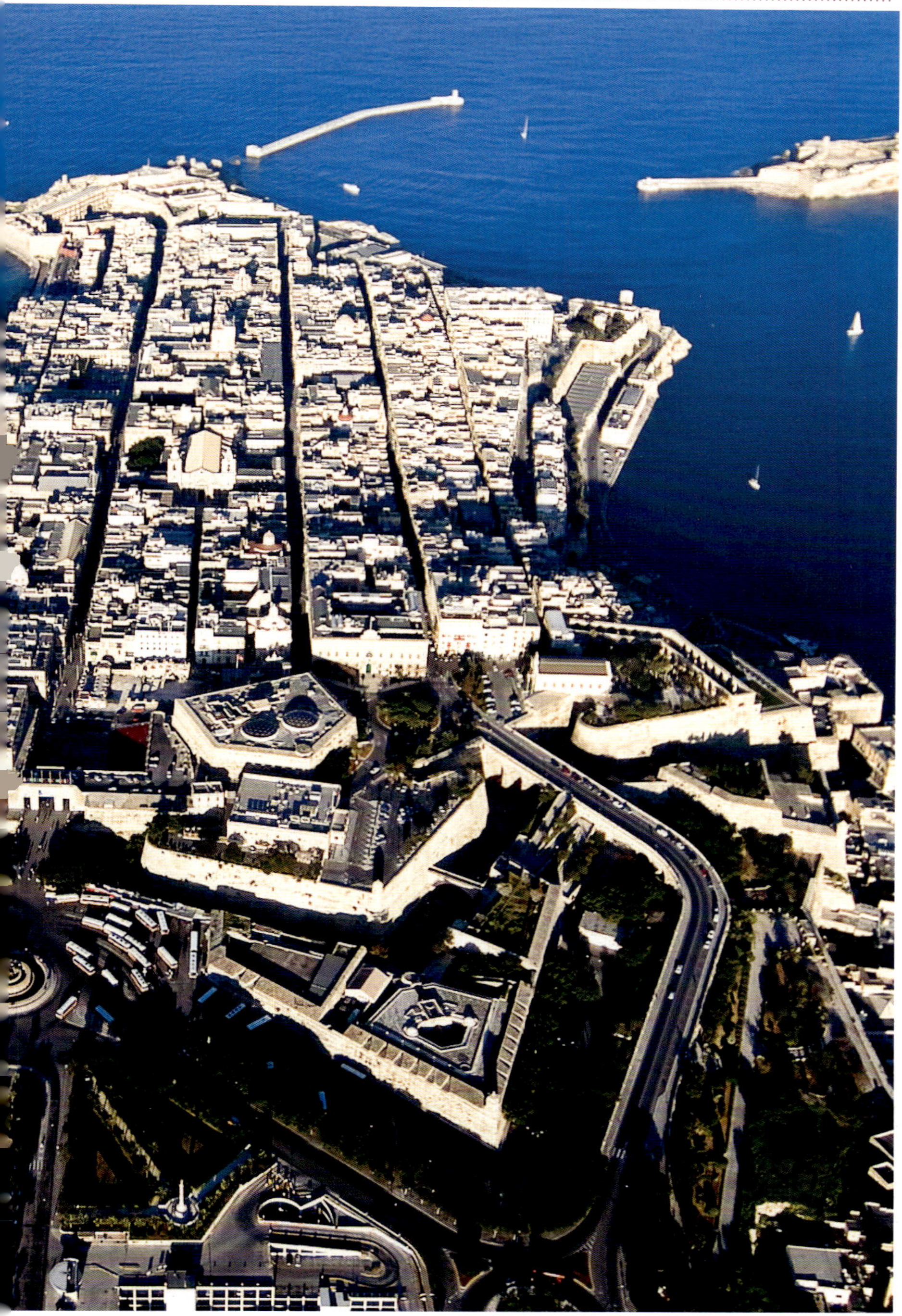

sometimes employed in the works. The big advantage of building projects in Malta was the softness of the local stone. The building was not stopped when Valette died in 1568. At the end of 1569, when most of the basic structures and lines were nearly completed, Laparelli left Malta but not before having trained the Maltese architect Gerolamo Cassar to finish the works. Cassar proved to be a most talented architect and it was he who constructed most of the palaces, auberges of the knights, and official edifices in the new city. His masterpiece is the conventual church of St John's. The parts of Laparelli's design which were not executed were the *Manderaggio*, or galley-pen, and an arsenal. In 1571 the convent moved from Birgu to Valletta as the new city was called in honour of its founder.

With the building of Valletta the whole defensive character of Malta changed. It became the new centre of defence of the island and everything which had to be build now would automatically have a subsidiary role to it.

The history and development of Valletta also reflects the history of early modern art and architecture in Malta. Their genesis is connected with some of the greatest architects and artists who worked on the island. At least since the Great Siege, Malta had carved its name in the European consciousness as a place of military strength and fortitude. Very often the name 'Malta' itself became synonymous with 'fortress' or 'bulwark of Christendom'. Its massive fortifications lent support to that idea. Many palaces and auberges in Valletta, however, show another

Even although modern changes and the tribute to modern traffic have altered the original lines of the fortifications of the land side of Valletta considerably, this aerial view still offers a good idea of the vastness and well-planned original construction.

side of the picture. With the gradual shift of the Order's life-style in the seventeenth and eighteenth centuries, the architecture and embellishment of the buildings also changed. In fact, at least with Nicolas and Rafael Cotoner in the late seventeenth century, the sombre austerity of sixteenth-century architecture gave way to more elaborate, resplendent, and spectacular rhetorical imagery. This is especially visible in the decorations of the palaces and auberges in Valletta. Maltese baroque is a special expression of this architectural and artistic intention which follows the style then prevailing in central and southern Catholic Europe and meant to impress upon the population the benevolent despotism of the State. Originally most of the buildings in Valletta, although imposing in mass and volume, lacked any bigger decoration which would have tempered their sombre atmosphere. This is still visible in the large construction of the *Sacra Infermeria*, the huge hospital of the Order, built in the 1570s. Later, buildings like the grand master's palace or the auberges were embellished with precious decorations and works of art and serve as symbols of how the princes of Malta started to adapt to the refined lifestyle of the European aristocracy.

Valletta is a fine example of a city planned according to the principles of Renaissance urban architecture. The grid plan of its streets and passages is typical for this sort of 16th-century architecture.

ST JOHN'S CO-CATHEDRAL
VALLETTA

St John's co-cathedral, the conventual church of the Order and the main temple of the Hospitallers in Malta, is situated in the centre of Valletta. The Maltese Gerolamo Cassar, who was originally trained as a military engineer, was entrusted with the planning of the church. He laid out a plan with a plain façade flanked by two large bell towers. The doorway is accompanied by a set of Doric columns supporting a balcony. The austere and sober character of the construction and façade still reflects the then prevailing monastic spirit of the Order. It was only later, in the baroque period, that the contrast between the sober façade and the festive mood of the interior, came about. The church has a rectangular floor plan with an apse at the east end. It has a wide nave, a barrel vault, and two aisles divided into side chapels. There appears to be some influence from the plan of the *Il Gesù* church in Rome.

Started in 1572, building was completed in 1577 during the magistracy of Jean Levesque de la Cassière. It was natural that the church should be dedicated to St John the Baptist, the patron saint of the Order. The building was consecrated by the archbishop of Monreale, Ludovico Torres, who came over to Malta for the occasion. The church was administered by a chapter of *cappellani maggiori* who were ordained members of the Order. These chaplains were headed by a prior, who

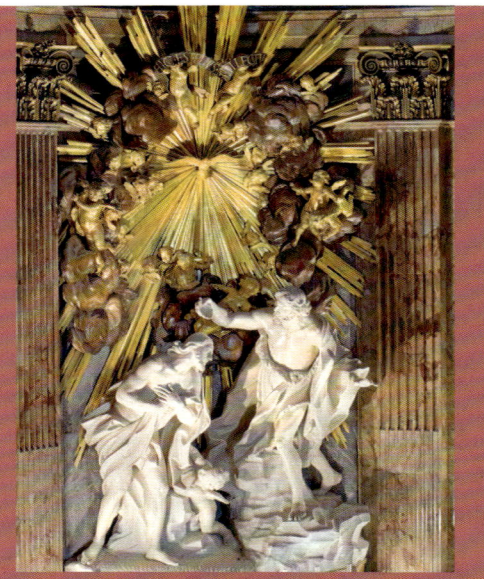

The fine high baroque altar of the chapel of the langue of Provence with the painting of St Michael the Archangel.

Left: The Baptism of Christ by John the Baptist *by Giuseppe Mazzuoli. The scupture was brought over from Rome in pieces and assembled* in situ *behind the main altar.*

The sanctuary of the church of St John's has had a number of changes in accordance with the Tridentine liturgical reforms, such as raising the high altar on a platform. Originally there was only one altar placed directly in the apse with an altarpiece depicting The Baptism of Christ. This painting now hangs in the museum. The apse now holds the impressive marble figures depicting The Baptism of Christ by John the Baptist by Giuseppe Mazzuoli, one of the leading sculptors of the 18th-century.

The altar of the chapel of the langue of Auvergne with the painting of St Sebastian.

The important icon of Our Lady of Philermos used to be held in this chapel. The icon was believed to have miraculous powers and had been in the Order's possession since its time in Jerusalem. Now it is exhibited in the Museum of Fine Arts of Montenegro.

ranked third in dignity after the grand master and the bishop of Malta. A chapel was assigned to each langue. However, it was not until 1603, during the magistracy of Alof de Wignacourt, that the various langues took responsibility to embellish their chapels. The connecting passages between the chapels were made in the early 1660s.

Originally the interior was modestly decorated. The lavish stone carving, gilding, and marble ornamentation were not added before the second half of the seventeenth century. The oratory and the sacristy were built in 1604 during the reign of Alof de Wignacourt, while the annexes were added in the early eighteenth century during the magistracy of Manoel de Vilhena, whose armorial shield can be seen on the doorway to these side annexes. Over the years, grand masters, dignitaries, and knights donated gifts of high artistic value and made enormous contributions to enrich it with the best works of art by the leading artists available to them. It was mainly during the rule of Spanish Grand Masters Rafael and Nicolas Cotoner after 1660 that a programme to redecorate the interior of the church was started. The seventeenth century had ushered in the new high baroque style and its flamboyant and demonstrative character provided ample material.

The appearance of the interior of St John's is linked to the famous artist Mattia Preti. At the end of 1661 the master from Calabria had come to Malta and started with the work which would take him until 1666 to finish. Contrary to what many books say Preti's painting of the vault are not frescoes, but painted directly in oils on the stone. Preti very aptly used the six bays of the vault of the

Several chapels in St John's are profusely decorated with rich sculptural motifs and they were gilded during the 1660 redecoration of the church. For example, in the chapel of the French langues the generous distribution of fleurs-de-lys in the passageways, as well as on the interior walls, proclaim the supremacy of the French crown.

ST JOHN'S CO-CATHEDRAL 261

The famous Italian artist Caravaggio is best known for his revolutionary light effect called chiaroscuro *and harsh realism which soon became hallmarks of baroque painting. The* Beheading of St John *is Caravaggio's largest and the only painting which bears his signature scrawled in the blood flowing from the Baptist's throat.*

Top: The oratory and the sacristy of St John's were built in 1604 during the reign of Grand Master Alof de Wignacourt.

Right: The ceiling of the church of St John's is a barrel vault. It was decorated by the Italian master Mattia Preti with episodes from the life of St John the Baptist.

262 The Sites Valletta

Preti painted saints, martyrs, and heroes of the Order on the cornice next to the oval windows. Above left: Frà Leone Strozzi, right: Pierre de Massues.

Below: The whole ceiling painted by Preti between 1662 and 1666 show the most important episodes in the life of the Order's patron saint St John the Baptist.

church to fit his narrative cycle. Each bay is subdivided into three sections. The story of St John the Baptist starts from the first bay on the north side with the vision of the priest Zachary and ends with the beheading of the saint in the last bay to the right of the altar. At the same time as this immense commission to paint the vault of the church, he was also commissioned to carry out various altarpieces for the side chapels. Over the next decades Preti was in charge for the supervision of the wall-carvings, the marble work, the gilding, and the overall decoration of the Order's prestigious conventual church. On designs prepared by Preti, the plain walls of the nave and chapels were decorated with elaborate motifs characteristic of baroque ornamentation, transforming the walls into a profile of richly gilded foliage, flowers, angels, and triumphal symbols of all kinds. The pilasters supporting the central nave were clad with the finest green marble, at the top of which the coat of arms of Grand Master Nicolas Cotoner are displayed.

Preti's arrival in Malta marked the beginning of an entire new era in Maltese art. Until the mid-seventeenth century a strong manneristic influence dominated the artistic scene. With Preti, the baroque filtered into Maltese art, as his manner and style were seized upon by numerous imitators. After his death in 1699, Preti was buried in St John's.

The entire floor of the church is covered with a unique collection of approximately 400 inlaid marble tombstones, made between the late seventeenth and the late eighteenth century to commemorate some of the most illustrious grand priors,

The entire floor of the church is covered with a collection of inlaid marble tombstones. There are approximately 400 tombstones. They commemorate some of the most illustrious knights of the Order, several of whom were members of the great aristocratic Catholic families of Europe.

ST JOHN'S CO-CATHEDRAL 265

admirals, and *balís*. Crowns and coronets indicate the most noble of the knights. Each tombstone is highly decorated with expressions of triumph, fame, and death. Skeletons and skulls are often included in the iconography.

The apse of the central sanctuary now holds the impressive marble figures of *The Baptism of Christ by John the Baptist* by Giuseppe Mazzuoli, a leading sculptor of the eighteenth century. The high altar is an extravagant piece composed of rare marbles and was a gift of Italian Grand Master Carafa. *St John Baptizing Christ* by Matteo Perez d'Aleccio, the church's original main altarpiece, was replaced by the large marble group of the Baptism. The choir stalls, installed in 1598, bear the arms of the reigning Grand Master Martin Garzes and Giorgio Gianpierei, the knight who financed them.

The chapels are arranged according to the seniority of the langues. The French langues were the most senior and the three chapels of France, Auvergne, and Provence were placed closest to the High Altar. The first chapel on the south side is dedicated to Our Lady of Philermos, where the miraculous icon of Our Lady of Philermos was kept. This icon drew great devotion and had been in the possession of the Order since its days in Jerusalem. Grand Master L'Isle Adam had brought this precious icon from Rhodes. Before battle the knights prayed to Our Lady of Philermos for victory. The chapel of Auvergne is dedicated to St Sebastian. The only grand master buried in this chapel is Annet de Clermont de Chattes Gessan whose white-marble monument is a typical early baroque design. The chapel of Aragon is dedicated to St George,

The increasing popular fashion in Rome of decorating churches in the new opulent baroque style did not fail to catch the Order's attention. Subsequently the Calabrian artist Mattia Preti was commissioned to transform the interior of St John's into a celebration of baroque art. The contrast between the sober façade and the festive mood of the interior makes St John's unique. Mattia Preti worked in St John's church for more than six years after 1663 to illustrate episodes of the story of St John the Baptist.

the patron saint of the Aragonese knights. The altar and its surrounds were redesigned during the magistracy of Ramon Despuig (1736–41) whose effigy can be seen at the base of the altar columns. The altarpiece, commissioned by Grand Master Martin de Redin in 1659, is one of Preti's first works in this church. It depicts St George on a white stallion after having killed the dragon. There are four grand masters buried in this chapel. Facing the altar to the left there is the monument to de Redin and opposite there is that of Rafael Cotoner. To the left of the outer arch is the famous monument for Rafael's brother Nicolas who succeeded him as grand master. Nicolas's gilt bronze bust is ensconced amongst an exuberant display of war trophies. Two slaves crouch underneath the weight of the weapons, representing the supremacy of the Order over Asia and Africa. The other monument to the right is that of Grand Master Ramon Perellos y Roccaful. The chapel of the langue of Castille, Leon, and Portugal is dedicated to the patron saint of Spain, St James. The altarpiece is by Preti. There are two grand masters buried in the chapel. On the left, close to the altar, is the monument to the Portuguese Antonio Manoel de Vilhena by the well-known Florentine sculptor Massimiliano Soldani Benzi. The monument commemorating Pinto on the left, close to the archway to the nave, has a note of neo-classical restraint.

The chapel of the Anglo-Bavarian langue was once known as the Shrine of the Holy Relics. It became the chapel of the newly formed Anglo-Bavarian langue in 1782 and is dedicated to St Charles Borromeo, cardinal archbishop of Milan, the

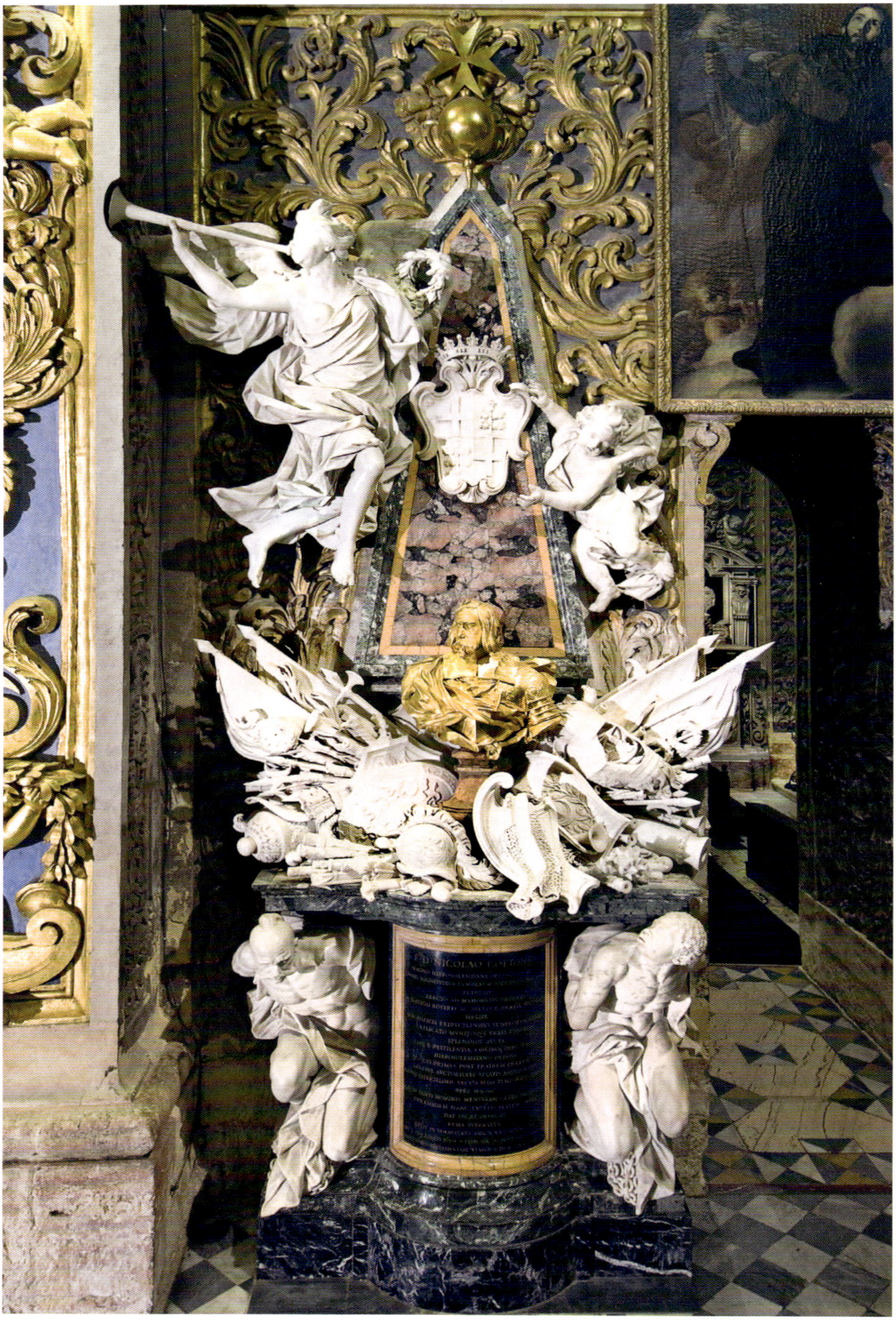

Left: Grand Master Nicolas Cotoner's gilt bronze bust is ensconced amongst an exuberant display of war trophies. Two slaves carry the weight of the weapons, representing the supremacy of the Order over the infidels.

Above: Before Mattia Preti was invited to Malta to decorate the conventual church of the Order, Grand Master Lascaris asked the artist to send him as a sample of his work, a painting of St George for the chapel of the langue of Aragon.

In the chapel of the langue of Castille is the elegant monument of Grand Master Pinto (1741–73). On the left is the monument of Grand Master Antonio Manoel de Vilhena (1722–36).

renowned Catholic reformer. The chapel of the langue of Provence is dedicated to St Michael the Archangel. The funerary monuments in this chapel belong to Grand Masters Antoine de Paule and Jean Lascaris Castellar. The chapel of France is dedicated to the Conversion of St Paul and has a fine altarpiece by Preti. The chapel holds three magnificent funerary monuments. The monument to Grand Master Adrien de Wignacourt, the nephew of Grand Master Alof de Wignacourt is sited on the epistle side. The pure-white-marble monument of Emmanuel de Rohan (1775–97) is situated on the right of the altar. The monument to the left of the altar is that of Marquis de Wignacourt, the brother of the grand master, who fell ill and died here during a visit in 1615. There is also the funerary monument of the

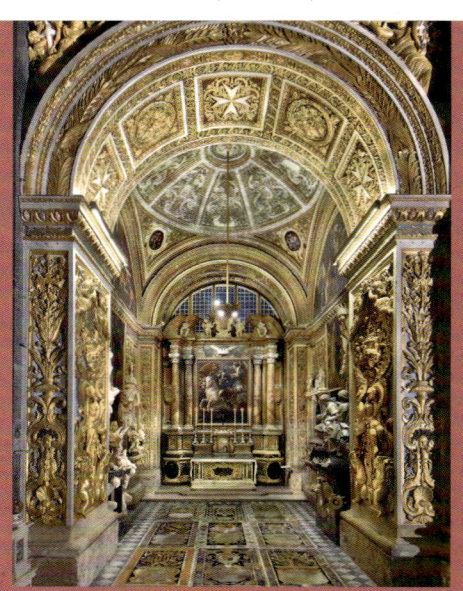

Above: The sarcophagus and bust of grand master de Rohan, the last Grand Master to be buried in Malta in 1797 in the chapel of the langue of France.

Left: The chapel of the langue of Aragon dedicated to St George. Five grand masters are buried here: de Redin; the Cotoner brothers Rafael and Nicolas; Perellos; and Despuig.

Vicomte de Beaujolais, the brother of King Louis Philippe of France, who died on 29 May 1808 when he was in Malta. The reclining figure of the count was commissioned by the king in 1843 from the French sculptor Jacques Pradier. The chapel of Italy is dedicated to the Immaculate Conception and St Catherine of Alexandria, the patron saint of the Italian knights. The altarpiece depicts *The Mystic Marriage of St Catherine* and is again by Preti. Most of the chapel was decorated in the mid-seventeenth century at the personal expense of Frà Francesco Sylos, ambassador to the viceroy of Sicily and commander of Palermo and Agrigento. Its altar consists of finely carved polychromized marble and is raised on three steps. The relics of St Euphemia are visible through an oculus on the altar front. The chapel contains the funerary

Detail from the monument of Vicomte de Beaujolais, the brother of King Louis Philippe of France, who died on 29 May 1808 while he was in Malta.

Above: The altar of the chapel of the langue of Germany dedicated to the Epiphany. The painting of The Adoration of the Magi *is by Stefano Erardi.*

Right: The chapel of the Holy Relics or of the Anglo-Bavarian langue. The altar was built during the reign of Grand Master Lascaris. The cross on the altar is by Alessandro Algardi.

272 The Sites Valletta

The spandrels of the dome of the chapel of the langue of Italy hold four escutcheons: those of the Order and of Grand Master Rafael Cotoner above the altar, whilst the two on the side of the nave represent the langue of Italy.

Above: The altarpiece in the chapel of the langue of Italy was painted by Mattia Preti and shows St Catherine of Alexandria, the patron saint of the Italian langue.

Left: The marble monument of the Italian Grand Master Gregorio Carafa (1680–90) depicts intricate designs of several war trophies.

monument of Grand Master Gregorio Carafa. The sarcophagus is in black marble and carries the bronze bust of the grand master accompanied by two putti, crushing a turban and a skull under their feet respectively. The chapel is mostly known because of the depiction of *St Jerome* which once adorned its walls. This painting originally formed part of the private collection of the Knight Ippolito Malaspina and was donated to St John's after his death in 1624. The painting of *St Jerome writing* by Michelangelo Merisi da Caravaggio is today kept in the oratory. In all probability Caravaggio was commissioned to carry out this work directly by Malaspina and it was intended to adorn the walls of his Valletta residence. The chapel of Germany, dedicated to the Epiphany, was originally assigned to the langue of England. The altarpiece, *The Adoration of the Magi*, depicts the moment when the three wise men from the East came to the place of Christ's birth guided by a bright star.

The oratory, a place of devotion for young novices, was started in 1602 and must have been finished by 1605 when, as the archives state, its windows were fitted with glass – then still a rare commodity. It was the ruling Grand Master Alof de Wignacourt who was searching for an artist to embellish the church and to produce a painting of the martyrdom of St John, the patron of the Order, for the novices to meditate on and to impress on their minds the devotion required to be a virtuous knight. This is how Caravaggio, who was then waiting for a papal pardon after having been accused of murder, came to Malta. The famous artist was probably attracted not only by the patronage of the Order but also by

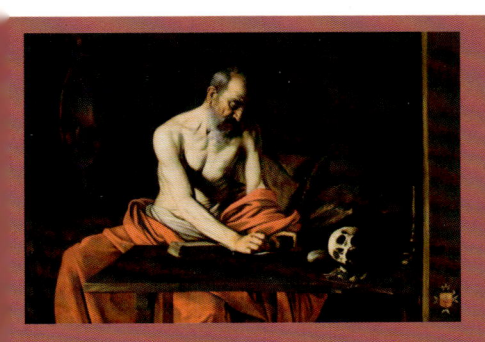

Above: Caravaggio's St Jerome writing *originally formed part of the private collection of Fra Ippolito Malaspina, an important and powerful member of the Order and was donated to St John's after his death in 1624.*

Right: The arch and pilasters of the chapel of Italy. All the walls of the church are masterpieces of baroque craftsmanship.

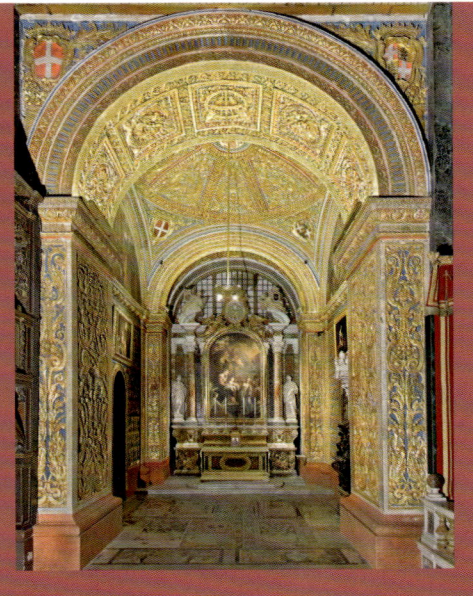

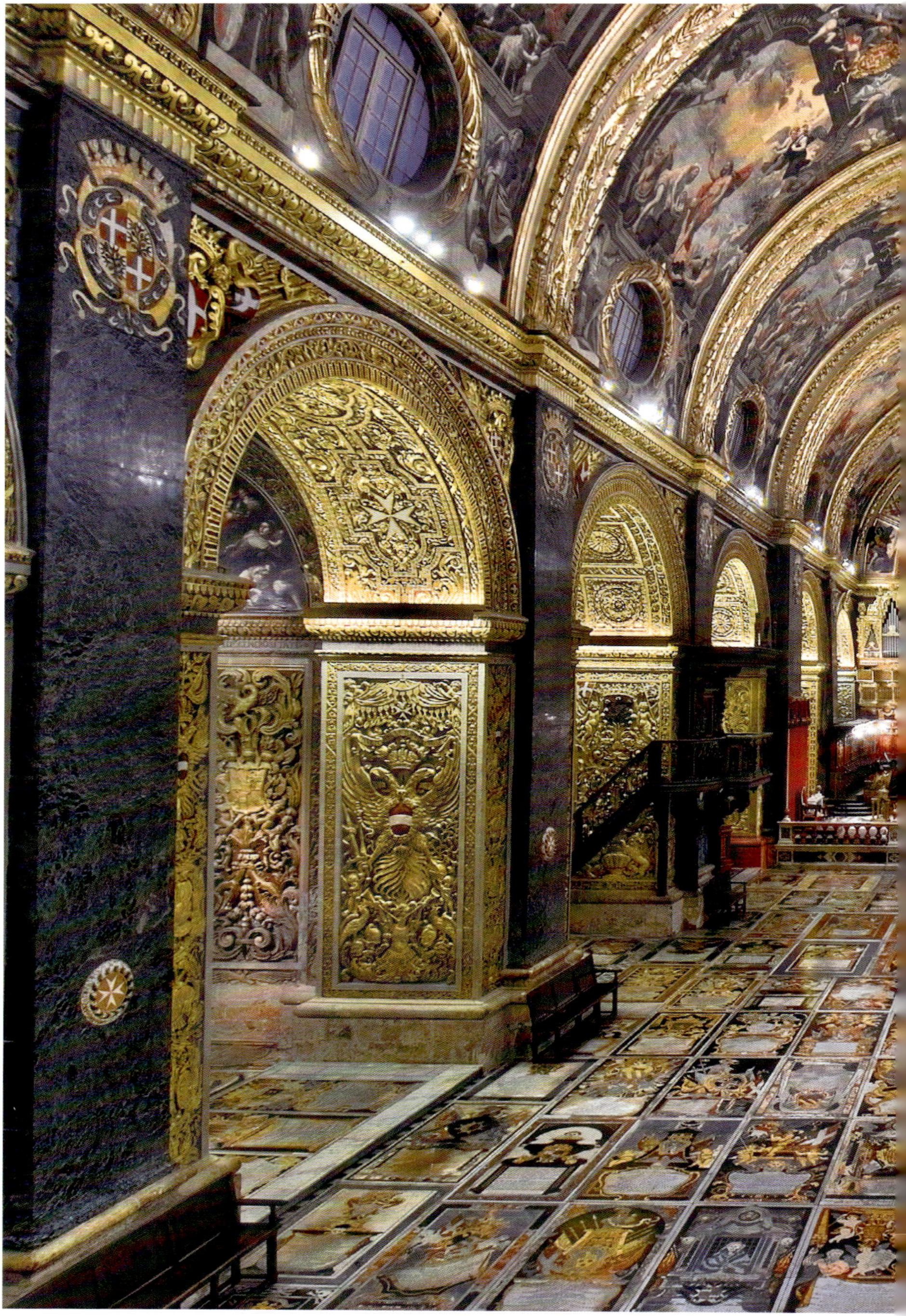

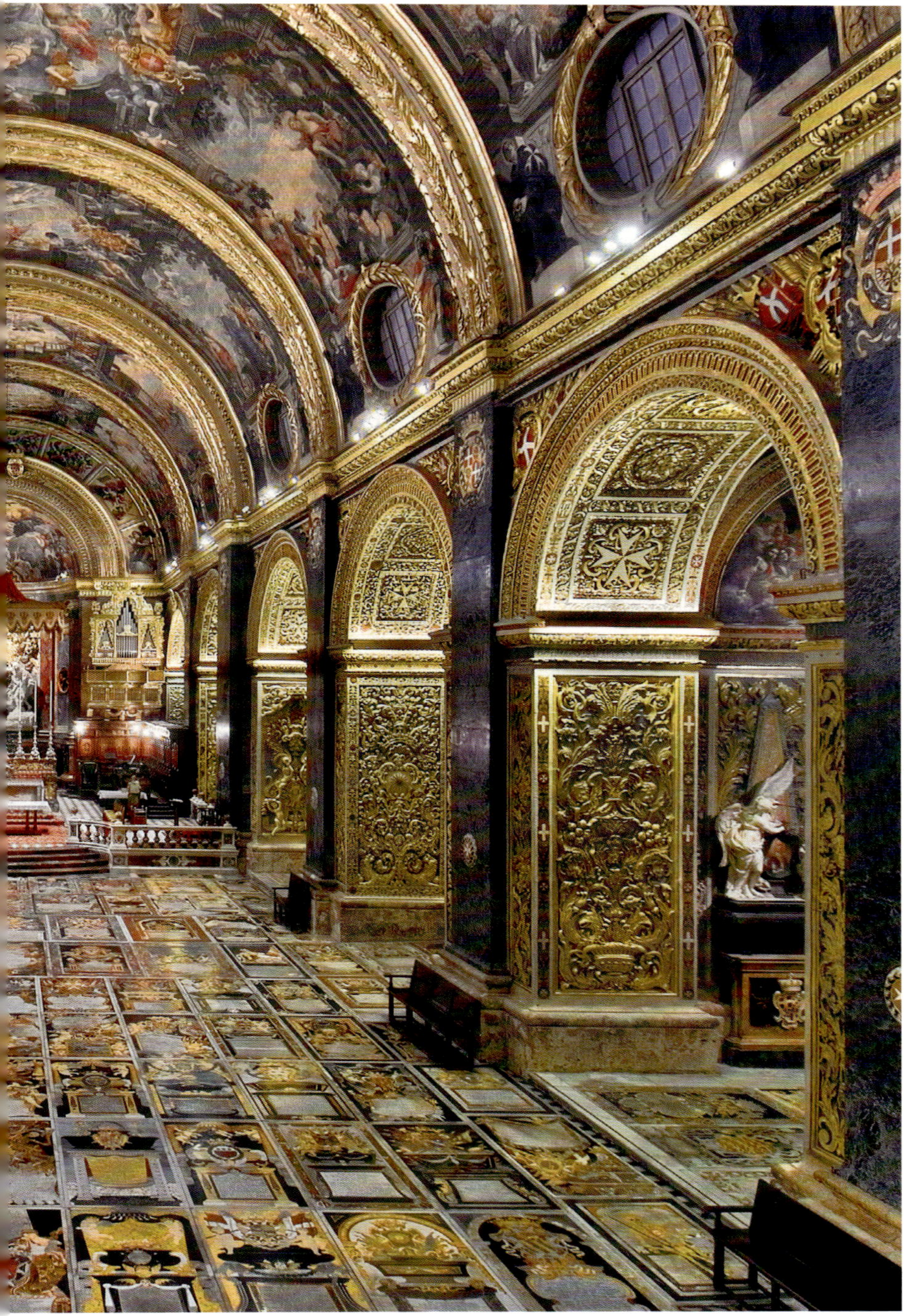

The crypt of St John's was excavated under the high altar and is reached through a flight of steps within the chapel of the langue of Provence. In the crypt lie the remains of 12 grand masters who ruled between 1522 and 1623. In the centre, exactly under the main altar, is the tomb of Grand Master Jean Levesque de la Cassière, builder of St John's. The ceiling decorations are by Nicolò Nasoni.

In its sobriety, the grand masters' crypt forms a harsh contrast with the baroque glory of the main church. It still evokes the medieval spirit and religiosity of the leaders of the Order. Amongst others, there are buried the remains of the famous Grand Masters Philippe Villiers de L'Isle Adam (1521–34) [above left] and Jean de Valette (1557-68) [above right], Jean Levesque de la Cassière (1572–81), the founder of the conventual church of St John's [centre top], Cardinal Hughues Loubenx de Verdalle (1582–95) [opposite right], and Alof de Wignacourt (1601–22).

the dream of knighthood. After having spent a year as a novice, he was invested into the Order as a knight of obedience on 14 July 1608, a ceremony that took place here in the oratory. A few weeks later, Caravaggio was involved in a fight during which a high-ranking knight was seriously wounded. He was arrested and imprisoned at Fort St Angelo from where he escaped in October 1608. The council, informed of his disobedience, immediately expelled him from the Order. Amongst the legacy which he left in Malta the *Beheading of St John the Baptist* in the Oratory is certainly the most impressive work. It is Caravaggio's largest work and the only painting which bears his signature scrawled in the blood flowing from the Baptist's neck. Most of the grand masters who ruled in the sixteenth century and the early seventeenth century over Malta are buried in the crypt under the main altar.

It is reached through a flight of steps in the chapel of Provence. There lie the remains of the 12 grand masters who ruled Malta between 1522 and 1623. In the four arches of the crypt there are the tombs of L'Isle Adam, Valette, de la Cassière, Verdalle, Alof de Wignacourt, Garzes, de la Sengle, del Monte, and de Homedes. Ximenes de Texada is buried beneath the pavement without a single line to mark the spot. Furthermore a small marble tablet commemorates the English knight Sir Oliver Starkey, Valette's *uditore* and Latin secretary, who is also buried here.

Overleaf: Four of the Flemish tapestries at St John's. The set forms the largest complete collection in the world, consisting of 29 pieces. It was ordered from the Brussels atelier of Judecos de Vos for 40,000 scudi and was based on cartoons by Peter Paul Rubens.

The beautifully sculpted mannerist marble and intarsio monument of Grand Master Martin Garzes in the crypt of the grand masters. The mausoleum is in the corner of the crypt. In the opposite corner is the monument of Grand Master del Monte.

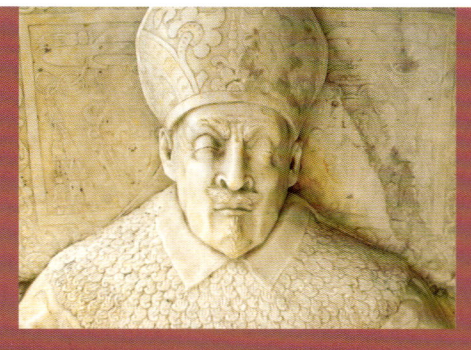

The face of Grand Master Hugues Loubenx de Verdalle scupted in white Carrara marble in the full body effigy of the grand master and cardinal in his mausoleum inside the crypt of the grand masters.

278　The Sites　Valletta

St John's Co-Cathedral

280 THE SITES VALLETTA

The Baptism of Christ by John the Baptist *by Giuseppe Mazzuoli.*

The Crypt of St John's was excavated under the high altar.

The beautiful mosaic in front of the main altar (now hidden under the new altar).

A wall from the chapel of Italy with the copy of Caravaggio's St Jerome *(now in the Oratory).*

Decoration under the main arch of the chapel of the langue of Castille, Leon, and Portugal.

The main sacristy with Stefano Pieri's Flagellation of Christ *on the main altar.*

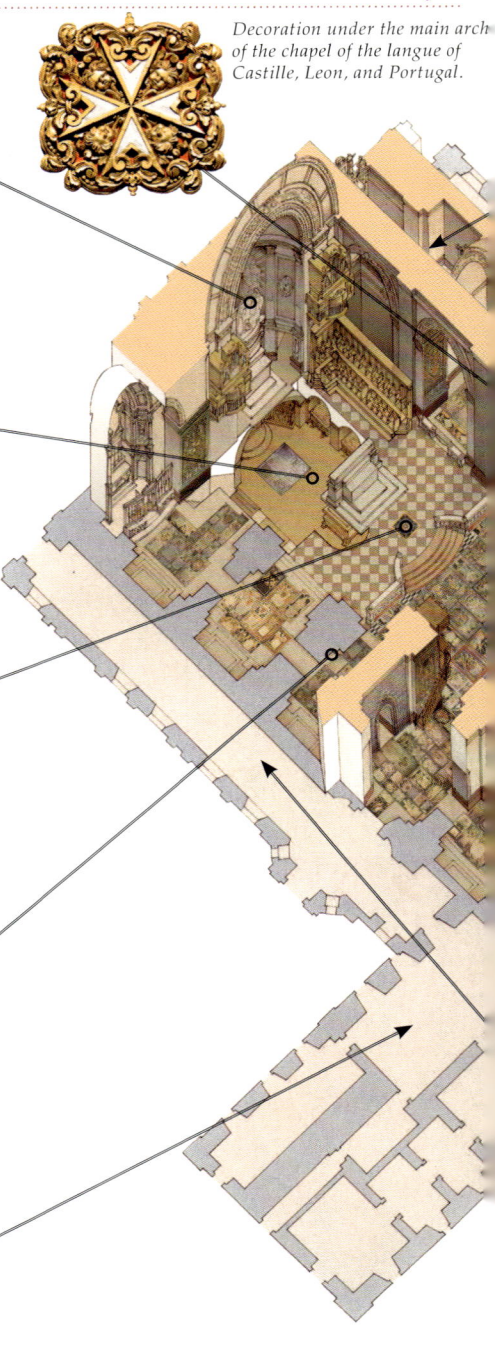

ST JOHN'S CO-CATHEDRAL   281

The famous silver gates in the chapel of Our Lady of Philermos.

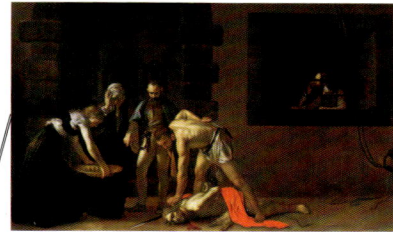

The **Beheading of St John** *is Caravaggio's largest painting. It is still in situ where he painted it.*

A detail from Caravaggio's **St Jerome Writing,** *now in the Oratory.*

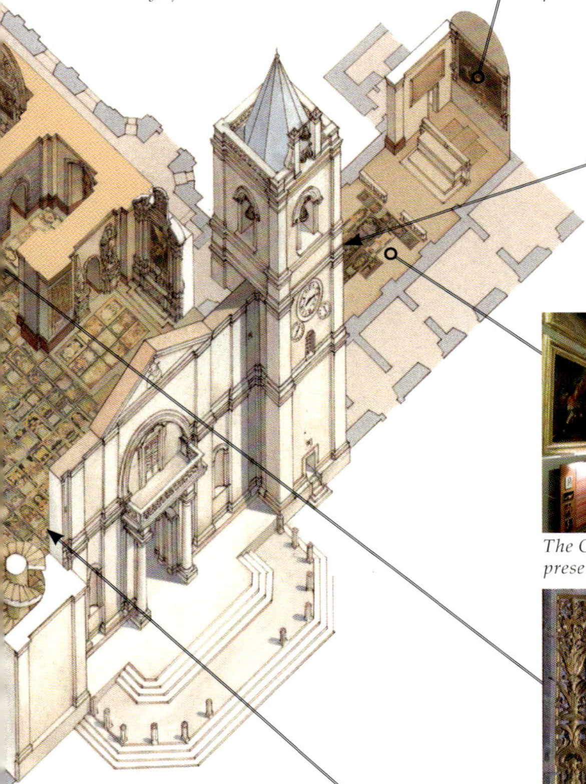

The Oratory, built in 1602 was given the present baroque appearance by Mattia Preti.

Above: The chapel of the langue of Aragon.
Below: Detail from Grand Master Zondadari's monument next to the main door.

The annex corridor next to the visitor's entrance is used for temporary exhibitions.

THE MAGISTERIAL PALACE
VALLETTA

The magisterial palace in Valletta has housed several rulers of Malta. For over 225 years (1573–1798), it was the residence of the grand masters. Between 1798 and 1800 the palace witnessed a short French *intermezzo* when Napoleon conquered Malta and General Vaubois in vain tried to resist the British taking Malta. From 1800 until 1964 Malta was a British colony and the British civil commissioners, later governors, resided here. After Malta's independence in 1964, it housed the governors-general and, since 1974, the building has served as the office of the president of Malta.

The beginning of the building was humble and certainly did not echo the power of the leaders of the Order. It was during the rule of Italian Grand Master Pietro del Monte (1568–72) that the idea was conceived to place the residence of the grand masters in the present site. Here, in the most level part of the city, there stood the private residence of del Monte's nephew, the Knight Eustachio del Monte and the first *Auberge d'Italie*. What made the grand master and council chose this place is not entirely clear. It might have been its level and central position. Originally the council had intended to build the palace on the site of the impressive *Auberge de Castille*. This was the highest point of the city but was certainly not central and, because of the bastions and bulwarks nearby,

It is generally maintained that the Maltese engineer and architect Gerolamo Cassar planned the magisterial palace in Valletta. Work was still in its initial stages when Grand Master Del Monte died on 27 January 1572. The main structure was completed under his successor, the Frenchman Jean Levesque de la Cassière (1572–81). Above the façade overlooking Pjazza San Ġiorgio.

THE MAGISTERIAL PALACE   283

The armoury corridor is the central corridor of the magisterial palace. This corridor is 62 metres long and 5 metres wide. The lunettes were created by the Italian painter Nicolò Nasoni.

The imposing triumphal doorway is a work of the Italian baroque architect Romano Carapecchia. The lunettes in this corridor were painted during the British period.

After ascending the staircase, one enters the **piano nobile** *of the magisterial palace — the upper storey of the palace. There were originally four corridors, but the one parallel to the entrance corridor was later divided into three rooms.*

Therefore today there is the entrance corridor in front of a rectangular lobby at the end of the staircase; the armoury corridor on the right side at the top of the staircase, and the Prince of Wales corridor on the right beyond at the end of the entrance corridor.

ill-placed, according to sixteenth-century treatises on architecture, for the erection of a huge palace with an adjacent ceremonial square. A place in the centre of Valletta was certainly more suitable.

By 1571 it was firmly decided that Eustachio del Monte's former residence should be converted into the magisterial palace. In this year the council bought the house and ground for this purpose. It is generally maintained that the Maltese engineer and architect Gerolamo Cassar planned the palace although there is no archival proof. Work was still in its initial stages when Grand Master Del Monte died on 27 January 1572. The main structure was completed under his successor, the Frenchman Jean Levesque de la Cassière (1572–81) but it took a long time to complete and furnish all the rooms.

The exterior of the building clearly reflects the fact that, in the late sixteenth century, the Order had not yet become an institution of proud *hommes du monde* with its splendid display of baroque and rococo tastes. The simple, massive, and ample square structure resembles more a fort than the contemporary refined palaces of the princes and dukes of central and southern Europe, then on the verge of absolutism. The Valletta palace originally was built around a central courtyard. As in many mannerist palaces in Italy and France, its four corners are accented by rusticated pilasters which run up the whole height of the building. The whole building occupies a space of 81 by 96 metres. In the tradition of many Renaissance palaces, the building has two storeys. On the first floor, the *piano nobile*, a suite of well-proportioned apartments

The winding oval staircase that connects the ground-floor loggia *to the stately rooms on the* piano nobile *is a fine example of Renaissance architecture. It consists of a series of wide marble steps with low risers that radiate out from the central cylindrical shaft.*

General view of the Neptune courtyard showing the observatory. Both courtyards of the palace are overlooked by balustraded windows. Historically, the name of the courtyard is somewhat misleading as it was not until 1861 that the bronze statue of Neptune was transferred to this place.

THE MAGISTERIAL PALACE

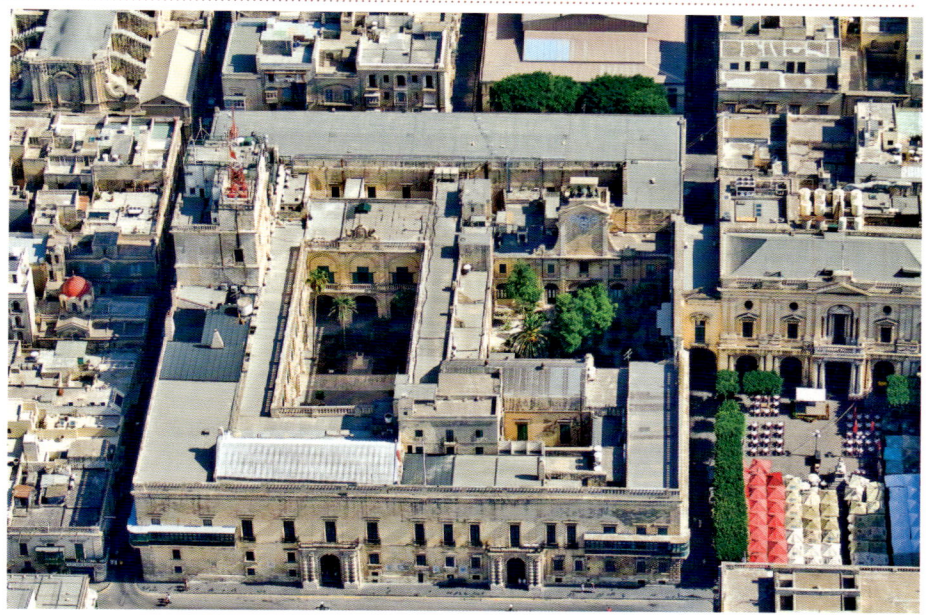

The main structure of the magisterial palace was completed under Grand Master Jean Levesque de la Cassière (1572–81). The exterior of the building clearly reflects the fact that, in the late sixteenth century, the Order had not yet become an institution of proud hommes du monde *with its splendid display of baroque and rococo tastes. The National Library added on the plan below is also visible on the right.*

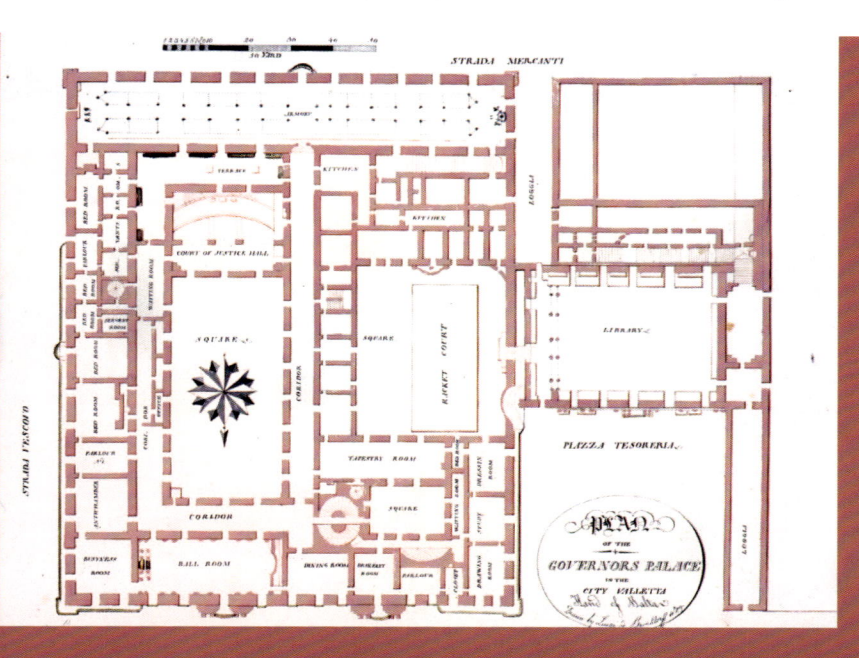

From the impressive hall of St Michael and St George, a door leads to the Ambassadors' room or state drawing room. This hall was most likely the place where the foreign envoys or charges d'affaires presented their credentials to the grand masters. This room is also known as the Red Room because its walls are covered with red damask brocade. The frieze paintings by Lionello Spada recall eight famous episodes in the chequered history of the Order:

The Pages Room with more frieze paintings by Lionello Spada recalling eight other episodes of the Order's history. The famous painting by Favray of Grand Master de Valette hangs between the doors of the long side-balcony.

The private study of the president of Malta at the east wing of the palace. Used as a drawing room during the British period, it was most probably used as a guest bedroom during the knights' period.

runs round the whole building. In the middle of the eighteenth century, under the rule of Portuguese Grand Master Pinto, the façade was drastically overhauled. Two entrance portals facing St George's Square were created and embellished with robust gateways. Both of them lead onto a courtyard. These gateways were adorned according to baroque taste with open balconies supported by Doric hard-stone rusticated columns. The other entrances are in the centre of each of the three remaining sides: along Archbishop Street, Merchants Street, and Old Theatre Street respectively. At each corner of the main façade facing St George's Square, there is a long, covered timber balcony which is supported by ornate and hefty corbels and heightens the visual appeal of the façade. The corbels are decorated with stucco work, consisting mainly of the banner of the Order and the escutcheons of grand masters.

The winding oval staircase that connects the ground-floor *loggia* to the stately rooms on the *piano nobile* is a fine example of Renaissance architecture. It is composed of a series of wide marble steps with low risers that radiate out from the central cylindrical shaft. Unlike the later fashionable baroque staircases for palaces which are more ornate and scenographic, the Valletta staircase relies on the spatial effect of a very gradual ascent to a higher level in an orbital fashion. Such structures are certainly more convenient for persons in heavy armoury or handicapped by old age. On the wall at the foot of the stairs is a marble slab with the names of the 28 grand masters who ruled over Malta. At the top is another slab with the names of the British governors.

The so-called Pinto Clock is attributed to the Maltese clockmaker Gaetano Vella and was installed on 22 June 1745. The clock has four dials. The principal one in the centre shows the hours and minutes. Above the principal dial is a smaller one which registers the phases of the moon.

The name Prince Alfred's courtyard recalls the first visit of the duke of Edinburgh, Prince Alfred, the second son of Queen Victoria, in November 1858. During this visit, the duke planted an Araucaria excelsa *in the centre of the courtyard.*

This staircase serves as a good document to show how distinguishable the original construction of the magisterial palace is from the many later baroque palaces constructed in Malta. In the late seventeenth and in the eighteenth century, palace staircases became more monumental and ornate. They were no longer perceived as utilitarian architectural elements to be hidden away from public view and to be absorbed in the building fabric. After ascending the staircase, one finds oneself in the *piano nobile* – the upper storey of the palace. There were originally four corridors, but the one parallel to the entrance corridor was later divided into three rooms. Therefore today there is the entrance corridor in front of a rectangular lobby at the end of the staircase; the armoury corridor on the right side at the top of the staircase, and the Prince of Wales corridor on the right beyond at the end of the entrance corridor.

The special attraction of the council chamber, the so-called tapestry hall, is certainly the set of Gobelins tapestries which deserve special attention. The famous *Tenture des Indes* set consists of ten panels. The subjects depicted are: *The Striped Horse*, *The Two Bulls*, *The Elephant*, *The Light Bay-Horse*, *The Indian Hunter*, *The Ostriches*, *Animals Fighting*, *The King carried in a Hammock*, *The Indian on Horseback*, and *The Fisherman*. These tapestries were woven in Paris after paintings by the Dutch artists Franz Post and Albert Eckhout. In 1708 Grand Master Perellos ordered these tapestries to embellish the chamber as part of his *gioia*, a gift all newly elected grand masters made to the Order. Another artistic gem is the hall of the supreme council or hall of St Michael and St George, the

The Council Chamber or Tapestry Hall houses the famous Tenture des Indes *set consisting of ten panels. These tapestries were woven in Paris after a series of paintings by the Dutch artists Franz Post and Albert Eckhout. In 1708 Grand Master Perellos y Roccaful ordered ten Gobelins tapestries to embellish the magisterial palace. This was part of his gioia, a gift all newly-elected grand masters made to the Order. The 'Maltese' set of Gobelins was worked in* haute lisse, *using a horizontal loom with the cartoon immediately underneath, which gives a reversed image.*

THE MAGISTERIAL PALACE

The special attraction of the Council Chamber is certainly the set of Gobelins Tapestries. The famous Tenture des Indes *set depicts the following subjects: The Striped Horse (470 by 505 cm), The Two Bulls (470 by 511 cm), The Elephant (470 by 408 cm), The Light Bay-Horse (470 by 298 cm), The Indian Hunter (470 by 350 cm), The Ostriches (470 by 313 cm), Animals fighting (470 by 458 cm), The King carried in a Hammock (470 by 450 cm), The Indian on Horseback (470 by 430 cm), and The Fisherman (470 by 400 cm).*

The tapestries were woven in Paris after a series of paintings by the Dutch artists Franz Post and Albert Eckhout. Post was responsible for the landscapes and Eckhout for the plants and animals. Between 1636 and 1644 Post and Eckhout formed part of the expedition corps accompanying Prince Johan Maurits of Nassau-Siegen to Brazil. In Brazil Post and Eckhout carried out hundreds of paintings and drawings depicting the local landscape with its exotic fauna and flora. Other tapestries with similar illustrations are found in many important collections yet this is the only full set.

name given to it in the early nineteenth century by the British. When George IV instituted the Order of St Michael and St George in 1818, the first and subsequent investitures of members of this Order were held in this hall. In the times of the Order, the hall was used for state functions. Its old name is derived from the sessions of the supreme council and the chapters general which were held there. It is decorated in the prevailing mannerist taste. Its highlights are the colourful frescoes carried out after 1576 by the Italian painter Matteo Perez d'Aleccio. Undoubtedly this frieze is d'Aleccio's major *oeuvre* in Malta. The 12 frescoes depict the various phases of the Siege of 1565. When Grand Master Cassière commissioned the work he wanted to make sure that the events of 1565 would remain fixed in the collective memory of the knights. The cycle starts with the depiction of the arrival of the Ottoman army on 18 May. It continues with depictions of the disembarking of the Ottomans at Marsaxlokk (20 May), the attack on Fort St Elmo (27 May), the fall of Fort St Elmo (23 June), the attack on Fort St Michael (27 June), the arrival of the Small Relief (*piccolo soccorso*) at Birgu (5 July), the attack on the posts of Castille and Germany (9 July), the assault on Fort St Michael by land and by sea (15 July), the assault upon the post of Castille (29 July), an overview of the battle scene, the arrival of the Great Relief (7 September), and the flight of the Ottoman forces (13 September). The 12 panels are separated by typical mannerist allegorical figures, representing religion, charity, hope, faith, temperance, fortitude, justice, prudence, happiness, fame, victory, virtue, patience, perseverance, and nobility.

In the 1570s the Italian artist Matteo Perez d'Aleccio decorated the hall of the Supreme Council in the Magisterial palace with a frieze showing the different stages of the Great Siege. His works were commissioned by Grand Master Cassière and are carried out in the then prevailing mannerist taste. The painting on the left side shows the Turks disembarking at Marsaxlokk. The one on the right side shows the fall of Fort St Elmo.

THE MAGISTERIAL PALACE

From the entrance corridor, one also enters the **Sala del Maggiore Consiglio** – the beautifully-proportioned Hall of the Supreme Council or Hall of St Michael and St George, as it is known today. This name was coined in the early nineteenth century when Malta was under British rule. When King George IV instituted the Order of St Michael and St George in 1818, the first and subsequent investitures of members of this Order were held in this hall. In the time of the Order the room was used for state functions. Today the hall is used for functions falling under the president of the Republic of Malta.

Above: A depiction of the entire war, showing the Turkish camp in the middle and Birgu and Senglea on the right side.

Right: The aged Grand Master Jean de Valette in full armour. Thanks to his courage, military competence, and steadfastness, the knights and Maltese stood firm against the much superior Turkish forces.

The famous armoury (or better what is left of it) of the knights of St John was moved to the ground floor of the rear side of the palace in 1975. In the middle of the sixteenth century, it was decreed that all arms (with the exception of swords and daggers) left by deceased knights belonged to the Order. These arms and the ones bought by the Order had to be available at the Order's headquarters in case of need. In the early seventeenth century the armoury was moved into a large hall on the first floor on the rear side of the magisterial palace.

'The Cuirassier Armour'	'The Verdelin Armour'	'The Wignacourt Armour'

The famous armoury (or better what is left of it) of the knights of St John was in 1975 moved to the ground floor at the rear of the palace. It runs parallel to Merchants Street. In the times of the knights and the British, the armoury was housed in the big hall situated at the end of the armoury corridor. This huge hall, 72 metres long and 12 wide, has since 1976 been serving as the chamber of parliament of the Republic of Malta. After the move to Valletta, the armoury was housed in a building in St George's Square, opposite the palace. Owing to lack of space, in the early seventeenth century the armoury was moved into a large hall on the first floor of the rear side of the palace. But arms were also kept on other places in Valletta, such as St James cavalier, or Birgu. The different brands, styles, and places of origin of the arms of the Order reflect the international character of the institution with its eight langues. There are pieces made in Spain, Italy, Germany, and France. One of the most precious items is the full suit of armour made by the Milanese armourer Spacini in the early seventeenth century for French Grand Master Alof de Wignacourt (1601–22). Just as precious is the complete early seventeenth-century suit of armour, also of Italian workmanship, made for the French Grand Commander Jean Jacques de Verdelin. Another magnificent item is the suit of armour of the Spanish Grand Master Martin Garzes (1595–1601), manufactured in the late sixteenth century by the Bavarian armourer Wolf. Also on display are the back and breastplates, of middle sixteenth-century Italian manufacture, once worn by legendary Grand Master Jean de Valette (1557–68), the hero of the Great Siege.

At least since the late seventeenth century, the administration of the Order kept lists of all the muskets and arquebuses delivered to professed knights and novices. For example, in 1674 8,938 muskets as well as 10,296 arquebuses and 4,000 pikes were gathered.
Right: The armoury as depicted by Charles Frederick de Brocktorff in the 19th century.

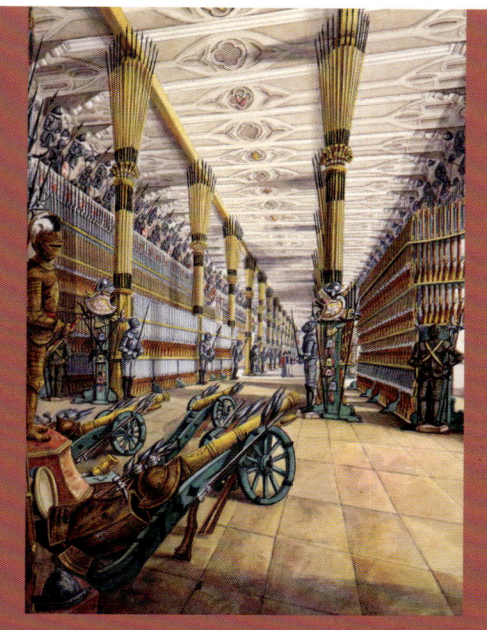

294 THE SITES VALLETTA

One of the earliest photographs of the Palace Armoury in the 19th century.

The main corridor of the palace.

The Sala del Maggiore Consiglio, *the Supreme Council or Hall of St Michael and St George, as it is known today.*

The painting of Grand Master de Valette by Antoine Favray (1706–98)

The Magisterial Palace 295

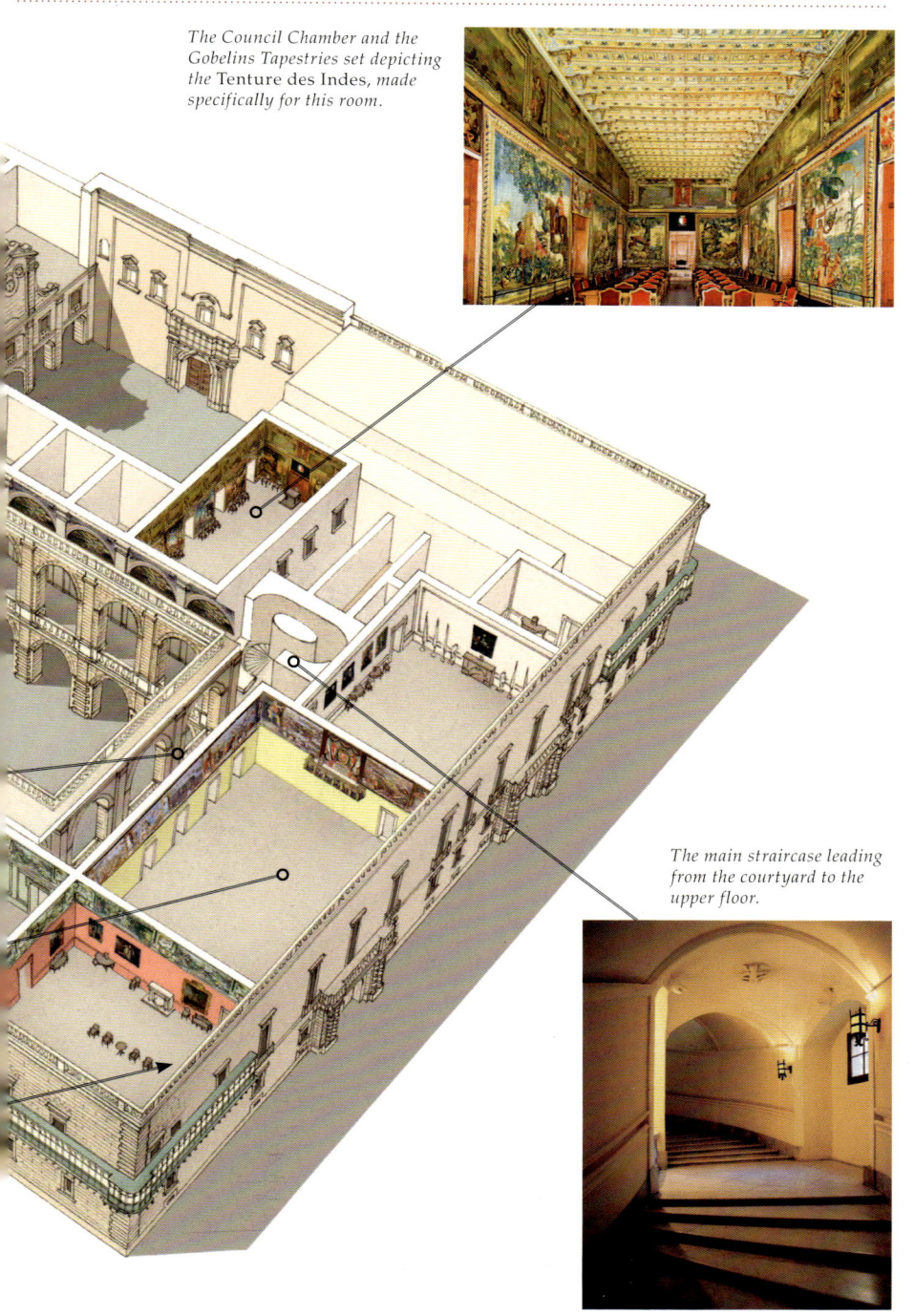

The Council Chamber and the Gobelins Tapestries set depicting the Tenture des Indes, *made specifically for this room.*

The main straircase leading from the courtyard to the upper floor.

FORT ST ELMO
VALLETTA

According to Spanish sources, there stood a watch-tower at the extreme end of the Sciberras peninsula, known as *Tarf il-Għasses*, already in the fourteenth century. After the Order took over, in the 1530s and 1540s the Florentine engineer Piccino and later the famous architect from Bergamo, Antonio Ferramolino, recommended the building of a fortress at the tip of the peninsula. But it was not before 1551 when Malta and Gozo suffered the disastrous raid led by the corsair Dragut that things started to move. Spanish Grand Master de Homedes asked Don Juan de Vega, the viceroy of Sicily, to send a competent military engineer to help design a fortress at Monte Sciberras. In January 1552 the viceroy sent Pedro Pardo who immediately started to work out a symmetrical star-shaped fort with narrow arms or bastions and a large internal *piazza*. On the southern front, the bastions were rounded off to provide orillion batteries. The fort was surrounded by a ditch. In mid-January the work on the new fort had commenced and by summer

Fort St Elmo is at the very bottom Republic Street, Valletta. Except for an area which is used by the War Museum (www.heritagemalta.org), the fort is closed for the public. A major restoration and upgrade is planned for Fort St Elmo.

most of the structure was ready. It was obvious that the most vulnerable side of the construction was the landward side. The fort did not rise high enough to command the high ground of the Sciberras peninsula.

Between 1554 and 1556, therefore, a large triangular cavalier was added on this side, connected to the fort by a drawbridge. In 1556 a ravelin was completed and, just a few months before the Great Siege, a ravelin on the eastern flank was hastily completed. The fort's force of fewer than 1,000 knights and soldiers showed a heroic defence during the siege but could not prevent defeat by the far superior number of Ottoman troops. After the siege the ruins of St Elmo were rebuilt and enlarged. The fort was fitted with barracks, ovens, and cisterns. A deep ditch was excavated on the western flank. In the early eighteenth century, the northern ramparts were demolished and two strong walls secured the cavalier to the fort. Some decades before, the so-called Carafa bastion was constructed to protect the fort against artillery attacks from the promontory known as Dragut Point.

Above: Fort St Elmo as seen from Fort St Angelo. The cement pillbox is an addition of World War II.

Opposite left: An aerial photograph of the fort. On the left is the main structure of St Elmo whilst the Carafa bastion is on the bottom right.

The fort's old chapel, known as Del Soccorso *(after the Madonna del Soccorso), has been recorded in existence since 1488. The chapel was re-dedicated to St Anne in the mid-sixteenth century and it is embellished with ornate stone carvings that date to the seventeenth century.*

FORT ST ANGELO – THE MEDIEVAL LEGACY
VITTORIOSA (BIRGU)

There is no archival proof when Fort St Angelo was started. Its origins might go back to the times of Arab occupation in the ninth and tenth centuries. The first documented evidence appears in the second half of the thirteenth century when the islands were ruled by the Angevins. In those times it was referred to as the *castrum maris*. The name Fort St Angelo does not seem to have been used before the knights arrived in Malta. It was a purely military establishment, governed by a castellan or captain, and manned by a garrison. This situation remained the same in the subsequent decades and centuries when Malta was ruled by the Aragonese. In the fifteenth century, the growing power of the Hafsids in Tunisia was increasingly threatening Malta, and the modest *castrum maris* was strengthened and refortified.

When the Hospitallers took over the fortress in 1530 it had two parts, an inner and an outer castle. The upper main enceinte was perched on the highest part of the promontory. The inner castle, the oldest part of the construction, formed a triangular enceinte that enclosed the residence of the castellan and a chapel. It was fortified by a number of wall-towers. The Hospitallers were not very satisfied with the state of the fort which they found 'half-ruined with age' and badly armed. The knights immediately spotted the importance of the castle for the entire control of the Grand Harbour area.

The medieval tower is a remnant of the **castrum maris** *of the 13th and 14th centuries. The commission sent by the knights to Malta in 1524 found it badly furnished and partly in ruins. The fort was refortified and strengthened after the Order moved to Malta and it withstood the Turkish assault of 1565.*

The interior of the chapel of St Anne. The grand masters who died before Valletta was built were buried in this chapel and their remains were later transferred to St John's. The De Nava family in 1534 built a chapel on the same site. The red granite column may have formed part of a Roman temple on the same site.

FORT ST ANGELO

What one sees today of Fort St Angelo is the result of changes and restructuring after the Great Siege and the adaptation of the fort to the posting of strong artillery. Already during the Great Siege there was a cannon posted on top of the fort. This cannon was of crucial importance for the defending Christians since it could fire from the highest point inside the Grand Harbour.

A look at Fort St Angelo and its conurbation unveils the strong maritime character of the Order. The creeks and bays near the fort and the town of Birgu offer relatively safe and sheltered places to anchor and berth. There were the anchorages of the famous galleys and sailing ships of the knights.

Also during the Great Siege the navy of the Order was anchored there.
Above left: The parvis and chapel of St Anne seen from the roof of the magisterial palace.
Above right: An aerial photograph of the fort with parts of Senglea in the foreground.

300 | THE SITES | THE GRAND HARBOUR CONURBATION

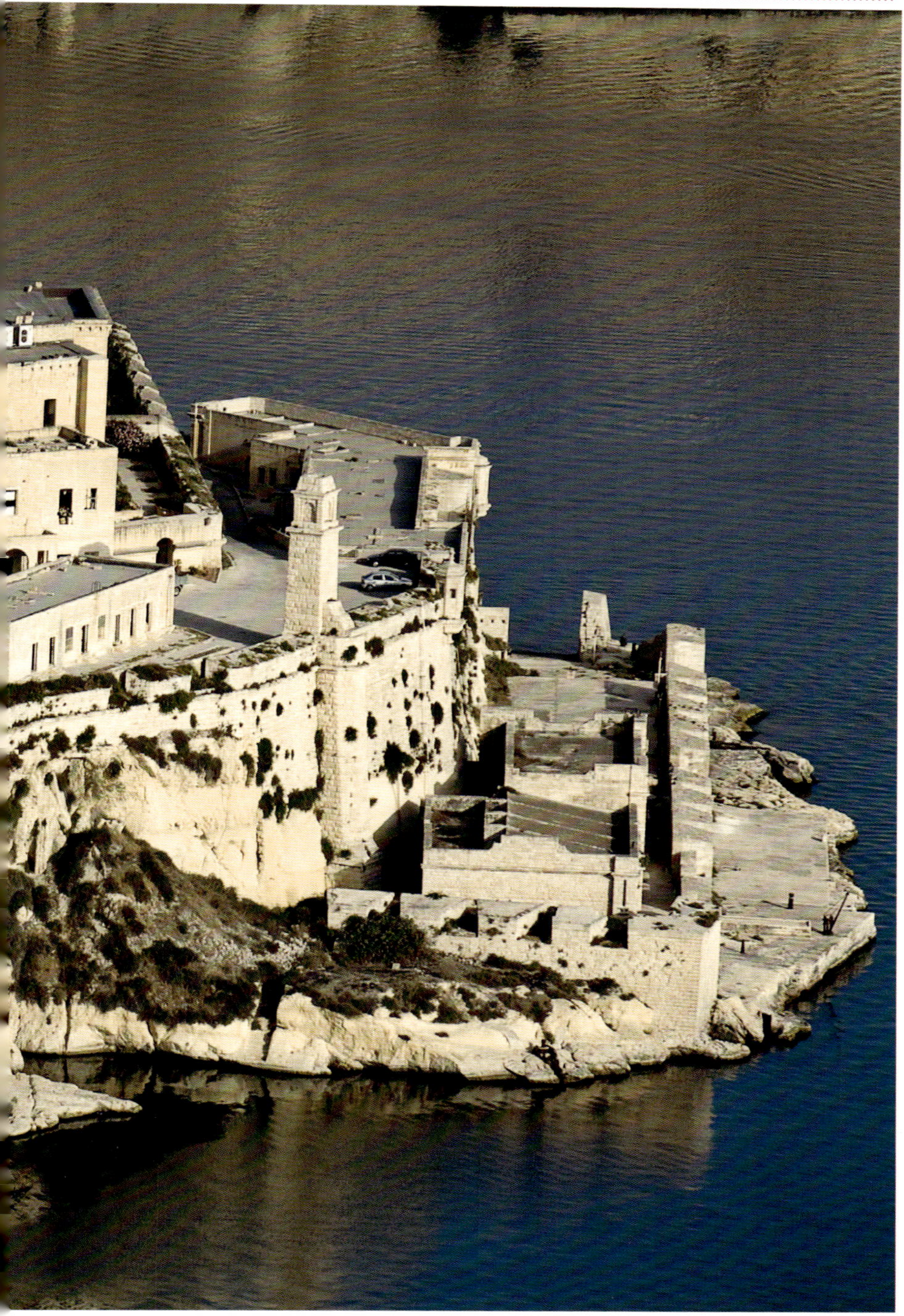

To protect it better from attacks from the landward side, in the 1530s the dry ditch was converted into a moat, thereby isolating the castle from the mainland.

Subsequently the ramparts facing Birgu were constructed. In front of the castle's outer gate a bastion, raised on two casemates, was erected and in 1540 a large cavalier was built on the gorge of the new land front. When the Ottoman assault started in May 1565, Fort St Angelo was anything but an impressive and impregnable stronghold but, against all prediction and thanks to the steadfastness of the knights and the Maltese garrison, it held out. Immediately after the siege, Valette ordered the repair and strengthening of the battered fortifications. New changes were made in the 1690s when the engineer to Charles II of Spain, Don Carlos de Grunenbergh

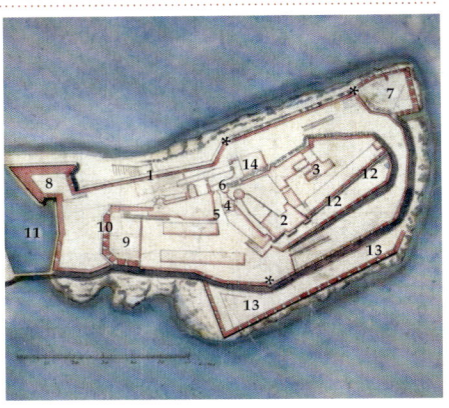

1. Main Gate, 2. Magisterial Palace, 3. Chapel of St Anne, 4. Chapel of the Nativity of Our Lady, 5. The *Guva*, 6. Remains of Medieval Round Tower 7. De Guiral's Battery, 8. D'Homedes Bastion, 9. Cavalier, 10. Great Siege Bell, 11. Moat, 12. Elevated Battery, 13. Sea-level Battery, 14. Polverista, * Sentinels.

reconstructed parts of the enceinte and the main gate and added more platforms for batteries. When the French conquered Malta in 1798, the fort had some 80 guns and four mortars.

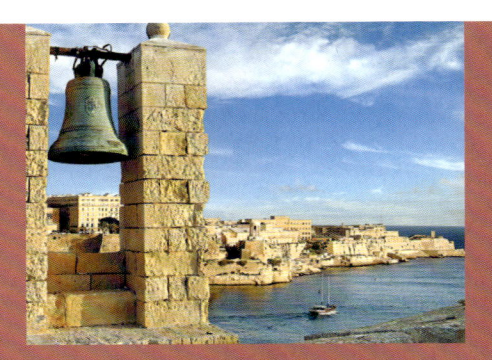

Fort St Angelo once housed the famous 'Great Siege Bell' which gave signals of alarm when the Turks arrived on 18 May 1565. The bell in a bell-cot on top of the cavalier of the fort displayed today is not the original 16th-century one but was cast in the 18th century.

The open staircase of the magisterial palace with the gothic quadripartite arched roof. Built in 1530–33 on the arrival of the Order to Malta by Frà Diego Perez de Malfreire who was L'Isle Adam's main architect.

FORT ST ANGELO 303

View of the inner courtyard and the magisterial palace. These buildings and the fort served as headquarters for the knights up to the early 1570s when the Order moved to Valletta.

That the Order until 1565 never had taken ambitious steps to augment and embellish Fort St Angelo shows the prevailing opinion that a return to Rhodes might be possible.

The main hall, one of the beautifully restored rooms of the magisterial palace. The upper section of Fort St Angelo was granted by the government of Malta in concession to the Order for a period of 99 years in 1988.

The upper section of the fort falls under the jurisdiction of the Sovereign Military Order of Malta. The lower area is curated by Heritage Malta. Even this fort is going through a restoration process to strengthen the structure of the main walls of St Angelo. Occasionally, on certain feasts or weekends, the fort is opened for visits. Check Heritage Malta's web-site at www.heritagemalta.org for opening days.

FORT ST MICHAEL
Senglea (L-Isla)

When the knights settled in Malta and made the harbour town of Birgu their first residence, the nearby tongue of land, then called *Isola* or *Monte del Mulino*, was hardly inhabited except for some huts. Its only fortification consisted of a small tower. Nonetheless the peninsula was strategically very important for the protection of Fort St Angelo and Birgu.

Shortly after the Ottomans tried in vain to conquer Malta in 1551, a small fortress was built on the peninsula and called Fort St Michael. It consisted just of a large squarish tower with a large battery on its roof. In 1556 French Grand Master de la Sengle ordered the peninsula to be enclosed with a bastioned enceinte. In the meantime more and more people had settled within its territory and the new settlement became known as *Città Senglea*. When the Great Siege started, the tip of Senglea was hastily refortified with a parapet and fighting platforms. The landfront then consisted of a large casemated central bastion flanked by two curtains and a small ravelin.

Little remains of the actual fort, yet a visit to Senglea is certainly worth it. One arrives at the Three Cities either by Triq Għajn Dwieli from Kordin, or through Triq Cospicua from Fgura. From Senglea Point one can enjoy the best view of Valletta.

Fort St Michael

The flank facing Birgu was left without fortification since the two towns were intended to protect each other. Despite of these quickly built provisional fortifications, Senglea and Fort St Michael managed to hold out. After the siege the badly damaged fortifications of the peninsula were reconstructed by the famous Maltese engineer Gerolamo Cassar. In the seventeenth and eighteenth centuries several additions and alterations were undertaken to modernize the construction. In the 1620s a large ravelin at the landfront; a *couvre port* or *tenaille* in front of the main entrance; and a counterguard protecting the demi-bastion facing Corradino Hill were added. In 1690 a large sea-level battery was built.

Matteo Perez d'Aleccio's fresco shows the Order's flag flying over Fort St Michael during the Great Siege. The cavalier is overemphasized in comparison with the rest of the bastions.

Although hastily fortified and provisionally augmented with bastions, Senglea and Fort St Michael managed to withstand the Turkish assault in the summer of 1565. The walls and bulwarks of Senglea were considerably reconstructed and changed after the Great Siege. Parts of them were planned and built by the Maltese Gerolamo Cassar who also was responsible for the planning and building of many of the fortifications, palaces and houses in Valletta. In the late 17th century, a large sea-level battery was added.

FLORIANA
Floriana

As the name indicates the building of this suburb of Valletta is closely linked with the famous military engineer Pietro Paolo Floriani. While he was working on the reconstruction of the fortifications of Ferrara, he was commissioned by Pope Urban VII to go to Malta to inspect the fortifications of Valletta and the *Porto Grande* and to discuss their improvement. Floriani arrived in Malta in May or September 1635 and began immediately to develop his plans and schemes. He did not deem Valletta able to resist a siege with modern techniques and arms and he proposed a completely new building of a line of defences towards the land front. The design consisted of a large entrenched centre bastion, flanked by two demi-bastions with adjoining curtain walls. In front of the curtains there were two large ravelins and beyond them a covertway with two salient crown-shaped place-of-arms. Although there was considerable opposition by other architects and some knights who found Floriani's scheme too costly and out of proportion, the council sanctioned

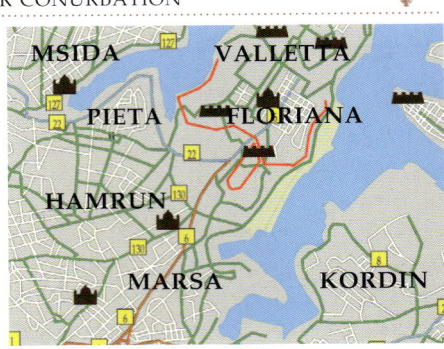

The best way to see the walls of Floriana is to walk along the bastions themselves. Parts of the Floriana lines are closed off as they are part of the police headquarters. The best place to see the walls closely is by visiting the Sa Maison Gardens on the road between Pietà and Floriana.

its construction on 10 December 1635. After his election to the magistracy, Lascaris had asked the pope to extend Floriani's stay in Malta for a few months, so that the fortifications could reach a more advanced stay. The building of the Floriana fortifications was started immediately after the councils' sanction but in the next years and decades were halted from time to time.

During his stay, Floriani also worked on plans for the land defence of Senglea and Birgu. His ambitious project consisted of five bastions, two demi-bastions, two cavaliers, and three ravelins. However the proposals for Birgu and Senglea were not accepted by the council. After Floriani left the island on 23 October 1636 for Ferrara, work on the Floriana lines was continued under the supervision of his assistant Giovanni Vincenzo Buonamici. Still the work continued in several stages well up to the eighteenth century when other architects and military engineers of European fame, such as Count Antonio Maurizio Valperga, Carlos de Grunenberg, and Louis François d'Aubigné de Tigné were involved. Valperga's designs for the Floriani lines included the construction of a crowned hornwork on the high ground overlooking the Grand Harbour and the formation of two new bastions. The whole of the front was to be further protected by the addition of a *fausse-braye*. Work on the crowned-hornworks started in 1671. It was helped considerably by the financial support of Juan Galdiano, prior of Navarra. In the eighteenth century several alterations and additions were made when a large retrenchment was constructed behind and above Quarantine bastion, facing Marsamxett harbour.

The building process of the walls and bastions of Floriana were started in the middle of the 17th century and continued in the following century, always adapting to the latest developments of artillery and siege techniques.

Porte de Bombes, *the main gate to Floriana was built around 1700 adapting the French baroque style which asserted the Order's power. The left side of the gate was reconstructed in the late 19th century to suit modern traffic.*

THE COTTONERA LINES
COTTONERA

When, in 1669, it became clear that the war of Candia had been an Ottoman victory and Venetian Crete was lost, the Order decided to strengthen the fortifications of Malta, especially the landward side of Senglea and Birgu. Grand Master Nicolas Cotoner requested the pope to send his military engineer Count Antonio Maurizio Valperga to examine the situation and to make proposals how to proceed. At the time of his coming to Malta, Valperga was also the chief military engineer for the house of Savoy. He arrived in early February 1670 and by March he must have already presented a scheme for a new trace of eight bastions, encircling the Sta. Margharita and San Salvatore heights and joining the outskirts of Birgu and Senglea. This was a much more elaborate and more ambitious scheme than that designed by the Italian military architect Vincenzo Maculano da Firenzuola in 1638. Valperga also presented plans for the new Fort Ricasoli at the entrance to the Grand Harbour. Valperga's scheme for the 'Cottonera lines'

The 5-kilometre-long lines are best seen from the fields outside the walls. From Triq Cospicua in Fgura and Triq Ghajn Dwieli (from Kordin) one can pass through British-cut tunnels in the walls. The width of these tunnels give an idea of the width of these bastions.

followed the old Dutch school in trying to impose a geometrically regular trace, however irregular the terrain.

Although this scheme was criticized by some members of the Order and foreign architects, it was approved by the council on 2 April 1670 and work had started by August. The building of the Cottonera lines on the southern side of the harbour became the greatest architectural project after the building of Valletta. The supervision of the work laid in the hands of the Orders' resident engineer Mederico Blondel. The costs for this prestigious project were enormous and in 1670 the Order obtained from the Holy Sea the permission to levy a tax on immovable property on the island. In 1673 this was commuted to a tax on *vendibili* and *comestibili*. As usual, the real costs were by far greater than the original estimates. By 1715, the fortifications had consumed in total the sum of 1,400,000 *scudí* but work on the fortifications continued incessantly.

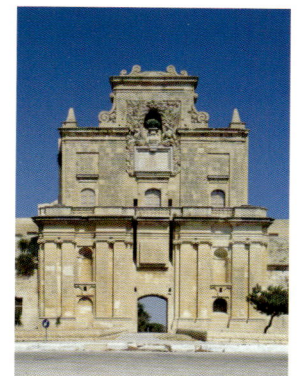

When Grand Master Nicolas Cotoner died in 1680, the main body of the enceinte had been laid down.

Top: Notre Dame Gate defending the Three Cities and Żabbar. This gate, the main one of the Cottonera lines has a bust of Grand Master Nicolas Cotoner and a marble plaque commemorating the building of the fortifications.

Overleaf: A parchment map of the Cottonera lines, the Three Cities, and Fort Ricasoli with a French legend. Unknown date. Heritage Malta Archives

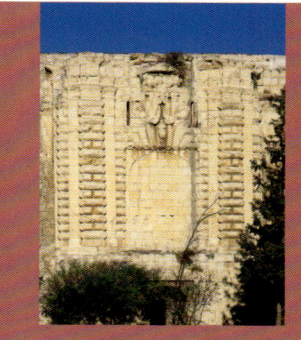

Left: View of the Three Cities and the Cottonera lines.

Top: Entrance portals or their imitations are important integral parts of an eloquent and sophisticated baroque stage-set. They also formed part of a triumphalistic military architecture. The building of the monumental Cottonera-lines started in 1670. The plan of the building by the military engineer Antonio Maurizio Valperga was, however, never completed. To defend this bulwark properly the Order would have needed more than 10,000 soldiers, a number which went beyond its realistic means.

310 THE SITES THE GRAND HARBOUR CONURBATION

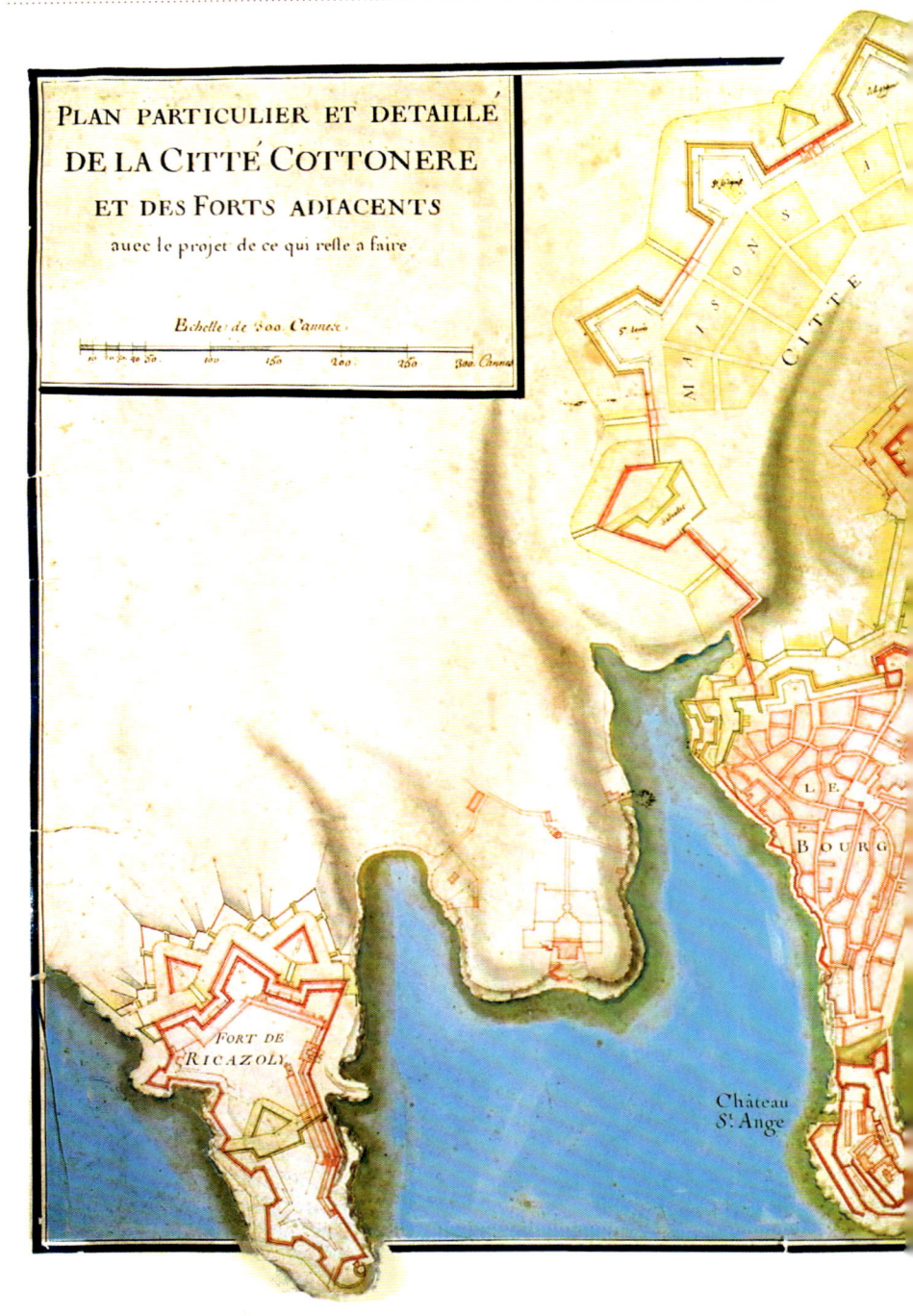

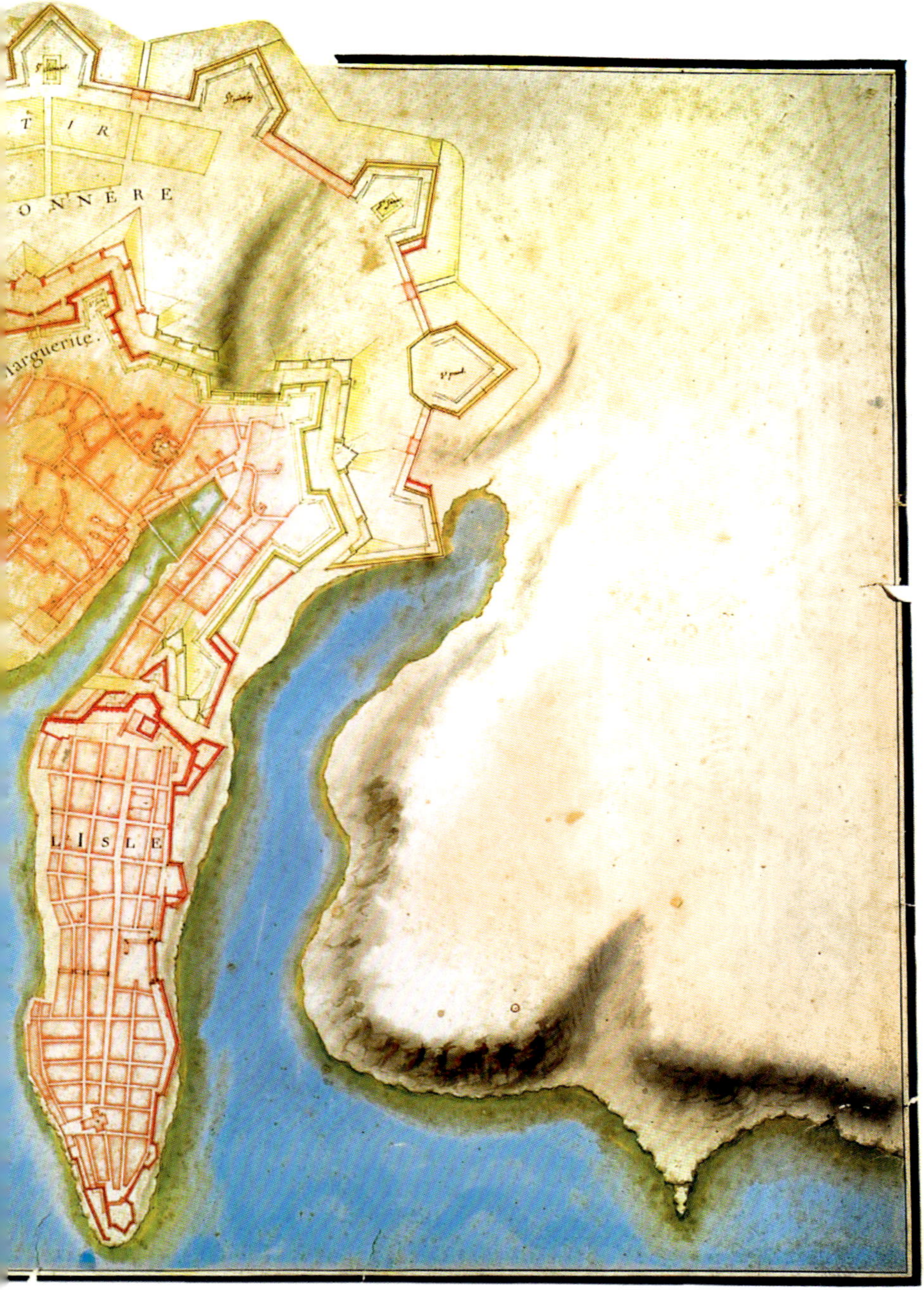
T I R
O N N E R E
Marguerite.
L I S L E

FORT RICASOLI
KALKARA

The promontory commanding the entrance to the Grand Harbour that used to be known as Gallows Point was left unfortified until the early seventeenth century. Its important strategic position was already clear during the Great Siege when the Ottoman troops occupied the site in June 1565 and established a battery from which to bombard Fort St Elmo on the opposite side of the harbour entrance. However – maybe because of lack of funds – it was not before 1602 that the council ordered a sea-level battery to be established at Gallows Point. Subsequently many local and foreign military engineers and architects proposed to fortify the site much more strongly. Finally the Order invited Count Antonio Maurizio Valperga in 1670 to present a detailed scheme to defend the harbour approaches. His plan consisted of a major defence line facing southwards. The land front was fortified by a *fausebraye*, two ravelins, a ditch, and a crownwork with a centre-bastion, connected by short curtain walls to two demi-bastions. A large number of bombproof casemated

Fort Ricasoli is closed to the public. In the last decade it has been used as a space for movies. The blockbusters *Gladiator* and *Troy* were filmed here. Driving from Kalkara, one can arrive to the main gate of the fort and walk along the walls. From here one can enjoy another beautiful view of Valletta.

barracks fitted the gorge of the bastions and the connecting curtains. The seaward side was protected by two small demi-bastions joined together to a form of a scissor-shaped front at the tip of the promontory. The interior of the fort contained two large barrack blocks, a powder magazine, a chapel, and a large *piazza*. The main gate facing the harbour was protected by a ditch and was fitted with a drawbridge. The mover of the project was the Knight Giovanni Francesco Ricasoli who donated 20,000 *scudí*, after whom the fort was named. In 1698 the construction works were finished and the same year the council appointed a governor to command the fort. In the eighteenth century, the walls of the fort were strengthened from time to time and the glacis heavily mined. When Napoleon attacked Malta, the fort was equipped with 75 cannon. Its governor, the *Balí* de Tillet managed to repel three French attacks and it surrendered only after the Order's capitulation.

Together with Fort St Elmo, Fort Ricasoli defends the entrance to the Porto Grande of the Order. Whilst Fort St Elmo was built immediately on the Order's arrival to Malta in the early 16th-century, it took until the late 17th-century to build a fort at Gallows Point. Its inner parts and buildings therefore show a different architectural scenography and rhetorical image than the older constructions at Fort St Elmo. They show influences of the then prevailing French baroque.
Above left: The main gate facing the Grand Harbour was reconstructed after it was hit during World War II.
Above right: The chapel in the fort.

MDINA
Mdina

The history and architectural profile of the old capital of Malta Mdina is connected with the Order of St John in several ways. Mdina was not conquered by the Turks in the epic Great Siege of 1565. It was ably defended by the French Knight Nicolas Durand de Villegagnon.

Later the Order contributed to reconstruct the original vertically built medieval bastions of the city into walls slightly at an angle to offer greater resistance against cannon balls. The Order also issued decrees not to extend gardens in the internal courtyards of the houses to save water. It was also ordered that the houses had to have underground reservoirs to collect rain water from the roofs in the winter months. Part of the old medieval city was destroyed by the earthquake of 1693. Besides the activities of the local Universitas, as the cathedral chapter and the resident religious orders it was Portuguese Grand Master Vilhena who implemented a grand plan for the urban renewal of Mdina.

Many of the new buildings were erected according to the plans of the French architect and military engineer François de Mondion (1683–1733). The architectural iconography of the then built imposing main gate of the city, the magisterial palace located right at the entrance, the *corte capitanale* and the *banca giuratale* are highly rhetorical and display intricate sculptures of war-trophies, festoons, torches, armoured breast-plates and Vilhena's coat of arms. The French influence is especially obvious in the prestigious building of the magisterial palace near the main gate.

The architect Mondion adopted the Parisian baroque *hôtel* typology with an ornate gateway leading to a forecourt. The *cour d'honneur* was aligned to the monument outer gateway and the inner entrance to the palace.

This sort of baroque architecture was always used as a langue of power and also the palace in Mdina was conceived as a strategically-placed landmark intended to impress upon the local population the absolutist power of the Order of St John.

The Banca Giuratale *known also as the* Casa della Città *was built between 1726 and 1728 by François de Mondion.*

Above: Mondion designed the new magisterial palace for Grand Master Vilhena. It was built between 1726 and 1728, replacing an older palace.

Opposite top: The elaborated sculptured coat of arms of Vilhena on the entrance archway leading to the courtyard of the magisterial palace.

Above: The Corte Capitanale *Palace (Law Courts) by Mondion was also built between 1726 and 1728. It shares the same courtyard of that of the magisterial palace. Opposite bottom: The main gate of Mdina also by Mondion. In 1725 it replaced the old medieval gate, seen now blocked to the right of the Baroque gate.*

316　The Sites　The minor palaces and fortifications

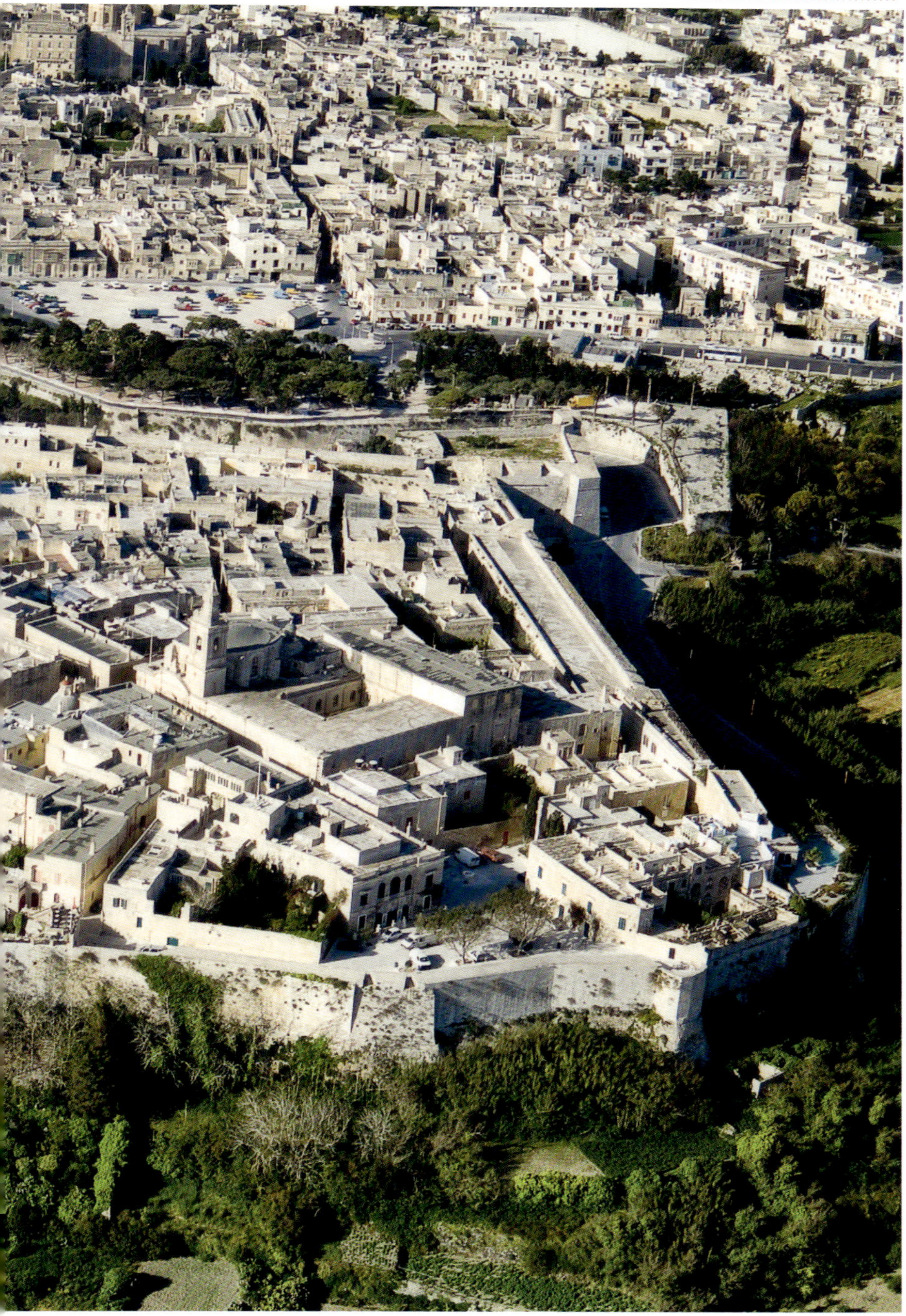

VERDALA PALACE
Rabat

Verdala Palace was built as a summer residence in 1585/86 by the French Grand Master Hughues Loubenx de Verdalle on property east of Rabat, then belonging to the *Mensa Vescovile*. It is situated on high ground overlooking Buskett valley, two miles from the old capital, Mdina. In Maltese, the palace is known as *Il-Palazz tal-Buskett*. Besides the hillside location with its fresh air and perfect views, the choice of the place was certainly also determined by the nearby wood, the *Buskett* or *Boschetto*. These characteristics made it possible for the residence to be used also to satisfy the favourite occupation of princes in the sixteenth and seventeenth centuries: hunting. In fact even before Verdalle made his choice, Buskett already had a certain hunting tradition among the knights. In the 1560s Grand Master Valette had built a hunting-lodge in the valley of Buskett, still known as *Il-Barumbara tax-Xerrufi* (The Pigeonry of the Overseer). It is traditionally believed that the famous Maltese falcons, which were sent every year to the viceroy of Sicily, were reared here.

Verdala Palace was planned as a fortified villa, strong enough to keep raiding groups away, but it could also function as a comfortable and distinctive summer villa. Despite of its being sometimes called a castle or fortress, Verdala Palace was certainly not meant as a fortified place. Although for some time

The builder of Verdala palace, French Grand Master Hughues Loubenx de Verdalle wanted an imposing manifestation of his sovereign authority and a monument for posterity. The Italian master Filippo Paladini's frescoes in the halls and chambers of the building depict events in Verdalle's career and document the French grand master's zeal for personal aggrandizement and love of glory. A special highlight was Verdalle receiving the cardinal's ring and hat from Pope Sixtus V as depicted in the picture on the left.

VERDALA PALACE

Above: The interior of the Cotoner palace chapel dedicated to St Anthony the Abbot. Verdala palace was built as a summer residence in 1585/86 by the French Grand Master Hughues Loubenx de Verdalle on property east of Rabat, then belonging to the **Mensa Vescovile**. *It is situated on high ground overlooking Buskett valley, two miles away from the old capital, Mdina.*

Verdala Palace was planned a rectangular fortified villa, strong enough to keep raiding groups away, but that could also function as a comfortable and distinctive summer villa.
In spite of it being sometimes called a castle or fortress, Verdala Palace was certainly not meant as a fortified place.

Although for some time cannon were placed on its roof, it could never withstand an attack by troops well-equipped with artillery. Besides the hillside location with its fresh air and perfect view, the choice of the place was certainly also determined by the nearby wood, the Buskett or Boschetto.

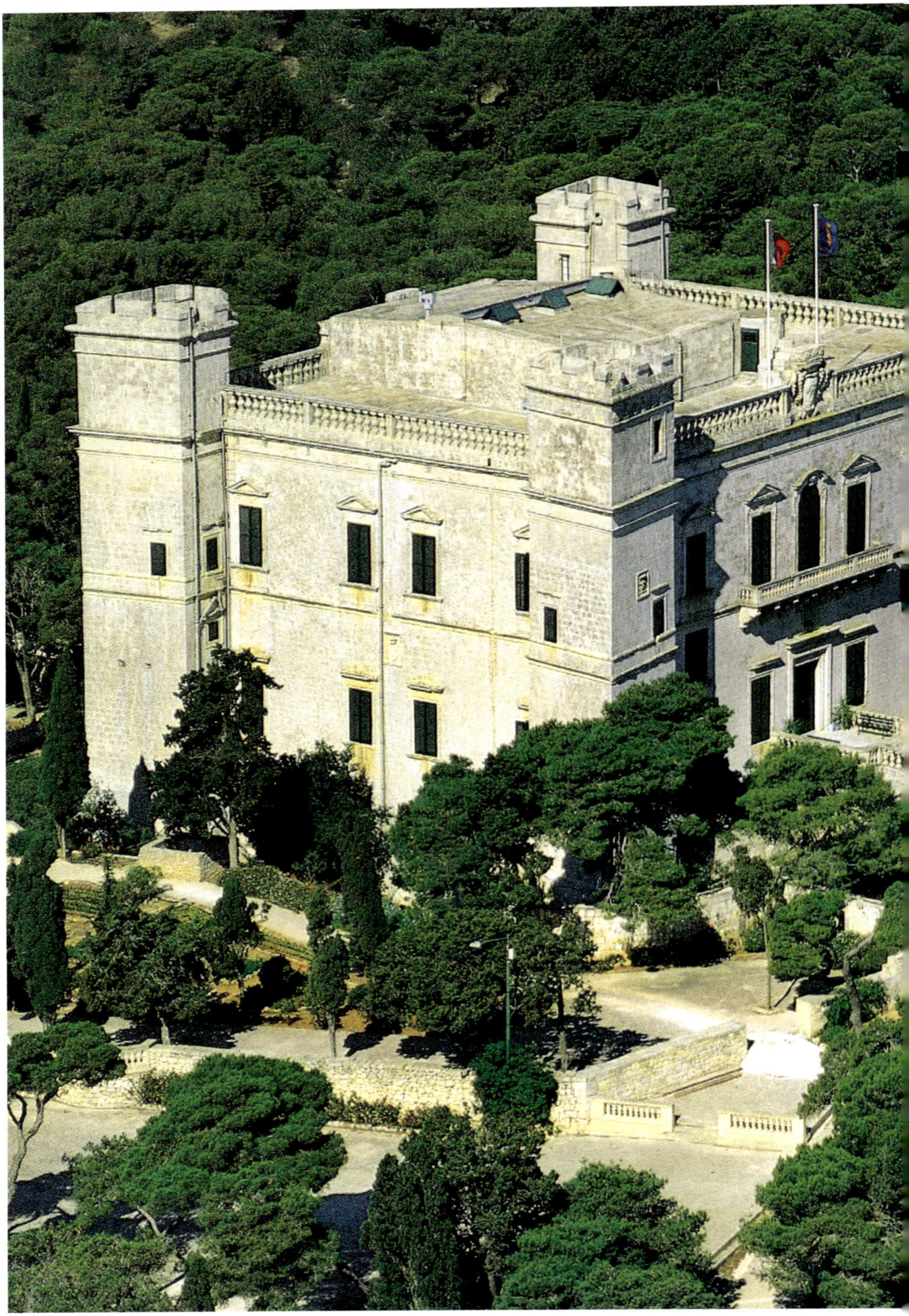

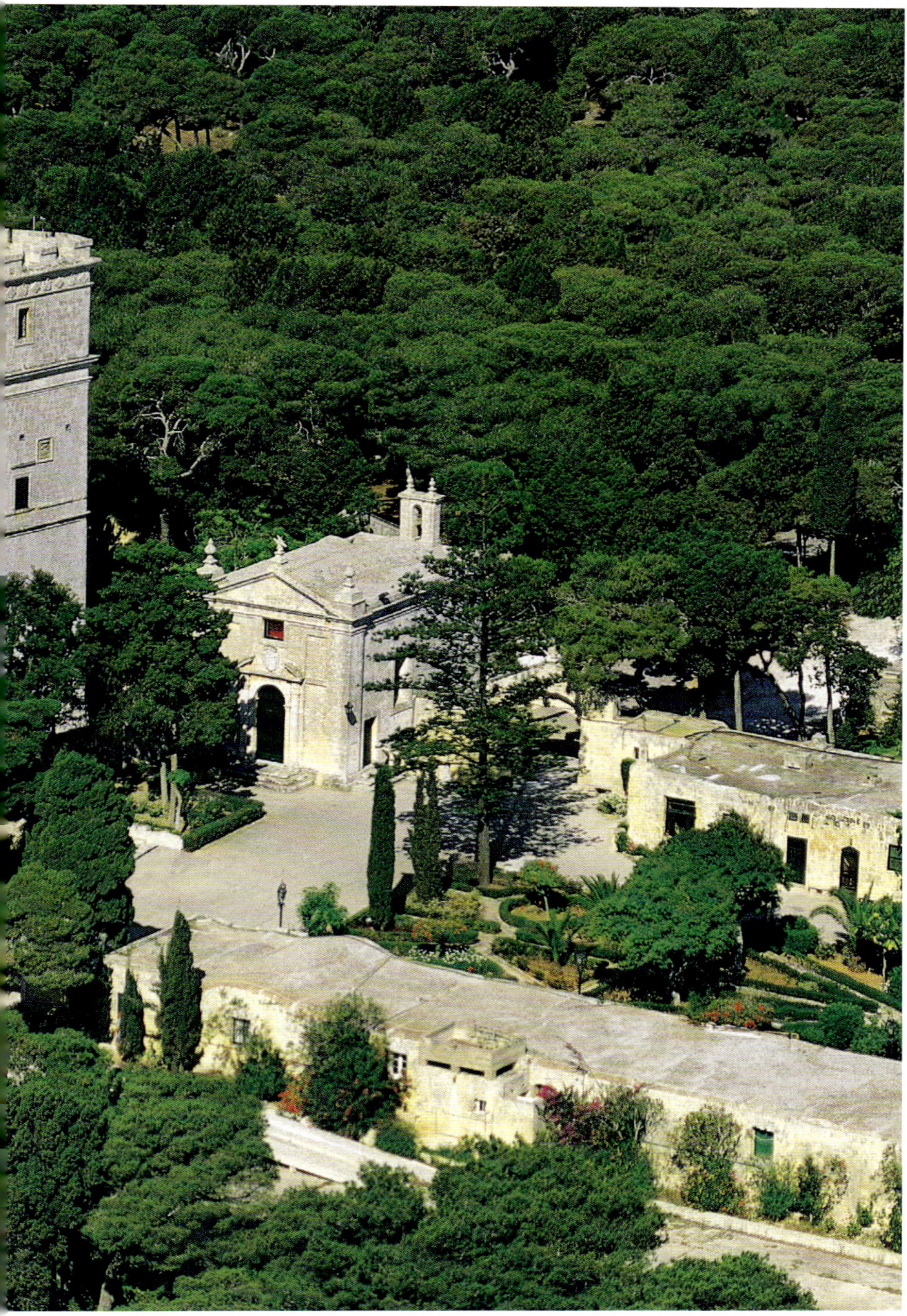

cannon were placed on its roof, it could never withstand an attack by troops well equipped with artillery. The building of this palace documents the change in attitude from the austere and monastic lifestyle of the former heads of the Order that took place in the late sixteenth century. The refined Verdalle certainly had good contacts with the latest artistic developments in France and Italy. While Valette was content with a small hunting lodge, Verdalle wanted an imposing manifestation of his sovereign authority and a monument for posterity. Filippo Paladini's frescoes in the halls and chambers of the building, depicting events in Verdalle's career, especially document the French grand master's zeal for personal aggrandizement and love of glory. Historians agree that its architect was the Maltese Gerolamo Cassar.

Verdala palace is almost square in plan, 176 by 188 feet large. The building consists of a basement and two other floors. At each corner there is an acute-angled battlemented tower, which rises by a further storey. The central building consists of two storeys, while the corner towers have a third storey. Decorated friezes run below the battlements. The flat roof was built strong enough to carry pieces of artillery. The plan shows an almost symmetrical disposition of the rooms and is clearly influenced by the concept of the sixteenth-century Italian country residence, namely Palladio's Veneto villas. The palace is approached by means of a flight of steps, and then by crossing a drawbridge over the ditch, to the main entrance. The inscription over the main portal greets the visitor with the words *Monti Verdalae ros et pluvial, MDLXXXVI* (Let dew and

At the palace of Verdala are displayed the escutcheons of Grand Masters Verdalle and Antonio Manoel de Vilhena (1722–36). Under the latter's rule, the palace not only underwent some structural modifications but many interior changes were also carried out.

On one side of the entrance hall, there is an oval staircase leading to the upper storey. In sixteenth- and seventeenth-century palaces and villas, staircases played an important role in matters of etiquette and protocol. In Verdalle's country villa, the staircase was designed wide enough for two persons of equal rank to go up or down side by side.

VERDALA PALACE

rain fall on Mount Verdala, 1586). On the far side of the building, there is a balcony with steps leading to the gardens across the ditch. Originally the building had one storey. The second storey with the balcony, the balustrades, the windows with the triangular pediments, and the balustrade on top of the building were added later in a different style from the original plainer mannerist design.

The nearby Buskett gardens were seen as an integral part of the concept of Verdalle's summer palace right from the beginning. Buskett and its gardens were changed and embellished by several grand masters and also by British civil commissioners and governors, thereby documenting the interest which the rulers of the island always showed for the place, a green paradise in a mostly arid landscape.

View of Verdala palace from the gardens. Even before Verdalle made his choice to build his palace there, Buskett had a certain hunting tradition among the knights. In the 1560s Grand Master Jean de Valette had built a hunting-lodge in the valley of Buskett.

A look in the Drawing Room or Upstairs Reception Chamber. Many rooms in Verdala palace were changed considerably under the rule of Grand Master Vilhena. His portrait near views of Mdina and Palazzo Manoel can be admired in the frieze. In the 19th century these rooms were used and also partly changed by the British governors of Malta.

The palace is open to the public only by invitation. Occasionally the President of Malta organizes open days for the public.
To easiest way to arrive to Verdala Palace is to leave from Rabat and go towards Buskett. Just before arriving at Buskett, one arrives at an open space with an iron gate. The castle grounds are behind this gate.

THE PALACE AND GARDENS OF SAN ANTON
ATTARD

The origin of San Anton Palace goes back to the early seventeenth century. In 1620 the Provençal knight, Antoine de Paule, built a villa to serve as his country retreat on land he had acquired some years earlier. After his election to the magistracy in 1623, he started to enlarge and embellish the villa, adding more rooms and building a squarish tower and extensively enlarging the garden with numerous fruit and ornamental trees. These included palms, jacarandas, cypresses, araucarias, oranges, citrons, pomegranates, and many other species.

De Paule also ordered the construction of fountains and pools as well as the placing of several statues, making it the largest garden area in Malta, situated on the confines of the villages of Attard, Balzan, and Lija.

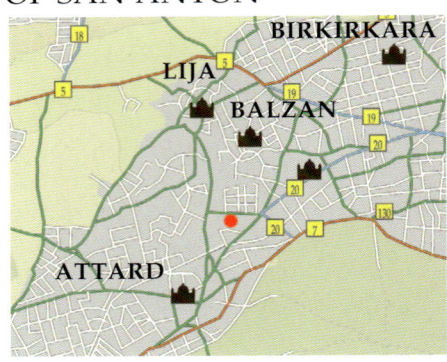

By car, one should drive along the main road between Mriehel and Mdina. Before arriving at Attard, the road next to the traffic lights forks towards Balzan. Driving along the Corinthia Palace Hotel, one finds the entrance to San Anton Gardens behind a high wall. The gardens are open daily yet the palace is the private residence of the president of Malta, and thus closed to the public.

The name San Anton is derived from that of de Paule's patron saint. De Paule subsequently acquired more land at Balzan and Lija to build reservoirs for the gardens. These reservoirs hold 20 million cubic litres of water and are still in use today. One can still see the elements of its seventeenth-century planning. Its site was certainly favoured by nature, being situated more or less in the geographical centre of Malta with the Great Ridge a few miles to the north protecting it from the north winds. A few months before his death in 1635, de Paule bequeathed his country residence and lands at San Anton to the Order.

Above: The main entrance to the palace from San Anton Gardens.

Left: The square tower overlooks the entrance courtyard and the gardens which surround the building. A long balustraded pathway was built around this yard.

Top: The private garden of the palace with its fountains and vine-covered pathways.

Above: The central round room which has four doors leading to the main rooms of the interior of the palace.

FORT MANOEL
GŻIRA

The earliest scheme to fortify the little island inside Marsamxett harbour dates to 1569 when an anonymous engineer pointed out that this side could be used to bombard Valletta's St Michael bastion. However, it was only in the 1640s that the Order started to use the *isoletto* in Marsamxett harbour to establish a quarantine hospital, later known as *Lazzaretto*. Although, in the late seventeenth century, celebrated architects and engineers like Valperga and Grunenbergh had stressed the importance to fortify the island, the Order was too busy with the Cottonera lines to get active in this direction. In 1723 finally Portuguese Grand Master Manoel de Vilhena offered to finance most of the project out of his own pocket. The fort thus got its name of Fort Manoel from its benefactor. The original design by the resident engineer Charles François de Mondion was modified by Louis François d'Aubigne de Tigné. Work progressed rapidly and by the early 1730s the work was nearly completed. It is composed of a square with four corner bastions. It

At the moment the fort is being restored to its former glory. It is not open to the public. The best way to see it is from Valletta along the Marsamxett coastline or, even better, from the heights of Hastings Gardens in Valletta.

has a tenaille and a ravelin in the ditch facing the land front and a small demi-lune facing the sea. The bastions facing the land front are strengthened with two cavaliers joined together by a long curtain wall. The garrison was accommodated in large bombproof barrel-vaulted casemates. The main entrance to the fort was through a baroque gateway in the centre of the east curtain.

The gate of Fort Manoel is a typical example of baroque ornate and ostentatious architecture. Architecture historians speak of a so called 'Vilhena style'. It is found in various buildings in Valletta and Mdina built in the early 18th century.

Opposite page: The main gate facing Valletta and the fort's chapel. This was dedicated to St Anthony of Padua and Lisbon. The builder of Fort Manoel, the Portuguese Grand Master Antonio Manoel de Vilhena had a special devotion to the saint, given his connection to his hometown, Lisbon.

Left and above: Fort Manoel was designed by the Order's resident engineer Charles François de Mondion. This plan was later modified by Louis François de Tigné. A major restoration project is going on at the moment on the fort which was severely damaged during World War II.

FORT TIGNÉ
SLIEMA

Fort Tigné, on the so-called Dragut Point, is the last major fortification completed by the Order in Malta. Although Dragut Point was a site of great strategic value to protect Fort Manoel and to defend the entrance to Marsamxett Harbour, it took the Congregation of War and Fortification until 1792 to decide to build a new fort there. The plans were drawn by the Order's chief engineer Stephane de Tousard. The work was supervised by the Maltese Antonio Cachia and was financed mainly out of the pocket of Grand Master Rohan and Balí Rene Jacques de Tigné. The fort is a strong casemated redoubt with four flanks. Its diamond-shape follows the latest development of fortress architecture at the end of the eighteenth century. At the rear end, facing the mouth of the harbour, it has a circular tower. The fort was surrounded by a dry ditch, commanded by three protruding counterscarp galleries. All the works were enclosed within a heavily mined glacis. The main entrance was protected by a drawbridge. Thanks to its well balanced, modern, and solid construction and the military qualities of its commander, Joseph Maria von Rechberg, Fort Tigné resisted repeated French assaults in June 1798 and only surrendered when its gun powder provisions were exhausted.

Fort Tigné's diamond-shaped casemated construction and the use of the polygonal fortification system show influence of the latest techniques of fortress building in the end of the 18th century. A 19th-century photo of the fort.

FORT TIGNÉ

Fort Tigné was the last major fortified work by the knights. It had been designed by the Order's chief resident engineer, Stephane de Tousard in 1792. Tousard then had entrusted its construction to the Maltese engineer Antonio Cachia. It was named after Balí Renate Jacques de Tigné who donated more than 1,000 scudi to its construction. In the last decade it has been restored and embellished.

The fort's guns (twelve 24-pounders, six 18-pounders, six 12-pounders, and four four-pounders) could do great harm to any ship entering Marsamxett Harbour and also to foreign troops attempting to land at St Elmo Bay at Valletta. The fort then was further armed with 12 mortars (six shell-firing and six petreros) of different calibre.

At the moment the fort is being restored to its former glory. It is not open to the public. It is part of the Tigné Point apartment project. Once the project is finished, the fort is to be opened to the public. To arrive at Tigné Point, drive to Sliema from Gżira and going along the Marsamxett waterfront, the fort is at the end of Triq ix-Xatt, beyond the Fortina Hotel.

THE GOZO *CASTELLO*
VICTORIA, GOZO

Although the site has been inhabited and fortified at least since Roman times, the present shape of the *Gran Castello* at Gozo comes from the time of the knights. It appears that before the Hospitallers' arrival, the town of Gozo, Rabat, was divided into an outer lower area and a castrum on the present site of the citadel. This castle on the rocky hill included a church, houses, a south-facing entrance, and a ditch. In times of raids, it had enough space to offer shelter for all people then living on Gozo. The ramparts were encumbered with a number of houses and some of the walls were formed by houses with windows which hindered its defence. Grand Master L'Isle Adam provided it with a garrison and new artillery but it still could not resist the disastrous Ottoman raid of 1551 when over 5,000 Gozitans were carried into slavery. The citadel subsequently was repaired but, because of lack of funds, nothing was done to improve and modernize the medieval structure to obey to the new techniques of war and bombardment. In the late sixteenth and the early years of the seventeenth century, the Italian architect Giovanni Rinaldini and the resident engineer of the Order, Vittorio Cassar, successfully presented plans to modernize the *Castello* and new demi-bastions, curtains, terrepleins, enceintes, and ravelins were built. The main land front with its central bastion was completed before 1610, St John cavalier by 1614, and St Martin cavalier by 1622. When Napoleon conquered the islands, the *Castello* was equipped with 40 cannon.

The dominant site of the Gozo **Castello** *was used already in Roman times. It formed part of the Roman town of Gozo. Later the Byzantines, Arabs, Normans, and Aragonese contributed to its fortifications.*

The **Castello** *includes several houses, the Gozo cathedral, a south-facing entrance, and a ditch. In late medieval times and up to the 17th-century, it had enough space to shelter all inhabitants of Gozo.*

GRAN CASTELLO AT GOZO 331

PROSPETTIVA DEL CASTELLO DEL GOZO,
come si vede dalla parte del Mezzogiorno.

1. Chiesa Collegiata
2. Chiesa di S. Giuseppe
3. Palazzo del Vescovo
4. Palazzo del Governatore
5. Orologgio
6. Ingresso al Castello
7. Chiesa di S. Barbara
8. Spedala de S. Cosimo e Damiano
9. Corte Governatoriale

Prospetiva del Castello del Gozo, from Il Gozo Antico e Moderno e Sacro (1746), by G.P.F Agius de Soldanis (1712–70). Gozo was victim of numerous raids by North African corsairs and Ottoman forces. In 1551 the castello was conquered by combined Turkish and North African forces and nearly all the 5,000 Gozitans which then had sought for shelter in its walls were carried into slavery. It took decades that Gozo then was properly repopulated.

Bernardo DeOpuo Street, one of the typical small streets of the Gozo Castello, with its houses dating back to the medieval period. The cathdral of Gozo with its 'flat' dome lies at the bottom of the street.

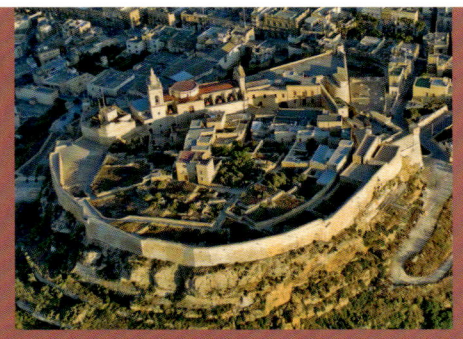

Aerial view of the Castello showing its round shape and its narrow and winding streets and alleys so typical for medieval times.

332　The Sites　The minor palaces and fortifications

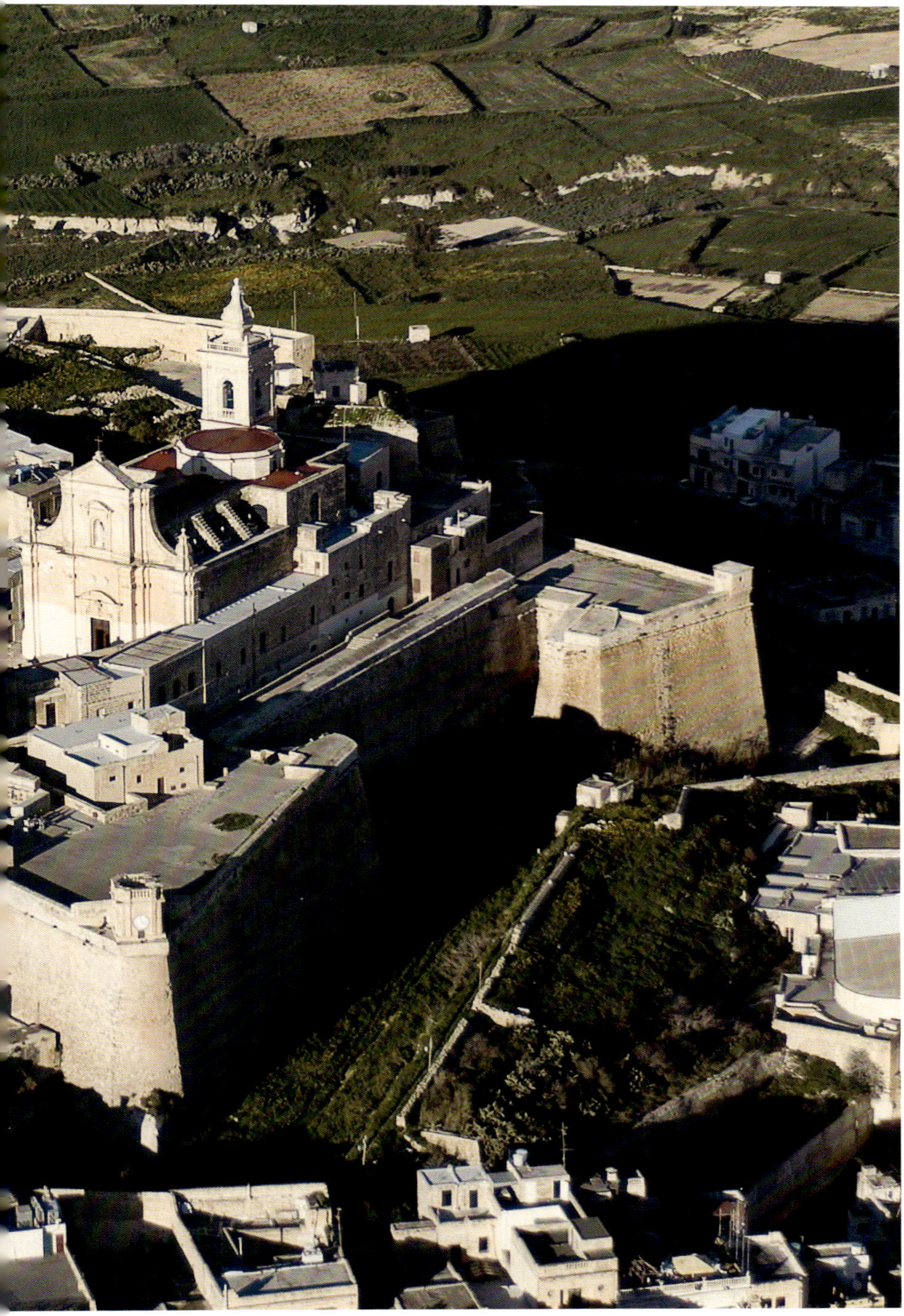

FORT CHAMBRAY
GĦAJNSIELEM

The history of Fort Chambray in Gozo is inseparably linked with the colourful life of one of the Order's most esteemed naval heroes, *Balí* Jacques François de Chambray. After his retirement from the Order's navy, Chambray held the post of lieutenant general of the defences. Besides his naval exploits, Chambray is remembered in Malta as a generous benefactor of churches. When he started to develop the plans for the strengthening of the coastal fortifications of Malta and Gozo, he was not the first one who had the idea to turn the little port of Mġarr into a fortified town protected by bastions and with a mighty citadel dominating both the land and sea approaches. But, without his insisting and contribution of huge sums of his own money, the project would never have come into gear properly. The concept to fortify the harbour itself was abandoned as too costly. The building of the citadel was started in 1749 and the first stone of the fortress was laid in January 1751. The fort as eventually built includes a large land-front facing northwards.

The fort is currently going through a complete refurbishing project. At the time of writing, it can only be accessed by residents of the newly built tourist village inside its walls. The best views of its walls are from Ix-Xatt l'Aħmar bay which can be accessed from Għajnsielem.

Fort Chambray

This land-front has a central bastion flanked by two bastions and two ravelins and is protected by a counterguard placed inside the wide ditch. The covertway has traverses and places-of-arms. The enceinte to the north-west consists of a long curtain. The enceinte, to the south, facing the cliff was not meant to be fortified. By 1761 Fort Chambray was fully completed but Chambray, who had died in 1758, did not witness the completion of his pet-project.

View inside the once spacious precincts of Fort Chambray. It was originally planned to build a full-fledged citadel which should be populated with settlers and craftsmen. This project had been developed in the times of the Portuguese Grand Master Vilhena but was then stopped owing to lack of funds.

By 1761 the building of Fort Chambray was finished. By then it was the best provisioned and defenced place on Gozo. By then it was still hoped that its spacious interior would be the home for settlers and it was planned to build a governor's palace, a parish church, and administrative buildings.

When, on 10 June 1798, the French attacked Gozo, Chevalier de Megrigny with a small garrison held Fort Chambray for a few hours. By the evening, General Reynier had captured Fort Chambray and the citadel of Rabat (Victoria).

THE WIGNACOURT AQUEDUCT
VARIOUS LOCATIONS

The provision of a fortress city like Valletta with fresh water was of utmost importance. In fact this was a weak spot of Malta's *città nuova* in the 1560s and 1570s. Most of the houses had cisterns and there was a spring in the vicinity of the *Porto Grande* and another one near the site of the *Auberge de Baviere* but, with the growing population of the city – in 1590 there were 4,000 inhabitants, by 1614 over 10,000 – the water-supply problem became more urgent. The order that every newly built house had to have a well did not help to solve the general problem. When Grand Master Aloph de Wignacourt came into power in 1601, a project to bring fresh water to Valletta to the capital from sources around Buskett near Rabat and behind Mdina was intensely discussed. Wignacourt promised to pay a part of the expenses out of his own pocket. In 1610 extensive excavation work started directed by the Sicilian Jesuit father and engineer Natale Tomasucci. By means of underground channels the water flowed easily down to Attard but to take it farther to Valletta was more difficult because of the uneven contours of the terrain.

It was the engineer from Bologna Bontadino de Bontadini who in the early 1610s, constructed stone conduits supported on a series of arches to carry the water from Balzan to Ħamrun. Close to Ħamrun, the line of arches turned at right angle to cross the road. The part of the aqueduct across the road formed an archway with a large central arch and two

The 5.2 km-aqueduct consists of a number of stone conduits, carried on a series of arches, all the way from Balzan to Ħamrun. From here the water went through underground channels down to Floriana and Valletta. The whole project was completed after five years of intensive work.

At Fleur-de-Lys, Santa Venera the three decorations on top of this stone arch – fleur-de-lys from Wignacourt's coat of arms – gave the name to the district. The gate was demolished during World War II after a RAF vehicle tried to pass through the gate, got stuck, and pulled the gate down.

small arched passageways. The construction was decorated with stone motifs, coat of arms, and plaques with Latin inscriptions commemorating the erection of the aqueduct. The three large *Fleur-de-Lys* – part of the coat of arms of Aloph de Wignacourt – later gave the name to this district. From Ħamrun the water was guided through underground channels to Valletta. After five years work the ambitious project was completed in the spring 1614, but apparently Bontadini did not see his work finished as he was mysteriously stabbed to death. Later commentators report that the final stages of the construction to take water to Valletta's *Piazza San Giorgio* in front of the palace of the grand master were supervised by some captured Turkish engineers. The inauguration of the project was celebrated with pompous festivities and the presence of the aged Grand Master Wignacourt on 21 August 1615. The fountain at *Piazza San Giorgio* was later decorated in baroque fashion. Another ornamental fountain was later erected in Valletta's suburb Floriana. The aqueduct was 5.2 kilometres long and cost the enormous sum of 155,000 *scudi*. The construction remained in use until the 19th century. In the 20th century it was replaced completely by the modern drainage and water supply systems. With the change of the urban landscape of Malta, parts of the aqueduct were removed and damaged.

Above: In 1616 at Floriana, Wignacourt's architect Bontadini constructed a water tower with a drinking-trough opposite the Sarria Church.

Right: The Wignacourt fountain that used to be at Piazza San Giorgio. *It was later dismantled and rebuilt at St Philip gardens, Floriana.*

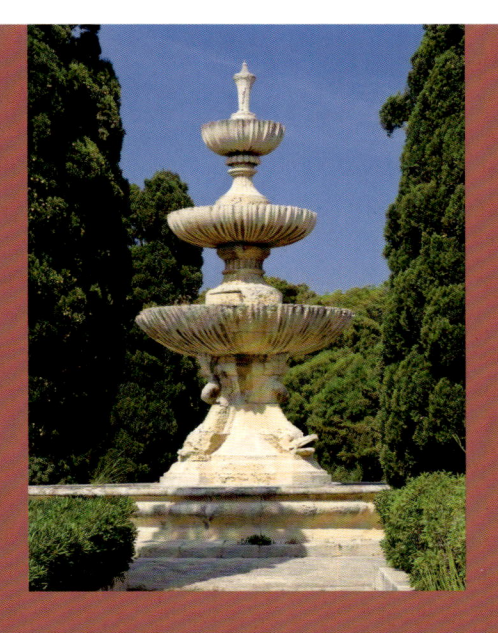

THE COASTLINE FORTIFICATIONS
MALTA AND GOZO

At first the knights concentrated on the fortification and protection of the conurbation of the *Porto Grande* and the port of Marsamxett. This was motivated by the fact that these ports were the hub of the island's economy and the main life-line between Malta and the outside world. It was essential to protect Birgu and Senglea (Isla) and the newly built capital of Malta, Valletta. There were also two other aspects which prevented the Order from taking also care of the protection of other areas of Malta and Gozo: lack of funds and the idea (which prevailed at least until the Great Siege) that one day they would return to their old possession, Rhodes. How vulnerable the regions outside the conurbation of the *Porto Grande* in fact were was shown in 1551 when Gozo was sacked by joint Ottoman and North African forces and the Gozo castello offered only a token resistance. Even in 1614 the Ottomans could land troops at Marsascala and raid its hinterland.

By then French Grand Master Aloph de Wignacourt had started a programme to fortify the coasts of the islands. In 1610 St Lucian tower at Marsaxlokk Bay and the tower at St Paul's Bay were built, followed St Thomas tower in 1614 and *Santa Maria delle Grazie* tower on Malta's south-eastern coast in 1620. The straits between Malta's north-east coast and Comino and

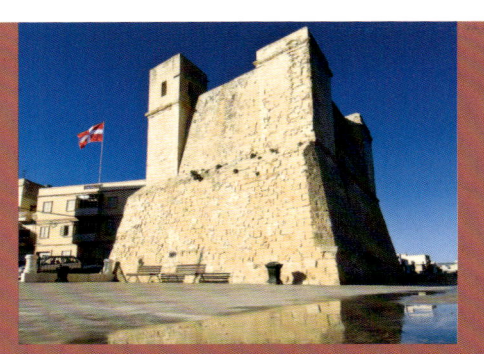

St Paul's Bay Tower, also known as Wignacourt Tower. Built in 1609, it was the first of the Wignacourt towers. Vittorio Cassar was its architect. The grand master donated 7,000 scudi for its building. The tower is now leased to Din l-Art Ħelwa (the National Trust of Malta). For opening hours check: www.dinlarthelwa.org

St Lucian Tower between Marsaxlokk and Birżebbuġja was built by Wignacourt in 1610. Just four years after it was built, its cannon warded off a fleet of some 60 Turkish vessels which tried to land in Marsaxlokk. The fort is now used as the base for 'The Malta Centre For Fisheries Sciences', and is not open to the general public.

The coastal towers formed significant strongpoints intended to protect vulnerable sections of the coast from attack. Many of them were built to be visible from one another in such a way to give the soldiers a possibility to signal one another in case of enemy attack. Here the Ghajn Tuffieha tower lines up with the Lippija tower, both built during Grand Master Lascaris' rule.

St Thomas Bay was not defended in any way, and the Turkish troops in 1614 after being repulsed from Marsaxlokk Bay by St Lucian tower, landed in St Thomas Bay. Soon after that year, work on the tower began under architect Gerolamo Bonici. It is now under the curatorship of Fondazzjoni Wirt Artna; www.wirtartna.org

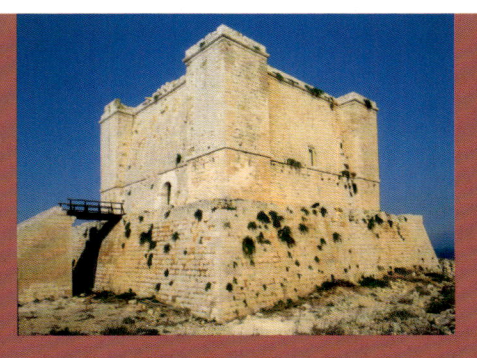

Comino Tower was built in 1618. It is also known as St Mary's Tower. It cost more than 18,000 scudi to built and the tower proved itself many times defending the Malta-Gozo channel. Built on the highest point of Comino, to gain even more height the tower was built on a base 8 metres high. Din l-Art Ħelwa takes care of this site. For visits go: www.dinlarthelwa.org

Mgarr were often visited by pirates and North African corsairs. To put a stop to that a tower was built overlooking the small port of Mġarr in 1609. A few years later a tower was built near Marsalforn at Gozo. In 1618 St Mary's tower was erected at Comino. This latter fortification was of great importance as it served as a look-out post and to protect the crossings between the islands. The building of the tower near Mellieħa dates to 1649 and to the period when Malta was ruled by Grand Master Lascaris. All of these buildings followed a more or less uniform construction. Their ground plan was rectangular and they had two storeys with the room in the basement used as a store. The entrance, in the second storey, was reached via an outside staircase. Some of the towers had a ditch with a drawbridge. In times of peace the company of each tower normally consisted of six men. The main armour, consisting of two guns firing balls of six *libres*, were placed on the roof. Besides their defence duties, the men in these towers were also responsible for signals, warnings, and various forms of communication. In case of danger they were obliged to raise flags or – at night – light fires.

After Wignacourt's death, the programme of coastal defences was continued. In the mid-17th century, smaller towers were built at Għajn Tuffieħa, Lippija, Qawra Point, St George's Bay, and Wied iż-Żurrieq, mostly in places where an enemy landing was possible but where it was rather difficult to move defensive troops by land. Much bigger was St Agatha tower (also called 'Red Tower') which was built in the late 1640s. The main building is surrounded by a star-shaped

Lippija Tower, also known as Ġnejna Tower since it overlooks the bay with the same name. Built in 1637 during the reign of Grand Master Lascaris, it was one of four towers built in the same shape and size. The other three are Għajn Tuffieħa (right), St George's Bay (opposite left), and Qawra Point (opposite right).

THE COASTLINE FORTIFICATIONS 341

The coat of arms of Grand Master Lascaris on the door (the ground door was opened later) of Lippija Tower with the inscription:

PAX FIAT IN VIRTUE TUA ET ABUNDATIO IN .... MDCXXXVII (Peace comes about in your honour and abundance... 1637).

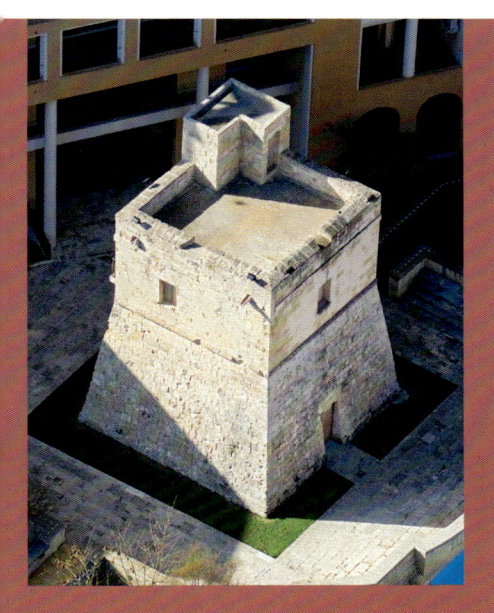

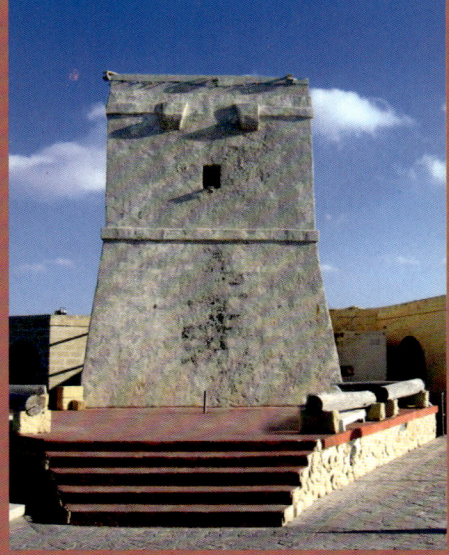

342   THE SITES   THE MINOR PALACES AND FORTIFICATIONS

*St Agatha Tower overlooking Mellieħa. Built in 1648 during the reign of Grand Master Lascaris. It is more commonly known as the Red Tower (*Torre Rossa*). It was painted red so that it would be more visible from the guards in the other towers. It served as a relay point to pass messages to Gozo. Open daily. The tower has been restored by* Din l-Art Ħelwa. *For opening hours check:* www.dinlarthelwa.org

Some of the De Redin towers. Above; Torri l-Abjad at Mellieħa built in 1658 (with Comino tower in the background); right: Qalet Marku tower also built in 1658; opposite left: Wardija Tower, also known as the Guardia Tower, built in 1659 the last of the 13 De Redin towers, and opposite right: Mġarr ix-Xini Tower, built strategically at the entrance of the little fjord in Gozo with the same name in 1661.

wall. During the reign of Grand Master Martin de Redin in the late 1650s, a building programme was started to complete the line of coastal defences and stations of communications leading to the erection of towers at Għajn Ħadid, Xrobb l-Għaġin, Triq il-Wiesgħa, L-Aħrax, Bengħisa, Madliena, Għallis, Marku, Qalet, St Julian's, Ħamrija, Wardija, and Delimara. Some of them were bigger than the towers built under Grand Master Wignacourt. They had one storey more and smaller towers on the four corners of the roof. In the late 17th and in the 18th century only a few other towers and coastal fortifications was added. Mġarr ix-Xini tower and Ta' Isopu tower near Nadur, both in Gozo, were built in 1661 and in 1667 respectively. In 1760 another tower was added near Marsalforn. In the 18th century a different concept of coastal defence was developed. It was observed that the existing towers possessed much too little firepower to stop enemy fleets from landing their troops.

To prevent enemy ships from anchoring and landing troops, a total of 34 coastal batteries were built, namely at Marsaxlokk, Marsascala, St Julian's Bay, St Thomas, Madliena, St Paul's and Mellieħa between 1715 and 1792. Twenty of these batteries were provided with shelters for infantry. Grand Master Vilhena was also decided to fortify some strategic important inland locations. In the second half of the 18th century, plans were developed to add 30 coastal batteries to protect the islands. This ambitious project, however, was never put into practice.

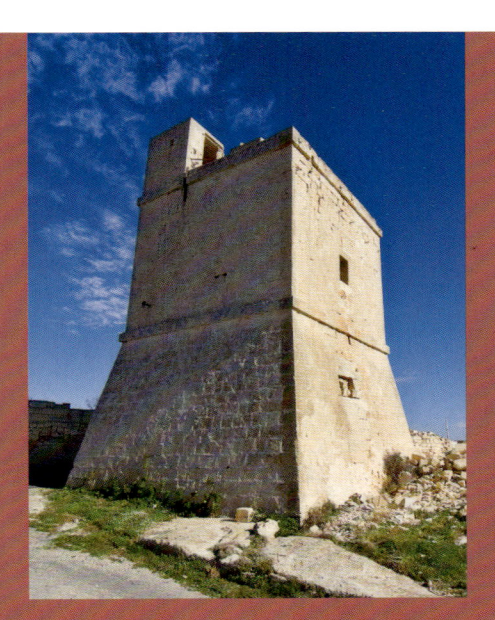

San Blas Tower at Nadur, Gozo known also by the locals as **it-Torri ta' Isopu**. Built in 1667 during the reign of Grand Master Nicolas Cotoner, it was paid for by the **Universitas** of Gozo, whilst the Order supplied the cannon. It was restored as a collaborative project between Din l-Art Ħelwa and the Nadur Local Council. For opening hours, check: www.dinlarthelwa.org

THE COASTLINE FORTIFICATIONS 345

Top: Marsalforn Tower, in Gozo. Built in 1724, it was completely demolished by the British in 1915 since it was in the way of a wireless station. The design of the tower was by Charles François Mondion.

Above: St Anthony's Battery as Ras il-Qala, in Gozo, as seen from the sea. Din l-Art Ħelwa, the Qala Local Council, and the Malta Environment and Planning Authority are restoring the 1732 battery.

346   The Sites   The minor palaces and fortifications

THE COASTLINE FORTIFICATIONS   347

In 1714 the Order started to built a battery on Comino to defend the Malta-Comino channel. Yet since the original site was not ideal, what had been built was dismantled and rebuilt in 1716 where St Mary's Battery lies today. It was equipped with two 24-pounder and four 6-pounder cannon. The battery was restored by Din l'Art Helwa. For opening hours check: www.dinlarthelwa.org

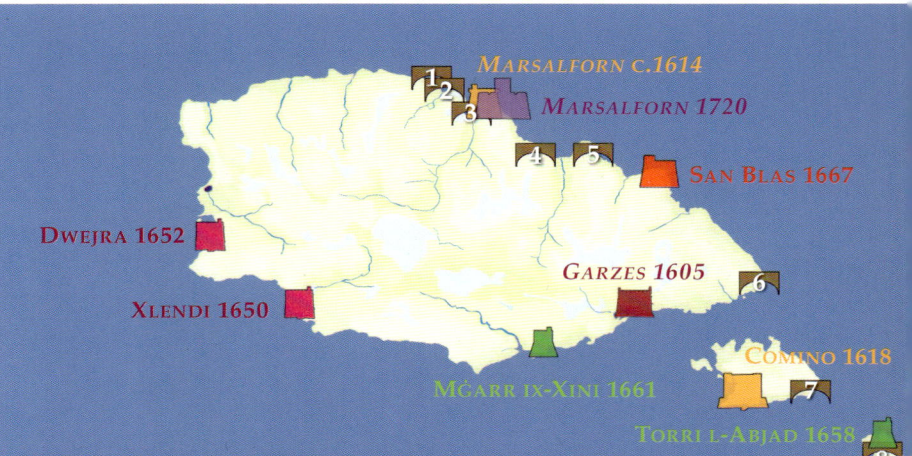

348 The Sites The minor palaces and fortifications

MARSALFORN c.1614
MARSALFORN 1720
SAN BLAS 1667
DWEJRA 1652
GARZES 1605
XLENDI 1650
MĠARR IX-XINI 1661
COMINO 1618
TORRI L-ABJAD 1658
RED TOWER 1648
GHAJN T
16
LIPPIJA 163

GRAND MASTER MARTIN GARZES/ALOF DE WIGNACOURT
1605

GRAND MASTER ALOF DE WIGNACOURT
1601–22

GRAND MASTER JEAN PAUL DE LASCARIS CASTELLAR
1636–57

GRAND MASTER MARTIN DE REDIN
1657–60

GRAND MASTER NICOLAS COTONER
1663–80

GRAND MASTER RAMON PERELLOS Y ROCCAFUL
1697–1720

DELIMARA 1659 Italic names mean that tower has been demolished.

THE COASTAL FORTIFICATIONS 349

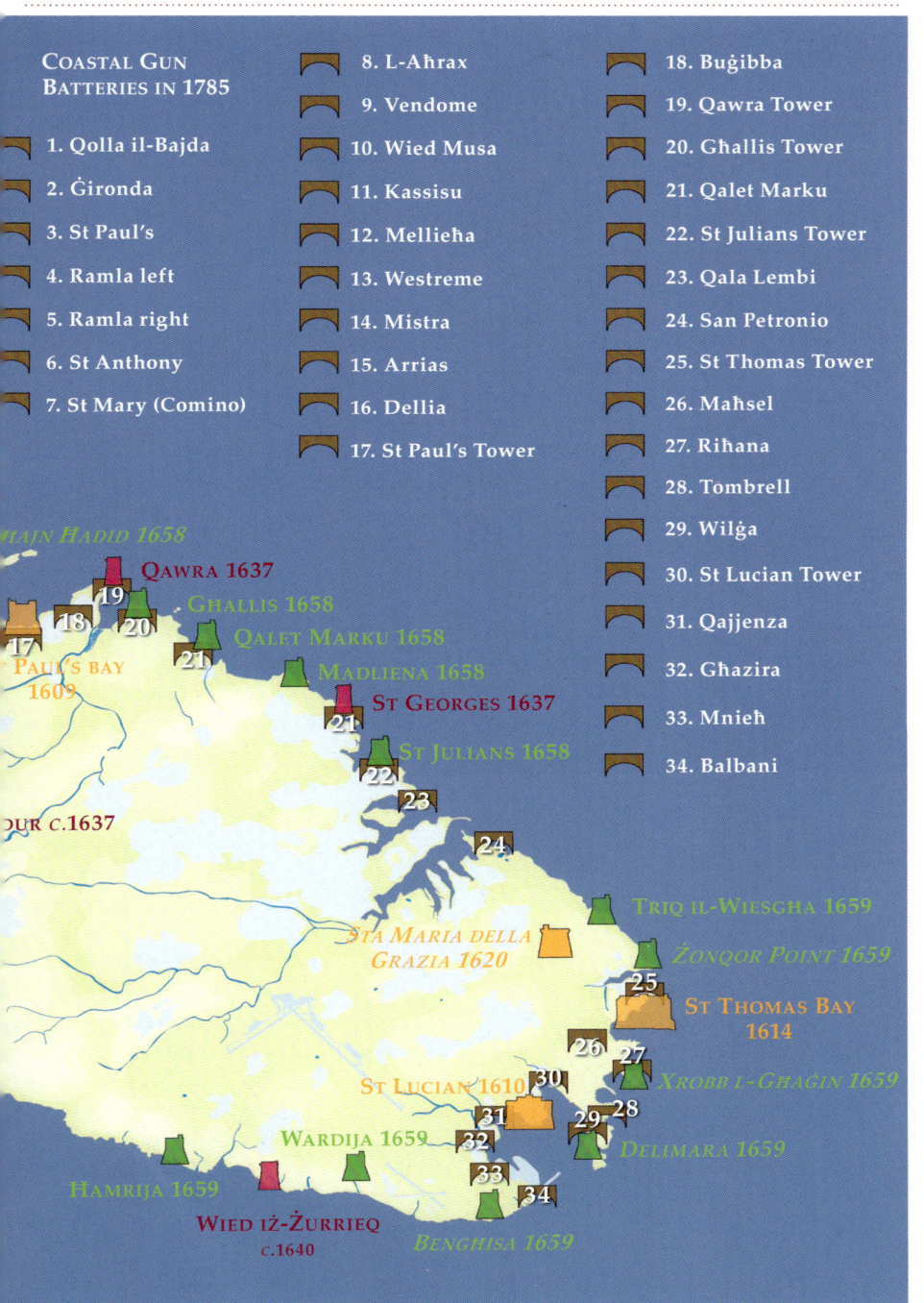

COASTAL GUN BATTERIES IN 1785

1. Qolla il-Bajda
2. Ġironda
3. St Paul's
4. Ramla left
5. Ramla right
6. St Anthony
7. St Mary (Comino)
8. L-Aħrax
9. Vendome
10. Wied Musa
11. Kassisu
12. Mellieħa
13. Westreme
14. Mistra
15. Arrias
16. Dellia
17. St Paul's Tower
18. Buġibba
19. Qawra Tower
20. Għallis Tower
21. Qalet Marku
22. St Julians Tower
23. Qala Lembi
24. San Petronio
25. St Thomas Tower
26. Maħsel
27. Riħana
28. Tombrell
29. Wilġa
30. St Lucian Tower
31. Qajjenza
32. Għazira
33. Mnieħ
34. Balbani

Ħajn Ħadid 1658
Qawra 1637
Għallis 1658
Qalet Marku 1658
Paul's Bay 1609
Madliena 1658
St Georges 1637
St Julians 1658
our c.1637
Triq il-Wiesgħa 1659
Sta Maria della Grazia 1620
Żonqor Point 1659
St Thomas Bay 1614
St Lucian 1610
Xrobb l-Għaġin 1659
Wardija 1659
Delimara 1659
Ħamrija 1659
Wied iż-Żurrieq c.1640
Benġħisa 1659

Sources and recommended reading:

Besides the extensive archival manuscript sources in the Archives of the Order of Malta integrated in the National Library of Malta (Valletta), the Archives of the Grand Magistry, Palazzo di Malta (Rome) and in several archives scattered all over Europe, especially in the Archivo Histórico Nacional, 'Sección de Ordenes Militares' (Madrid), Badisches Generallandesarchiv, 'Johanniter Orden' (Karlsruhe), and the Russian Imperial Foreign Policy Archive (Moscow) amongst others, there is a long list of historical works and studies dealing with the chequered history of the Order. Parts of it is listed in the bibliographical works by Franz Paul von Smitmer, *Catalogo della Biblioteca del S. Militare Ordine di S. Giovanni Gerosolimitano, oggi detto di Malta* (Rome, 1781) and Ferdinand de Hellwald, *Bibliographié Méthodique de l'Ordre Souverain de St Jean de Jérusalem* (Rome, 1885). Long and useful bibliographies of older works are also found in Louis de Boisgelin, *Ancient and Modern Malta*, 3 vols. (London, 1805) or Albrecht Christoph Kayser, *Neuestes Gemälde von Malta*, 3 vols. (Ronneburg–Leipzig, 1799–1800).

In the fifteenth and sixteenth century, some authors had already started to compile information on the Order's history and had published works on crucial events of its history. One might mention here Guillaume Caoursin, *Obsidionis Rhodiae Urbis descriptio* (Venice, 1480) and François Nicolas Durand de Villegagnon's description of the attack on Malta in 1551 and the loss of Tripoli (*De bello Melitensi et ejus eventu Gallis imposito commentarius*, Lyon, 1552). In the mid-sixteenth century the knights Giuseppe Cambiano and Antoine Geoffroi were commissioned to write a history of the Order, but Geoffroi's death aborted his project and Cambiano's compilation remained unpublished. In 1556 a Catalan knight, Joan Antoni Foxa, was commissioned to finish the work started by Geoffroi. Foxa's 'Ystoria dela sacra Religione y milicia de sant Joan bautista de hierusalem ...' (*c*.1556) was never published. In 1581 Heinrich Pantaleon, the Protestant scholar from Basel, published *Militaris Ordinis Joannitarum Rhodiorum aut Melitensium equitum ... Historia Nova*. Between 1594 and 1602 there appeared the voluminous *Historia della Religione et Ill.ma Militia di S. Giovanni Gerosolimitano*. It was a milestone in the publications on the Order and also contributed considerably to make the Hospitallers' new headquarters Malta more known in Europe. Its author was Giacomo Bosio who had long been in contact with the Order. In the 1580s Bosio had worked on a literary apotheosis of the moral values of the knights. This compilation of short essays (*La Corona del Cavalieri Gierosolimitano*) appeared in 1588 in print. In 1589 he published in Italian a compilation of the statutes of the Order, *Li Privilegi della Sacra Religione di S. Gio Gerosolimitano*. By 1594 Bosio had published the first two volumes of the *Historia della Religione et Ill.ma*

Militaria di S. Giovanni Gerosolimitano dedicated to Grand Master Verdalle. In 1602 the third volume was published. The announced fourth volume was never published. In 1621 Bosio edited a reworked and augmented version of the first volume of the *Historia*. In 1630 Carlo Aldrobandini edited a revised version of the second volume. A new edition of the first volume was printed in Naples in 1684.

In the seventeenth century many historians used Bosio's works as a basis for their histories of the Order. One may here list Pierre Boissat de Livieux (*Histoire des Chevaliers de l'Ordre de l'Hospital de St Jean de Hierusalem, contenant leur admirable institution et police*, 2 vols. (Lyon, 1612), Jean Baudoin, *Histoire des Chevaliers de l'Ordre de S. Jean de Hierusalem* (Paris, 1624), and Ignazio Agostin de Funes, *Corónica de la illustrissima Milicia y Sagrada Religion de San Juan Bautista de Ierusalem*, 2 vols. (Valencia–Saragossa, 1639). In the mid-seventeenth century the German knight of Malta Christian von Osterhausen published several works on the statutes of the Order which also included long chapters on the history of the Order (*Statuten, Ordnungen und Gebräuche des hochlöblichen Ritterlichen Ordens St Johannes von Jerusalem zu Malta,* (Frankfurt, 1644); *Eigentlicher und gründlicher Bericht dessen, was zu einer vollkommenen Erkenntnis und Wissenschaft des hochlöblichen Ritterlichen Ordens St Johannis von Jerusalem zu Malta vonnöten* (Augsburg, 1649). The next important work was Bartolomeo dal Pozzo's *Historia dellaSacra Religione militare di S. Giovanni Gerosolimitano detta di Malta*, 2 vols. (Verona 1703–15). The Veronese Dal Pozzo was a knight of the Order. In the same period there appeared Johann Christoph Beckmann's *Anmerkungen von dem Ritterlichen Johanniter-Orden und dessen absonderlichen Beschaffenheit in dem Herren-Meistertum derselben in Mark, Sachsen, Pommern und Wendland* (Frankfurt an der Oder, 1693, also 1695 and 1728); Johann Georg Dienemann's *Nachrichten vom Johanniterorden, insbesondere in dessen Herrenmeisterthum in der Mark, Sachsen und Wendland* (Berlin, 1767), Johann Christoph Dithmar's *Geschichte des Ritterlichen Johanniter-Ordens* (Frankfurt an der Oder, 1728), and Heinrich Ludwig Gude's *Staat des Malteser oder Johanniter-Ordens* (Halle, 1708).

In 1726 there was published possibly the most famous historical work on the Order: René Aubert, Abbé de Vertot's *Histoire des chevaliers hospitaliers de St Jean de Jerusalem*, 4 vols. (Paris, 1726). It was translated into English and German and used extensively by many other authors and historians who aimed to write on the Order. In the last years of the 18th and the early years of the 19th century – after the Order had been expelled from Malta – many authors felt the need to present new histories of the knights, very often for political motives. These include Gregoryi Krayevski's *Kratkoye Tipograficheskoye, Istoricheskoye i Politicheskoye Opisaniye Ostrova Malti*, 2 vols. (St Petersburg, 1800–01)

(Volume two concentrates entirely on the history of the Order of St John), the above mentioned works by Boisgelin, Kayser, and Joseph Charles Meyer de Knonau's *Révolution de Malte en 1798; gouvernement, principes, lois, statuts de l'Ordre. Réponse au manifeste du Prieuré de Russie* (Trieste, 1799), Johann N. Längenfeld's, *Kurzgefaßte pragmatische Geschichte des hohen Malteserordens* (Munich, 1783), Joseph de Maisonneuve's *Annales Historiques de l'Ordre Souverain de St Jean de Jerusalem depuis l'année 1725 jusqu'au moment présent* (St Petersburg, 1799), Heinrich Czermack's *Kurzgefaßter Begriff von dem hohen Orden der Johanniter- oder Malteser-Ritter* (Munich, 1782), and Joseph Anton Sauter's *Über den Maltheserorden und seine gegenwärtigen Verhältnisse zu Deutschland* (Frankfurt–Leipzig, 1804).

In the 19th and 20th centuries and up to recently, a huge number of histories of the Order have been written. Their number is too extensive to be listed here. For English readers interested in general presentations, one may mention Elizabeth Schermerhorn's *Malta of the Knights* (Surrey, 1929, reprint London 1978), Victor Mallia-Milanes's (ed.), *Hospitaller Malta 1530–1798. Studies on Early Modern Malta and the Order of St John of Jerusalem* (Malta, 1993), Roderick Cavaliero's *The last of the Crusaders. The Knights of St John and Malta in the eighteenth century* (London, 1960), H.J.A. Sire, *The Knights of Malta* (New Haven–London, 1994). There are also many Italian, Spanish, French, and German general works, such as Francesco Gazzoni, *L'Ordine di Malta* (Milan, 1979), Claire Éliane Engel's *L'Ordre de Malte en Mediterranée (1530–1798)* (Monaco, 1957), id., *Les Chevaliers de Malte* (Paris, 1961), Aain Blondy's 'Malte et l'Ordre de Malte a l'épreuve des idées nouvelles (1740–1820)', Université de Sorbonne 1992–93, unpublished habilitation thesis. 4 vols.), id., *L'ordre de Malte au XVIII ème siècle : des dernières splendeurs à la ruine* (Paris, 2002), Jaime Salva's *La Orden de Malta y la acciones espanoles contra Turcos y Berberiscos en los siglos XVI y XVII* (Madrid, 1944), Karl Falkenstein's *Geschichte des Johanniter-Ordens* (Zeitz–Leipzig, 1867), Gottardo Bottarelli's *Storia politica e militare del Sovrano Ordine di S. Giovanni di Gerosolemme detto di Malta* (Florence, 1940), Rudolf von Finck, *Übersicht über die Geschichte des ritterlichen Ordens St Johannis vom Spital zu Jerusalem und der Balley Brandenburg* (Leipzig, 1890), Walter G. Rödel's *Der Ritterliche Orden St Johannis vom Spital zu Jerusalem. Ein Abriß seiner Geschichte* (Nieder–Weisel, 1989), A. Wienand, C.W. von Ballestrem, and Chr. von Imhof (eds.), *Der Johanniter-Orden. Der Malteser-Orden. Der ritterliche Orden des Hl. Johannes vom Spital zu Jerusalem. Seine Aufgaben, seine Geschichte* (Cologne, 1970, also 1988), Michel de Pierredon's *Histoire politique de l'Ordre Souverain de Saint-Jean de Jérusalem (Ordre de Malte) de 1789 à 1955*, 2 vols. (Paris, 1956–63), I.K. Antochevsky's *L'Ordre Souverain de Saint-Jean de Jérusalem, dit Ordre de Malte* (St Petersburg, 1914), Paul

Gauger's *Der Ritterorden des Hl. Johannes oder die Malteser* (Karlsruhe, 1844), Bernhard G. Hafkemeyer's *Der Malteser-Ritter-Orden* (Hamburg, 1956), and Wilhelm von Mirbach's *Geschichte des Johanniterordens* (Bad Pyrmont, 1957).

The medieval period of the Hospitallers is discussed in Jonathan Riley-Smith, *The Knights of St John in Jerusalem and Cyprus c.1050-1310* (London, 1967), Anthony T. Luttrell, *Latin Greece, the Hospitallers and the Crusade: 1291-1440* (London, 1982), id., *The Hospitallers in Cyprus, Rhodes, Greece and the West 1291-1440* (London, 1978), id., *The Hospitallers of Rhodes and their Mediterranean World* (London, 1992), Eric Brockman, *The two sieges of Rhodes, 1480 & 1522* (London, 1969), Jean Delaville le Roulx, *Les Hospitallers à Rhodes jusque'à la mort de Philibert de Naillac: 1310-1421* (Paris, 1913). On the Hospitaller's early period there is the most useful edition of documents by Jean Delaville le Roulx (ed.), *Cartulaire général de l'Ordre des Hospitaliers de St Jean de Jérusalem*, 4 vols. (Paris, 1894–1906).

The foreign contacts and relations of the knights is discussed in Victor Mallia-Milanes, *Venice and Hospitaller Malta. 1530-1798. Aspects of a Relationship* (Malta, 1992), Alfredo Mifsud, *Knights Hospitallers of the Venerable Tongue of England in Malta* (Malta, 1914), Andrew P. Vella, *An Elizabethan-Ottoman Conspiracy* (Malta, 1972), id., *The Tribunal of the Inquisition in Malta* (Malta, 1964), id., *Malta and the Czars. Diplomatic relations between the Order of St John and Russia, 1697-1802* (Malta, 1972), Guzeppi Schembri, *The Malta and Russia Connection* (Malta, 1990), Walter G. Rödel, *Das Großpriorat Deutschland des Johanniter-Ordens im Übergang vom Mittelalter zur Reformation anhand der Generalvisitationsberichte von 1494/95 und 1540/41* (Cologne, 1972), Alexander Bonnici, *Medieval and Roman Inquisition in Malta* (Malta, 1998), Julius von Pflugk-Harttung, *Die Anfänge des Johanniter-Ordens in Deutschland besonders in der Mark Brandenburg und in Mecklenburg* (Berlin, 1899), Carmel Testa, *The French in Malta. 1798–1800* (Malta, 1997), Thomas Freller, *The Anglo-Bavarian Langue of the Order of Malta* (Malta, 2001), Desmond Gregory, *Malta, Britain, and the European Powers, 1793–1815* (Madison, n.y.), Ernst von Berg, *Der Malteserorden und seine Beziehungen zu Russland* (Riga, 1879), Ernst Opgenoorth, *Die Ballei Brandenburg des Johanniterordens im Zeitalter der Reformation und Gegenreformation* (Würzburg, 1963), Frederick W. Ryan, *The House of the Temple. A Study of Malta and its Knights in the French Revolution* (London, 1930), Robert Dauber, *Der Johanniter-Malteser Orden in Österreich und Mitteleuropa*, 3 vols. (n. pl., 1996–2000).

On the statutes of the Order concentrate the studies by E.J. King, *The Rule, Statutes and Customs of the Hospitallers, 1099–1310* (London, 1934), M. Barbaro di San Giorgio, *Storia della Costituzione del Sovrano Militare Ordine di Malta* (Rome, 1927), M. Ambraziejuté, *Studien über die*

Johanniterregel Diss. (Freiburg, 1929), Hans Prutz, *Die exemte Stellung des Hospitaliter-Ordens. Ihre Entwicklung, ihr Wesen und ihre Wirkung* (Munich, 1904), Berthold von Waldstein-Wartenberg, *Rechtsgeschichte des Malteserordens* (Vienna, 1969), Heinrich von Ortenburg, *Der Ritterorden des Hl. Johannes von Jerusalem. In seiner Verfassung und Geschichte dargestellt* (Ratisbon, 1866), Jürgen Sarnowsky, *Macht und Herrschaft im Johanniterorden des 15. Jahrhunderts. Verfassung und Verwaltung der Johanniter auf Rhodos (1421–1522)* (Münster, 2001).

There are numerous studies on the different aspects of the rule of the Order in Malta. The maritime aspect is covered in valuable works by Joseph Muscat, 'The Warships of the Order of St John 1530–1798', in *Proceedings of History Week 1994* (Malta, 1996), Joseph Muscat and Andrew Cuschieri, *Naval Activities of the Knights of St John. 1530-1798* (Malta, 2002), Ubaldo Mori Ubaldini, *La Marina del Sovrano Militare Ordine di San Giovanni di Gerusalemme, die Rodi e di Malta* (Rome, 1971), Michel Fontenay, 'Corsaires de la foi ou rentiers du sol? Les chevaliers de Malte dans le corso méditerranéen au XVIIe siècle', *Revue d'Histoire Moderne et Contemporaine*, xxxv (July–September 1988), 361–84, Ettore Rossi, *Storia della marina dell'Ordine di S. Giovanni di Gerusalemme, di Rodi e di Malta* (Rome–Milan, 1926), Joseph Wismayer, *The Fleet of the Order of St John 1530–1798* (Malta, 1997).

With the charity and sanitary work of the Knights is dealt with in Paul Cassar, *Medical History of Malta* (London, 1964), id., *The Holy Infirmary of the Knights of St John, La Sacra Infermeria* (Malta 1994), Jesko von Steynitz, *Mittelalterliche Hospitäler der Orden und Städte als Einrichtungen der sozialen Sicherung* (Berlin-Munich, 1970), and Edgar Erskine Hume, *Medical Work of the Knights Hospitallers of Saint John of Jerusalem* (Baltimore, 1940).

There are furthermore many monographs on important and influential personalities of the Order: Winston L. Zammit, *Malta under the Cotoners 1660–1680.* (Malta, 1980), Johann Albert von Ittner, *Paul der Erste, russischer Kaiser, als Großmeister des Malteserordens* (Aarau, 1808), Carl Pfaff, *Philipp Villiers de l'Isle-Adam und Johann de la Valette. Zwei Heldenbilder aus dem sechszehnten Jahrhundert* (Schaffhausen, 1851), Michael Galea, *Grandmaster Philippe Villiers de l'Isle Adam* (Malta, 1997), id., *Grand Master Emanuel de Rohan. 1775–1797* (Malta, 1996), id., *Grandmaster Hughues Loubenx de Verdalle. 1582–1595* (Malta, 2000), id., *Grand Master Anton Manoel de Vilhena 1722–1736* (Malta, 1992), id, *Großmeister Ferdinand von Hompesch* (Malta, 1996); André Plaisse, *Le Rouge de Malte ou les curieux mémoires du bailli de Chambray* (Paris, 1991), Michel Bertrand, *Suffren 1729–1788. De Saint-Tropez aux Indes* (Paris, 1991), Carmel Testa, *The Life and Times of Grand Master Pinto 1741–1773* (Malta, 1989), Claire Èliane Engel, *Knights of Malta. A Gallery of Portraits* (London, 1963), Robert L. Dauber, *A Knight of Malta in Brazil. Ambassador* and Admiral. Comm. Frà François de Villegagnon (1510–1571) (Malta, 1996), Alain Blondy, Hugues de Loubens de Verdalle: 1531–1582–1595: cardinal et grand maître de l'ordre de Malte, un prince de la Renaissance à l'aube de la Contre-Reforme (Saint-Denis, 2005).

Important contributions to the fortifications of the knights in Malta, the monuments erected by the Order and the knights urban development programmes are by Albert Ganado, 'Matteo Perez d'Aleccio's Engravings of the Siege of Malta of 1565', Proceedings of History Week 1983 (Malta, 1984), 125-61; Roger de Giorgio, A city by an Order (Malta, 1986); Alison Hoppen, 'Military Engineers in Malta, 1530-1798', Annals of Science No. 38 (1981), 413-433; id., The Fortification of Malta by the Order of St John 1530-1798 Edinburgh, 1979); Denis De Lucca, Conrad Thake, The Genesis of Maltese Baroque Architecture: Francesco Buonamici (Malta, 1994); Quentin Hughes, The Building of Malta 1530–1795 (London, 1956); B. Lintorn Simmons, Description of the Governor's Palaces in Malta, of Valletta, St Antonio and Verdala and Catalogue of the Pictures (Malta, 1895); Leonhard Mahoney, 5000 years of Architecture in Malta (Malta, 1996); Stephen Spiteri, Fortresses of the Cross (Malta, 1994); id., The Art of Fortress Building in Hospitaller Malta (Malta, 2008); id., The Great Siege: Knights vs Turks MDLXV (Malta, 2005); id., The Palace Armoury (Malta, 1999, also revised edition Malta, 2003); Conrad Thake, 'Girolamo Cassar (1520s-1592). Architect of the Order', Treasures of Malta, vi, 2 (Easter 2000), 29–34.

Photo Credits

(not specified in caption of image):
p: page,
t: top,
c: centre
l: left,
r: right,
b: bottom

pg. 2-3: NMAL, pg. 6 SJF, pg. 10 all WC, pg. 11tr ASMOM, pg. 12-13 SJF, pg.14 WC, pg. 15 WC, pg. 25 WC, pg. 26 GE, pg. 31 WC, pg. 48 www.jeudiland.com, pg. 49t WC, pg. 49b WC, pg. 51 GE, pg. 58 WC, pg. 59 adapted from artwork by Mario Fabretti, pg. 79 WC, pg. 80 HMA, pg. 106 NMAL, pg. 116 WC, pg. 121 WC, pg. 124 WC, pg. 127 WC, pg. 162 WC, pg. 167 NMAL, pg. 210 WC, pg. 227 WC, pg. 228 ASMOM, pg. 230 ASMOM, pg. 241 traced and re-coloured from http://cilialacorte.com/grandmasters.html, pg. 242 all ASMOM, pg. 243 adapted from artwork by Mario Fabretti, pg. 285 MNL, pg. 293 br MNL, pg. 294 tl MNL, pg. 302 t NMAL, pg. 308 b GE, pg. 327 t NMAL, pg. 328 NMAL, pg. 331 MNL, pg. 336 br NMAL, pg. 345 t NMAL.

Photos of St John's Co-Cathedral: St John's Co-Cathedral Foundation

MNL: National Library of Malta,
NMAL: National Museum of Archaeology Library;
MM: Maritime Musueum,
HMA: Heritage Malta Archives,
ASMOM: Archives of the Sovereign Military Order of Malta,
GE: Google Earth,
WC: Wikipedia Commons.

A

Aachen 18
Abela, Leonardo 139
Acre 6, 37, 42, 47
ad-Dihn, Muslih 55
Agius de Soldanis, G.P.F. 331
Aleppo 47
Alexander, Carl 224
Alexander I (Czar) 213
Alexandria 47
Alfonso I of Aragon 23
Algardi, Alessandro 191, 271
Amadeo V (Duke of Savoy) 44
Amalfi 17, 18, 21, 31, 38
Amalfi Cross 17
Ambassadors' Room 286
Anastasius II 44
Anglo-Bavarian langue 126
Anjou, Charles of 37
arm of St Paul 190
armoury 292
Ascalon 30
Augustine 16
Aventine Hill in Rome 227

B

bagnio 109
Balaguer, bishop of Malta 179
Balbi di Correggio, Francesco 91
Ball, Alexander Sir 77, 212
Barberini, Antonio 163
Barcelona 47
Bari 47
Bayezid II (Sultan) 51, 52
Beaujolais, Vicomte de 271
Bech, Theoderich 179
Bechir Hoggia 105
Beit-Jibrin Castle 24
Benzi, Massimiliano 267
Bernard of Clairvaux 15
Bertucci, Antonio 125
beylerbeys 138
Bibliotheca 188
Blondel, Mederico 309
Blondy, Alain 144
Boccage, Chevalier de 179
Bodrum 45
Boissat, Pierre 108
Bonello, Antonio 86
Bonnici, Alexander 170
Bontadini, Bontadino de 336, 337
Book of Hours 47
Book of Navigation 78
Borg, Filippo 164
Borgia, Alessandro 225
Borromeo, St Charles 265
Bosio, Giacomo 18, 33, 72, 108, 176, 348

Bosredon, Pierre 47
Brandenburg 122, 124
Braudel, Fernand 81, 129
Breydenbach, Bernhard von 31
Brocktorff, Charles Frederick 199, 293
Buonamici, Francesco 184
Buonamici, Giovanni Vincenzo 181, 307
Buonaparte (Napoleon) 6, 7, 8, 119, 162, 206, 209, 210, 211, 212, 214, 219, 282, 313, 330
Busca, Antoine 219

C

Cachia, Antonio 188, 328
Cagliares, Baldassare 160, 161, 190
Cambrai 52
Campo, Girolamo 72
Cancelleria, Vecchia 186
Candida, Carlo 223
Caoursin, Guillaume 50, 52
Caracciolo, Giuseppe 219
Caracciolo, Ricardo 50
Carapecchia, Romano 184, 185, 186, 283
Cars, Laurent 107
Casa Rocca Piccola 172
Cassar, Carmel 170
Cassar, Gerolamo 103, 183, 250, 256, 258, 282, 284, 305, 322, 355
Cassar, Vittorio 330
Castagna, P.P. 106, 213
Castelfranco 77
Catherine the Great (Czarina) 204
castrum maris 85, 86, 151, 152, 154, 296
Chambray, Fort 5, 113, 210, 244, 332, 333
Chambray, Jacques François de 112, 185
Chapel of St Anne (Fort St Angelo) 296
chapter-general 33, 58, 63, 64, 73, 148, 164, 200, 213
Charles V 8, 52, 68,73, 75, 77, 78, 79, 80, 81, 82, 83, 122, 126, 135, 148
chebec 119, 120
Chigi Albani della Rovere, Ludovico 162, 163, 177, 225, 228
Chigi, Fabio 162, 163
Chios 135
Codex Laparelli 252
Codice de Rohan 64, 200
Collacchio (in Rhodes) 49

Colloredo, Philipp von 223
Comino Tower 339
Constantinople 44, 47
Corona Ottomana 197
corso 5, 47, 49, 67, 68, 78, 103, 104, 105, 106, 108, 109, 110, 112, 113, 119, 120, 193, 354
Cortés, Fernando 83
Cottonera Lines 5, 129, 130, 159, 246, 307, 309, 311, 326
Council Chamber 288
Council of Lyons 40
Crac de Chevaliers 4, 25, 40
Cronoligiche dell' Origine degli Ordini Militari 66
Cyprus 6, 40, 41, 43, 50, 99, 135, 351

D

Dalmatia 137
dal Pozzo, Bartolomeo 109, 158, 351
D'Aramont, August 89, 91
D'Avity, Pierre 171
Deaulx, F. Scipione 110
de la Corna, Ascanio 98
de la Ferté, Gabriel 177
del Monte, Eustachio 282, 284
Demandolx, Baldassare 132
De Opuo, Bernardo 89
de Vos, Judecos 169, 275
di Giovanni e Centelles, Andrea 219, 220, 222
Diego, Baldassare 132
Din l-Art Helwa 340, 339, 342, 345, 345
Dodecanese 45
Dragut Reis 88, 89, 91, 92, 93, 100, 101, 152, 296, 328
Dusina, Pietro 158, 160, 162

E

Eckhout, Albert 288, 289
Ekkehard 18
el-Kamil (Sultan) 35
Engel, Claire Éliane 66
Epernay Town Hall 35
Erardi, Stefano 271

F

Famagusta 47
Favray, Antoine 21, 133, 186
Ferdinand of Mantua (Italian Duke) 190
Ferdinand II (German Emperor) 148
Ferramolino, Antonio 248, 296

Ferrara 222
Fiorini, Stanley 154
Firenzuola, Vincenzo Maculano 308
Flemish tapestries 277
Fleur-de-Lys 336, 337
Floriana 185, 306
Floriana lines 307
Floriani, Pietro Paolo 65, 184, 306
Fondazione Cotoner 167
Fondazzjoni Wirt Artna 339
Fontenay, Michel 142
Fortizza di Gozo 153
Fort Manoel 326
Fort Ricasoli 312
Fort St Angelo 298
Fort St Elmo 252, 296
Fort St Michael 304
Fort Tigné 328
Franz II (Emperor) 213
Franz Joseph (Emperor) 223
Frederick II (Emperor) 35, 36, 37
Friedrich, Duke Elector of Brandenburg 125
Frutolf 18
Funes, Juan Agostin de 108

G
Galdiano, Juan 307
Galleria degli Uffizi, Florence 248, 249
Ganado, Albert 248
Genga, Bartolomeo 181, 184, 246
Genoa 37, 38, 47, 55, 82, 113, 134, 135, 142, 170
Gerard, Blessed 18, 19, 21
Gersdorff, Rudolf Christoph Freiherr von 227
Għajn Tuffieħa, tower 339, 340
Gianpieri, Giorgio 266
Giustiniani, Bernardo 66
Giustiniani, Giustino 107
Gnejna Bay 91
Gnien is-Sultan 169
Gobelin Tapestries 168
Gori Pannelini, Galeazzo (Inquisitor) 179
Gozo 73
Gozo *Castello* 246, 330, 331, 338
grain 167
grand council 61, 63
Grand Masters:
  Alfonso of Portugal 33, 58
  Bertie Willoughby, Ninian 229
  Carafa, Gregorio 6, 111, 130, 137, 195, 240, 272, 273, 297

Chattes Gessan, Annet Clermont de 239, 266
Chigi Albani della Rovere, Ludovico 225
Cotoner, Nicolas 6, 111, 130, 144, 145, 183, 184, 213, 238, 245, 260, 263, 269, 308, 309
Cotoner, Rafael 130, 184, 238, 243, 260, 267
d'Assailly, Gilbert 27
d'Aubusson 4, 35
de la Cassière, Jean l'Evesque 106, 107, 233, 235, 241, 258, 276, 277, 282, 284, 285, 290
de la Sengle, Claude 101, 158, 235, 241, 248, 277, 304
del Caretto, Fabrizio 55
del Monte, Pietro 234, 235, 241, 277, 282, 284
Despuig, Ramon 144, 239, 241, 267, 270
Festing, Matthew 4, 229, 230
Garzes, Martin 143, 236, 241, 266, 277, 293
Homedes, Juan de 78, 89, 91, 101, 107, 233, 234, 277, 296
Hompesch, Ferdinand von 4, 6, 159, 204, 207, 208, 209, 210, 211, 212, 214, 218, 240, 355
Mojana di Cologna, Angelo de 228
Moulins, Roger de 24, 26
Naillac, Philibert de 45, 50, 351
Paule, Antoine de 237, 268, 322
Perellos y Roccaful, Ramon 113, 119, 123, 144, 166, 168, 169, 185, 194, 195, 196, 239, 241, 267, 269, 288
Pinto de Fonseca, Manoel 6, 117, 144, 148, 159, 188, 197, 198, 199, 200, 203, 208, 240, 241, 267, 269, 287, 355
Puy, Raymond de 21, 24, 30, 33, 61
Rohan, Emanuel de 64, 117, 155, 159, 164, 169, 199, 200, 202, 204, 208, 229, 240,241, 267, 270, 328, 343, 354
Saint Jaille, Didier de 234
Thun und Hohenstein, Galeazzo von 225
Tommasi, Giovanni Battista 211, 218

Valette, Jean de 6, 78, 91, 99, 100, 101, 103, 159, 164, 181, 233, 235, 248, 250, 253, 256, 276, 277, 286, 291, 293, 302, 318, 322, 323, 354
Verdalle, Hughues Loubenx de 107, 171, 173, 182, 185, 236, 241, 276, 277, 318, 319, 322, 323, 351, 355
Vilhena, Antonio Manoel de 6, 115, 144, 185, 195, 196, 239, 258, 260, 265, 268, 312, 314, 322, 323, 326, 327, 333, 335, 341, 343, 353,
Villaret, Foulques de 40, 41, 44
Villeneuve, Helion de 50
Villiers de L'Isle-Adam, Philippe de 6, 55, 57, 68, 77, 78, 83, 86, 105, 126, 155, 233, 234, 266, 276, 277, 330
Wignacourt, Aloph de 6, 107, 111, 125, 168, 182, 190, 191, 195, 199, 236, 238, 260, 261, 270, 273, 276, 277, 293, 336, 337, 338, 340, 342, 343
Ximenes de Texada, Francisco 144, 198, 199, 200, 240, 277
Zacosta, Ramon 63
Zondadari, Marc'Antonio 239
Grotto of St Paul 173
Grunenbergh, Carlos 302, 326
Guevara-Suardo, Innico Maria 218
Guidotti, Opizio 175

H
Ħamrun 336, 337
Hedscha 53
Heitersheim 121, 125
Hercolani-Fava-Simonetti, Antonio 228
Herrmann, Friedrich 221
Hitler, Adolf 226, 227
Hohenstaufen, (dynasty) 14, 37
Homem, Diogo 194
hospital 42

I
Imbroll, Salvatore 108
Inguanez, Ingeraldo 86
Inquisition 138, 161, 162, 170, 353
Ittar, Stefano 184, 188

J

Jaffa 47
Jerusalem 26
Jesuits 132, 146, 163, 179, 197
Johanniter-Unfall-Hilfe 226, 227
Joseph II (German Emperor) 181, 200
Judeo-Arabic script 140

K

Kansuk Ghani 53
Kheiredin Barbarossa 83
Kings:
 Alfonso V (Aragon) 141
 Baldouin (Jerusalem) 21
 Charles III (Spain) 197
 Christian IV (Denmark) 111
 Ferdinand IV (Two Sicilies) 77
 Francis I (France) 52, 55, 79, 81
 Friedrich Wilhelm III (Prussia) 224
 Friedrich Wilhelm IV (Prussia) 224
 Fulques (Jerusalem) 24, 43
 George III (England) 214
 George IV (England) 288, 289
 Gustav Adolf (Sweden) 111
 Henry II (Cyprus) 43
 Henry VIII (England) 66, 125, 126, 176
 Louis XV (France) 144, 146, 148, 198, 200
 Louis XVI (France) 203
 Philip II (Spain) 101, 114, 134, 181, 248, 250, 251
 Philip IV (France) 40, 45, 143
 Rudolf of Hapsburg (Germany) 42
Knonau, Charles Joseph Meyer de 204, 206

L

Lagow (commandery) 123
Lanci, Baldassare 246, 249, 250
'langues' of the Order 58, 59
Laparelli, Francesco 103, 182, 184, 249, 250, 253
Lepanto, battle of 99, 109, 134, 135, 137
Limassol 42, 43
Lippija Tower 340, 340
Litta, Giulio 206
Loo, Charles A.P. van 148
L'Orient (French flagship) 210
Loyola, Ignatius of 140
Lucini, Antonio Francesco 99
Lull, Ramon 68
Luttrell, Anthony T. 104

M

Maghreb 38
Magisterial palace 4, 152, 169, 243, 244, 282, 283, 285, 287, 289, 291, 292, 293, 295, 303
Magri, Domenico 139
Maisonneuve, Joseph de 206, 352
Malaspina, Ippolito 273
Malfreire, Diego Perez de 302
Malteserstadt (Heitersheim) 121
Manderaggio 256
marble tombstones 264
Margat (fortress) 33, 40, 43, 58
Marmol y Carvajal, Luis del 171
Marsalforn 343
Marsaxlokk 91
Massuez Vercoyran, Pierre de 92, 262
Mazzuoli, Giuseppe 258, 259, 262
Mdina 314
Mecklenburg 124
Medieval Tower 298
Megrigny, Chevalier de 335
Mehmet II (Sultan) 51, 52, 53
Mehmet IV (Sultan) 132
Melo, Diego de 132
Mergentheim 45
Merisi da Caravaggio, Michelangelo 65, 182, 183, 261, 273, 277
Metternich, Klemens Wenzel von 221
Militia Dei 15, 16, 17
Mondion, Charles François 314, 315, 326, 327, 345
Monroy-affair 85
Morea 137
Moriscos 134
Murad Agà 78
Muristan 26
Muscat, Gio Niccolò 200, 202
Muscat, Joseph 110
Mustapha Pasha 91, 93, 98, 100
Myriti, Giovanni 181

N

Nasoni, Nicolò 185, 186, 276, 283
Naviglio del Secolo XVII 175
Neitzschitz, Georg Christoff von 105, 108
Nemerow (commandery) 123
Neptune's courtyard 284
Nice 83
Nicopolis 51

O

Order of St Anthony of Vienne 200
Oskar von Preussen 227
Osterhausen, Christian von 125, 351
Otranto 47
Our Lady of Philermos 259

P

Padre Ottomano 132
Paladini, Filippo 182
Palan, Jeronimo 178
Palazzo Malta 222
Palestine 37
Pantaleon, Heinrich 108
Pappalardo, Diego 172
Pardo, Pedro 248, 296
passagio 65
Paul I (Russian Czar) 206, 207, 209, 210, 211
Pauline Cult 189, 191
Perez d'Aleccio, Matteo 92, 93, 98, 99, 100, 153, 182, 266, 290, 305, 355
Pialí Pasha 91, 93, 98, 100, 152
Pignatelli, Antonio 162, 163
Pignatelli, Ettore 68
Pinto Clock 287
Piranesi, Giovanni Battista 225
Pisa 38, 50
plague 1675 185
Popes:
 Alexander III 25, 28
 Alexander IV 33
 Alexander VII 162
 Anastasius IV 22, 23, 33
 Benedict XIII 196
 Clement V 40, 41, 44
 Clement VII 72, 77, 170
 Clement VIII 125
 Gregory IX 35
 Gregory X 38
 Gregory XIII 162, 171
 Hadrian VI 68
 Innocent II 21, 22, 33
 Innocent XII 162
 Julius III 107
 Leo X 52
 Paschal II 9, 18, 21, 28
 Pius IV 101, 250
 Pius V 134

INDEX   359

Pius VI   210
Sixtus V   171, 318
Urban VII   306
Urban VIII   148, 164
population growth   158
Post, Franz   288, 289
Pradier, Jacques   271
Preti, Mattia   65, 130, 183, 260, 261, 262, 263, 266, 267, 269, 270, 271, 272
Priuli, Girolamo   141
Provence   58
Prutz, Hans   47
Psaro, Antonio   204

Q
Qalet Marku Tower   342
Quadra, Diego   158
quarterings   65
Quinsani da Montalcino, Antonio   248
Quintin d'Autun, Jean   73, 87, 181

R
Ragusa   47
Rechberg, Joseph Maria von   328
Reis, Piri   78
Reuwich, Erhard   31
Reynier, Jean-Louis-Ébénézer   335
Rhodes   4, 6, 10, 41, 42, 44, 47, 50, 51
Ricasoli, Giovanni Francesco   313
Riley-Smith, Jonathan   28, 67
Rinaldini, Giovanni   330
Rocchi Drawing   248
Rödel, Walter G.   122
Rudolph II (German Emperor)   148
Rudolf of Hapsburg   42
Russian Grand Priory   202

S
S. Maria de Latina   18
Saewulf   22, 28
Sal-ad-Din   36
Sala del Maggiore Consiglio   291, 294
Salelles, Sebastiano   179
Salih Pasha   88
San Anton (the palace and gardens of)   324
San Blas Tower   346
Sandrart, Joachim von   183
Sanuto, Marino   68
Schellinkx, Willem   86, 157
Schivelbein (commandery)   123
Schlegelholtz, Heinrich   45
Selim I (Sultan)   51, 52

Serbelloni, Gabrio   125, 253
Sheremetev, Boris Petrovitch   195
Sinan Pasha   88, 89, 101
Sinan Rais   104
Siege of Algiers   82
Smyrna   51
snake tongues   172
Soltikov, Nicholas   213
Spada, Lionello   22, 23, 24, 33, 36, 37, 40, 41, 42, 44, 55, 57, 83, 182, 183, 286
Specklin, Daniel   182
Spinola, Paolo Rafael   186
spoglio   66
Stabilimenta Rhodiorum Militum   53, 61, 63, 67
St Agatha Tower   342
St Angelo, Fort   4
Starkey, Oliver   277
Statuta Hospitalis Hierusalem   60
St Gilles   58
St Jean d'Acre   33, 43
St John's Co-Cathedral (Conventual Church)   4, 6, 103, 131, 169, 258, 258-281
St John the Almoner   28
St Lucian Tower   338
St Mary's Battery   347
St Paul's Bay Tower   338
St Peter   45
Strozzi, Leone   262
St Thomas Bay Tower   339, 349
Sublime Porte   82, 116, 137
Suffren de St Tropez, Pierre André   112
Suleiman II (the Magnificent)   6, 51, 52, 53, 55, 68, 78, 88, 89, 91, 100, 105
Sword of the Grand Masters   101
Sylos, Francesco   271
Syria   37

T
Tadino, Frà Gabriele   72
Templars   35
Terra di S. Paolo   172, 173, 191
Terra Melitensis   172
Teutonic Knights   13, 14, 44, 45, 124, 147, 204, 206, 216
Tigné, Louis François d'Aubigné   307, 326, 327
Tigné, Rene Jacques   328
Tillet, Balí   313
Toledo, Diego de   72, 250
Toledo, Garcia de Toledo, Viceroy   91, 98, 253

Tolomaide   40, 42
Tomasucci, Natale   336
Topkapı Palace   116
Torres, Ludovico   258
Towers:
 Għajn Tuffieħa   339, 340
 Lippija   340
 Marsalforn   340
 Qawra Point   340
 St George's Bay   340
 St Paul's Bay   338
 St Thomas   338, 343
 Torri l-Abjad   342
 Wied iż-Żurrieq   342
Treaty of Amiens   214, 218
Treaty of Karlowitz   194
Tripoli (Libya)   73, 78
Troisi, Pietro Paolo   185, 196

V
Valabre, Gautier   146
Valencia   47
Vallier, Gaspard de   89, 91
Valperga, Antonio Maurizio   130, 184, 307, 308, 309, 312, 326
Vasari, Giorgio   77
Vassalli, Mikiel Anton   200
Vaubois   282
Vega, Juan de   296
Vella, Andrew P.   170
Vella, Gaetano   287
Venegas, Juan de   189, 190
Venice   37, 38, 47, 55, 66, 82, 106, 107, 113, 114, 115, 132, 134, 135, 141, 142, 170, 193, 222, 350, 353
Venuti, Filippo   251
Verdala Palace   318
Vertot, Abbé Réné-Aubert   27, 38, 68, 71, 107
Vignoli, Vignolo de   44
Villavicencio, Pedro Nuñez de   183
Villegagnon, Nicolas Durand de   89, 314, 350
Viterbo   57, 72, 83
Vitry, Jacob of   21
Voltaire   99

W
Waldstein-Wartenberg, Berthold   25, 28
Wardija Tower   340
War of Candia   132, 135, 137, 306
Wignacourt Aqueduct   244
Wignacourt Fountain   337
Wignacourt Tower   338
William of Tyre   17, 18, 28, 30
Worontzoff, Mikhail   213
Würzburg, Johannes of   26

Malta's Living Heritage Series is produced by
Midsea Books Ltd with the collaboration with

Heritage Malta

Malta's Living Heritage Series
Edited by Louis J. Scerri

MALTA: THE ORDER OF ST JOHN
First published in Malta in 2010
Midsea Books Ltd

ISBN 978-99932-7-297-7 Hardback
ISBN 978-99932-7-298-4 Paperback
©2010 Midsea Books Ltd

Text Thomas Freller

Illustrations by Inklink, Florence

Main photography, artwork, & maps
© 2010 Daniel Cilia

Copyright and authorship of other images:
see page 355

Malta's Living Heritage Series was originated and
designed by Daniel Cilia, all rights reserved.

The publishers, author, and all collaborators would like to thank
Ms Maroma Camilleri, Rev Mgr John Azzopardi, and Mr Joseph Muscat
for their valid help and contributions in the production of this book.

No part of this book may be reproduced or utilized in any form or by any means mechanical or electronic, including photocopying, digital scanning, recording or by any information storage and retrieval system now known or invented in the future, without the prior written permission of the above. All copyrighted images in this publication have been digitally watermarked.

Printed and bound at NOVA Arti Grafiche s.r.l.
Signa, Florence, Italy